RESTRAINT OF TRADE

RESTRAINT OF TRADE

Michael Jefferson

JOHN WILEY & SONS
Chichester • New York • Brisbane • Toronto • Singapore

Published in the United Kingdom
1996 by

John Wiley & Sons Ltd,
Baffins Lane, Chichester,
West Sussex, PO19 1UD, England

National   01243 779777
International (+44) 1243 779777
e-mail (for orders and customer service enquiries):
cs-books@wiley.co.uk
Visit our Home Page on http://www.wiley.co.uk
or
http://www.wiley.com

Other Wiley Editorial Offices

John Wiley & Sons Inc., 605 Third Avenue,
New York, NY 10158-0012, USA

Jacaranda Wiley Ltd, 33 Park Road, Milton,
Queensland 4064, Australia

John Wiley & Sons (Canada) Ltd, 22 Worcester Road,
Rexdale, Ontario M9W 1L1, Canada

John Wiley & Sons (Asia) Pte Ltd, 2 Clementi Loop #02-01,
Jin Xing Distripark, Singapore 0512

British Library Cataloguing in Publication Data

A catalogue record for this book is available from the British Library

ISBN 0-471-96271-6

Typeset in 10/12 Baskerville by York House Typographic Ltd
Printed and bound in Great Britain by Bookcraft (Bath) Ltd, Midsomer Norton
This book is printed on acid-free paper responsibly manufactured from sustainable
forestation, for which at least two trees are planted for each one used for paper
production.

CONTENTS

PREFACE

This book restates the English law concerning restraint of trade between employers and employees and related areas in a manner which is accessible to practitioners. It does not deal in depth with the general law of civil litigation, drafting and tactics of trial but it does point out matters of litigation and drafting technique which are particularly concerned with covenants potentially in restraint of trade.

In the words of Hoover J in the Common Pleas Court, Cuyahoga County, in *Arthur Murray Dance Studios of Cleveland Inc* v *Witter*, 105 NE 2d 685 (1952), "this [area of law] is not one of those questions on which the legal researcher cannot find enough to quench his thirst. On the contrary, there is so much authority it drowns him. It is a sea – vast and vacillating, overlapping and bewildering. One can fish out of it any kind of strange support for anything, if he lives so long". In one of the most recent reported cases, *Panayiotou* v *Sony Music Entertainment (UK) Ltd* [1994] EMLR 229, 320, Parker J said that "capacity for change is ... of the nature of the doctrine". While it remains true to say that some aspects of the doctrine are unsettled the core is easy to state, if difficult to apply. Cases are noted only if relevant today. I have included reference to Commonwealth authority where English or Scottish law is uncertain or non-existent. I have striven not to include too many cases or articles from the United States.

The text dealing with express clauses is structured around the six principal problems which may be faced when considering whether a covenant potentially in restraint of trade is enforceable or not after termination of employment:

(1) Does the clause protect a legitimate proprietary interest which will normally be a trade secret or trade connection?
(2) Is the clause reasonable between the parties?
(3) Is the clause reasonable in the public interest (an issue not normally relevant in employment law)?
(4) If part of the clause is invalid, may it be severed?

(5)   How is the covenant to be construed? and

(6)   If the term is valid, which remedy or remedies may the employers obtain?

The book considers also covenants during employment, implied terms both during and after employment, various drafting tips, the effect of the Transfer of Undertakings (Protection of Employment) Regulations 1981, the definition of particular words in the covenant, the consequences of invalidity of a clause, and the effect of wrongful dismissal.

In the appendix are several precedents kindly supplied by Chris Tulley of Dibb, Lupton, Broomhead, Solicitors, of Leeds. The clauses have proved successful in the past but the warning, which is sounded on several occasions in the following chapters, is that covenants must be adapted to fit the circumstances of the employee (after all the threat to the business differs depending on the person who makes it: an accountant may take a client with her when she leaves but a typist may well not do so), and if a so-called "boiler-plate" covenant is used for every employee from cleaner to director, the likelihood is that it will be held to be unenforceable.

On some occasions I have written of an employee or former employee as being female, on others as being male. I have generally treated the person or persons employing the employee as if she, he or they were always plural. In these ways I have sought to avoid both sexist language and infelicities of style. Quotes remain unaltered. In sum female includes the male, the male embraces the female, and the plural encompasses the single.

I would like to thank Jean Hopewell, Shirley Peacock and Janet Rayner who typed the manuscript. I dedicate the book to my wife, Francesca, and my children, Lucy and William, all of whom suffered or perhaps enjoyed being deprived of my company. In the interests of scholarship I should perhaps add that my interest – a word on which he has speculated at length – was partly kindled by reading Dyson Heydon's *The Restraint of Trade Doctrine*, published a quarter of a century ago and long since out of print. He was one of two interviewers I had for a place at college. Unfortunately I cannot remember a word he uttered and indeed he was hidden in a wing chair placed sideways on to me!

I have sought to state the law as it appeared to me on 30 September 1995.

MICHAEL JEFFERSON
University of Sheffield
15 November 1995

TABLES OF CASES

UK Cases

Commonwealth and other jurisdictions

TABLES OF LEGISLATION

United Kingdom Legislation

Part 1

COVENANTS DURING AND AFTER EMPLOYMENT

Contents of Chapter One

INTRODUCTION

Chapter One

INTRODUCTION

Employers who see their employee leave to set up a rival firm or join a competitor may be tempted to try and stop such behaviour. The departing employee may see the chance of greater income by leaving than by staying. The employers may seek a legal remedy against the former employee, who may wish to defend herself. In the twentieth century judges have trod a line whereby they have upheld some attempts at restricting an employee's freedom to do as she pleases after employment but have struck down others. The principal mechanism by which they differentiate between successful and failed attempts is the restraint of trade doctrine. The doctrine has several facets and is at the same time both policy-oriented and mechanical in its operation. Judges often stress a former employee's freedom to trade, the freedom to compete, and they sometimes refer to inequality of bargaining power; but they also state that they will prevent harm to the employers' interests. These policies underlie the conflicting interests of employers and employees post-employment. Associated with these policies are subsidiary factors such as the employee's freedom to compete, which includes the former employee using the skill and knowledge which she has acquired while working for her ex-employers. There is, however, no bright line between the freedom to compete, which the employee desires, and the ability to trade free from what might be called illegitimate competition, which is the desire of employers. Similarly, there is no clear line between trade secrets, which employers can protect, and information which has become part of the "employee's make up", as Harvey CJ in Eq put it in *Ormonoid Roofing & Asphalts Ltd* v *Bitumenoids Ltd* (1930) 31 SRNSW 347, 354, such as skill and knowledge, which belongs to the employee and may be used for her own or another's advantage to the detriment of her former employers. Much of the argument in reported cases deals with such disputes. The mechanical aspect of the doctrine can be seen especially in relation to severance, the method by which English courts cut away invalid parts of the covenant to leave a grammatically sound and legally valid clause. Many of the law districts of the United States adopt the rule that covenants may be modified in coverage to save them. A covenant may be reduced from, say, an unlawful four counties to a lawful area within a radius of three miles from the plaintiffs' factory. This partial enforcement of covenants is rejected in England, though there is a growing jurisprudence on it in respect of the way in which remedies are framed in the order of the court.

The threats to a firm's competitive advantage over rivals which a departing employee may pose to her former employers are multifarious. She may have acquired trade secrets which she can sell to rivals or use in a business which she has established. An example of a technical trade secret is the design for clamps and interfaces for swimming pools in *Cranleigh Precision Engineering Ltd* v *Bryant* [1965] 1 WLR 1293. The former employers may be affected in several ways. Where it can be said that the business is the trade secret (or the trade secret is the business) the employers may suffer irremediable loss. If the Coca-Cola Co had its recipe for its principal beverage divulged to competitors, perhaps the firm would not survive. Alternatively, the loss may be negligible, as when a former employee discloses confidential information which would, the day after, be revealed by the employers putting on sale the item which contained the secret. Other scenarios can be envisaged. An employee may be the point of contact between the customer and the firm. An oft-used illustration is the milkman. The housewife may not even know that he works for a certain company but may follow him to a new firm if he changes jobs. The milkman may be able to exert the influence he has built up over the years with customers to induce them to follow him from his old employers to the new. A more modern illustration is insurance brokers. Some employees may, however, have little influence over clients. It may be readily understood that one is unlikely to follow the employee of an estate agent from one firm to another. Similarly, if a lecturer were to change jobs, it is highly improbable that students would leave one educational institution for another. Perhaps assistant solicitors fall into a borderline category. Some clients may go with her, some may not. In all instances the question is one of fact, and cases which hold, for example, that a certain milkman had a loyal following should not be treated as precedents automatically applying to all milkmen. Another threat which may be raised by a departing employee is that she may take with her part of the workforce, thus undermining the employers' ability to compete. The defection of a team working on a project can be met by well-drafted restraint of trade clauses, provided that the conditions for enforceability of such clauses are met. It is certainly best for employers' advisers to utilise covenants at the commencement of employment than at the date of termination, by which time it may be too late to prevent the employee from decamping with highly confidential information such as lists of customers or with such influence over clients that they will leave with her or from enticing her workmates away with her to form a new rival firm or to join one.

What is a Covenant in Restraint of Trade?

A covenant in restraint of trade in a contract of employment (also called a contract of service or a service agreement) is an express term which is intended by the employers to prevent an employee from entering into certain competitive activities after the termination of the employment. By definition an implied term cannot constitute a covenant in restraint of trade: *Burton, Rowe & Viner Ltd* v *Brereton* (1946) 79 Ll LR 438, 444, *per* Hallett J. The applicability of the doctrine to independent contractors is unclear. There is a growing number of authorities in which judges have recognised that the restraint of trade doctrine applies during employment too, though different principles govern terms applying during employment from those affecting a former employee. This issue is discussed below.

The doctrine extends to independent contractors, as the recent case of *Marshall* v *NM Financial Management Ltd* [1995] 1 WLR 1461 (Ch D) demonstrates. The plaintiff was a self-employed salesman for the defendants' life assurance and pension plan policies. He sought a declaration that a term in his contract was void or unenforceable for restraint of trade. Sumption QC, sitting as a deputy High Court judge, granted the declaration without considering whether the principles applicable to independent contractors differed from those applying to employees. The law governing directors and partners is dealt with in Chapter 5.

It could be argued that all contracts restrain trade for by them one party surrenders the capability of dealing with others. For example, if the newsagent sells me a magazine, he cannot sell it to you. However, not all contracts fall within the restraint of trade doctrine. Indeed, the general policy of the law continues to be the upholding of contracts freely entered into, and judges cannot, at common law, make or amend contracts. Public policy may, however, be used to strike down contractual terms which are in restraint of trade. Therefore, a definition is required to distinguish between the two classes of contractual clauses. The leading definition is that put forward by Diplock LJ in *Petrofina (Great Britain) Ltd* v *Martin* [1966] Ch 146, 180: "a contract in restraint of trade is one in which a party (the covenantor) agrees with any other party (the covenantee) to restrict his liberty in the future to carry on trade with other persons not parties to the contract in such manner as he chooses" (see also Lord Denning MR at 169). This definition was criticised by Lord Wilberforce in *Esso Petroleum Co Ltd* v *Harper's Garage (Stourport) Ltd* [1968] AC 269, 331 (HL), because the attempted definition was really a formulation of the issue, not a definition. Lords Reid, Morris and Hodson spoke of giving up a freedom. Lord Morris (at 307) said that Diplock LJ's exposition was "helpful", but it must be used "rationally and not too literally." He exemplified his point thus: "if A made a contract under which he willingly agreed to serve B on reasonable terms for a few years and to give his whole working time to B it would be surprising indeed if it were sought to describe the contract as being in restraint of trade ... Yet Counsel [for the defendants] did not shrink from the assertion that every contract of personal service is a contract in restraint of trade. I cannot think that either authority or logic requires acceptance of so extreme a view". The House went on to consider contracts which did not fall within the doctrine and did not essay a definition of those that did. It may be that no further analysis is possible. While the application of the doctrine to some categories is in doubt, there is no doubt that it applies to covenants by a servant not to compete with his master after employment and to covenants by the vendor of a business not to compete with the purchaser (see Lord Reid in *Esso* at 293). Accordingly the principal subject-matter of this book falls within the doctrine. Once one has determined that the doctrine applies, special rules take effect. As Lord Reid put it in *Esso* (at 295) "this rather anomalous doctrine of restraint of trade" places the clause in a category separate from other contractual terms and subjects it to the tests of reasonableness discussed below. It is uncertain which party bears the burden of proving that a term falls within the doctrine.

It is also possible for the doctrine to apply pre-contract. The primary authority is *Nagle* v *Feilden* [1966] 2 QB 633 (CA), where a woman was several times refused a licence to train horses by the Jockey Club because she was not a man. The most vociferous champion of this wide approach and the leading judge in this case was Lord Denning MR. He stated that individuals have a right to work, and that right is not defeated by, for instance, a union's closed shop: *Edwards* v *SOGAT* [1971] Ch 354 (CA). This particular development had to be blocked by statute, now the Trade Union and Labour Relations (Consolidation) Act 1992, s 11; otherwise trade unions would be unlawful since their purposes could be seen as being in restraint of trade.

An agreement by an actor or similar not to use a pseudonym also falls within the restraint of trade doctrine. In *Hepworth Manufacturing Co Ltd* v *Ryott* [1920] 1 Ch 1 (CA), the defendant promised that he would not use his pseudonym (Stewart Rowe) after termination of his contract and that he would not work for others unless they agreed not to use his pseudonym. The court held that these covenants were unenforceable. There was a restraint of his *trade*. What seems to have weighed heavily with them was that his value as an actor was reduced by more than half if he could not use his alias. Warrington LJ (at 24) said that the covenant was in restraint of trade because it was "an interference with the right of the defendant to use those qualifications of which he is possessed to the best advantage for himself and for the public, and as such is contrary to public policy". He relied on the restraint cases of *Nordenfelt* v *Maxim Nordenfelt Guns and Ammunition Co* [1894] AC 535 (HL) and *Mason* v *Provident Clothing and Supply Co Ltd* [1913] AC 724 (HL).

Lord Reid said in *Esso Petroleum Co Ltd* v *Harper's Garage (Stourport) Ltd*, above at 298 (HL) of the restraint of trade doctrine that "its application ought to depend less on legal niceties or theoretical possibilities than on the practical effect of a restraint in hampering that freedom which it is the policy of the law to protect". This statement continues to encapsulate the law and it was approved in *Panayiotou* v *Sony Music Entertainment (UK) Ltd* [1994] EMLR 229, 320 (Parker J). Lord

Wilberforce in *Esso* (at 331) added that "the doctrine of restraint of trade is one to be applied to factual situations with a broad and flexible rule of reason". The outcome is that a contract which is restrictive of trade falls within the doctrine unless there are good grounds for excluding it. Such grounds include precedent. For further study see Heydon, *The Restraint of Trade Doctrine* (Butterworths, 1971).

A Brief History of Covenants in Restraint of Trade

Any attempt to trace historically the development of the common law attitude towards "restraints" of different kinds would be out of place here, and generalisations as to it are hazardous (Lord Wilberforce in *Esso Petroleum Co Ltd v Harper's Garage (Stourport) Ltd* [1968] AC 269, 333).

This section considers the development of the restraint of trade doctrine.

The Unlawfulness of the Covenant

The earliest reported case (for an unreported one see *Pecche* cited in the *Case of Monopolies* (1603) 11 Co Rep 84, 88) which is generally taken to be one involving a restraint of trade is *Anon* usually called *The Dyer's Case* (1414) YB 2 Hen 5, fol 5b, pl 26. The court held to be unlawful a condition in a bond which prohibited the defendant from acting as a dyer for six months within the town where the plaintiff, his master, worked. Hull (or Hall) J is reported to have said: "Per Dieu, si le plaintiff fut ici, il irra al prisone, tanque il ust fait fyne au Roye" (By God, if the plaintiff were here he would be sent to prison until he had paid a fine to the King": my translation). Commentators have noted that the opinion that the restraint was illegal was expressed by only one judge ("a ma intent") ((1888) 3 LQR 240, 241), but Frederick Pollock, one of the greatest medievalists, wrote that outbursts such as that of Hull J were not uncommon in the early rolls: *Principles of Contract* (13th ed, Stevens & Sons, 1950) 328 n 19. Covenants such as that in *The Dyer's Case* were contrary to the apprenticeship laws, which obliged a worker to follow his trade through the guild system, and these early cases seem to reflect the judges' reluctance to permit evasion of the system of apprenticeship. Carpenter, an American academic, wrote in "Validity of Covenants not to Compete" (1928) 76 U Pa LR 244, 244–5, that the early authorities: "represent reactions by the judges against the erosions in the actions of the guilds by aggressive craftsmen . . . they show judicial support of the customary concepts of 'fair' commercial activity of the late medieval period". Employers were attempting to prevent competition by their journeymen. Today a covenant which is in restraint of trade is invalid but has no criminal consequences. There is debate whether a clause which is caught by the doctrine is void or (merely) unenforceable but it is not illegal if by illegal one means that the employers suffer a criminal penalty for incorporating the clause in the contract. It seems that a covenant which is in restraint of trade continues in existence until the restricted party chooses to resile from it. See especially *Esso Petroleum Co Ltd* v *Harper's Garage (Stourport) Ltd* [1968] AC 269, 297. If both parties wish for a restraint to continue in force, the court will not prevent them from so doing, at least when no third party is thereby injured: *Boddington* v *Lawton, The Times*, 4 February 1994.

Consideration

For at least two centuries English courts held that a covenant would not be enforced where the consideration for it was inadequate. For example, in a case involving the vendor of a business, *Prugnell* v *Gosse* (1649) Aleyn case no 68, 82 ER 919 (CP), the plaintiff brought an action on the case for breach of a promise by the defendant that on the assignment of her shop in Basingstoke she would not trade there. Rolle J said that: "[w]here a bond or promise restrains the exercise of a trade, although it be to a particular place only, yet if it be upon no consideration, the bond etc is void". An employment case is *Colmer* v *Clark* (1735) 7 Mod 230, 87 ER 1209 (KB). The plaintiff, a tally man, took the defendant into his home and instructed him in his trade. The defendant promised to serve him for five years and not to exercise the trade for seven years after that time within the City and liberty of Westminster. However, he breached that covenant. The court held that the requirement of good consideration for the promise existed. The necessity for adequate consideration applied not just to a covenant on termination of the contract but also to one during it, as is demonstrated by *Young* v *Timmins* (1831) 1 Cr & J 332, 148 ER 1446. Vaughan B in the Exchequer stated that the question whether a covenant is good or bad depends on the adequacy of the consideration (at 343, 1452). Soon afterwards the rule was changed. In *Hitchcock* v *Coker* (1837) 6 Ad & E 438, 112 ER 167, the plaintiff, a druggist, engaged the defendant as his assistant. The latter promised that he would pay £500 as liquidated damages if at any time after the end of the contract he worked as a chemist within three miles of Taunton. He did so. The plaintiff sued in *assumpsit*. Tindal CJ *per curiam* (at 454, 173) in the Exchequer Chamber held the court did not investigate the adequacy of the consideration. The new rule was swiftly followed. It was applied to partnerships in *Leighton* v *Wales* (1838) 3 M & W 545, 150 ER 1262 (Ex), and to covenants not to work for another during employment in *Pilkington* v *Scott* (1846) 15 M & W 657, 183 ER 1014 (Ex). The rule has been accepted by the House of Lords. For example, in one of the cases which settled the modern doctrine of restraint of trade, *Herbert Morris Ltd* v *Saxelby* [1916] AC 688 (HL), Lord Parker stated that "[t]he court no longer considers the adequacy of the consideration ... ", a proposition which was applied by the Court of Appeal in *M & S Drapers (A Firm)* v *Reynolds* [1957] 1 WLR 9, 11, *per* Hodson L J. There is a dictum of Lawrence L J in the common law retail price maintenance case of *Palmolive Company (of England) Ltd* v *Freedman* [1928] 1 Ch

264, 286, that " ... the consideration for imposing a restraint should not be merely colourable. There should be some good consideration, though in an agreement between businessmen regulating their trade relationship the Court would not go with any particularity or nicety into the adequacy of the consideration". This statement, which is somewhat opaque, is incorrect insofar as it holds that a covenant requires adequate consideration.

While consideration need not be adequate, the quantum is relevant to the reasonableness of the covenant, and this issue is later discussed in that context. Lord Macnaghten in *Nordenfelt v Maxim Nordenfelt Guns and Ammunition Co* [1894] AC 535, 565 (HL) said that " ... of course the quantum of consideration may enter into the question of the reasonableness of the contract". This rule has become an accepted part of the modern law of restraint of trade in England and the Commonwealth. For example, in *Amoco Australia Pty Ltd v Rocca Bros Motor Engineering Co Pty Ltd* (1972–3) 133 CLR 288, 306, Walsh J said in the High Court of Australia in relation to a solus tie that: "the quantum of the benefit which the covenantor receives may be taken into account in determining whether the restraint does or does not go beyond adequate protection for the interests of the covenantee". Gibbs J (at 316) said that "it is permissible, in asking whether a restraint is reasonable in the interests of the parties, to consider as part of the circumstances of the case against which the question of reasonableness is to be decided, the quantum of consideration received by the covenantor and the effect of the agreement on the position of the covenantor ... ". In *Clifford Davis Management Ltd v WEA Records Ltd* [1975] 1 WLR 61 (CA), an exclusive services case, Lord Denning MR stated (at 65) that property in 11 Fleetwood Mac songs was transferred for a "grossly inadequate" consideration (one shilling each). The sum was so small because of the unequal bargaining power of the parties. He refused to enforce the assignment of copyright. The case is only an interlocutory one but it reflects judicial thinking of the time.

In contracts of service, consideration is provided by employment or continued employment. The usual requirements of the doctrine of consideration apply. For example, past consideration is no consideration. There is no English case, but for an American example see *Timenterial Inc v Dagata*, 277 A 2d 512 (1971) (Conn). Exceptionally (separate) consideration is required for a deed under seal, though no modern case exists.

Bonds and Mutual Contracts

In the seventeenth century there developed the doctrine that "[a] man may contract or promise that he will not use his trade, but he cannot bind himself in a bond not to do it; for if he do so it is void". Thus spoke Reeve J in *Barrow v Wood* (1643) March NR 191, 193, 82 ER 470, 471 (CP). He relied on a case called *Clegant v Batcholler*, Mich 44 Eliz Rot 3715 (KB), which is reported as *Claygate v Batchelor* (43 & 44 Eliz) Owen 143, 74 ER 961 and as *Colgate v Bacheler*, Cro Eliz 872, 78 ER 1097, where the judges refused to enforce a covenant that the defendant's son would pay £20 if he entered into the trade of haberdasher as journeyman, servant, apprentice or master in Kent within four years of the making of the bond, and on *Bragge* v *Stanner* (1622) Palmer 172, 81 ER 1031, where a majority of the King's Bench held that the plaintiff had a *bon assumpsit* where the defendant promised on the sale of his haberdashery business to the plaintiff for £500 that he would pay him £100 if he exercised his trade of linen draper in the same area – Newgate Market – which he did.

The distinction between bonds and covenants was exploded by Parker CJ in *Mitchel* v *Reynolds* (1711) 1 P Wms 181, 185, 24 ER 347, 349, which was applied to a bond in *Davis* v *Mason* (1793) 5 Term Rep 118, 120, 101 ER 69, 70 (KB).

General and Partial Restraints

At first all restraints were invalid and *The Dyer's Case* was generalised from apprenticeship law to that covering all workers, but by the early seventeenth century a distinction was drawn between general and partial restraints. The King's Bench in *Rogers* v *Parry* (1614) 2 Bulst 136, 80 ER 1012, said "A man cannot bind one, that he shall not use his trade generally ..., but that as this case here is, for a time certain and in a place certain, a man may be well bound and restrained from using of his trade". Parker CJ, later Lord Macclesfield, in *Mitchel* v *Reynolds*, above (at 186, 349), stated that *Rogers* v *Parry* was wrongly reported because of the omission of a reference to adequate consideration (see above) but he adopted the distinction that general covenants were void but particular ones were valid (at 185, 349). At 190–1, 350, he enquired: "for what does it signify to a tradesman in London, what another does at Newcastle?" An England-wide, or general, restraint was therefore invalid.

Mitchel v *Reynolds* quickly came to be seen as the source of the general/partial distinction. It was applied by the King's Bench in *Colmer* v *Clark*, above, which involved what can now be called a training contract, and by the Common Pleas to an employed dentist in *Horner* v *Graves* (1831) 7 Bing 725, 131 ER 284. It was applied to a covenant during the running of a contract in *Young* v *Timmins*, above. The Privy Council applied the rule in *Collins* v *Locke* (1877) 4 App Cas 674, 686, a case involving stevedores in Melbourne who had parcelled out the work among them to keep prices up. As late as 1887 Cotton L J in *Davies* v *Davies* (1887) 36 Ch D 359, 383–6, was strongly supporting the distinction. At 386 he gave his reasons for the rule (1) "No man ought to be prevented during his life from earning his livelihood by carrying on his trade"; (2) "the public ought not to be prevented from the benefit which they might get from a man who is skilled in a trade carrying on that trade". There are many other similar cases.

Doubts as to the wisdom of the rule surfaced in *Proctor* v *Sargent* (1840) 2 M & G 20, 133 ER 647 (CP). Maule J (at 67, 654) said in relation to a covenant at the end of a cowkeeper's contract of employment: "Perhaps the best way would have been to hold that all contracts of this nature to be legal that do not interfere with the rights of individuals". James V-C in *Leather Couch Co* v *Lorsont* (1869) LR 9 Eq 345 (the case is often called *Leather Cloth*) granted an injunction to restrain the defendant from acting in breach of a covenant not to manufacture and sell leather cloth in Europe. He added (at 354) that a person could bind herself not to reveal a secret anywhere in the world. Wickens V-C in *Allsopp* v *Wheatcroft* (1872) LR 15 Eq 59, 64, reasserted the distinction and criticised James V-C, holding that his remarks were *obiter*. Fry J in the Chancery Division in *Rousillon* v *Rousillon* (1880) 14 Ch D 364 noted that many cases had accepted the distinction. Some but not all (*Allsopp* v *Wheatcroft*, for example) could be explained on the basis not that the clause was general but that the employers had sought to impose unreasonable restrictions. He noted that some cases were inconsistent with the rule such as *Whittaker* v *Howe* (1841) 3 Beav 383, 49 ER 150, which involved an attorney promising not to practise for 20 years anywhere in Great Britain. Because of the division in the cases Fry J (at 369) considered that he had a choice and he chose to assimilate general and partial restraints. Fry J held, granting an injunction and damages of one shilling, that a covenant by the defendant not to establish himself in the champagne trade for 10 years was binding. In terms of policy, trades which extended throughout England and Wales would not be protected if the dichotomy was correct (at 366). He said (at 367) that: "The rule [is] really an artificial one without principle". Fry LJ, as he by then was, adhered to his view in *Davies* v *Davies*, above (at 396), though he refused to express a decided view. Cotton LJ (at 398) in a famous phrase interjected: "I meant to decide the question". In other words he strongly supported the general/partial distinction. Chitty J in *Badische Anilin und Soda Fabrik* v *Schott, Segner & Co* [1892] 3 Ch 447, a case involving a restraint in the context of agents, held that *Rousillon* v *Rousillon* had not been overruled by the Court of Appeal in *Davies* v *Davies*. At 450 he said: "There is no absolute rule that a covenant in restraint of trade is void merely because it is unlimited in regard to space". Therefore, if the covenant was limited as to time, it did not matter that it was unlimited as to space: it, like partial covenants, was subject to the reasonableness test. On the facts the plaintiffs' business was worldwide. Therefore, since as the judge held a worldwide covenant was reasonable, an injunction was granted prohibiting them from breaching a covenant for one year after the termination of the agreement from entering upon a similar business or giving information of any kind about the business. Chitty J stressed (at 452) that restrictions as to space became less important as communications improved: "What might in former ages have been considered an unreasonable restriction would not necessarily be so held in the altered circumstances of the present time".

By the early 1890s there was accordingly a division in the judges. Some, largely common law ones, preferred to maintain the general/partial distinction; others, mainly equity lawyers, preferred not to use this "hard and fast" rule, as it had come to be known. The showdown came in *Nordenfelt* v *Maxim Nordenfelt Guns and Ammunition Co*, above, in the House of Lords, a case involving the sale of business. In the Court of Appeal, where the names were reversed, [1893] 1 Ch 630, Bowen LJ examined the authorities at length and concluded that the common law rule held sway, subject to an exception for trade secrets. Lindley LJ also examined the

cases but concluded that the equity view prevailed. A L Smith LJ on the whole
supported Lindley LJ. In the House, Lord Herschell C, referring to the example
quoted above in *Mitchel* v *Reynolds*, said:

> regard must be had to the changed conditions of commerce and of the means of
> communication which have developed in recent years. To disregard these would be
> to miss the substance of the [general/partial] rule in a blind adherence to its letter.
> Newcastle-upon-Tyne is for all practical purposes as near to London today as towns
> which are now regarded as suburbs of the metropolis were a century ago ... [T]hat
> which would have been once merely a burden on the covenantor may now be
> essential if there is to be reasonable protection to the covenantee.

Accordingly both types of covenant were to be assessed by asking whether the
clause went beyond protection of the covenantee. Lord Macnaghten (at 571) said
that:

> it is no wonder that judges of former times did not foresee that the discoveries of
> science and the practical results of those discoveries might in time prove general
> restraints in some cases to be perfectly reasonable. When that time came it was only
> a legitimate development – it was hardly even an extension – of the principle on
> which exceptions were first allowed to admit unlimited restraints into the class of
> allowable exceptions to the general rule.

Lord Morris (at 575) said: "we have now reached a period when it may be said
that science and invention have almost annihilated both time and space. Consequently there should no longer exist any cast-iron rule making void any agreement not to carry on a trade anywhere. The generality of time or space must
always be a most important factor in the consideration of reasonableness though
not *per se* a decisive test". Accordingly, "the time for a new departure has arisen
and ... it should be now authoritatively decided that there should be no
difference in the legal considerations which would invalidate an agreement
whether in general or partial restraint of trading. These considerations ... are
whether the restraint is reasonable and is not against the public interest".

The *Nordenfelt* exposition of the general/partial distinction has not since been
questioned. The retreat from the distinction was signalled in the United States by
Andrews J in *Diamond Match Co* v *Roeber*, 13 NE 419 (1887) (CA NY). He stated (at
421) that steam and electricity had deprived the distinction of its efficacy and (at
423) that "the boundaries of the State are not those of trade". The US Supreme
Court approved *Nordenfelt* in *Dr Miles Medical Co* v *John D Park & Sons Co*, 220 US
373, 406 (1911) (Holmes J dissenting but not on this point), a case on resale price
maintenance. Bradley CJ *per curiam* averred that the argument that, to enforce a
covenant covering the whole of a state would oblige an employee to uproot
himself and settle in another state, was weak because the United States was one
country, "especially in all matters of trade and business". The victory of the
Nordenfelt test was slow to come in some states. For example, Illinois kept the
distinction in *Parish* v *Schwartz*, 176 NE 757 (1931) but the First District upheld a
statewide covenant in a secret formula case, *Pharmacal Distrib Co* v *Killey*, 125 NE 2d

309 (1955), and a more than statewide covenant was upheld where the employee breached "fiduciary duty" (in English, duty of faithful service) by financing a more efficient vending machine for his employers' rivals during employment: *Vendo Co v Stoner*, 321 NE 2d 1 (1974) *cert den'd*, 420 US 975 (1975). As stated above, one of the reasons for abolishing the distinction was the invention of railways. Advances of technology continue to support the abolition of the distinction. Birrell J said in *Droba v Berry*, 139 NE 2d 124, 127 (1955) (CP) that "possibly the advent of the automobile has extended the reasonableness of the distances". Computer wizardry means that the rule is gone forever, though the issue was clear a century ago.

Modern Law

Much of modern law was settled in the years surrounding the First World War. Important cases from that period include *Nordenfelt*, above, *General Billposting Co Ltd v Atkinson* [1909] AC 118 (HL), *Mason v Provident Clothing and Supply Co* [1913] AC 724 (HL), *Attorney-General of the Commonwealth of Australia v Adelaide SS Co Ltd* [1913] AC 781 (PC), *Herbert Morris Ltd v Saxelby* [1916] AC 688 (HL), *Attwood v Lamont* [1920] 3 KB 571 (CA), and *Fitch v Dewes* [1921] AC 158 (HL). The principles in these authorities remain relevant today and are discussed in the following chapters, which deal with the common law of restraint of trade between employers and employees and former employers and former employees. The non-employment parts of the doctrine are now heavily controlled by legislation, both English and European Community. For an overview see D D Prentice in *Chitty on Contracts* (27th ed, 1994), ch 16, pp 841 *et seq*.

The contrast between the restraint of trade doctrine and the classic nineteenth century *laissez-faire* attitude towards sanctity of contract could not be more pronounced. Jessel MR famously stated in *Printing and Numerical Registering Co v Sampson* (1879) LR 19 Eq 462, 465: "if there is one thing which public policy requires, it is that men of full age and competent understanding shall have the utmost liberty of contracting and that their contract, when entered into freely and voluntarily, shall be sacred". The restraint doctrine can be seen in several different ways in relation to the doctrine of freedom of contract. It can be viewed as a fossil from an earlier age just as the relationship between master and servant survived from an earlier era: the killing of a master by a servant was petty treason until the early nineteenth century and servants who broke their contracts were liable to imprisonment until the final quarter of that century. The restraint doctrine can also be seen as an attempt to bolster freedom of contract in this sense: the former employee by engaging in competition with her former employers is exercising her freedom to trade, and customers have another party with whom to contract and thus freedom to contract is enhanced. Policy issues are further discussed in Chapter 9, but it is worth nothing here how far English courts have moved from striking down all restraints to upholding those where the term is no wider than is reasonably necessary to protect the employers' interests.

As the legislature intervened more and more in the twentieth century between contracting parties, the restraint of trade doctrine has come to be seen as part of the decline of freedom of contract. Both legislation and the doctrine may be considered as manifestations of public concern at inequality of bargaining power. The doctrine was certainly not aimed at striking down unconscionable bargains originally, though it is sometimes so categorised nowadays. There is something of a return to taking consideration into account. Lord Diplock in *Macaulay* v *A Schroeder Music Publishing Co Ltd* [1974] 1 WLR 1308, 1315, stated: "the public policy which the court is implementing is not some 19th century economic theory about the benefit to the general public of freedom of trade, but the protection of those whose bargaining power is weak against being forced by those whose bargaining power is stronger to enter into bargains which are unconscionable". This approach has been called "welfarist". Insofar as the doctrine now rests on inequality of bargaining power, covenants between vendors and purchasers cannot normally be assessed in the same way as can the relationship between employer and employees, for there may well be no such inequality. A modern way of considering covenants between vendors and purchasers is to say that vendors cannot derogate from their grant, that is they cannot compete with their former business for doing so would undermine what the buyers had purchased from them. The courts have also placed contracts among partners, and more recently contracts between employers and employees who partly own the company through shares, in categories separate from employers and employees. This book concentrates on employers and employers and former employees and former employees but does compare their position with that occupied by others included within the sweep of the restraint of trade doctrine and cases involving solus ties (exclusive supply agreements) and similar arrangements are noted when appropriate. The categories of contractual terms which fall within the restraint doctrine are not closed; nor is there any limit on the types of clauses which employers may use. The different types of covenants are discussed next.

Contents of Chapter Two

THE DIFFERENT TYPES OF COVENANT

Chapter Two

THE DIFFERENT TYPES OF COVENANT

The restraint of trade doctrine applies to clauses however they are drafted. The courts look at the substance of the term, not at its form. Lord Wilberforce advised in the Privy Council case of *Stenhouse Australia Ltd* v *Phillips* [1974] AC 391, 401, that "[w]hether a particular provision operates in restraint of trade is to be determined not by the form the stipulation wears, but . . . by its effect in practice". Form is of importance for as discussed below some "normal" or "usual" forms which apply during employment are not subject to the doctrine. The formulation of covenants is also important because at times judges have struck down one type of covenant on the basis that a different type should have been used. The following section presents a selection of clauses divided into several categories. These classes represent methods by which ex-employers can meet threats to compete by former employees.

Area Covenants

This category of covenants is one which prohibits an employee from working within a certain area. There might, for example, be a restriction on working within a radius of five miles from Piccadilly Circus or within a certain geographical area such as County Durham. A case law illustration occurred in *Lawrence David Ltd* v *Ashton* [1991] 1 All ER 385:

> for a period of two years after the termination of this agreement for any reason whatsoever, Mr Ashton shall not without the written consent of the Board, either alone or in partnership, undertake to carry on or be employed in any capacity or be interested directly or indirectly in the design or development, manufacture or supply of any sliding door vehicle body . . . within the UK.

In the most famous US case, *Arthur Murray Dance Studios of Cleveland Inc* v *Witter*, 105 NE 2d 685 (1952), the clause read:

The employee agrees that upon the termination of his employment for any cause and for a period of two (2) years thereafter, he will not teach dancing or accept employment in any matter relating to dancing, dancing engagements, or exhibitions, dancing lessons or instruction or lectures in dancing in any form whatsoever, or become engaged directly or indirectly in business in any respects relating to dancing at any hotel, resort, ship or establishment, nor solicit business for himself or any other business in any manner related to dancing, nor directly nor indirectly engage in teaching dancing to anyone within a radius of twenty-five (25) miles of employer without the written consent of employer.

The final covenant is an area one. It should be noted that this single clause, a "rolled-up" one, is not recommended to employers for it is better for them to have separate clauses. Then, if one is struck down for being unreasonable, the rest may survive, and there is no difficulty in attributing consideration to the remainder. In other words it is easier to sever one separate covenant than one part of a lengthy clause which seeks to cover all eventualities.

This category of covenants is useful in respect of trade secrets, and it may be of help in relation to trade connections where the employee has built up influence over clients, as in *Fitch* v *Dewes* [1921] 2 AC 158 (HL) (*cf. SW Strange Ltd* v *Mann* [1965] 1 WLR 629 (Stamp J)). Otherwise a non-solicitation or non-dealing covenant is more likely to be upheld as being of a less restrictive nature than an area covenant.

This type of covenant may be so worded as to prevent the employee from contacting both clients and persons who are not clients. Therefore, if the employers are seeking only to prevent the employee's soliciting clients, an area covenant is inappropriate. In *Office Angels Ltd* v *Rainer–Thomas* [1991] IRLR 214 Sir Christopher Slade said (at 220) that in relation to an area covenant "the Court *is* [his emphasis] entitled to consider whether or not a covenant of a narrower nature would have sufficed for the covenantee's protection". An area covenant was held to be unreasonable, whereas covenants preventing soliciting and dealing with clients would have been successful. In *SW Strange Ltd* v *Mann*, above, the employee covenanted that he would not act as a bookmaker within 12 miles of Cheltenham for three years after the termination of his contract of employment. He successfully challenged the covenant. One ground given by Stamp J was that the employee had no personal relationship with the punters. Therefore, the clients would not seek him out after he had left his employers. Therefore, an area covenant went further than was legitimate to protect the employers' trade connections. It would have been sufficient if they had adopted a non-solicitation covenant, which would have prevented the employers' clients being approached by the former employee.

An area covenant must be drafted with particularity. A tip is: think of the employee's territory and halve it! A covenant will not be upheld if it is uncertain in its scope. Take a covenant drafted to apply to an area within 25 miles of London, Does that phrase mean a radius of 25 miles from Charing Cross or within 25 miles of inner London or 25 miles of the boundaries of greater London or some other area? It is suggested that a specific location from where a radius is measured should be stated: for example, 25 miles from the employers' premises on Farringdon Road.

Non-Competition Covenants

An example of this type of covenant occurred in *London & Solent Ltd* v *Brooks*, 27 October 1988, LEXIS (CA). An employee was prohibited from

> during the period of one year after termination of his employment, in any way be[ing] concerned or interested in any business competing with that of the Company (meaning a business identical or similar to any business which shall, at the date of such termination, be carried on by the Company) provided however that nothing in this provision shall prevent the holding, for investment purposes only, of not more than five per cent in nominal amount of the issued equity share capital of a company listed on a recognised stock exchange, or a beneficial interest in such a holding.

This type of clause is effective in protecting trade secrets and trade connections. For a franchise case where a non-competition clause to protect goodwill was upheld see *Kall-Kwik Printing (UK) Ltd* v *Rush* [1996] FSR 114 (Ch D). Judge Cooke said that a non-solicitation covenant would be impossible to police (at 124). In *Forster & Sons Ltd* v *Suggett* (1918) 35 TLR 87, the clause prohibited the employee from carrying on or being interested in glass bottle manufacture or any other business connected with glass making within the United Kingdom for three years after the termination of the contract. The restraint did not specifically deal with trade secrets, but by prohibiting the former employee from working for a competitor it indirectly gave protection to the former employers' information. This type of covenant is extremely useful to employers because it prevents a former employee from joining a rival firm, unlike a clause which may be expressed as applying only on her using or disclosing the confidential information, a stage later than that of joining the competitor. See *C R Smith Glaziers (Dunfermline) Ltd* v *Greenan*, 1993 SLT 1221, 1223 and *Scotcoast Ltd* v *Halliday*, 10 January 1995, LEXIS (Outer House).

Of all categories of restraint clause the non-competition covenant is the one most likely to be closely examined by the court. With regard to trade connections it is more likely that a non-solicitation covenant will be upheld than a non-competition one because the employers have a legitimate proprietary interest in the goodwill attaching to their business: see *Herbert Morris Ltd* v *Saxelby* [1916] 1 AC 688 (HL). Moreover, a non-solicitation covenant need not be restricted to a certain area but a non-competition clause must normally be so for without such a restriction it will be construed as a worldwide restraint and rarely will the employers' business interests be worldwide.

Non-Solicitation and Non-Dealing Covenants

A non-solicitation covenant is designed to prevent the employee from canvassing or soliciting orders from customers or suppliers. It is often restricted but need not be to a specific area. An employee may be restricted in approaching the employers' clients within a certain district. For example, the clause might read that the former employee is not, for one year after termination, to solicit persons who within the six months prior to termination were clients of the employers at their branch in the Arndale Centre, Manchester. In *London & Solent Ltd* v *Brooks*, above, one clause prohibited a director from the following behaviour: "during the period one year after termination of his employment, directly or indirectly solicit or endeavour to entice away from or discourage from dealing with the Company any person who, during the period of two years immediately preceding such termination, shall have to his knowledge been its manufacturers, suppliers, customers, clients, distributors or agents or have had any dealings with it".

A non-dealing covenant prohibits a former employee from treating with the employers' clientele or suppliers. An example is also found in *London & Solent Ltd* v *Brooks*, above. The leader of a marine reinsurance broking team covenanted *inter alia* that he would not deal with his former clients for two years after the termination of his contract of employment. The court heard that clients soon heard of managers leaving one outfit and joining another and they often followed them.

This type of covenant is different in effect from an area clause. The latter prohibits the former employee from working at all in the relevant trade for a certain length of time. A non-solicitation covenant merely prevents her from approaching her former clients and it does not prevent them from approaching her, and it does not prevent her from working at all in the restricted area. Furthermore, new customers are not prohibited by a non-solicitation covenant from approaching the defendant on the recommendation of those who were her customers when she worked for her former employers.

It may be difficult to prove solicitation by the former employee. For that reason the employers will find it easier to prove a breach of a non-dealing covenant than a non-solicitation one, for "dealing" can be commenced by either side, whereas solicitation must be done by the former employee.

In *Scorer* v *Seymour Jones* [1966] 1 WLR 1419 the Court of Appeal upheld an area covenant on the grounds that a non-solicitation covenant was difficult to police. The facts were that the defendant had set up in competition with his former employer immediately on dismissal. He contended that the covenant not to undertake or carry on or be employed or interested in the business of auctioneer, surveyor or estate agent was unenforceable. Salmon LJ (at 1427) said that a covenant preventing the employee from doing business with his former clients was too narrow to be of use because it was "almost impossible to prove that the defendant was whittling away the plaintiff's trade connection". He noted that the covenant in *Fitch* v *Dewes*, above, was in similar form and had not been criticised on that score. The authority of *Scorer* v *Seymour Jones* is questionable in the light of recent cases such as *Office Angels*, noted above.

Non-solicitation and non-dealing covenants may be used to protect the employers' connection with both existing and potential clients. It is suggested that two covenants, one for existing customers and one for possible future ones, should be included so that if the latter is struck down, the former may survive as an independent stipulation. Such covenants need not be limited to the area where the employee worked but may extend to areas into which the employers hoped their business would extend: for example *Ropeways Ltd* v *Hoyle* (1919) 88 LJ Ch 446 and *Connors Bros Ltd* v *Connors* [1940] 4 All ER 179 (PC).

While most non-solicitation and non-dealing covenants are directed at protecting trade connections, they may be used to safeguard trade secrets. For example, a clause which prevents a former employee from dealing for one year with those who had been customers for six months preceding termination will not allow him to use a confidential list of customers he has surreptitiously taken from his former employers. In this respect a covenant not to deal is easier to police than one against using or disclosing trade secrets for the latter permits the ex-employee to have contact with the clients and he may reveal secret information to them.

Despite the difference stated above between non-solicitation and non-dealing covenants the Privy Council in *Stenhouse Australia Ltd* v *Phillips*, above (at 403), was of the opinion that "the presence of one restraint diminishes the need for the others, or at least increases the burden of those who must justify these others". It was partly on this ground that a non-dealing covenant was struck down whereas a non-solicitation covenant was upheld. However, where a non-solicitation covenant would be inefficacious a non-dealing convenant may be reasonable. In *London & Solent*, above, the Court of Appeal determined that clients of marine insurers would follow former employees into their new employment because of the nature of their contact. Non-dealing covenants were accordingly upheld, and the employee's contention that a non-dealing covenant should not be upheld when there was a non-solicitation covenant was disapproved on the facts.

It should be noted that the customer connection protected by these types of covenant need not be longstanding. Moreover, the connection may exist despite the customers' resorting also to other sources.

Non-Enticement Covenants

A type of clause which has come into prominence in recent years is one in which the employers seek to prevent the employee from poaching her colleagues on leaving employment. The covenant may be drafted thus: "on termination of employment you will not make contact with your co-workers who were employed in the department in which you were employed for six months preceding the termination of your employment". Such a clause, it is thought, must be restricted to colleagues over whom the employee had influence, and it is suggested that such a clause may well be inappropriate in relation to members of staff whom the employers can easily replace: cleaners may be instanced.

This type of covenant is intended to prevent the employers losing their workforce to a competing firm. It demonstrates that the interests which the employers can protect are not restricted to trade connections and trade secrets. The list of legitimate propriety interests is not closed.

The principal English non-poaching case is one between two employers: *Kores Manufacturing Co Ltd* v *Kolok Manufacturing Co Ltd* [1959] Ch 108. The arrangement, expressed in an exchange of letters, was that each company would "refrain from engaging any person or persons who have been in the employ of either firm during the previous period of five years". The arrangement was struck down by the first instance judge because the duration of five years was too lengthy. Lloyd-Jacob J stated at [1957] 3 All ER 158, 163, that the covenant was contrary to the public interest because it obliged workpeople to work at inconvenient distances from home. He also thought (at 162) that employers might have no protectable interest (applying *Mineral Water Bottle Exchange & Trade Protection Society* v *Booth* (1887) 36 Ch D 465 (CA)). On appeal the court (at 124) held that the covenant was void and unenforceable because it applied to employees who had no "trade secrets or confidential information". In a joint judgment Jenkins, Romer and Ormerod LJJ said *obiter* (at 125): "The danger of the adequacy and stability of his complement of employees being impaired through employees leaving his service and entering that of a rival is not a danger against which he is entitled to protect himself by extracting from his employees covenants that they will not, after leaving his service, enter the service of any competing concern". The employers could not obtain this result indirectly by reaching an agreement among themselves. The court assimilated an agreement between manufacturers of stationery products with covenants affecting employees on the termination of their contracts.

The case may be distinguished as not involving a covenant between employers and employees, and the court's statement on the issue of legitimate proprietary interest is *obiter*. There are indications in more recent cases that employers do have such an interest in the stability of their workforce. In *Office Angels Ltd* v *Rainer-Thomas*, above, the Court of Appeal said *obiter* that an employment agency could protect its trade connection with the temporary workers it had on its books. The temps were not employees of the agency; nor indeed were they clients. The court (at 219) distinguished *Kores* on the basis that it did not involve a contract of service. Sir Christopher Slade stated that the interests which the employers can protect are not restricted to trade connections and trade secrets but included the connection with a pool of temporary workers. However, the clause was construed to cover only the connection with clients, not with temps.

At first instance in *Rex Stewart Jeffries Parker Ginsberg Ltd* v *Parker*, 12 June 1986, unreported, Lewis Hauser QC sitting in the Queen's Bench Division granted an interlocutory injunction restraining a former employee from enticing former colleagues to join him. The Court of Appeal [1988] IRLR 483 merely noted that the order had expired. No attempt was made by Glidewell LJ to justify such an order, which is strange considering that there was no covenant to that effect in the contract. The case was only an interlocutory one, and judgment was apparently not reserved. Perhaps counsel missed the issue. The issue may now be taken to have been settled. In *Ingham* v *ABC Contract Services Ltd*, 12 November 1993, LEXIS (CA) Leggatt LJ said that employers "have a legitimate interest in maintaining a stable, trained workforce in ... a highly competitive business". *Ingham* was followed in *Alliance Paper Group plc* v *Prestwich* [1996] IRLR 25 (Ch D), where contrary authority was discountenanced.

There are potential problems with non-enticement covenants. For example, for how long should protection extend? Since the employers are seeking to prohibit the former employee from utilising her knowledge of her former workmates, in most circumstances only a short duration will be needed for many work relationships do not survive one employee's leaving. The solidity of the relationship will have to be considered.

Trade Secrets Covenants

A clause may be included in a contract of service which prohibits an employee from using or disclosing a trade secret belonging to her employers. A simple illustration is a covenant which prevents the employee using blueprints owned by her former employers after employment. One of the most famous restraint of trade cases, *Nordenfelt* v *Maxim Nordenfelt Guns and Ammunition Co* [1894] AC 535 (HL), while not an employee case but one between the vendor and purchasers of a business, is illuminating. The covenant provided that the vendor would not for 25 years "carry on business, engage ... in the trade or business of a manufacturer of guns ... explosives or ammunition or in any business competing or liable to compete in any way with that for the time being carried on by the company ... ". Indirectly this covenant prevented the employee from using trade secrets world-wide for 25 years. In *London & Solent Ltd* v *Brooks*, above, clause 10(1)(b)(ii) prohibited the defendant from the following conduct. He should not:

> during his employment by the Company or at any time after the termination of his employment, take away, conceal, destroy, make use of, retain or disclose to any person ... any information whatsoever concerning the business, activity or identity of any of the company's manufacturers, suppliers, customers, clients or other persons, with whom the Company has dealt in the course of any business carried on by it and which he has acquired or which has come to his knowledge during the course of his employment by, or activity in, the affairs of the Company ... .

A third example is from *Lawrence David Ltd* v *Ashton* [1991] 1 All ER 385. Clause 5 read: "Mr Ashton shall not at any time during or after the termination of his employment under this agreement disclose to any person whatsoever any information relating to the Company or its customers of any trade secrets of which he becomes possessed while acting as Sales Director ... ". A trade secret covenant need not be restricted in duration or territory: see for example *Herbert Morris Ltd* v *Saxelby* [1915] 2 Ch 57, 77 (Joyce J). Nevertheless a worldwide restraint will require justification: *Commercial Plastics Ltd* v *Vincent* [1965] 1 QB 623, 643.

It is more likely that a well-drafted trade secret clause will be upheld than one involving trade connections such as an area or non-solicitation clause. A confidentiality clause is more easily upheld than a non-competition clause. It is improbable nowadays that an area covenant extending to the whole world will survive challenge, whereas a worldwide trade secrets clause is readily upheld: how else can the employers protect their confidential material by contract? Furthermore, a clause relating to customers is expected to be limited in time. After a certain period the influence which employees such as milkmen have over customers may well evaporate, but a trade secret may require protection until its nature is disclosed. A covenant is useful to distinguish protection from other information. The principal drawback, however, of a trade secrets covenant is that the court may rule that there is no secret at all or that what was confidential during employment is, after employment, part of the employee's skill and knowledge, which the employers cannot restrain. These issues are considered later. No injunction will be granted to enforce a trade secret clause where the confidential information is not defined with sufficient precision. Balcombe LJ in *Lawrence David* stated that this difficulty was one justification for the use of an area covenant even when that clause was principally directed at protecting trade secrets. Similarly spoke Lord Denning MR in *Littlewoods Organisation Ltd* v *Harris* [1977] 1 WLR 1472, 1479.

If a trade secret covenant falls, the implied duty of confidentiality may spring up. The principal English authority is *Thomas Marshall (Exports) Ltd* v *Guinle* [1979] Ch 227. While, as stated above, the courts have recently stated that one type of clause will not be upheld when a narrower type should have been adopted, there is nothing to prevent employers inserting clauses of all forms. If one type falls, another may survive and give the employers the protection they desire. Area, non-solicitation and non-dealing covenants are useful to employers because it is not always easy to determine whether or not a former employee has breached a covenant protecting trade secrets. They may be used to prevent an ex-employee working for a rival at all, whereas a clause prohibiting her using or disclosing trade secrets does not prevent her joining a competitor. Therefore, she may join that firm and the former employers may not be able to uncover any breaches of the covenant. After all, they do not, for example, have access to their rivals' laboratories. There may, further, be grave difficulty in distinguishing between the employee's skill and knowledge, which she may use after employment, and other, protectable, information. Yet the distinction has to be drawn for trade secrets covenants can protect only trade secrets and other highly confidential information, and the employee's general skill and knowledge do not fall within those categories. *Cf. Metrans Pty Ltd* v *Courtney-Smith* (1983) 8 IR 379 (Kearney J). This problem does not arise in respect of the other types of clauses for the former employee is prohibited totally from working in the designated trade or industry (depending on the wording of the covenant). There is no need to distinguish between the trade secrets and skill and knowledge for none may be used in the prohibited employment. A further difficulty with trade secrets clauses is the necessity to identify with particularity the items which comprise the protected information. An area covenant could be upheld in such circumstances. Moreover, it would be upheld even though the principal proprietary interest protected by that covenant was the former employers' confidential information.

Conclusion

Employers seeking to protect their interests should choose the type or types of covenants most likely to protect them. For instance, a clause preventing a senior manager from soliciting her employers' clients will fail if she had never met those clients during employment. However, she may have confidential information which the employers wish to keep secret from their competitors. They should have utilised a covenant preventing her from using or disclosing such information. The selection of the appropriate type of covenant is thus of the utmost importance. For this reason it is suggested that the nature of the activity which the employers seek to prohibit should be at the forefront of the drafters' minds. Once the correct type is (or depending on the facts the correct types are) chosen, other issues tend to fall into place. For example, if the employers wish to restrain their employee from dealing with customers after employment, a non-dealing covenant will be selected. There then follow other queries: dealing in which goods? (and will these change over time?); who will the customers be? (perhaps they will change during the worker's employment); where will she operate and will this territory change? The possibility of change may mean that at each alteration the covenant may have to be varied in the usual contractual manner such as by providing extra pay to encourage the employee to consent to the variation.

Contents of Chapter Three

THE APPLICABILITY OF THE RESTRAINT OF TRADE DOCTRINE DURING EMPLOYMENT

Chapter Three

THE APPLICABILITY OF THE RESTRAINT OF TRADE DOCTRINE DURING EMPLOYMENT

It may be expected that during employment the employee will not attempt to compete with her employers. In that sense the interests of both parties converge. After employment, however, an employee may wish to compete with her former employers and therefore their interests diverge: *Stenhouse Australia Ltd* v *Phillips* [1974] AC 391, 400 (PC). For this reason the judiciary has adopted different principles in relation to covenants potentially in restraint of trade during employment from those applying after employment. The result is that clauses during employment are more likely to be upheld than ones applying after employment. This principle is particularly applicable when the clause is one which is adjudged to be a "normal" one in a contract of employment. A clause which instructs an employee to devote her full time and attention to the company is so very much a usual incident of the employment relationship that in respect of senior staff the clause is at present virtually unchallengeable. Similarly there may be qualifications on the right to hold shares in competing firms and on the right to divulge the employers' confidential information. Lord Wilberforce said in *Esso Petroleum Co Ltd* v *Harper's Garage (Stourport) Ltd* [1968] AC 269, 335 (HL), in relation to tied public houses, leases and documents conveying the freehold that covenants "have become part of the accepted machinery of a type of transaction which is generally found acceptable and necessary, so that instead of being regarded as restrictive they are accepted as part of the structure of a trading society. If in any individual case one finds a deviation from accepted standards, some greater restriction of an individual right to 'trade', or some artificial use of an accepted legal technique, it is right that this should be examined in the light of public policy". Restraints in employment contracts can in like fashion become incidents of such agreements. It is strange that the doctrine renders unenforceable contracts willingly entered into if its ambit is determined by normal commercial practice: one would not expect such contracts to be unenforceable. Lord Wilberforce (at 333–4) stated:

the development of the law does seem to show that judges have been able to dispense from the necessity of justification under a public policy test of reasonableness such contracts or provisions of contracts as, under contemporaneous conditions, may be found to have passed into the accepted and normal currency of . . . contractual . . . relations . . . That such contracts have done so may be taken to show with at least strong *prima* [*scil facie*] force that, moulded under the pressures of negotiation, competition and public opinion, they have assumed a form which satisfies the test of public policy as understood by the courts at the time . . . Absolute exemption . . . is never obtained: circumstances, social or economic, may have altered, since they found acceptance, in such a way as to call for a fresh examination: there may be some exorbitance or special feature in the individual contract which takes it out of the accepted category: but the court must be persuaded of this before it calls upon the relevant party to justify a contract of this kind.

Lord Wilberforce's words are directed at distinguishing between those contracts which fall within the restraint of trade doctrine and those which do not – employment contracts do. However, one may apply the thinking to terms in employment contracts. For example, although a "full time and attention" clause may be usual for senior managers, one should be wary of incorporating one into a manual worker's contract, for the judiciary has been careful not to impose restrictions on spare-time work which does not compete with the employers. This policy has the potential to encompass non-manual workers too. If employers sought to prevent a top manager from serving behind the bar at a gym in reliance on a full time and attention covenant, they may not succeed in the light of the policy of keeping some time free of employers' demands.

A similar policy can be seen even at a time when an employee is preparing to leave to establish or join a rival firm. The courts draw a line between permissible and impermissible behaviour, and employers will be disappointed by the law which allows a substantial amount of preparation before leaving even though the effect is to give the employee *carte blanche* to leave the company one evening and open up in competition the next morning. There does come a stage at which the courts are prepared to intervene, especially when a person in employment has copied the names and addresses of her employers' customers in preparation for leaving and setting up a rival firm which will use the list to contact those clients.

It is suggested that separate covenants should be drafted to cover situations during and after employment, even though the type of competition is the same. The legal analysis is that stated above: the converging and diverging interests of both parties. This advice is supported by the proposition that if one clause is too wide to be enforced after the doctrine of severance has been applied, a separate covenant may survive testing by the restraint of trade jurisprudence better than a rolled-up clause.

The application of the restraint of trade doctrine to situations during the currency of the contract may be taken to have been settled in *Esso Petroleum Co Ltd* v *Harper's Garage (Stourport) Ltd*, above, which was a case involving a solus tie. Though there are earlier cases such as *McEllistrim* v *Ballymacelligott Co-operative Agricultural and Dairy Society* [1919] AC 568 and *English Hop Growers Ltd* v *Dering*

[1928] 2 KB 174 (neither case involved employees), Lord Pearce (at 328–9) stated that the doctrine does not apply to all contracts which absorb an employee's services with the effect that he is prevented from trading with others.

> It was the sterilising of a man's capacity for work and not its absorption that underlay the objection to restraint of trade ... The doctrine does not apply to ordinary commercial contracts for the regulation and promotion of trade during the existence of the contract, provided that any prevention of work outside the contract, viewed as a whole, is directed towards the absorption of the parties' services and not their sterilisation ... When a contract only ties the parties during the continuance of the contract, and the negative ties are only those which are incidental and normal to the positive commercial arrangements at which the contract aims, even though those ties exclude all dealings with others, there is no restraint of trade within the meaning of the doctrine ... If, however, the contract ties the trading activities of either party after its determination, it is a restraint of trade ... So, too, if during the contract one of the parties is too unilaterally fettered so that the contract loses its character of a contract for the regulation and promotion of trade and acquires the predominant character of a contract in restraint of trade.

The effect is that if the clause is classified as being in restraint of trade it is *prima facie* unenforceable, whereas a normal clause is valid, unless it is held to be void for some reason.

Case law emphasises that the doctrine does not apply to "normal" or "usual" clauses in contracts of employment except in exceptional cases. The Court of Appeal in *Electronic Data Systems Ltd* v *Hubble*, 20 November 1987, unreported, a case dealing with the repayment of training expenses on a sliding scale, applied the well-known words of Lord Diplock in *Macaulay* v *A Schroeder Music Publishing Co Ltd* [1974] 1 WLR 1308, 1315–6, where he instanced the restraint of trade rules as one part of the law on unconscionable bargains. Mustill LJ said of the plaintiffs' claim to enforce a promissory note the defendant had given that the bargain was unconscionable. There was no equality of bargaining power, and the repayment of the loan was a barrier to resignation. The amount to repay was half the salary. The defendant had little choice but to continue in his job for at least two years after he had ceased training; the sum, £4,500, was not the cost of the programme or the value of it to him. The employers' motive "was not to get their money back, but to make sure that persons who by working in their organisation had learned their ways and had developed skills did not go off to use their knowledge and skills in the employment of competitors". The court granted the employee leave to defend the plaintiffs' application under Order 14 RSC. For an unconscionable bargain between a boxer and a promoter see *Watson* v *Prager* [1991] 1 WLR 726. English cases tend to involve the exclusive services of young musicians.

Where the parties are both business people or firms of equal bargaining power, the judiciary has said that "it regards the parties as the best judges of what is reasonable as between themselves" (*per* Lord Haldane C in *North Western Salt Co Ltd* v *Electrolytic Alkali Co Ltd* [1914] AC 461, 471 (HL)). Similar is the view of Lord Hodson in *Esso Petroleum*, above (at 320), where he approved the proposition of

Lord Haldane, though he weakened the statement by referring to the parties as *usually* the best judges.

Express Terms During Employment: Advantages over Implied Terms

Employers may use express terms to protect their interests. These terms may be written or oral. Putting terms into writing prevents disputes which are costly in time and money. Express terms hold several advantages over implied ones.

(1) The employee may be warned off from acting in a manner inconsistent with the interests of the employers: Rideout, *Principles of Labour Law*, (2nd ed, 1976), 89, called this effect a "burglar alarm". The employee is informed that if she, for example, misappropriates confidential information, she will legally be in the wrong. Implied terms, which are rarely known and understood by employees or employers, do not affect the mind of the defendant in the same way for she is not put on notice of the possibility that there may be a breach of contract if she proceeds. Not just advertent but inadvertent breaches may be prevented.

(2) The express term may have "a chilling effect on negotiations with a prospective employer, who may wish to avoid even the threat of litigation", as the District of Columbia Circuit put it in *Maloney* v *E I du Pont de Nemours & Co*, 352 F 2d 936, 939 (1965). The employers-to-be are less likely to be aware of implied terms.

(3) There will rarely be direct evidence that either a former employee has breached the implied duty of confidentiality by using or disclosing trade secrets or she may do so. It will usually be easier to show that she has acted or will act in breach of an express term such as one not to work for others. In contested cases the width of the implied duty of faithful service is uncertain until the court determines the outcome of the trial. Express terms can succinctly encapsulate the various heads of the implied duty into a more concrete form with the result that the employee is given notice of the stage when she is in breach of the terms: she knows what is allowed and what is not. A written clause may even put into express form the whole of the implied duty. A clause that the employee will "faithfully serve" the firm will do so. The advantage of such a broad clause is that if only certain headings of the implied obligation are expressly incorporated, an employee may be misled into thinking that she is not bound by the ones not expressly stated. The clause obviates any false impression.

(4) Employers may more easily gain an injunction when the protected material is included expressly than otherwise because the courts know what is to be forbidden and so are able to frame the order with no difficulty.

(5) It is arguable that an implied term should be of narrower width than a covenant because while at least in theory an employee has the opportunity to object to an express clause, there is no such opportunity in respect of an implied one: *Balston Ltd* v *Headline Filters Ltd* [1987] FSR 330, 352.

(6) An express term may cover more information than an implied one. A term will not be implied when information which is to be protected is not readily separable from information in the public domain. Nevertheless, a covenant may be upheld.

The lack of an express restraint clause may be evidence that the employers have not taken sufficient measures to protect information which would otherwise be protectable under the implied duty of confidentiality. See for example *Printers & Finishers Ltd* v *Holloway* [1965] RPC 239. This lack also may result in the information being protected only when it passes the *Faccenda Chicken Ltd* v *Fowler* [1987] Ch 117 (CA) test, whereas, though the point is moot, it may be protected by a covenant. See Chapter 11.

An express clause will not be construed to obviate the deficiencies of poor draftsmanship. A clause prohibiting "disclosure" does not extend to use: *Thomas Marshall (Exports) Ltd* v *Guinle* [1979] Ch 227. Nevertheless, as that case demonstrates, the utilisation of an express term does not *pro tanto* abolish the implied term. The latter remains, ready to spring up to mend the defect: on the facts "use" was prevented by the implied term.

Express Terms

Whole Time and Attention Clauses and Exclusive Services

A clause stating that an employee will devote her whole time and attention to the business is a common-form one in the contracts of managers but not of employees of junior status. From an industrial sociology perspective one might expect that senior people would devote their whole time and attention to the employers, whereas junior workers would not.

The phrase "whole time and attention" is something of a misnomer. No employer could expect an employee to work 24 hours a day, seven days a week, 52 weeks a year for them – death would supervene – and the law draws a line in relation to implied terms between contractual hours and spare time. The law on express terms is not so clear because of the paucity of cases. With regard to spare time the implied term permits the employee to engage in activities which do not cause serious harm to the employers. Similar thinking, it is suggested, pervades the express term. The employee may be prohibited from competing during contracted working hours, a phrase which includes overtime agreed by the parties. The furthest extent of the clause is dependent, it seems, on reasonableness. In the event of the employee being an executive, a clause stating that she must devote her whole time and attention to the employers' business at such times as the employers reasonably determine may well be upheld. Similarly a clause stating that a senior employee would work unpaid overtime would be upheld. In that eventuality, those hours remain, as it were, the employers'. The employee is forbidden to work for others during that time. A clause stating that the employee is bound to devote her whole time and attention to the employers' business when she is performing her duties would presumably be upheld.

All these different framed clauses are apt to cover both activities which compete with the employers and those which do not. They will, for example, prevent an executive who works for a drugs firm from serving in a pub at lunch-time as well as forbidding her from engaging in directly competitive activities for a rival firm. Such clauses serve to preserve any competitive advantage the employers have.

Recent cases are few but on the whole support the above analysis. In *Johnstone* v *Bloomsbury Health Authority* [1992] QB 333 the Court of Appeal by a majority upheld a clause that the plaintiff, a junior hospital doctor, would work for 40 hours per week and in addition be available for work on average for 48 hours per week. In other words the average was 88 hours but for some weeks he would work for considerably longer to make up any deficit in the hours. Stuart-Smith LJ, dissenting, said that the express term was subject to the implied duty to take reasonable care for the safety of the employee (at 343–4). Leggatt LJ (in the majority on this point) said: "as a matter of law reliance on an express term cannot involve breach of an implied term. The defendants cannot be said by the mere fact of requiring the plaintiff to work no more hours than he had contracted to work, to be in breach of any contractual duty owed to him . . . In the result if the plaintiff fell sick during the performance of his employment . . . because it was too arduous for him, he did not do so by reason of any relevant breach of duty on the defendants' part" (at 349). Browne-Wilkinson V-C (at 350–1) construed the express and the implied terms to avoid a conflict, but if they did conflict, the express term would prevail.

The *Johnstone* case is one among several where the courts have been invited to rule whether an express term can be cut down by an implied one. In orthodox law such a qualification is not possible; however, in employment law there have been several cases over the past decade where the court has been persuaded that an implied term can modify an express one. The issue has arisen particularly in the construction of mobility and flexibility clauses. For example, in *United Bank Ltd* v *Akhtar* [1989] IRLR 507 (EAT) an express term that the employers could move the employee at will was held to be subject to an implied term that they would not do so unreasonably. The orthodox position continues to receive support. One illustration is *Rank Xerox Ltd* v *Churchill* [1988] IRLR 280 (EAT) where it was held that an unambiguous express term could not be limited by an implied duty not to exercise powers under that term unreasonably. A compromise was reached by the EAT in *White* v *Reflecting Roadstuds Ltd* [1991] ICR 733. It was held that *United Bank*'s ratio was that the employers could not enforce an express clause in a manner which prevented the employee from performing her side of the contract.

The amount of spare time an employee has may depend on the existence and enforceability of a "whole time and attention" clause. With regard to such leisure time as remains, there are legal difficulties in the way of express terms prohibiting the employee from engaging in work. The restraint of trade doctrine may apply to clauses which prevent the employee from engaging in activities which will lead after employment to competition with the present employers. For example, certain preparatory acts are not forbidden under the implied duty of fidelity: may they be stopped by an express clause? The law is unclear but it appears that such a term is valid provided that the effect is not to make the employee comply with it or starve: *Young* v *Timmins* (1831) 148 ER 1446 (Ex). Lord Reid said in *Esso Petroleum Co Ltd* v *Harper's Garage (Stourport) Ltd* [1968] AC 269, 294, that an employee:

> may enter into a contract of service or may agree to give his exclusive services to another: then during the period of the contract he is not entitled to engage in other business activities. But no one has ever suggested that such contracts are in restraint of trade except in very unusual circumstances, such as those in *Young* v *Timmins*, where the servant had agreed not to work for anyone else but might have been given no work and received no remuneration and thus have been deprived of a livelihood . . .

Lord Reid returned to the issue in *Macaulay*, above at 1314. "Any contract by which a person engages to give his exclusive services to another for a period necessarily involves extensive restriction during that time of the common law right to exercise any lawful activity he chooses in such manner as he thinks best. Normally, the doctrine of restraint of trade has no application to such restrictions: they require no justification. But if contracted restrictions appear to be unnecessary or to be reasonably capable of enforcement in an oppressive manner, they must be justified before they can be enforced." Lord Pearce in *Esso* (at 328) applied his distinction between sterilising an employee's ability to work for others during employment and the absorption of her work into the enterprise of which she was an employee. "It was the sterilising of a man's capacity to work and not its absorption that underlay the objection to restraint of trade. This is the rationale of *Young* v *Timmins*, where a brass foundry was during the contract sterilised so that it could only work for a party who might choose not to absorb its output at all but to go to other foundries with the result that the foundry was completely at the mercy of the other party and might remain idle . . . ." The language can be used of natural persons: if the contract permits the employers to use others but the employee may work only for them, the restraint of trade law applies. *Ehrman* v *Bartholomew* [1898] 1 Ch 671 (Romer J) is illustrative. The court refused to grant an injunction to a wine merchant who sought to enforce a covenant that his commercial traveller would not be employed in any other business or transact any business because the clause was not restricted to the business sought to be protected. The covenant thus was "unreasonable". He followed the approach of Lindley MR in *Whitwood Chemical Co* v *Hardman* [1891] 2 Ch 416 that: "cases where negative stipulations in contracts of service are enforced by the Court ought not to be extended, and are to be regarded as anomalies which it would be very dangerous to extend. To enforce such a general negative stipulation as I find here would be . . . a dangerous extension, for here the stipulation extends to business of any kind, while the negative stipulations enforced in the prior cases ... were confined to special services''.

Employers often insert clauses which curtail the width of forbidden activities outside employment. One such clause is a term that the employers may give their consent to such activities. This type of clause may produce some goodwill for the employers and it does not harm them for they will refuse consent for competitive behaviour. Sometimes a consent clause is drafted with the proviso that agreement will not be unreasonably withheld. Such a term leaves the way open for employees to challenge management discretion to refuse consent and may lead to time-consuming and expensive disputes. For example, an employee who is a human resources management expert in a certain firm may argue that his teaching part-time on, say, a Higher National Certificate course in business management should be permitted but his employers may contend that the teaching will inevitably reveal their organisational methods, which are the foundation of their success. The resolution of such dispute is uncertain. Therefore, employers are advised that if they wish to preserve their freedom to grant or refuse consent to outside working the term should be baldly stated; for instance, ''consent may be given to outside activities at the employers' absolute discretion''. Moreover, since employers are very likely to ban competitive behaviour but may well not forbid non-competitive conduct, there seems to be no point in incorporating a clause that consent will not be withheld unreasonably, for it would generally not be unreasonable to prevent competition but it might be so to forbid non-competitive behaviour. In this sense such a clause adds nothing.

One issue which has arisen in relation to consent clauses is whether such terms save bans on working for others or oneself at times which do not ''belong'' to the employer. The principal authority remains *Chafer Ltd* v *Lilley* (1946) 176 LT 22. Roxburgh J held that a covenant was unenforceable because it did not protect a lawful subject-matter but ''an unlawful subject-matter, namely, direct competi-tion''. He added that a consent clause could not render lawful that which was unlawful: since the covenant was invalid, it could not be rendered valid by the proviso. While this case concerned covenants in restraint of trade post-employment, there is no reason to doubt that it applies also to clauses during employment. Another post-employment covenant case is *Technograph Printed Circuits Ltd* v *Chalwyn Ltd* (1967) 84 RPC 339. Plowman J said (at 344) that an unenforceable agreement was not saved by a consent provision, applying *Chafer Ltd* v *Lilley* and *Perls* v *Saalfeld* [1892] 2 Ch 149 (CA). In the latter case Lindley LJ had said that the proviso as to consent was meaningless unless the covenant was wider than was reasonable; since the covenant did not protect the employers' business, the proviso fell with the consent (at 152). There is one contrary authority, *Kerchiss* v *Colora Printing Inks Ltd* [1960] RPC 235, a first instance decision also involving a post-employment covenant. Diplock J held (at 240) that a covenant not to enter into the employment of a manufacturer of any type of ink in 16 countries for three years after termination of the contract would have been invalid because the plaintiff worked on only certain types of ink whereas the covenant prohibited his working on all types. However the covenant was saved by the proviso as to consent. The House of Lords in *General Billposting Co Ltd* v *Atkinson* [1909] AC 118 had the opportunity of clarifying this issue but did not take it.

An express clause which is coming to be common form in managers' contracts acts, it may be said, in a way similar to consent clauses. It permits an employee to invest in shares on a recognised Stock Exchange such as London. Such clauses often have a cap of 5% of the share capital.

Disclosure of Misconduct

An express term obliging the employee to report her colleagues' misconduct such as engaging in competitive activity may give her pause for thought before she undertakes competition and may extend the implied duty of faithful service. It may be argued that adding a duty to disclose one's own misdeeds is superfluous for the employee is unlikely to be prevented from misdeeds by contract, but such a clause may act as a deterrent.

The law is not pellucid and cases are few. In *Swain* v *West (Butchers) Ltd* [1936] 3 All ER 261 the Court of Appeal construed a duty to disclose to the board the unlawful orders of his superior, the managing director, under whose supervision he worked, out of an express term that he would "do all in his power to promote, extend and develop the interests of the company". It is suggested that a court will read such a clause as giving effect to a duty to reveal misdeeds of fellow employees only when the relevant employee is in a senior position. The employee in *Swain* was a general manager, a position high in the corporate hierarchy. In relation to junior employees the Scottish EAT held in *Distillers Co (Bottling Services) Ltd* v *Gardner* [1982] IRLR 47 that the duty to report a fellow worker who stole from the employers had to be one clearly placed on the employee. A prohibition on stealing did not give rise to such an obligation. Lord McDonald (at 50) emphasised that "[i]t is asking a lot of an employee to require him to report the misdemeanours of his colleagues, but if it is to be the rule, it should ... be very clearly spelled out".

The implied duty to disclose wrongdoings does not extend to an obligation to reveal one's own misconduct. An express clause obliging the employee to do so is unlikely to stop her misbehaving when she is preparing to establish a rival business but it alerts her that her conduct is not tolerable and accordingly may help prevent activities which are intended to ripen into competition. Employers would be well advised to include such a clause. The effect of *Distillers* is to impel employers towards inserting a specific express term detailing the obligation to reveal colleagues' wrongdoings. A clause may be so worded as to prohibit activities which are lawful under the implied duty such as leasing premises where competitive activity is to take place. In addition employers may wish to embody the term which gave rise to the duty in *Swain*, one to "promote, develop and extend the interests" of the employers.

Confidential Information

During employment the employers can protect more information than after-wards. A clause preventing the employee from using or disclosing any informa-tion acquired during employment from his employers or their suppliers, dis-tributors or customers is likely to be upheld on the basis that the restraint of trade doctrine does not touch such normal clauses.

There is some debate whether such a clause prevents the disclosure of informa-tion freely available to the public such as a client's telephone number which appears in *Yellow Pages*. Full force has not been accorded to clauses in this area, and it may be that information which is in the public domain cannot be the subject of injunction, though the possibility of a (nominal) monetary remedy remains. It is hard to see what purpose would be served by a term preventing the disclosure of material in the public domain except that the employee may be put on notice not to reveal any information whether public or private. In any case she is subject to the springboard doctrine (see below) if she has herself put con-fidential information into the public domain.

Surrender

It is usual and useful to insert a clause into a contract of employment that the employee will return all the employers' property on termination. An illustration is a term that the employee shall "on termination of the contract of employment deliver up to the employers all documents, blueprints, and other property of the employers which are in the possession of the employee. The employee shall make no copies".

Intellectual Property

A clause that the employee must disclose inventions and discoveries to the employers should be inserted. A similar clause can be used to cover improve-ments to inventions and discoveries. The Patents Act 1977 supersedes incon-sistent contractual terms. A clause might read: "Any invention, discovery, design or improvement made or discovered by the employee shall be the employers' property (subject to s 39 of the Patents Act 1977), provided that it relates to the employers' business".

In respect of intellectual property rights such as copyright, design right and trade marks, statute decrees that ownership resides in the employers if it was created by the employee in the course of employment. To cover matters arising outside of the course of employment employers may insert an express clause that intellectual property created in such circumstances belongs nevertheless to the employers.

Garden Leave

The aim of a garden leave clause is to prevent an employee from making contacts or gaining information from the employers in the time after she has been recruited to join another firm or has decided to set up in competition and until she leaves. The clause permits the employee not to work for the employers during the notice period but provides her with a salary and other contractual benefits to meet the objection that if she is not working and thereby earning money, she must be starving and the law does not permit a choice between working for one particular employer or starving. The employee may tend her garden, go on holiday or whatever, provided that she does not engage in a competitive activity. It would seem that any full time and attention clause is displaced. A drafting tip is that the clause should expressly provide that the employee may do anything which is not competitive with her employers. Such a clause may make the court look more favourably on a garden leave clause than would otherwise be the case. If the clause is upheld, the effect is to stop the employee from gaining confidential information during the notice period and may prevent contact between suppliers, customers, colleagues and her, thereby diminishing the employers' competitive capability. The popularity of this type of clause is a function of the public policy against covenants in restraint of trade. The courts are more willing to uphold express clauses applying during employment than those applying post-termination.

Cases are rare, though the clauses are quite common in executives' contracts of employment. One of the principal authorities is *Provident Financial Group plc* v *Hayward* [1989] ICR 160 (CA). The employee was the financial director of the plaintiffs. He gave the six months' notice as required by the contract. During his garden leave he tried to join a firm, the business of which was similar to that of his employers. The court would have granted an interlocutory injunction preventing him from so doing if the plaintiffs' competitive edge would have been dented by the employee's defection. The court held, however, that their market position would not be undermined. The confidential information the employee had was of no use to his new employers, and so no detriment to his present employers would be occasioned by his working for his new ones. Corporate plans, group strategies, profitability and developments did not comprise information which the new employers could use because they operated out of supermarkets, not out of estate agents' offices as the current ones did.

A case which at first sight looks like a garden leave one but in fact is not is *Evening Standard Co Ltd* v *Henderson* [1987] ICR 588 (CA), where the plaintiffs were ready for the employee to continue working on their premises. The facts of the case are not complex but the argument requires study to understand the court's reasoning. The employee desired to join a rival of his employers. By contract he had to give 12 months' notice. He sought to give only two months' notice. His doing so would have been a breach of contract. The employers decided not to accept the breach of contract, the legal basis, which is disputable, being that a breach of a fundamental term of a contract of employment does not automatically terminate it but gives the injured party the option to terminate or to keep the contract in existence. The court granted the plaintiffs an interlocutory injunction. It accepted their undertaking to pay the employee's salary during the notice period. This undertaking applied whether the employee came in to work for them or not. If he did not the employers undertook not to sue for damages. The court stated (at 594) that the employers were not gaining specific perform-ance of the contract of service, which the law forbids. In these circumstances the implied duty of faithful service as well as any express term will apply to prevent the employee from utilising confidential information and trade connections.

One difficulty which has arisen in relation to garden leave clauses is the effect of any contractual right, implied or sometimes express, that the employee has to work. If the employers fail to accord their right to employees during the notice period, they run the risk of being in breach of contract and, if this breach is repudiatory, the contract, including the garden leave clause, will fall. The issue was discussed in *Spencer* v *Marchington* [1988] IRLR 392 (Ch D). The employee sought to argue that she had a right to work because she was paid by a share of the profits. Her contention was that her employer's request that she should not work out the last two months of her contractual 12 months notice period was a breach of a fundamental term, her right to work. Mowbray QC sitting as a deputy High Court judge held that the breach was not repudiatory ostensibly on the grounds that she had agreed to two months' garden leave and that she did not accept this breach, if any, which under the elective theory of repudiation she had to do. The way round the difficulty seen in *Spencer* v *Marchington* is the provision that the employers are under no duty to provide work once notice has been given even if the case is one of the exceptional ones such as where the employee is paid only by commission, when the employers are under such an obligation.

The courts have also stated that they will not enforce garden leave clauses which result in skilled workers losing their aptitudes. In *Provident* Taylor LJ (at 170) spoke of the employee's skills becoming rusty. The courts have thus provided themselves with a weapon to strike down lengthy garden leaves. Employ-ers should consider how long it would be before the employee's skills begin to become rusty. If it is three months, leave should last for only that duration. The outcome is that although the notice period is lengthy, say 12 months or two years, the garden leave may apply only to the last three or six months of that period. This analysis is in line with the rationale of such clauses: the protection of customer connection, trade secrets and confidential information. If the employee poses no danger, the clause is worthless. For remedies for breach of garden leave clauses see Chapter 13.

The Effect of Striking Down an Express Term

If the express term is for whatever reason void or unenforceable, the implied duty of faithful service may spring up. The incorporation of an express term does not, therefore, abolish the implied term *pro tanto* but displaces it. The classic definition of this point is the judgment in the patents case of *Triplex Safety Glass Co Ltd* v *Scorah* [1938] Ch 211, 217. Farwell J said "it cannot be that merely because a servant covenants in his contract of service to behave properly and honestly towards his employer, and that contract of service happens to be too wide to be enforceable, that he is thereby entitled to be as dishonest and to act as unfairly as he pleases towards his employers. That obviously could not be so".

A more up-to-date authority is *Thomas Marshall (Exports) Ltd* v *Guinle* [1979] Ch 227. Megarry V-C held (at 247) that an express prohibition on disclosure did not prohibit the employee from using it. However, the defendant's use of confidential information was forbidden by the implied duty of fidelity. As *Guinle* demonstrates, the implied term can at times supply the defects in the draftsmanship of express terms. For the reason stated above it is wise to incorporate express terms, using the implied duty as a fall-back position.

In *Provident Financial Group plc* v *Hayward*, above, the defendant's counsel contended that an order to enforce a negative covenant (one not to work for anyone else during the contract of employment) had to be phrased in the very words of the agreement. Dillon LJ (at 167) accepted that the argument was correct in relation to a restraint clause but that it was incorrect where the express negative clause was the same as an implied one, here the employee's obligation of good faith. That implied obligation was enforceable by an injunction preventing the employee from working for rivals, applying *Hivac Ltd* v *Park Royal Scientific Instruments Ltd* [1946] Ch 169 (CA) and *Guinle*, above. Therefore, the injunction to enforce the express term could also be framed in such a way, that is to forbid the employee from working for named rivals or all rivals.

While the implied duty of fidelity is only displaced by the express term, and the implied term springs up if the express one is void or unenforceable, a clause stating *ex abundanti cautela* that express terms operate without prejudice to implied terms can be incorporated to warn off the employee from acting in a way incompatible with the contract.

Summary

Parker J in *Panayiotou* v *Sony Music Entertainment (UK) Ltd* [1994] EMLR 229, 335, stated that "while the mere fact that the operation of a restraint is limited to the period of the contract may not suffice to justify the restraint, it is ... a factor to be brought into account on the side of justification ... ".

Contents of Chapter Four

TERMINATION OF THE CONTRACT OF EMPLOYMENT

Chapter Four

TERMINATION OF THE CONTRACT OF EMPLOYMENT

When is the Contract Terminated?

The moment of termination of an employment contract is not always clear, yet it is at that point when the duty of faithful service ceases and when covenants for the period after termination take effect. Moreover, repudiation by the employers which destroys covenants depends on there being a contract to repudiate, and employers can gain injunctions to enforce garden leave clauses when there is a contract to enforce.

Where the parties terminate the contract by mutual agreement, they may include in a document a date on which the service contract is to end, and normally there will be no problem in determining the date of the cessation of the contract. Where the contract is terminated on the expiry of a fixed term, by definition the contract ends on that ascertained date. A contract of employment is terminated by frustration at the moment of frustration. Neither party need perform any act to bring the agreement to a close. A contract is terminated even though it is impossible to say exactly when frustration occurred: *Marshall* v *Harland & Wolff Ltd* [1972] 1 WLR 899 (NIRC). A contract of employment is terminated by the death of either the employee or the employer, by the dissolution of a partnership (provided that the obligations under the partnership agreement were personal to the deceased partner: see *Phillips* v *Alhambra Palace Co* [1901] 1 QB 59 (QBD)), and by the compulsory winding up of a company and the appointment by the court of a receiver. There is complex law relating to the appointment of a receiver by the debenture holders. Where either the employers or the employee gives contractual notice of the termination of the contract, the parties can agree that the notice period need not be worked out or that the period be abridged.

The date of termination is dependent in the normal run of cases (where the employee is dismissed or resigns) on whether repudiation terminates the contract of employment automatically or whether the innocent party is given the choice whether to accept the repudiation or not. The effect on remedies is discussed in Chapter 12. Dicta are divided on which theory is correct. If the employers' wrongful breach of contract automatically terminates it with the result that the employee is dismissed no matter how ready and willing she is to work, the logical position is that covenants fall and the employee loses any right to pay post-termination including, for example, commission from insurance premiums. Cases in support of the automatic theory include *Denmark Productions Ltd* v *Boscobel Productions Ltd* [1969] 1 QB 699 (CA). The argument accepted was dependent on mutuality. Since employers cannot obtain specific performance of their employee's contract, similarly an employee cannot obtain specific performance of the employers' obligations. In *Sanders* v *Ernest A Neale Ltd* [1974] ICR 565, 571 (NIRC) Donaldson P said: " ... the repudiation of a contract of employment is an exception to the general rule. It terminates the contract without the necessity for acceptance by the injured party". Some authorities such as *Decro-Wall International SA* v *Practitioners in Marketing Ltd* [1971] 1 WLR 361 (CA) and *Gunton* v *Richmond-upon-Thames LBC* [1981] Ch 448 (CA, by a majority) support the elective theory, the best brief statement of which was given by Asquith LJ in *Howard* v *Pickford Tool Co* [1951] 1 KB 417, 421: "[a]n unaccepted repudiation is a thing writ in water and of no value to anybody ... ". The lack of clarity is exacerbated by the law sometimes laid down that where the employee has broken the contract, the innocent party may elect to keep the contract alive with the effect that covenants continue to apply: *Thomas Marshall (Exports) Ltd* v *Guinle* [1979] Ch 227, 242–3 (Megarry V-C). It cannot be said that the issue is settled. In the latest case, *Boyo* v *Lambeth LBC* [1994] ICR 727 (CA), the elective theory was applied because of precedent but two members of the court would have used the automatic theory, had they not been bound (see Staughton LJ at 747 and Sir Francis Purchas at 750). The case did not involve covenants.

An issue which has arisen quite recently is whether every dismissal without notice constitutes a repudiation. In *Lawrence David Ltd* v *Ashton* [1991] 1 All ER 385 the defendant, a sales director, covenanted with the plaintiffs, manufacturers and sellers of vehicle bodies, that he would not *inter alia* reveal their trade secrets or for two years after termination "carry on or be employed in any capacity or be interested directly or indirectly in the ... manufacture or supply of any sliding door vehicle body ... ". The plaintiffs dismissed him. He received a job offer from a competing company. They sought an interlocutory injunction to enforce the clauses. Balcombe LJ (at 394) stated that not every breach of a contract of employment was repudiatory and held that there was a serious question to be tried within *American Cyanamid Co* v *Ethicon Ltd* [1975] AC 396 (HL) whether on the facts the particular breach, dismissal without proper notice, was repudiatory. If there was no repudiation, employers would be able to enforce covenants in restraint of trade.

A similar theory applies during the running of the contract to putting an employee on garden leave under the contractual notice provisions. Where an employee has a contractual right to work, failure to accord him the right constitutes repudiation. In *Provident Financial Group plc* v *Hayward* [1989] ICR 160

(CA) Dillon LJ (at 168) noted that cases which state that employers must provide work normally involve actors and others who need publicity (see for example *Herbert Clayton and Jack Waller Ltd* v *Oliver* [1930] AC 209 (HL)), but he thought that employers had a duty to provide work to chartered accountants for otherwise their skills would atrophy. Dillon LJ might also have mentioned piecework (see for example *Devonald* v *Rosser & Sons* [1906] 2 KB 728 (CA)) and commission (see for example *Turner* v *Goldsmith* [1891] 1 QB 544 (CA)), but the general rule remains that classically stated by Asquith J in *Collier* v *Sunday Referee Publishing Co Ltd* [1940] 2 KB 647, 650: "provided I pay my cook her wages regularly, she cannot complain if I choose to take any or all of my meals out".

If the employee departs without adhering to the notice period the contract ends either automatically or on the employers' acceptance, depending on which theory is adopted. When it is the employee who gives notice, rules similar to those stated below in relation to the employers' giving notice govern. The contract ceases when the notice period expires, if the employee works out the period. If the employers agree to let the employee not work out that period but be paid normally, the contract terminates when the period elapses. If the employers pay the employee's salary in a lump sum with the proviso that the employee leaves immediately, *semble* the contract continues until the end of the notice period. If, however, there is a repudiation by the employers, the contract terminates automatically or on acceptance (see above).

Where the employers give the requisite period of notice under the contract and whether or not the employee is obliged to work out the notice or not, the contract terminates on the expiry of the notice, subject to the rule that if the employers' words or conduct are repudiatory of the contract, the contract may well continue until the employee accepts the breach. In the event of the contract's continuance, the employee is still bound by contractual duties such as the obligation of faithful service. In the event of the employers dismissing the employee, they may provide wages in lieu of notice. The law, which is complex, was laid down in *Delaney* v *Staples* [1992] AC 687 (HL):

(1) If the parties agree that the employment contract is to cease on a certain day, it does so.
(2) If the employers give the employee the correct length of notice but give her pay in lieu, the contract terminates at the expiry of the notice period. The pay is deemed to be an advance of salary or wages.
(3) If there is an express contractual term permitting the employers to give pay in lieu of notice, the contract terminates on the date when the employee stops working; that is, before the end of the notice period: *Rex Stewart Jeffries Parker Ginsberg Ltd* v *Parker* [1988] IRLR 483 (CA). The defendant's contract included a term that his employment could be "determined by the giving in writing of six calendar months' notice on either side or the payment of six months' salary in lieu thereof". He was dismissed for redundancy with one week's notice. He was given, according to the letter terminating his contract, six months' pay in lieu of notice in accord with his contract. The

defendant contended in one of his arguments that by giving him only one week's notice (and not the six months' notice) the plaintiffs were in breach of a fundamental term of his contract with the result that he was no longer bound by a non-solicitation covenant. Glidewell LJ (at 485) – the other judge merely said that he agreed – distinguished *Dixon* v *Stenor Ltd* [1973] ICR 157 (NIRC) as being a case in which the contract itself did not provide for payment in lieu. The instant clause gave the plaintiffs an option, which they took. By doing so they were exercising their rights under the contract. Therefore, there was no breach. The court rejected the argument that where the contract provides for money in lieu, it merely quantifies the amount of damages due for failure to give the correct period of notice. The court ruled that the option was not contrary to statute. Section 49(3) of the Employment Protection (Consolidation) Act 1978 reads in part: " ... this section shall not be taken to prevent either party from waiving his right to notice on any occasion, or from accepting a payment in lieu of notice". The clause as to payment in lieu applied even though it was in the contract at the commencement of employment: it need not be part of the agreement terminating it. As this case demonstrates, payment in lieu based on an express term is not a repudiatory breach of contract. Therefore, covenants in restraint of trade survive. Employers are well-advised to insert such a clause.

(4)   If the contract has no express term permitting pay in lieu of notice, the contract terminates immediately, if the automatic theory of termination is adopted, or at the latest when the employee accepts the repudiation, if the elective theory is followed. Pay is deemed to be damages for breach of contract. The authority is *Dixon* v *Stenor Ltd*, above.

Somewhat similar to *Rex Stewart* is *Spencer* v *Marchington* [1988] IRLR 392, 395, a decision of Mowbray QC in the Chancery Division. He ruled that the defendant's asking the employee to stay away from her desk for one week out of a 12-month contract did not amount to a "fundamental breach". Since there was no repudiation, the clause stood. Even if there was a repudiation, the employee did not accept it. This elective theory of termination of employment contracts works hardship on employees in this context. *Spencer* v *Marchington* is an illustration of where payment in lieu means that there is no dismissal: the employee simply serves his or her period of notice by staying at home. Unless there is a duty to provide work, the employers are not in breach of contract and so *General Billposting* (see below) is inapplicable. This approach is contrary to that of Sir John Donaldson, as he then was, in *Dixon* v *Stenor Ltd* above, who held payment in lieu to be payment for breach of contract. There was a dismissal and so *General Billposting* applied. The difference between these two approaches to payment in lieu is said to reside in the wording of the contract. If that is correct, employers would be well-advised to do what the employers did in *Rex Stewart*: insert a term providing for pay in lieu. In that eventuality, employers can rely on covenants.

It is not always easy to slot the facts into a particular category. The principal problem is to differentiate between (2) and (4). It has been said that the question is resolved by construing the document through which notice was given or the verbal situation in which the employers gave notice. There is a suggestion that where the facts are not clear-cut, the courts will strive to hold that dismissal with pay for the period which the employee would otherwise have worked under her contract will lead to the contract being terminated with immediate effect (that is the facts fall within (4)): *Berkeley Administration Inc* v *McClelland* [1990] FSR 505. The result on the facts of the case was that the employee was permitted to use confidential information he had acquired during employment for his own purposes during the notice period. If the facts had fallen within (2), he would not have been so permitted.

It should be noted that where there is an express term permitting the employers to dismiss by notice or by giving a sum in lieu, the amount in lieu does not represent damages for wrongful dismissal but represents the sum due under the contract. Therefore, no mitigation is required: *Abrahams* v *Performing Rights Society* [1995] IRLR 486 (CA). In these circumstances termination is lawful, not wrongful. Leave to appeal was refused.

Wrongful Dismissal and Covenants

If the employers do not give notice or they give insufficient notice, that is they dismiss summarily, the contract terminates immediately if the dismissal was justified; if, however, the dismissal is wrongful, termination occurs either on dismissal or on acceptance depending on which theory of termination is adopted. Repudiation by the employers signifies that the covenants in restraint of trade fall: *General Billposting Co Ltd* v *Atkinson* [1909] AC 118 (HL). The defendant, manager of the plaintiffs, covenanted that he would not carry on a business similar to that of his employers for two years after the termination of his contract of employment within a certain radius without their permission. They dismissed him without notice. The House of Lords (of which there were only three members) in very brief speeches dismissed the plaintiffs' appeal. Lord Collins (at 122) said that once the plaintiffs had evinced an intention no longer to be bound by the contract as they did by dismissing the defendant in breach of the notice period, he "was thereupon justified in rescinding the contract and treating himself as absolved from the further performance of it on his part". He rejected the argument of the plaintiffs that this rule applied only when the clauses were interdependent. Lord Robertson (at 121) stated that the covenant was ancillary to the contract and "once the contract of service is rescinded the other falls with it". *General Billposting* continues to apply today: see *Unigate Dairies (Western) Ltd* v *Cooter*, 21 July 1982, LEXIS (CA). Scotland provides several authorities including *Scotcoast Ltd* v *Halliday*, 10 January 1995, LEXIS (Outer House).

The width of *General Billposting* is uncertain. Express clauses fall, but what of implied terms? If implied terms fall too, do any equitable duties of confidentiality survive? The following cases are a sample of those where the courts have held that there has been repudiatory behaviour (with the effect that covenants fall).

- Reduction in pay: *Industrial Rubber Products* v *Gillon* [1977] IRLR 389.
- Change in the employee's contractual duties: *Pedersen* v *LB of Camden* [1981] ICR 674 (CA).
- Dissolution of a partnership: *Briggs* v *Oates* [1990] ICR 473 (Ch D). The plaintiff informed the other party that he did not wish to continue in partnership. The defendant, an assistant solicitor (a salaried employee, not a partner), left to set up a new firm of solicitors, 120 yards from his former firm. The plaintiffs sought to enforce a covenant that the employee would not practise for five years after termination within five miles of Market Place, Huddersfield, and would not accept instructions from his former clients for five years. Scott J held that in the light of the personal nature of the partnership the dissolution determined the contract of employment, unless there was an express term to the contrary. He applied *Bruce* v *Calder* [1895] 2 QB 253 (CA).
- Winding-up of a company: *Measures Bros Ltd* v *Measures* [1910] 2 Ch 238 (CA). This case, which was applied in *Briggs* v *Oates*, held that since the defendant, a director, no longer held office because of the compulsory winding-up of the company, he was no longer bound by a covenant not to compete for seven years after ceasing to hold office.

Summary

If there is no express clause permitting the employers to terminate the contract summarily for whatever reason with pay provided in lieu of notice, they are in repudiatory breach of contract: *Dixon* v *Stenor Ltd*, above. In the event of a repudiatory breach, covenants in restraint of trade fall: *General Billposting Co Ltd* v *Atkinson*, above. Accordingly, employers should insert a clause that payment in lieu is permitted. In that case the covenant survives: *Rex Stewart Jeffries Parker Ginsberg Ltd* v *Parker*, above. An interesting if perhaps academic issue not discussed in the cases is whether a covenant rendered unenforceable by *General Billposting* may be saved, should subsequently discovered facts justify a previously wrongful dismissal under the rule in *Boston Deep Sea Fishing & Ice Co Ltd* v *Ansell* (1888) 39 Ch D 339 (CA). One argument is that the covenant is suspended for a time but then made enforceable restrospectively.

May *General Billposting* be Evaded by Careful Drafting?

There have been many suggestions that a well-drafted covenant will not fall when the employers have wrongfully dismissed the employee. In *Lawrence David Ltd* v

1991

Ashton, above, the clause 11 purported to apply when the contract was terminated "for any reason whatsoever". In *Arthur Murray Dance Studios of Cleveland Inc* v *Witter,* 105 NE 2d 685 (1952) the covenant was drafted to apply when the covenant had been terminated "for any cause". This issue is discussed below.

One suggestion is that the difficulty posed to employers by *General Billposting* may be solved by the use of a collateral contract. In this context wrongful repudiation would terminate that contract but the collateral contract would survive, for plaintiffs can rely on a collateral contract even though the principal contract cannot be enforced: *Strongman (1945) Ltd* v *Sincock* [1955] 2 QB 525 (CA). It is suggested that this legal device would be unsuccessful. The law of restraint of trade looks to substance, not to form: see Lord Wilberforce in *Stenhouse Australia Ltd* v *Phillips* [1974] AC 391, 402. The substance is that the collateral agreement is merely a smokescreen: the truth is that employers are seeking to disapply *General Billposting,* which is not possible. It is also possible that the contract of employment and the collateral contract will be seen as in truth one contract: they are really two sides of the same issue, the agreement under which the employee works. If the courts accept this contention, the failure of the clauses in the contract of employment on wrongful dismissal will result in the failure of the covenant(s) in the collateral contract. This argument is bolstered by the proposition that a restraint of trade covenant is not the sort of provision which one would expect to see in a collateral contract. The usual instance of a collateral contract is when the defendant has induced the plaintiff to enter into a contract. The pre-contractual negotiations are statements by which the plaintiff was persuaded to agree, and her so agreeing is the consideration for the collateral contract. That situation is not reflected in a restraint of trade case. One might argue too that even if the contracts are separate, there is an implied term in the collateral contract that the employers will not terminate the principal contract through a wrongful dismissal. Even if all of these contentions fail, it is posited that breach of this collateral contract would sound only in damages. The employers would not obtain an injunction, whether temporary or permanent, because they have not acted equitably.

Since the early 1980s there has been a small amount of debate whether by express words in the contract the effect of *General Billposting* can be avoided. Might a covenant apply in the event of a wrongful repudiation if it was stated to do so in the event of a breach "howsoever caused" or "however arising"? The solution to this problem depends on the effect of *Photo Production Ltd* v *Securicor Transport Ltd* [1980] AC 827, a decision of the House of Lords dealing with exclusion clauses, not with covenants. The principal thrust of that decision is the rejection of the substantive doctrine of fundamental breach, that is that exemption and limitation clauses in contracts did not apply where the contract was terminated by a fundamental breach. Instead even where such a breach had occurred, the parties were free to determine on whom the risk should lie by means of exclusion clauses. Such choice was not defeated by the doctrine of fundamental breach. On the facts of *Photo Production* the defendants did not bear the risk of one of their employees setting fire to the plaintiffs' factory because that event was covered by their agreement. Therefore, whether the exception clause applied was a matter of construction of the term.

Two limitations on *Photo Production* ought to be brought out, and these two matters have not always been emphasised in academic analyses. First, the judiciary has eschewed law-making "in commercial matters generally, when the parties are not of unequal bargaining power, and when risks are normally borne by insurance", as Lord Wilberforce put it (at 843). None of these conditions, and especially not the third, necessarily applies to covenants between employers and employees. While one ought to be careful of the transplant of a legal phrase out of one context into another, it may be of significance that the Rome Convention on Contractual Obligations 1980 gives special protection to employees and consumers (part of UK law under the Contracts (Applicable Law) Act 1990, in force 1 April 1991). As the House noted in *Photo Production*, Parliament has enacted the Unfair Contract Terms Act 1977, which was not in force at the time of the facts of the case. In their Lordships' view such intervention signified that judicial legislation was not required either for consumers (who are protected by the Act) or for businesses (which are not). While the current government does not seem willing to protect employees' rights, except when obliged to do so by EC law, one can perhaps draw from the present state of the law that covenants fall neither under the Act nor under this aspect of *Photo Production*. Therefore, there is room for judicial manoeuvre. Secondly, since the effect of exception clauses depends on their construction, judges could if they wished construe them *contra proferentem* and hold that the covenant does not apply after breach where the occurrence is not foreseen expressly in the contract. Such interpretation is bolstered by the presumption of invalidity of covenants, that is employers bear the burden of proving that the clause is reasonable in the interests of the parties. Certainly, the clause will not apply by interpretation to a breach. Stress should be laid on that fact, as stated already, that *Photo Production* is distinguishable as being a case on exemption clauses. Lord Diplock (at 850) defined an exemption clause as "one which excludes or modifies an obligation . . . that would otherwise arise under a contract or by implication of law". A covenant in restraint of trade, in any case, cannot be implied by law, and it is not a clause which excludes or modifies an obligation but it extends it. Lord Diplock also stated (at 848) that "[a] basic principle of the common law of contract, to which there are no exceptions that are relevant in the instant case, is that parties to a contract are free to determine for themselves what . . . obligations they will accept". In the area of restraint of trade, however, the parties are not free to contract as they please. The common law requires a proprietary interest and a term which is reasonable in the interest both of the parties and of the public. It may be that one of the exceptions, therefore, to Lord Diplock's basic principle is covenants in restraint of trade. Similar words may be written of the speech of Lord Salmon (at 853): "[a]ny persons capable of making a contract are free to enter into any contract they may choose: and providing the contract is not illegal or voidable, it is binding upon them". Being charitable, one might say that covenants fall within that exception, though in law restrictive covenants are neither illegal nor voidable. Since the question is one of construction and covenants are to be construed against employers, the adoption of a *Photo Production* approach might not help employers.

Employers have attempted to evade *General Billposting* by phrasing the clause to cover circumstances of wrongful dismissal. Take for example a covenant which is to apply "however the contract is terminated". The employers are seeking thereby to rely on the covenant despite there being a breach. Although the question is moot, the courts may interpret the clause as applying only where there is a lawful termination. Accordingly, where there is an unlawful, that is wrongful one, the principle of *General Billposting* will apply. A similar argument would apply to other clauses, for example "whether or not the employers are in breach". If the employers are in breach, *General Billposting* says that the covenant goes. Accordingly, this part of the covenant also goes. If it is contended that the parties intended by express terms that the covenant should apply after unlawful termination, that argument might be met by saying that it is contrary to the policy of English law for the wrongdoer, that is here employers, to rely on their wrongful acts, that is breaches of contract, and so the covenant falls. In *Briggs* v *Oates*, above, the clause was worded that the defendant-employed solicitor would not practise, etc, for five years after the termination of his contract "for whatever reason". Scott J held that since the employee had lost the benefit of the covenant through his employers' breach, they had deprived him of the full consideration under the agreement; and since the employee had accepted the breach as terminating the contract, the clause did not survive that termination. Moreover "[a] contract under which an employee could be immediately and wrongfully dismissed, but would nevertheless remain subject to an anti-competitive restraint seems … grossly unreasonable". Therefore the covenant fell. Scottish cases such as *Living Design (Home Improvements) Ltd* v *Davidson* [1994] IRLR 69, 71 and *Lux Traffic Controls Ltd* v *Healey*, 1994 SLT 1153 have followed the reasoning in *Briggs* v *Oates*, but some judges have construed similar clauses as applying only to lawful termination: *NCH (UK) Ltd* v *Mair*, 20 September 1994, LEXIS, *Aramark plc* v *Sommerville*, 1995 SLT 749 and *PR Consultants Scotland Ltd* v *Mann*, 15 August 1995, LEXIS.

Another possible way round *General Billposting* is to consider whether the covenant is an independent promise and so one which survives termination by the employers. As stated above, in *General Billposting* that argument was unsuccessful. The principal speech was delivered by Lord Collins (at 122). He rested his decision on the employers having demonstrated that they no longer wished to be bound by the contract and correspondingly the employee was no longer bound. He put on one side cases of independent covenants because the employee had served the employers in return for his salary. He had therefore done something in return for consideration and so he was not getting something for nothing, which was the basis of the independent covenant rationale. The other speech, that of Lord Robertson, said (at 121) that the covenant was ancillary to the employment contract and so was not independent. In the partnership case of *Kaufman* v *McGillicuddy* (1914–15) 19 CLR 1, the High Court of Australia held that the covenant was one contract with several stipulations, and that the covenant was not an independent contract. If, however, the covenant had been independent and there had been consideration, the employers could have relied on it, despite there being a breach on their part. *Measures Bros Ltd* v *Measures*, above, is similar, except the Court of Appeal was divided on the issue. Buckley LJ dissented on the grounds that the covenant was independent of a clause in the contract which provided that the employee, a director, was to hold office for seven years. Kennedy LJ held that the terms were interdependent and the failure to continue the employee in employment meant that the covenant fell: *General Billposting* was applied. The other judge of the majority, Cozens-Hardy MR (at 254), said *obiter* that the clauses were not independent but based his judgment on the failure by the plaintiffs to perform their part of the bargain. Their failure meant that it would be inequitable to award an injunction. Kennedy LJ (at 262) stated that the difference between independent and interdependent covenants was to be judged "according to the intention of the parties and the good sense of the case", a not very exact test, as can be seen from the fact that Buckley LJ dissented on this point.

Breach of the Covenant by the Employee

Before a covenant is enforced, the employee must actually or potentially be in breach of it. Whether she is depends on applying the wording of the covenant to the facts. Normally there is no difficulty. For example, in an American case, *Traweek* v *Shields*, 380 SW 2d 131 (1964), an employee undertook that he would not "solicit, divest or take away, or attempt to take away, any of the customers of the Employer". Evidence was that he had called on two customers and induced them to contract with him. The Court of Civil Appeals, Texas, held that there was a breach and remanded the case with a direction to convict. Similarly, in a vendor case *B & Y Metal Painting Inc* v *Ball*, 279 NW 2d 813 (1979) (Minn) the seller agreed not to compete but established a competing business in the same building! There was no doubt as to breach. For further analysis, see Chapter 6.

Contents of Chapter Five

COVENANTS IN RESTRAINT OF TRADE AFTER EMPLOYMENT

Chapter Five

COVENANTS IN RESTRAINT OF TRADE AFTER EMPLOYMENT

Express terms in contracts of employment are void or unenforceable if they seek to restrain a former employee's freedom to compete after the termination of employment unless they protect a legitimate proprietary interest and do not extend beyond such protection as is reasonably necessary to safeguard that interest. The covenant must furthermore not infringe the public interest. Authorities to this effect are legion. For example, Viscount Haldane C in *Mason* v *Provident Clothing and Supply Co* [1913] AC 724, 731, said that covenants "are invalid if they go beyond what is necessary for the protection of the rights of the employer". He, like many others, including Lord Shaw (at 739) approved the proposition of Lord Macnaghten in *Nordenfelt* v *Maxim Nordenfelt Guns and Ammunition Co* [1894] AC 535, 565: "It is ... the only justification if the restriction is reasonable – reasonable, that is, in reference to the interests of the parties concerned and reasonable in reference to the interests, so framed and so guarded as to afford adequate protection to the party in whose favour it is imposed, while at the same time it is in no way injurious to the public". Lord Atkinson in the next House of Lords' authority, *Herbert Morris Ltd* v *Saxelby* [1916] 1 AC 688, 699, also approved this passage. Lord Parker in *Herbert Morris* (at 707) said the covenant must "afford *no more than* [his emphasis] adequate protection to the party in whose favour it is imposed". He added: "So conceived the test appears to me to be valid both as regards the covenantor and covenantee, for though in one sense no doubt it is contrary to the interests of the covenantor to subject himself to any restraint, still it may be for his advantage to be able so to subject himself in cases where, if he could not do so, he would lose other advantages, such as ... the possibility of obtaining employment or training under competent employers".

Consideration

In General

A covenant must be supported by consideration. Highly exceptionally even a covenant in a deed must be supported by consideration: *Mitchel* v *Reynolds* (1711) 1 P Wms 181, 192–3, 24 ER 347, 351. It is suggested that the need for consideration in a deed is inconsistent with modern thinking and the authority (and there are others) would not be followed. It has several times been said that consideration must be legal. See, for example, Jessel MR in *Gravely* v *Barnard* (1874) 43 LJ Ch 659, 661, following *Hitchcock* v *Coker* (1837) 6 Ad & E 438, 457, 112 ER 167, 175 (Ex Ch).

In most instances there is no difficulty as to the adequacy of the consideration. A covenant included in a contract of employment from the start is related to the offer and acceptance of the job. Similarly a covenant inserted into the contract after the commencement of employment has consideration for it; namely, the continuation of the employee's working in that post. An illustration from Northern Ireland is *Norbrook Laboratories Ltd* v *Smyth* (1987) IRLIB 335, 17 (High Court). Murray J said that he accepted the evidence of the employee's manager that the employee would have been dismissed had he not submitted to a confidentiality agreement prohibiting his use or disclosure during or after employment of "any confidential information obtained by him during the course of his employment with Norbrook". Continuing to employ him was a promise of value given in return for the covenant. An older English case is *Woodbridge & Sons* v *Bellamy* [1911] 1 Ch 326 (CA). Eve J held that a firm of solicitors would not have continued to keep a solicitor as a clerk unless he signed a covenant in restraint of trade. The employers no doubt intended that the covenant would apply from the beginning of employment and indeed the covenant was expressed to be "in consideration of your agreeing to employ me". However, the clause was shown to the employee a fortnight after he had agreed to accept employment with the firm. Continued employment was sufficient consideration.

It is arguable that these cases do not truly represent the law. Take a company with 20 employees. In the past, 19 have refused to accept a covenant being inserted into their contracts during employment. The 20th refuses and is dismissed. Can it truly be said that the consideration for the covenant is continuing employment? While no specific part of the consideration need be appropriated to the covenant, on these facts it is untrue to state that continuing employment is the consideration for the covenant when no one has lost employment through refusing to agree to a restraint of trade clause. One way around this problem is to provide specific consideration on the introduction of a covenant. For example, a clause might be utilised to the effect that the employers have produced a (small) sum of money in consideration of the new term. A second, perhaps less to be recommended, option is for the employers to dismiss the employee. If the notice period is short, the maximum amount of damages in a wrongful dismissal action is likely to be small. In an unfair dismissal claim employers should be able to demonstrate that the dismissal was for "some other substantial reason", and provided that they acted reasonably within section 57(3) of the Employment Protection (Consolidation) Act 1978, they will be able successfully to defend such a claim. Similar problems may arise when the employers seek to impose a covenant at the termination of the contract. The solution is to tie the covenant to the employment of the worker as a consultant. Another suggestion is to provide a pension plan predicated on the employee's acceptance of the covenant. For more on these devices, see "Covenants during and on termination of employment", below.

Adequacy

Modern law provides that for contracts consideration need not be adequate. In one of the most authoritative restraint of trade cases, *Herbert Morris Ltd* v *Saxelby*, Lord Parker (at 707) specifically rejected the old view that consideration had to be adequate for covenants. In *M & S Drapers (A Firm)* v *Reynolds* [1957] 1 WLR 9 the Court of Appeal held that the inadequacy of the consideration, the brevity of the period of notice to be given to the employee, was not to be taken into account in determining the reasonableness of the covenant. Hodson LJ (at 11) stated that "the court will not . . . weigh the advantages accruing to the covenantor under the contract against the disadvantages imposed on him by the restraint". The substantive fairness of the bargain is not investigated in employment cases.

In *Allied Dunbar (Frank Weisinger) Ltd* v *Weisinger* [1988] IRLR 60 (Ch D) Millett J held that covenants were not to be struck down on the grounds of proportionality. The defendant, who was not an employee but an independent contractor, worked for Allied Dunbar as a sales associate, selling financial services. He sold his practice including goodwill to them for a capital sum (£386,000). He earned some £194,000 from commission in the year of the sale. He agreed not to compete in any way with Allied Dunbar or with their subsidiary, the plaintiffs, which had bought him out. The judge said (at 65): "the now fashionable concept of proportionality . . . is a novel and dangerous doctrine. It is . . . perhaps more accurately a revival, in modern dress, of an obsolete and discredited theory. There is no trace of it in the modern cases". Approving what Lord Parker said in *Herbert Morris*, Millett J continued thus:

> It was at one time thought that in order to ascertain whether a restraint was reasonable in the interests of the covenantor, the court ought to weigh the advantages accruing to the covenantor under the contract against the disadvantages imposed on him by the restraint, but any such process has long since been rejected as impracticable . . . If it be reasonable that a covenantee should, for his own protection, ask for a restraint, it is . . . equally reasonable that the covenantor should be able to subject himself to this restraint. The test of reasonableness is the same in both cases.

The judge also considered that the concept of proportionality was "dangerous" since "it calls upon the court to perform a balancing exercise which is not in reality capable of being carried out and which is best left to the parties to solve by the process of negotiation". On the facts of the case the defendant, a man of 52, was being asked to take a two-year sabbatical for £394,000. Millett J inquired whether even assuming that two years without work was a detriment, how could one weigh it against the protection afforded to the plaintiffs? Negotiation was the best way of settling the balance between protection for the employers and detriment to the defendant. The price agreed for the business "is the best means of adjusting the otherwise disproportionate advantages and disadvantages of the other terms of the contract".

Adequacy and Reasonableness

While consideration need not be adequate for the covenant to be valid, the reasonableness of the convenant may be affected by the adequacy of the consideration. In a vendor case, *Nordenfelt*, above, Lord Macnaghten (at 565) said that "the question of the consideration may enter into the question of the reasonableness of the contract". More recently the House of Lords approved this proposition in *Esso Petroleum Co Ltd* v *Harper's Garage (Stourport) Ltd* [1968] AC 269 (Lord Reid at 300, Lord Hodson at 318, and Lord Pearce at 323) and see *A Schroeder Music Publishing Co Ltd* v *Macaulay* [1974] 1 WLR 1308 (exclusive services). The Privy Council in *Amoco Australia Pty Ltd* v *Rocca Bros Motor Engineering Co Pty Ltd* [1975] AC 561, 579, adopted the same view. In *Deacons* v *Bridge* [1984] 2 All ER 19, 25, Lord Pearce said that the Judicial Committee found "no reason to consider that the restriction was unreasonable between the parties by reason of the consideration paid to the defendant having been inadequate". This case involved partners. Lawton LJ expressed what may be called a summary of modern law in *Office Overload Ltd* v *Gunn* [1977] FSR 39, 43: " . . . there is a line of cases which says that when the court comes to consider what is reasonable it shall look at the consideration, and if the employee or the purchaser is getting virtually nothing out of the contract, and all the advantages are on the side of the employer or the vendor . . . then the court should take that factor into consideration". The law is not totally clear but it seems to be that adequacy is a relevant factor when determining reasonableness. Accordingly, "the size of the consideration may be a positive factor tending to justify the restraint. If the consideration for the restraint is so substantial that by any objective standard it is in the interests of the party receiving the consideration to subject himself to the restraint, then that must . . . be a factor pointing in the direction of justification" (*Panayiotou* v *Sony Music Entertainment (UK) Ltd* [1994] EMLR 229, 330).

Covenants in Severance Agreements and Similar Arrangements

A covenant may be in a document other than a written contract of employment. Whether a clause is in restraint of trade is determined by substance, not by form.

In *Stenhouse Australia Ltd* v *Phillips* [1974] AC 391, 402 (PC), Lord Wilberforce opined to that effect. On termination of his employment the defendant agreed in clause 5 of an agreement between the parties that he would pay to the company half of the commission he received from any client of the company. The Judicial Committee advised that the clause was unenforceable. Lord Wilberforce (at 402–3) said of this profit-sharing arrangement that, though the clause was not *ex facie* in restraint of trade in the sense that it constrained competition, nevertheless it was likely to cause the employee to refuse business which he would otherwise have taken; in other words, his prospects of employment were reduced. "First, ... the employee comes under an obligation to pay ... even if business is obtained without his knowledge. Secondly, the proportion which he is committed to pay ... is 50 per cent of the gross commission regardless of the size of the financial benefit obtained by him. Thirdly, the clause may operate for a period of five years and thereafter the obligation to pay continues for a further five years. All these provisions ... contain in aggregate a substantial element of restraint of trade." The clause was "severe" on the employee and was unenforceable. Similarly in *PSGB* v *Dickson* [1970] AC 403, 440, Lord Wilberforce stated that the clause is judged "by reference to the practical working of the restraint, irrespective of the legal form". This statement was approved by Gibbs J, dissenting, in *Amoco Australia Pty Ltd* v *Rocca Bros Motor Engineering Co Pty Ltd* (1972–3) 133 CLR 288, 314 and Sumption QC applied the principle in *Marshall* v *NM Financial Management Ltd* [1995] 1 WLR 1461, 1467.

The most famous cases on this topic involve pensions. In *Wyatt* v *Kreglinger and Fernau* [1933] 1 KB 793 (CA) the defendants promised to pay the plaintiff a pension of £200 per year provided that "you do nothing at any time to our detriment (fair business competition excepted)". During the depression the pension was discontinued. The plaintiff sought a declaration that the defendants were liable to pay the pension and damages for breach of contract. The defendants argued *inter alia* that the agreement was void as being in restraint of trade. The court held that, although the clause was not expressed as an agreement not to enter the wool trade but as one which gave a financial benefit which the plaintiff would not otherwise enjoy if he refrained from so doing, it was in truth an agreement not to enter the wool trade, and accordingly it fell within the restraint of trade doctrine. That being the case, the whole agreement was unenforceable because it was contrary to public policy. As Scrutton LJ put it (at 807), "the country is thereby being deprived without any legitimate justification of the services of a man of sixty years who is quite competent to enter into business ... ". The learned commentator (presumably Goodhart) in (1933) 49 LQR 465, 466–7, asked:

What interference with individual liberty is there if the pensioner is at any time free to enter the trade on giving up the pension? The restraint at best is a voluntary one, for the only interference with liberty is that the promisee "restrains himself" ... because of the greater benefit to be got from the pension ...

... [A] quasi-restraint, ... so obviously reasonable in the interests of the parties that the party said to be restrained is seeking to enforce it, is held to be against public policy because of some supposed injury to the public.

And where do we find this injury to the public? It is based on the ground that, if it were not for the agreement, the plaintiff "might continue to serve the community in the wool business ... " [I]t is hardly a valid argument in 1933 when there are nearly 2,000,000 unemployed.

Wyatt was followed by the Ontario High Court in *Furlong* v *Burns & Co Ltd* (1964) 43 DLR 2d 689, though Hughes J noted that it had come under criticism because there was no injury to the public. He was able to sever the offending clause with the result that the plaintiff continued to receive a pension. The clause severed made his pension conditional on not engaging in conduct detrimental to the company: he had become the manager of one of its competitors. *Wyatt* was applied to independent contractors, though the point was not discussed, in *Marshall* v *NM Financial Management Ltd*, above.

The contrasting English case to *Wyatt* is *Bull* v *Pitney-Bowes Ltd* [1967] 1 WLR 273 (QBD). The plaintiff received a pension from the defendants. One rule of the pension fund provided that the committee administering the fund was entitled to withdraw the benefit if a member "is engaged or employed in any activity or occupation which is in competition with or detrimental to the interests of the company". On retirement the plaintiff entered the employ of a rival company. He sought a declaration that the rule was in restraint of trade. The defendants contended that the rule defined those not entitled to a pension; it was not an undertaking not to engage in certain activities such as joining a competing firm. Thesiger J (at 285) said that the rule:

> would have been regarded by the Court of Appeal that decided *Wyatt*'s case as equivalent from the public point of view to a covenant in restraint of trade. The state of affairs in 1933 in which that court was then criticised for so holding as a matter of public policy that the covenant was unenforceable ... no longer prevails in this country. So far as that aspect of the decision is concerned there is no inducement for me in 1966 to try to distinguish *Wyatt*'s case. It would be a difficult, if not impossible, task in any case, and the inducement is rather the other way.

Accordingly, the rule was one which fell within the restraint doctrine. The judge held it to be unreasonable and so unenforceable. The employee could therefore continue to receive the pension. It should be noted that both *Wyatt* and *Bull*, which were decided on public interest grounds, could have been decided on the ground that the covenants, not being limited in area or time, were unreasonable in the interests of the parties. *Wyatt*, which was followed by Eve J in *Re Prudential Assurance Company's Trust Deed* [1934] 1 Ch 338 (Ch D), which in turn was followed in *Marshall* v *NM Financial Management Ltd*, above, and *Bull* were applied by the New South Wales Court of Appeal in *Ronayne* v *Howard F Hudson Pty Ltd* (1969) 71 SRNSW 269, where a term that a pension would not be paid if the employee engaged in or was concerned with marketing or selling builders' or architects' hardware within Australia was held to fall within the doctrine.

The doctrine was applied to post-termination commission in *Sadler* v *Imperial Life Assurance Co of Canada* [1988] IRLR 388 (QBD). In the plaintiff's contract as an insurance agent there was a clause stating that he could be paid commission for the first 10 years of a policy he had sold. Therefore, if he left, he would still receive commission after termination of his contract. He covenanted that on his entering into a contract of service or for services "directly or indirectly with any limited company, mutual society, partnership or brokerage operation involved in the selling of insurance" the payment would cease. The plaintiff breached the covenant. P J Crawford QC held that the covenant was unreasonable and followed *Bull* v *Pitney-Bowes Ltd.* Even though there was a monetary benefit to accepting the covenant, the term was unenforceable as being in restraint of trade. The judge went further and held that the fact that he had struck down the covenant did not mean that the clause concerning the payment of commission was also invalid on the ground of failure of consideration. He stated (at 392) that: "there is ample other consideration to support the defendants' continuing obligation to pay post-termination commission. The structure of [the clause] is such as to operate as an inducement to the employee to complete at least 10 years of service". A similar case is *Marshall* v *NM Financial Management Ltd*, above. Payment of post-termination commission was conditional on (1) the plaintiff's not acting as a financial intermediary or being employed by an organisation which competed with the defendants, *or* (2) his not being 65. The judge held that the provisos were linked, and could be severed and the remaining clause was supported by consideration. Accordingly, the self-employed agent received commission after he had resigned despite his joining a rival firm. Continuing to receive commissions was dependent on his having gained clients during his agency. Allowing him to work for a rival did not therefore destroy consideration for the continued payment of commission.

The same principle applies to a promise to repay training expenses, should the employee leave the employers within a certain period. In *Electronic Data Systems Ltd* v *Hubble*, 20 November 1987, LEXIS (CA), the employers sought summary judgment to enforce a promissory note given by the defendant by which he promised to pay £4,500 if he resigned within 24 months of the commencement of training. Mustill LJ stated that the clause compelled the employee to continue working for the company for at least two years after the training and he gave the employee leave to defend the action.

It can, accordingly, be stated that employers cannot evade the doctrine of restraint of trade by devices which in form are not restrictive covenants.

Covenants During and on Termination of Employment

Most covenants will be present at the start of employment. Sometimes covenants may be put into the service agreement at a later stage: see, for example, *R S*

Components Ltd v *Irwin* [1974] 1 All ER 41 (NIRC). There is also the possibility that a covenant will be negotiated or imposed at the termination of the contract, perhaps as a *quid pro quo* for the employee receiving a golden handshake. The basic rule is that such a covenant is not against public policy. The case establishing this principle is *Spink (Bournemouth) Ltd* v *Spink* [1936] Ch 544. For a consideration of £100 the defendant agreed to be subject to a restraint of trade covenant when he resigned as a director and employee. The covenant stated that the defendant, director and manager of the plaintiffs, garage proprietors and car dealers, covenanted on leaving that he would not for five years "carry on or assist in carrying on the business either as a director, partner, manager, servant or agent or a garage proprietor, motor-car seller or motor-car distributor within a radius of ten miles from the General Post Office, Bournemouth". Luxmoore J said (at 548) that: "[s]uch a covenant cannot affect adversely any member of the public or the person who, with his eyes open, takes the consideration and gives the covenant". He thought (at 547) that the covenant was like one on the sale of goodwill of a business but, even if it was assumed to be an employment covenant, it was nevertheless valid.

A more modern case is *J A Mont (UK) Ltd* v *Mills* [1993] IRLR 172 (CA). The defendant was the sales and marketing director of a firm which amalgamated with the plaintiffs. His employment was terminated. In a severance package he was given a year's salary, and he submitted to a term in it that: "This total payment is made on condition that you do not join another company in the tissue industry within one year of leaving our employment". After leaving he was appointed as joint managing director of a company in the retail trade of selling tissues. The court held that the clause was unenforceable and that relief by way of interlocutory injunction could not be granted in terms narrower than that stated in the contract.

Summary of the Legal Protection of Information During and After Employment

Current law based on *Faccenda Chicken Ltd* v *Fowler* [1987] Ch 117 (CA), while not pellucid, may be summarised thus. After employment the employers cannot stop the employee from using or disclosing what has become his own skill and knowledge. Trade secrets and information of a similar nature is protected both during and after employment. Unlike the next category it is protected after employment even though there is no express covenant in restraint of trade. The implied obligation of faithful service extends beyond the termination of employment but only to (highly) confidential information: in this book this obligation is called the duty of confidentiality. However, information, even information which is confidential but not amounting to a trade secret or similar, is protected during employment either by an express term or by an implied one. Such information is not protected after employment except where there is a covenant in restraint of trade or an express confidentiality clause. Even then a line is drawn between confidential information and the employee's skill and knowledge; the former is protectable, the latter not. To the rule that confidential information cannot be protected after employment there is the exception known as the "springboard" doctrine. An employee is not permitted after employment to use or disclose confidential information she acquired during employment *even though that information is no longer confidential*. The aim is to prevent an ex-employee from utilising misappropriated data to gain a competitive advantage or head start. For example, if the employee takes a list of clients with her on termination she is under a duty not to use that list even though the names on that list can be compiled from public sources such as telephone directories. In other words established competitors can use this information because it is public knowledge but the former employee cannot, even though she too could have compiled the list from publicly available sources. Discussion of the springboard doctrine also occurs in Chapter 12 on remedies, below.

Legitimate Proprietary Interest

In one of the cases which laid the foundations of the modern law, *Nordenfelt*, above, (at 565) Lord Macnaghten said that members of "the public have an interest in every person's carrying on his trade freely; so has the individual. Interference with individual liberty of action in trading, and all restraints of trade of themselves, if there is nothing more, are contrary to public policy, and therefore void". This chapter investigates what employers have to rely on to show that there is something else which goes beyond restricting competition by the former employee. The courts tend to denominate these additional elements legitimate proprietary interests, the main ones being trade connections and trade secrets. The list of such interests is not closed. In *Panayiotou v Sony Music Entertainment (UK) Ltd* [1994] EMLR 229, 360–1, counsel for the defendants submitted that they had 12 interests. The judge did not disagree. He thought it "too formalistic" to dismiss any of the suggestions as not being a legitimate interest. He did not, however, attempt to uphold all 12 interests. Earlier authorities are *McEllistrim v Ballymacelligott Co-operative Agricultural and Dairy Society* [1919] AC 548, 574 and *English Hop Growers Ltd v Dering* [1928] 2 KB 174, 180. None of these cases involves employees. For a Scottish case where there was no protectable interest see *Scotcoast Ltd v Halliday*, 10 January 1995, LEXIS. Even though the employers can demonstrate that the clause protects a legitimate interest of theirs, the clause must also pass the other requisites for a valid covenant such as reasonableness between the parties and reasonableness in the public interest, and it must cover the alleged breach. The requirement of a proprietary interest has been criticised on the ground that a person should be able to surrender her freedom to work in return for a substantial sum of money even where no recognised protectable interest prevails. It may be difficult to envisage a former worker bringing an action to declare the restraints unenforceable in such circumstances, but if the covenant is anti-competitive, it may be struck down on public policy grounds for it is not in the public interest, it may be argued, for employers to keep a former employee idle either generally or in the trade in which she was accustomed to work. The requirement of a proprietary interest was not part of early law but *Herbert Morris* decisively settled the issue. No matter how valuable the employers' interests are they will not be protected unless they fall within a legally recognised class.

The speech of Lord Parker in *Herbert Morris*, above (at 709), provides authority that trade connections and trade secrets are protected. He stated that covenants were enforced on the grounds that the ex-employee "might obtain such personal knowledge of and influence over the customers of his employer, or such acquaintance with his employer's trade secrets as would enable him if competition were allowed, to take advantage of his employer's trade connection or use information confidentially obtained". The policy behind the prerequisite of a legitimate proprietary interest was stated by Lord Wilberforce in *Stenhouse Australia Ltd* v *Phillips* [1974] AC 391, 400: "the employer's claim for protection is based on the identification of some advantage or asset inherent in the business which can properly be regarded as, in the general sense, his property, and which it would be unjust to allow the employee to appropriate for his own purposes, even though he, the employee, may have contributed to its creation". As a result Diplock LJ in *Petrofina (Great Britain) Ltd* v *Martin* [1966] Ch 146, 188, held that "[t]he interests of the appellants in selling as large a quantity of their petroleum products as they can is one which they have a right to have protected". Commercial interests are therefore protectable. In other words "proprietary" adds nothing to "legitimate interest".

Trade Connection

This term covers both links with customers and suppliers, compendiously goodwill. Without a covenant the former employee is free to canvass clients of her former employers; see, for example *Wessex Davies Ltd* v *Smith* [1935] 2 KB 80 (CA). A non-solicitation covenant protects the former employers' connection with them. No protection is afforded in respect of the former employee's skill and experience.

The difficulty is to judge whether people have become so attached to the employers' business that they can be called "customers". In *Herbert Morris*, above, Lord Parker (at 709) required the employee to have acquired "personal knowledge of and influence over the customers of his employer". Lord Sumner (at 712) agreed with Lord Parker. Romer LJ expressed himself more broadly in *Gilford Motor Co Ltd* v *Horn* [1933] Ch 935, 966: " . . . when an employee is being offered employment which will probably result in his coming into contact with his employer's customers, or which will enable him to obtain knowledge of his employer's customers, then the covenant against solicitation is reasonably necessary for the protection of the employer". Romer LJ therefore thought that contact without influence was sufficient to constitute this legitimate proprietary interest. If influence is the touchstone, this statement is incorrect.

In some cases such as *Marion White Ltd* v *Francis* [1972] 1 WLR 1423 and *Home Counties Dairies Ltd* v *Skilton* [1970] 1 WLR 521, which are discussed below, it is hard to say that the employees had influence over their customers. In the opinion of the writer, while it may happen that a customer seeks out a hair stylist, it will rarely, if ever, happen that customers will put any effort into finding where their milk roundsperson has gone: indeed they may never see her except once a week (or less) when paying. These cases are inconsistent with Lord Parker's emphasis on *Herbert Morris* on influence. They may be based on the judges' disapproval of the employees' conduct. Harman LJ (at 530) and Cross LJ (at 537) in *Home Counties* said that the defendant was in flagrant breach of covenant. Buckley LJ in *Marion White* (at 1428) said that the defendant's conduct was "ethically . . . quite inexcusable". However, if the judges' reliance on behaviour which is displeasing to them is a reason for upholding trade connections, *Herbert Morris* can no longer be regarded as authoritative. As a matter of precedent *Herbert Morris* is more authoritative than those cases. See also *Marley Tile Co Ltd* v *Johnson* [1982] IRLR 75 (CA). The cases also cast doubt on the almost universally accepted proposition that covenants are judged at the time when they are entered into, not at the time of the breach. If *Home Counties* and *Marion White* are correct, it can no longer be said that a covenant is either valid or unenforceable *ab initio*, but one has to wait, as with innominate terms, until the alleged breach to see whether the covenant is valid or not.

When considering trade connections, one must take care with regard to statements about no protection being given against the employee's skill and experience. While it is true that skills and experience on the one hand and trade secrets on the other may have to be distinguished, in relation to trade connections there is not a similar line to be drawn. The connection may be one which was created and fostered by the employee's own attributes. For example, in *Home Counties*, above, Harman L J (at 578) spoke of a milkman's acquiring "a clientele along his round who, if he is an agreeable and competent man, will tend to rely on him for his arrival and to follow his departure to serve another employer". On the facts of the case the defendant had done just that. He left the plaintiffs, a few days later joined a rival firm and started selling milk in the area he had formerly served. The business which the defendant had gained for the plaintiff had become "very much a part of the employer's goodwill which he is entitled to protect, for it is his most saleable asset". It is, however, doubtful that customers would so readily transfer their allegiance to the former employee's new employers. Surely it will rarely happen that they will go to another part of town to place their order with him. Similarly in *Marion White*, above, a hairdresser acquired influence over her clients through her personality. The covenant provided that she would not for 12 months after the termination of her contract work in any capacity for a ladies hairdresser within half a mile of the plaintiffs' establishment. Buckley LJ (at 1429) said that the employers were entitled to protect against the employee using her personality and skills as an assistant hairdresser to attract customers to follow her into a new salon. The "personal contact" between hairdresser and clients "constitutes an important element of the goodwill of the business; and that is an interest which the employer is entitled to have protected". The customer connection does not seem strong in *Marion White*: would customers really have sought out the employee in her new salon some distance away, especially when they were accustomed to going to their usual one? The connection does, however, seem stronger than in *Home Counties*. Perhaps clients are more ready to accept solicitation by a hairdresser than by a milkman. The House of Lords has recognised that influence may derive from the employee's own competence. In *Mason* v *Provident Clothing and Supply Co Ltd* [1913] AC 724 Viscount Haldane C said (at 731) that the employee's influence was "due mainly to natural gifts as a canvasser ... The training which his employers had given him was secondary to his natural talents". Nevertheless, he could be restrained, provided the covenant did not extend beyond what was necessary for the protection of the rights of the employer. On the facts the character of the business was not such that protection was necessary across the whole area within 25 miles of London. See further *Cantor Fitzgerald (UK) Ltd* v *Wallace* [1992] IRLR 215 and the cases discussed below

The courts look for situations in which the employee acquired influence over customers through her job. One aspect of influence is recurring contact. If the transaction between the employee and the client related to a single event, it is unlikely that there is a sufficiently close connection to be protectable under the restraint of trade doctrine. For example, in *Bowler* v *Lovegrove* [1921] 1 Ch 642 (Ch D) P O Lawrence J struck down a clause in the contract of an employee of an estate agent. House vendors and purchasers came to him at one time and often did not return. No trade connection had been built up, and the employers had to tout for custom, as was indeed shown by the title of the employee's job – canvassing clerk. Sometimes, however, influence can be built up quickly without the need for recurring contact. The usual illustration is a solicitor. Clients may come back to her even though they have seen her on only one occasion. For example, a visit on a conveyancing matter may lead to further consultations about, say, divorce. Recurring contact is not, however, sufficient *per se*, for there may be no influence, as in *S W Strange Ltd* v *Mann* [1965] 1 WLR 629 (Ch D).

The case of *John Michael Design plc* v *Cooke* [1987] ICR 445 (CA) causes difficulty with regard to the definition of "customer". The plaintiffs sought to enforce the following covenant: "At no time within two years of the termination of this contract (however ended and whether or not John Michael shall be in breach of this contract) shall the employee directly or indirectly canvass, solicit or accept from any client who is or was in the four years prior to the termination of this employment a client of John Michael any business in competition to [*sic*] or similar to that of John Michael". The plaintiff sought an interlocutory injunction to prevent customers placing their business with the defendant. The court awarded relief. The remedy prohibited him from accepting clients who did not wish to place orders in the future with the plaintiffs. The court argued that in relation to those customers who would continue to trade with the plaintiffs there was no need for an interlocutory injunction. However, with regard to the client who would not, the remedy was specifically intended to cover those who wished to transfer their custom. There is much to be said for the proposition that customers who will not return do not form part of the employers' trade connection. The first instance judge had granted the order but had excluded the client who no longer intended to trade with the plaintiffs. If, as seems more and more likely, the remedy can be granted in terms which are of less width than those stated in the covenant, that judgment is sensible in that it makes clear the meaning of the phrase "trade connection", permits to a former employee an opportunity of competing with his former employers, thereby encouraging the free market, and is consistent with the definition of goodwill, which is concerned with the possibility of business recurring.

As stated above, the fact that an employee was using her innate talents as a salesperson during employment does not mean that the employers cannot enjoin her afterwards in accordance with the terms of a restraint of trade clause. It is for this reason that *Cantor Fitzgerald (UK) Ltd* v *Wallace*, above, looks suspect. The plaintiffs were a firm of Eurobond brokers. The first to fifth defendants were former employees who all left on the same day to join the sixth defendant, a firm engaged in the same business. The first to fifth defendants had covenanted that they would not compete for six months after leaving the company. Judge Prosser QC sitting as a deputy Queen's Bench Division judge ruled (at 217) that the job of trader depended on the employee's "personality and character". The employee's "reputation, the speed, ease of dealing with, manner of dealing, trustworthiness in the sense of giving confidence to his client" was what mattered. There was accordingly no legitimate proprietary interest. Surprisingly the judge partly based his conclusion on two cases noted above, *Home Counties* and *Marion White*, which go the other way. A similar case is *Hanover Insurance Brokers Ltd* v *Schapiro* [1994] IRLR 82 (CA). Without reference to these cases Holland J in *G F I Group Inc* v *Eaglestone* [1994] IRLR 119 (QBD) said of a firm dealing largely in over-the-counter options that it had a customer connection based on a good working relationship between the defendant, a broker, and traders. The connection was "based on trust and empathy between the two individuals . . . fostered by communication by way of a direct telephone line and by the expenditure by the plaintiffs of very substantial sums on achieving mutual socialising" (at 120). This case was followed in *Euro Brokers Ltd* v *Rabey* [1995] IRLR 206, 208, by Reid QC sitting as a deputy High Court judge in the Chancery Division. Both of the latter cases involve garden leaves but in neither (and also not in *Schapiro*) was *Cantor Fitzgerald* referred to. It is suggested that *Cantor Fitzgerald* is incorrect insofar as it holds that the employee's skills cannot lead to the formation of a customer connection. There is no difference in this regard between a Eurobond broker and a milkman.

A non-solicitation covenant by definition protects a legitimate proprietary interest where one exists. A non-competition one, however, prevents a former employee from setting up or joining a rival business. Since the enforcement of a non-competition covenant prevents the employee from earning wages or a salary, Lord Shaw in *Mason*, above (at 741), expressed the view that a reasonable non-solicitation covenant would have been upheld when he struck down a non-competition clause that the defendant, a canvasser, would not be employed or engage in any business similar to that of the plaintiffs within 25 miles of London for three years after the termination of the contract. Certainly a non-competition covenant can protect trade secrets, for it prohibits an employee from joining a rival of the employers and then whether knowingly or unwittingly revealing their trade secrets to the new employers. The reasoning of Lord Shaw has, however, not always been followed. For example, in *Marion White*, above, the Court of Appeal upheld a covenant which *inter alia* prohibited a hairdresser from being engaged or concerned or interested in, in any capacity, the business for 12 months after termination within half a mile of the plaintiffs' salon. Non-solicitation and non-dealing covenants would have given them what they wanted – the preservation of goodwill. A covenant not to be involved in any way was surely too broad.

In sum, whether there is a trade connection is dependent on the facts of the case. For example, in the Commonwealth a customs broker was held by Sullivan J in the Supreme Court of British Columbia in *Lock* v *Nelson and Hardy Ltd* (1950) 22 DLR (2d) 298 to have such contact, whereas the Full Court held in *Aloha Shangri-La Atlas Cruises Ltd* v *Gaven* [1970] Qd R 438 that cruise passengers would not seek out the ship's captain. As *Lock* among other cases demonstrates, there can be a protectable connection despite its being built up by the employee. Accordingly, as Harvey C J put it in *Coote* v *Sproule* (1929) 29 NSWLR 578, 580:

> An employer is entitled to hold his employee to an agreement not to injure the former's business connection by virtue of the special relationship which has existed between the employee and the employer's customers as a consequence of his employment ... A man's trade connection consists of those members of the public who are trading with him or who would in the ordinary course return to trade with him if, for any transitory reason, they had ceased to trade with him.

To determine whether there is a special relation the judge must in the words of Long Innes C J in *Cash Orders (Amalgamated) Ltd* v *Haynes* (1937) 37 SRNSW 157 "consider the circumstances of each case, and, in particular, the character of the business carried on by the employer and the nature of the employment".

The following is a list, with a selection of authorities, of vocations and trades where it has been held that there was a trade connection:

- doctors: *Routh* v *Jones* [1947] 1 All ER 758, *Deacon* v *Crehan* [1925] 4 DLR 664 (Ont);
- insurance agents: *Burton, Rowe & Viner Ltd* v *Brereton* (1946) Ll LR 438 (Hallett J), *Orville Kerr Ltd* v *DeWitt* (1970) 8 DLR 3d 436 (Ont);
- accountants: *Taxation Services of Australia Ltd* v *Townsend* (1936) 37 SRNSW 98; (for a case on partners see *Bassman* v *Deloitte Haskins & Sells* (1984) 4 DLR (4th) 558 (Ont));

- estate agents: *Scorer* v *Seymour Jones* [1966] 1 WLR 1419, *Calvert Hunt &*
  Barden v *Elton* [1975] EG Dig 219, *Curson & Poole* v *Rash* (1982) 263 EG 518,
  Hilbery Chaplin & Co v *Trowbridge* (1983) 264 EG 50, and *Anscombe &*
  Ringland Ltd v *Butchoff* (1984) 134 NLJ 37. *Contra* is *Phillip M Levy Pty Ltd* v
  Christopoulos [1973] VR 673;
- articled clerks: *Fitch* v *Dewes* [1921] AC 158;
- managing clerks: *Howard* v *Woodward* (1864) 34 LJ Ch 47 (Wood V-C);
- sales staff: *Standex International Ltd* v *Blades* [1976] FSR 114, *Spafax Ltd* v
  Harrison [1980] IRLR 442 (CA), *Gestetner (Canada) Ltd* v *Henderson* [1948] 3
  DLR 64 (Alta A D);
- travellers: *Mallan* v *May* (1843) 11 M & W 653, 152 ER 167, *Parsons* v *Cotterill*
  (1887) 56 LT 839;
- compilers of business dictionaries: *Baldwin* v *McIver* [1937] NZLR 265;
- milkmen: *Cornwall* v *Hawkins* (1872) 41 LJ Ch 435, *Evans* v *Ware* [1892] 3 Ch
  502, *Home Counties*, above, *Dairy Crest Ltd* v *Pigott* [1989] ICR 92 (CA), *Coote*
  v *Sproule*, above, and *Woodmason's Melrose Pty Ltd* v *Kimpton* (1924) 30 ALR
  356;
- breadcarters: *Marquett* v *Walsh* (1929) 29 SRNSW 298;
- hairdressers: *Marion White*, above, *Tony Standish Ltd* v *Arthur* [1976] Bar
  Library Transcripts no 293, *Cope* v *Harisimo* (1964) 48 DLR (2d) 744
  (BCCA);
- designer of bedrooms: *A & D Bedrooms Ltd* v *Michael* (1984) unreported
  (CS);
- removals man: *Stevens* v *Allied Freightways Ltd* [1968] NZLR 1195.

A case illustrative of facts where no trade connection was found is *Clarke, Sharp &*
Co Ltd v *Solomon* (1921) 37 TLR 176 (CA): a commercial traveller in coal had no
influence over customers. For a Scottish case which turned on the definition of
"customers" see *Aramark plc* v *Sommerville*, 1995 SLT 749.

Trade Secrets

In *Herbert Morris*, above, Lord Shaw (at 714) said that:

> Trade secrets, the names of customers – all such things which in sound philosophical
> language are denominated objective knowledge – these may not be given away by a
> servant; they are his master's property and there is no rule of public interest which
> prevents transfer of them against his master's will being restrained. On the other
> hand, a man's aptitudes, his skill, his dexterity, his manual or mental ability – all
> those things which in sound philosophical language are not objective but subjective
> – they may and ought to be relinquished by a servant; they are not his own property;
> they are himself.

Therefore, a line is drawn between trade secrets and the employee's skills. How
then are the two concepts distinguished? In a case not involving restraint of trade

but breach of confidence, *Thomas Marshall (Exports) Ltd* v *Guinle* [1979] Ch 227, 248, Megarry V-C laid down a four-part test for trade secrets:

(1) the owner of the information must believe that the release of the information would harm him or be advantageous to rival businesses;
(2) the owner must believe that the information is confidential;
(3) the belief in (1) and (2) must be based on reasonable grounds; and
(4) the confidentiality of the information is judged from the viewpoint of the trade or industry concerned.

Megarry V-C did not distinguish between trade secrets and (merely) confidential information. He said (at 248): "costs and prices which are not generally known may well constitute trade secrets or confidential information": *cf. Faccenda Chicken Ltd* v *Fowler* [1987] Ch 117 (CA). The criteria for trade secrets are different from those in *Faccenda*. For example, the owner's belief is taken into account under *Guinle* but not under *Faccenda*. A legal way of reconciling the cases is to say that the ratio of *Guinle* is concerned with activity during employment, whereas *Faccenda* is an authority on the position after cessation of employment.

Trade secrets have long been protected by restraint clauses. In *Bryson* v *Whitehead* (1822) 1 Sim & St 72, 57 ER 29, Leach V-C said (at 77, 31) that: "although the policy of the law will not permit a general restraint of trade, yet a trader may sell a secret of business and restrain himself generally from using that secret". On the facts the secret was that of dyeing cloth such as bombazine. Therefore, even before it had been held that general covenants were acceptable, a covenant to protect a trade secret was permissible. In the later case of *Badische Anilin und Soda Fabrik* v *Schott Segner & Co Ltd* [1892] 3 Ch 447 Chitty J said that if such clauses were not enforced, the defendants, the plaintiffs' English agents, would be "dangerous customers" and he upheld a covenant preventing them from giving information of any kind about the business.

If there is no trade secret, the covenant falls. A Commonwealth illustration is *Maguire* v *Northland Drug Co* [1935] 3 DLR 521. A druggist covenanted that he would not engage in the business of a retail drug store within 25 miles of the Flin Flon Mine in Northern Manitoba for five years after the termination of his employment contract. He left and joined the drugstore next door. The Supreme Court of Canada held that although "proprietary rights, such as secrets of manufacturing processes, secret modes of manufacturing clearly come within the group of rights entitled to protection" (*per* Dysart J at 325), there were no such rights on the facts.

Examples from the cases of trade secrets are:

– a glass engraving process: *Phillips* v *Stevens* (1889) 15 TLR 325;
– the method of making carbon paper and ribbons: *Caribonum Co* v *Le Couch* (1913) 109 LT 385;
– the mode of production of PVC calendering: *Commercial Plastics Ltd* v *Vincent* [1965] 1 QB 623;

- a list of names of clients: *Computer Center Personnel Ltd* v *Lagopoulos* (1975) 58 DLR (3d) 352 (Ont) and *Spencer* v *Marchington* [1988] IRLR 392;
- forms devised for preparing income tax returns: *H & R Block Ltd* v *Sanott* [1976] 1 NZLR 213;
- a mail order catalogue prepublication: *Littlewoods Organisation Ltd* v *Harris* [1977] 1 WLR 1472 (CA);
- blends of polymers and profit margins: *Poly Lina Ltd* v *Finch* [1995] FSR 751 (QBD).

Skill and Experience

There are many expressions in the cases of a hard and fast line being drawn between trade secrets (or trade connections) and the employee's own skills and experience. Lord Parker in *Herbert Morris*, above (at 711), distinguished between "the general skill and knowledge which an employee of any ability must necessarily obtain [and] knowledge of any matter or skills in any process in which the company could be said to have any property at all". Lord Shaw in *Mason* v *Provident Clothing and Supply Co*, above at 740–1, approved the proposition of Farwell LJ in *Sir W C Leng & Co* v *Andrews* [1909] 1 Ch 763 that the restraint of trade doctrine "does not mean that an employer can prevent his employee from using the skill and knowledge in his trade or profession which he has learned in the course of his employment by means of directions or instructions from the employer. That information and that additional skill he is entitled to use for the benefit of himself and the benefit of the public who gain the advantage of his having held such admirable instruction". He continued: trade secrets cases:

> are ... widely distinguished from the other cases of an employee who, by faithful and industrious exercise of his powers, becomes mentally, or even manually, well equipped as a servant. The distinction between that case and the former is as wide as the psychological distinction between subjective and objective knowledge ... For, in the former case, the equipment of the workman becomes part of himself ... But in the other case the knowledge of trade secrets may be as real and objective as the possession of material goods, and the law would much more readily support a restraint of liberty which would, or might, be likely to include the transfer of this to others, with the danger of consequent loss.

The distinction continues today: see for example *Ixora Trading Inc* v *Jones* [1990] FSR 251, 258–9.

The distinction between trade secrets on the one hand and skill and experience on the other is connected with the previous topic that employers are not entitled to protect themselves from competition *per se*. Lord Wilberforce emphasised this point in *Stenhouse*, above, (at 400): "The accepted proposition that an employer is not entitled to protection from mere competition by a former employee means that the employee is entitled to use to the full any personal skill and experience even if this had been acquired in the service of his employer: It is this freedom to use to the full a man's improving ability and talents which lies at the root of the policy of the law regarding this type of restraint".

Though the distinction is clear-cut in theory, in practice the line is hard to draw and that line may be drawn only after litigation. For example, in *Liverpool Victoria Legal Friendly Society* v *Houston* (1900) 3 F (Ct of Sess) 42, 47, 48, the judges were divided. As Heydon wrote in *The Restraint of Trade Doctrine* (Butterworths, 1971) 101, "the chief problem in practice is to determine whether information is a trade secret or is merely part of the employee's stock of knowledge and skill". An analysis of the cases is not helpful, because they turn on their own facts. What the employers cannot, however, restrain is the employee's "natural gifts" or "natural aptitude" as opposed to "any special knowledge of the kind recognised as a trade secret", as Lord Haldane C put it in *Mason*, above, at 731–2. Other phrases abound such as "intelligence, industry and persuasive manner" (*per* Richards JA in *New Method Cleaners and Launderers Ltd* v *Hartley* [1939] 1 DLR 711 (Man CA)).

The distinction is long-standing. Parke B in *Mallan* v *May* (1843) 11 M & W 653, 655, 152 ER 167, 172, spoke of "skills and experience". A consideration of one authority may be helpful. In *Phillip M Levy Pty Ltd* v *Christopoulos* [1973] VR 673 the defendant covenanted with his employers, real estate agents, that he would not operate as an agent within one mile of any of their offices for one year after the termination of his contract. He departed and began to compete. Kay J in the Supreme Court of Victoria stated that the publicity the employers had given to the defendant in the Greek community was not a proprietary interest. He said (at 687): "any benefit gained by the defendant by such publicity was similar to the proficiency in his trade and added skill which he derived by experience as a salesman in the employment of the plaintiff. This was a personal advantage which became part of him ... The defendant's skills and ability belong to him and are not the property of his employer".

It has been held that clients which the employee brought with her on taking employment are not the employers' property: *M & S Drapers (a Firm)* v *Reynolds* [1957] 1 WLR 9, 15, and *Northern Messenger & Transfer Ltd* v *Fabbro* (1944) 45 DLR (3d) 73, 98 (Man). However, in *Oswald Hickson Collier & Co* v *Carter-Ruck* [1984] 2 All ER 15, 17, the Court of Appeal suggested that the result might be different if "the fact that the employee is bringing new customers to the business will form an essential part of the original bargain".

As Turner, *The Law of Trade Secrets* (Sweet & Maxwell, 1962) 120, noted, the distinction between confidential information, which is protectable, and personal skill and experience, which is not, depends on the width given to the latter concept. The wider its ambit, the less the employers can protect. It should, however, be remembered that if the employers manage to have a covenant upheld (or if the former employee does not breach it, whether the clause is reasonable or not), the effect will be to constrain her use of skill and knowledge in the area and for the time agreed. In *Nordenfelt* v *Maxim Nordenfelt Guns and Ammunition Co* [1894] AC 535, a vendor case, the defendant was not only prohibited from utilising trade secrets and connections but was prevented from using the skill and knowledge in armaments manufacture. With respect to the metaphor of drawing the line, the problem is not to outline the law but to apply it to specific facts. The courts, by using phrases such as "general information as distinguished from special information", as Farwell J put it in *Triplex Safety Glass Co Ltd* v *Scorah* (1938) 55 RPC 21, 27, are not helping practitioners to advise clients.

One troublesome aspect of the "skills and experience" debate is the situation where the employee either recalls or consciously memorises information: does it become part of her skill and experience which she can use for herself or others after employment? In *Herbert Morris*, above, Lord Atkinson (at 702) said that on the facts various matters such as tables detailing the strength of materials "were highly confidential ... The information they contain is so detailed and minute that it would be impossible for any employee to carry away in his head. He might retain the recollection of the general character and principle of the elaborate scheme of organisation, but no more". Confidential information was contrasted with "the skill and knowledge which he had acquired by the exercise of his own mental faculties on what he had seen, heard or had experience of in the employment" (at 698), "the impressions left on his mind by his experience in the ... works" (at 702), and "the superior skill and knowledge he had acquired of [the employers'] scheme of organisation and methods of business" (at 704). Lord Atkinson's remarks were directed at the recollection of information, not at the memorising of it. As with the law on implied terms, a distinction is made between the two. For example, in *Printers & Finishers*, above, the judge (at 256) said that formulae were not part of the employee's stock of knowledge simply because they were remembered. Turner in his book (at 141) made the point:

> ... if memory is admitted *in toto* to personal skill, knowledge and experience, the bounds of unrestrainable use would be far too wide: a fortuitous measure of memory in such cases would decide whether a secret was protectable. Certainly memory is not irrelevant to personal skill, knowledge or experience, because if a person cannot in fact remember information and has therefore resorted to keeping records and so on of what he observes in his current employment those records will not be part of his skill, knowledge and experience. All skill, knowledge and experience must be contained in the memory, but it is submitted that everything in the memory does not qualify as personal skill, knowledge or experience.

Megaw LJ in *Littlewoods Organisation Ltd* v *Harris* [1977] 1 WLR 1472, 1485, said that the law on trade secrets applied despite the fact that "the information may be carried in his head ... ". He added that it is irrelevant that the former employee finds extreme difficulties separating confidential information from skills and experience.

Business methods and Schemes of Organisation

Lord Atkinson in *Herbert Morris*, above (at 703) stated that a former employee's general impressions of the ways in which his former employers carried on their business were not so confidential as to constitute trade secrets. On the facts he instanced details of manufacture, charts of the strength of materials, facts ascertained by experience, composition and dimensions of machines, cost of machinery, details of jobs tendered for or obtained, records of instructions as to how to do work, and requirements of customers. These impressions "are part of himself". Lord Parker (at 712) said that: "all he could carry away was the general method and character of the scheme of organisation practised by the plaintiff company. Such scheme and method can hardly be regarded as a trade secret".

Farwell L J said in *Sir W C Leng & Co* v *Andrews* [1909] 1 Ch 763, 773, in a passage which was approved by Lord Atkinson in *Herbert Morris* at 704–5, that:

> A man who goes into an office is entitled to make use in any other office ... of the knowledge which he has acquired in the form of details of office organisation, such as the establishment of one department with a chief or head and grades of subordinates under him ... To acquire the knowledge of the reasonable mode of general organization and management of a business ... , and to make use of such knowledge, cannot be regarded as a breach of confidence ... although the person may have learnt it in the course of being taught his trade.

Connection with Staff

There is a growing recognition that there is a third legitimate proprietary interest, that of preventing an employee from poaching her former colleagues. Such departures may be extremely injurious to firms. In *Office Angels Ltd* v *Rainer-Thomas* [1991] IRLR 214 (CA) there was evidence, which was unchallenged, that a consultant, the second defendant, who dealt with the placement of temps would develop a personal relationship with them and some of them would move with her when she obtained another job. Sir Christopher Slade (at 219) rejected the defendants' contention that a pool of temporary workers was not part of the plaintiffs' goodwill and therefore was not a legitimate subject of protection. He said that he could see no reason why the plaintiffs' trade connection with temps "should not in law be incapable of protection by a restriction no greater than is reasonably necessary for such purpose". The Court of Appeal thought similarly in *Ingham* v *ABC Contract Services Ltd*, 12 November 1993, LEXIS.

What of a covenant purporting to prevent an employee from soliciting former colleagues, an activity often known as "poaching"? Employers may argue that they have a valuable asset to protect. That asset is the preservation of a stable workforce. Losing key workers is disastrous for enterprises, and the recruitment and training of new ones is expensive and time-consuming. There is, it may be contended, a legitimate proprietary interest just as worthy of protection as trade secrets and trade connections. Indeed, it may be argued that a clause stipulating that an employee should not after employment entice former workmates away is common form as are restraint of trade terms against soliciting customers and using or disclosing trade secrets. There is a case from the 1950s on poaching but it involved two employers agreeing not to poach the other's employees. In *Kores*

Manufacturing Co Ltd v *Kolok Manufacturing Co Ltd* [1959] Ch 108 the Court of Appeal held that there was no protectable interest and therefore the agreement was unenforceable. The employers could protect trade secrets and "the adequacy and stability of the ... complements of employees ... But ... [t]he danger of the adequacy and stability of his complement of employees being impaired through employees leaving his service and entering that of a rival is not a danger against which he is entitled to protect himself by exacting from his employees covenants that they will not ... enter the service of any competing concern" (Jenkins LJ *per curiam*, at 125). More recently the Court of Appeal held in *Hanover Insurance Brokers Ltd* v *Schapiro*, above, that on the facts a covenant against soliciting colleagues was unenforceable because the employers had no proprietary interest to protect. The Court of Appeal considered the clause to be a pure covenant against competition: see the next section.

Competition *per se*

Lord Parker in *Herbert Morris*, above (at 709) stated that covenants were not enforced on the mere ground that the former employee "would by reason of his employment or training obtain the skill and knowledge necessary to equip him as a possible competitor in the trade ... ". Lord Wilberforce in *Stenhouse Australia*, above said (at 400) that the law was based on the policy of allowing the employee "freedom to use to the full a man's improving ability and talents ... ". In relation to a covenant given by the vendor of a business the Privy Council struck down a covenant on the sale of a licence to brew beer that the vendors would not compete for 15 years on the ground that they had never brewed beer; accordingly, there was no interest to protect: *Vancouver Malt and Sake Brewing Co* v *Vancouver Breweries Ltd* [1934] AC 181. Lord Macmillan said (at 313): "the agreement is nothing more or less than a contract whereby in consideration of a sum of money [the defendants] undertake for a period of 15 years not to engage in the business of brewing beer". The clause was a bare covenant against competition. (In any case the covenant was unreasonable because it was worldwide.) Accordingly, if the covenant does not protect a legitimate proprietary interest, it will fall.

Similarly, as is shown below, a covenant will fall if it is not reasonable in the interests of the parties or if it offends the public interest. Again it may be said that the clause is a restraint on competition *per se*. An illustrative case is *Curson & Poole* v *Rash* (1982) 263 EG 518. The plaintiffs sought an interlocutory injunction to prevent the defendant from contravening a covenant that he would not solicit or act for any client within three miles of the office where he had worked for one year after termination of his contract. Vinelott J said: "The firm ... has a very wide geographical spread ... To prohibit the defendant from acting for anyone who at any time had been a client of the firm is in effect to prohibit competition, and not merely to protect the legitimate interest of the plaintiffs". Better put, estate agents can acquire a trade connection but the clause was wider than was reasonably necessary for its protection.

There are many English and Commonwealth cases which prohibit what are sometimes known as "bare" covenants (see, for example, Oliver LJ in *Milthorp International Ltd* v *Mann*, 19 May 1982, LEXIS, and Dixon L J in *Butt* v *Long* (1953) 88 CLR 476, 486).

A recent authority is *Marshall* v *NM Financial Management Ltd* [1995] 1 WLR 1461 (Ch D). Sumption QC, sitting as a deputy High Court judge, stated in relation to the plaintiff who was an independent contractor exclusively sold the defendant's pensions and assurance policies that: "[t]he plaintiff's business as an agent, including the goodwill arising from his reputation and connections, was his own property and not the defendant's". The defendants' interest lay in the protection of its existing client base. A clause extending beyond such protection was unreasonable. English examples of bare covenants include: *Hadsley* v *Dayer-Smith* [1914] AC 979 (HL) (partners), *Attwood* v *Lamont* [1920] 3 KB 571, 581, 586, *Marchon Products Ltd* v *Thomes* (1954) 71 RPC 445, *Vandervell Products Ltd* v *McLeod* (1957) 74 RPC 60, 65, *Kerchiss* v *Colora Printing Inks Ltd* [1960] RPC 235, 238–9, *Gledhow Autoparts Ltd* v *Delaney* [1965] 3 All ER 288, 291, *Printers & Finishers Ltd* v *Holloway* [1965] 1 WLR 1, 6, *S W Strange Ltd* v *Mann* [1965] 1 WLR 629, 638, *Home Counties Dairies Ltd* v *Skilton* [1970] 1 WLR 526, *Marion White Ltd* v *Francis* [1972] 1 WLR 1423, 1429, *Standex International Ltd* v *Blades* [1976] FSR 114, 126, *Office Overload Ltd* v *Gunn* [1977] FSR 39, *Littlewoods Organisation Ltd* v *Harris* [1978] 1 All ER 1026, 1032, *Flexiveyor Products Ltd* v *Owens*, 4 May 1982, LEXIS and *Marley Tile Co* v *Johnson* [1982] IRLR 75, 77. It is suggested that the phrase "competition *per se*" is to be understood as referring to lack of a protectable interest or a covenant which is unreasonable in terms of scope, duration or area, rather than to a separate ground of invalidity.

In sum, the employer "is undoubtedly entitled to have his interest in the trade secrets protected, such as secret processes of manufacture, which may be of vast value ... He is also entitled not to have his old customers ... enticed away from him ... But freedom from all competition *per se* ... , he is not entitled to be protected against" (*Brunner & Lay Inc* v *Chapin*, 172 NE 2d 652 (1961) (Ill App), which has been approved in cases such as *Central Keystone Plating of Illinois Inc* v *Hutchinson*, 210 NE 2d 239 (1965)). The restraint doctrine prohibits unfair competition, not competition *per se*.

Are the Interests of the Former Employee Taken into Account?

The criteria for the validity of covenants in restraint of trade are often stated to be that they must protect a legitimate proprietary interest, they must be reasonably necessary for its protection, and they must be reasonable in the interests of the public. The first two requirements are often expressed as: covenants must be reasonable between the parties. The formulations are, however, different. A test looking at protection of the employers' interests does not on its face take into account any interest the ex-employee may have, whereas a test of reasonableness between the parties does. There are statements of high authority which call on the courts to take the former employees' interests into account. In *Fitch* v *Dewes* [1921] AC 158, 163, Lord Birkenhead C inquired whether the covenant exceeded "what is necessary for both the parties". Younger LJ in *Attwood* v *Lamont* [1920] 3 KB 571, 589, said that:

> ... the restraint must be reasonable not only in the interests of the covenantee but in the interests of both the contracting parties. This disposes of the almost passionate protest of Neville J in *Leetham* v *Johnstone-White* [1907] 1 Ch 189, 194, that no agreement was invalid, provided that the restriction was reasonably necessary for the protection of the employer, however oppressive to the employee and fatal to his change of obtaining his own living in this country it might be.

Lord Shaw in *Herbert Morris*, above (at 716), noted that the celebrated words of Lord Macnaghten in *Nordenfelt*, quoted at the start of this chapter, specifically referred to the interests of both parties: "But the interest of the covenantor entirely equates, in kind although not in degree, with the interest of the public". His interest renders the covenant unenforceable if the restraint "would be injurious to society at large".

Modern cases normally make no reference to the interests of the employee when discussing whether the covenant was reasonable between the parties. The formula agreed between the parties in *Rex Stewart Jeffries Parker Ginsberg Ltd* v *Parker* [1988] IRLR 483, 486 (CA), was "the restriction being in restraint of trade, it is *prima facie* contrary to public policy and will be void unless it is shown to be no wider than is reasonably necessary for the protection of the employer's legitimate interests".

Despite the different formulations used over the last century – both parties, interests of the ex-employee equated with the public's interest, and only the employers – the employee's interests may in truth be considered at several stages including the inquiries into whether the covenant is a bare one directed at competition *per se* and whether the court should order an interlocutory or final injunction as well as at the stage of considering whether the covenant is reasonable in all the circumstances. Thus the court may consider whether if the restraint were to be upheld, the employee could fall back onto other skills: see *Commercial Plastics Ltd* v *Vincent* [1965] 1 WLR 623.

Subsidiary and Associated Companies

May an employee be prevented by a covenant from competing after employment not just against the firm for which she used to work but also against companies in the same group? The basic rule is that subsidiary or associated companies cannot acquire protection in this way. The principal authority in recent times is a Scottish one. In *Hinton & Higgs (UK) Ltd* v *Murphy*, 1989 SLT 450 the Court of Session was faced with a covenant which stated: "It is a condition of your employment that upon leaving you will not work for any previous or present clients of the Hinton

& Higgs group of companies . . . for a period of at least 18 months". The court held that "in the absence of some special circumstances there is no ground for considering it necessary for the protection of the interests of the pursuers that the defenders be restricted for working for any client of any company in the same group as the pursuers" (*per* Lord Dervaird at 453). In the English case of *Business Seating (Renovations) Ltd* v *Broad* [1989] ICR 729, 734, Millett J said that a covenant was void when it extended to the non-solicitation of customers of associated employers. An older case is *Henry Leetham & Sons Ltd* v *Johnstone-White* [1907] 1 Ch 322 (CA). The court struck down a covenant within the United Kingdom and Ireland to engage in the business of flour miller for five years after termination in competition with "the principal or subsidiary companies". Farwell LJ considered that the clause was a covenant in gross because it protected a business in which the defendant was not employed. Buckley LJ said *arguendo* (at 324) that: "The fact that these companies have a common management and are interested in each other's businesses seems to me to have nothing to do with this case . . . ". The defendant had worked only for a subsidiary company, not for the parent company, the plaintiffs. Therefore, they had no legitimate proprietary interest to protect.

As might be expected Lord Denning MR has expressed an opinion on this point. In *Littlewoods Organisation* v *Harris* [1977] 1 WLR 1472 (CA) he said that the firm which the defendant had joined was part of a single entity – GUS. Accordingly, a clause applying to the subsidiaries and not just the company he had joined was not unreasonable. The group was under "unified control", and employees could be˜switched from one company to another within the group without difficulty. He relied on *DHN Food Distributors Ltd* v *London Borough of Tower Hamlets* [1976] 1 WLR 852 (CA), a decision which the House of Lords criticised in *Woolfson* v *Strathclyde Regional Council*, 1978 SC 90. Megaw LJ, the other judge in the majority, held that the phrase "any company subsidiary thereto" meant "any subsidiary which at any relevant moment in time during the period covered by the covenant is concerned wholly or partly in the mail order business carried on in the United Kingdom". In this way he was able to hold that the activities of the former employee constituted a breach of covenant. The dissentient, Browne LJ, did not mention the issue. He would have struck down the covenant on the grounds that it was worldwide and could not be saved by the methods of interpretation the majority used.

Though the basic rule remains that a covenant cannot protect the interests of associated companies, the position may be different in respect of holding and service companies. The facts of *Stenhouse*, above, were these. The holding company had a number of subsidiary companies. The covenant stated that the employee would pay over half the commission he received from clients who at a certain date were clients of the Stenhouse group of companies. The Privy Council held that the holding company directed the activities of the subsidiaries. Their profits were sent to it. Lord Wilberforce (at 404) distinguished *Henry Leetham* as being a case where the agreement as interpreted was with one company in the group, whereas the covenant was expressed to protect all the companies in the group. In the instant case "the subsidiary companies were merely . . . instrumentalities through which the appellant company directed its integrated business". Therefore, the employers had a legitimate interest in protecting its clientele who were serviced by the subsidiaries.

A service company is one which, for example, employs employees who work for a group of companies of which the service company is one. The employees thus work for one company in the group but are employed by another. If there is a covenant between the service company and the employee preventing her utilising trade connections, or secrets belonging to the company in the group for which she has been working, it is thought that the service company will be able to obtain an injunction (provided the covenant is properly drafted), for in reality she has access to those trade secrets and connections through her attachment to a company in the same group.

Severance of the offending words may be possible as occurred in *Ingham* v *ABC Contract Services Ltd*, 12 November 1993, LEXIS (CA).

Reasonableness between the Parties

In determining what is reasonable the goddess of justice that hovers over the . . . courthouse with scale in hand has a delicate job of weighing; and it is a three, not a two, pan scale for she must balance the conflicting interests of employers, employee and public (*Arthur Murray Dance Studios of Cleveland Inc* v *Witter*, 105 NE 2d 685 (1952) *per* Hoover J).

Once the employers have proved that the covenant protects a legitimate proprietary interest, they must demonstrate that the covenant is reasonable between the parties. This issue may be divided into (1) the scope of the covenant; (2) its duration; and (3) its territorial extent.

The Scope of the Covenant

Lord Moulton aptly expressed this issue in *Mason* v *Provident Clothing and Supply Co Ltd* [1913] AC 724, 732: "what is the critical question which the Court ought to put to itself in such a case as this [?] It is as follows: are the restrictions which the covenant imposes upon the freedom of action of the servant after he has left the service of the master greater than are necessary for the protection of the master in his business? The first task of the Court, therefore, is to ascertain the nature of the master's business and of the servant's employment therein".

The prohibited activity must not be one which extends beyond the employers' business. A simple illustration is the partnership case of *Jenkins* v *Reid* [1948] 1 All ER 471 (Ch D). The plaintiff brought an action to determine the validity of a covenant which prohibited her from practising "at any time . . . as a physician, surgeon or apothecary" within five miles of two post offices. Romer J applied

Routh v *Jones* [1947] 1 All ER 758 (CA). The covenant prohibited a doctor from working as a consultant but she had acted only as a GP; therefore it was too wide and was unreasonable. The case involved a partnership but the same principle applies to employment.

The employers' business activities are closely scrutinised. For example, in *Rogers* v *Maddocks* [1892] 3 Ch 346 a covenant prohibited the employee, a traveller, from being concerned in the selling of malt liquor or aerated waters for two years within 100 miles of Cardiff. The Court of Appeal held that the prohibition did not extend to two different activities, wholesale and retail, but rather wholesale and retail were simply methods of pursuing the one business, that of selling malt liquor (the part as to aerated waters was severed). The covenant was not restricted, as the trial judge had thought, to the wholesale business, which was the trade in which the defendant had been engaged. A modern illustration is *Technograph Printed Circuits Ltd* v *Chalwyn Ltd* [1967] RPC 339 (Ch D).

The topic of the range of the covenant may also be seen as falling within the section on legitimate proprietary interest. If the employers try to take too much, they have no interest in the business for which they sought protection.

Time

The duration of the covenant is an important factor in determining the reasonableness of the covenant: *Macaulay* v *A Schroeder Music Publishing Co Ltd* [1976] AC 1308, 1312 (HL). However, as Lord Birkenhead C delivering the principal speech in the Lords put it in *Fitch* v *Dewes* [1921] 2 AC 158, 166–7, it is "quite impossible to be dogmatic upon the period proper to each individual case", and "the Courts long since determined that they would lay down no hard and fast rule either in relation to time or in relation to space, but that they would treat the question alike of time and of space as one of the elements by the light of which they would measure the reasonableness of the restriction taken as a whole". *Cf. Zang Tumb Tuum Records Ltd* v *Johnson* [1993] EMLR 61. In a trade connection case the available length of the covenant was succinctly summarised by Lord Wilberforce sitting in the Privy Council in *Stenhouse Australia Ltd* v *Phillips* [1974] AC 391, 402: "The question is not how long the employee could be expected to enjoy a competitive edge over others seeking the client's business. It is, rather, what is a reasonable time during which the employer is entitled to protection against solicitation of clients with whom the employee had contact and influence during employment and who were not bound to the employer by contract or stability of association". With regard to this type of interest the courts have stated that the duration permitted will normally be the length of time a replacement for the covenantor would take to acquire the influence over the customers which the latter had, though Lord Wilberforce's test and this one may lead to different results.

There is little to be gained from looking at a list of cases but one or two may be chosen to illustrate the law. In *Kall-Kwik Printing (UK) Ltd* v *Bell* [1994] FSR 674

(Ch D), a franchise case, Harman J considered that 18 months was not too long for the protection of the plaintiffs' goodwill from former franchisees. In a case reported in the *Yorkshire Evening Post*, 8 October 1986, the High Court sitting in Leeds granted an injunction to prevent a hairdresser from breaching a covenant not to work for six months after the termination of a contract as a hairdresser within a half-mile radius of the Essanelle salon within Fenwick's store, York. A limit of 15 years on a contract to deliver records was said not to outrage the court in *Panayiotou* v *Sony Music Entertainment Ltd* [1994] EMLR 229, 366, the George Michael case. Parker J said that he found it "impossible to be outraged at the prospect of Mr Michael being denied the opportunity, once he has achieved success under the provisions of his existing recording agreement, to capitalise on that success in the open market by commanding even greater financial returns than he has so far enjoyed". Michael Smith, however, commented in his case-note [1994] 8 EIPR D-211 that "[n]otwithstanding the decision in this case, it has been noted that since George Michael issued proceedings standard record company contracts have become more reasonable in terms of duration … ". *Cf.* Coulthard (1995) 58 MLR 731 n 4. The author (at 740) also noted that the approach adopted by the judge would justify the lifelong restraint of a successful artiste. After all, similar clauses but of shorter duration than the one in this case have been held to be unenforceable. *Cf. Zang Tumb Tuum Records Ltd* v *Johnson*, above, and *Silvertone Records Ltd* v *Mountfield* [1993] EMLR 152.

In respect of trade secrets the point to bear in mind is that covenants protecting such a legitimate proprietary interest may vary in their permitted duration but the length is dependent on the trade secret remaining confidential. Once the secret enters the public domain, it is no longer confidential to the employers. Therefore, a lengthy restraint is reasonable when it is expected that the information will be kept private for a long time, whereas a covenant of only a short duration is appropriate when the item containing the information is to be put onto the market, when it is easily reverse-engineered, or when an article detailing it is about to be published in the trade press.

It is unusual for a covenant lasting for the remainder of the employee's life to be upheld: *Sir W C Leng & Co Ltd* v *Andrews* [1909] Ch 763 (CA). It is nevertheless possible for a lifelong restraint to be valid, even in relation to clients, as can be seen from *Fitch* v *Dewes*, above. The defendant, a solicitor's clerk, covenanted that he would not on the expiry of his contract "be engaged or manage or concerned in the office, profession or business of a solicitor, within a radius of seven miles of the Town Hall of Tamworth". Lord Birkenhead C said that the covenant did not exceed the protection of the covenantee and was not against public policy, noting (at 166) that it was impossible to lay down any strict limit on duration. Without the covenant the clerk would be able to compete at any time by soliciting his former clients. Lord Parmoor (at 69–70) stated that the clause "is no more than adequate protection for a solicitor who desires to protect his professional secrets and to protect his clients from being enticed away by a former clerk who has had access to all his papers and has been in direct personal relation with a number of clients".

Assessing the Duration

Lord Wilberforce in *Stenhouse,* above (at 402), said that the duration of the covenant cannot:

> advantageously form the subject of direct evidence. It is for the judge, after informing himself as fully as he can of the facts and circumstances relating to the employer's business, the nature of the employer's interest to be protected, and the likely effect on this of solicitation, to decide whether the contractual period is reasonable or not. An opinion as to the reasonableness of the elements of it, particularly of the time during which it is to run, can seldom be precise, and can only be formed on a broad commonsense view.

Nevertheless, Lord Fraser in *Deacons* v *Bridge* [1984] AC 705, 717 (PC), said that there was no case in which a restraint was held to be unreasonable solely on the ground of duration.

Correctly judging the requisite period may be difficult. Among factors which the courts take into account are the frequency of the ex-employee's contact with the customers and the nature of that contact. For example, a milk roundsperson may quickly build up influence over customers but that influence may be easily lost. Similar thinking affects trades such as garage mechanics. Some jobs provide an employee with less contact with clients but the influence may be longer lasting than these tradespeople. For example, clients of a solicitor may follow her into a new firm and a quite lengthy covenant against canvassing or dealing may be appropriate. There is a view that the covenant should last as long as it would take a replacement to acquire the same influence over the clients that the former employee had: *Middleton* v *Brown* (1878) 474 LJ Ch 411, 413; normally the duration is judged by referring to the time over which influence would be exercised. For a Scottish case see *Malden Timber Ltd* v *Leitch,* 1992 SLT 757.

The judges have set their face against using previous cases as precedents on time. In *Dairy Crest Ltd* v *Pigott* [1989] ICR 92 (CA), the court allowed an appeal from the first instance judge who had followed earlier authorities to hold that a covenant lasting two years was enforceable in relation to a milkman. The covenant prevented the employee within two years of cessation of employment from soliciting or serving with milk or dairy produce any person who during the employee's service and within one year of the termination had been supplied by the employee. Warner J granted an interlocutory injunction in terms of the clause. He relied on earlier cases where covenants lasting for one year or two years were upheld. Balcombe LJ said that the test for enforceability "makes it a matter for the judge to decide, upon the appropriate evidence, whether in the particular circumstances of the case before him, a restraint is or is not unreasonable". Nevertheless, the courts have sometimes considered the authorities on the length of the covenant. In particular the House of Lords did so in *Esso Petroleum Co Ltd* v *Harper's Garage (Stourport) Ltd* [1968] AC 269, a case involving the sale of petrol to a filling station. Lord Hodson (at 320) said that he had been influenced by the number of reported cases of like nature to the one at issue, and he referred to *Biggs* v *Hoddinott* [1898] Ch 307 where a covenant for five years in a mortgage deed was held to be reasonable. Lord Pearce (at 322) placed Commonwealth authorities at the forefront of his speech.

Trebilcock wrote in *The Common Law of Restraint of Trade* (Carswell, 1986), 106 that " . . . there is considerable uncertainty concerning the appropriate test for duration in the customer connections cases. In practice, however, the determination of appropriate duration in accordance with these tests is generally so difficult and subjective a judgment, and liable to vary so much depending on the facts of a particular case, that the formal character of the test is not likely to be of great consequence". A decade later this opinion remains true.

Area

As with time the prohibited space in an area or other covenant must not extend beyond that which is reasonably necessary for the protection of the employers' legitimate proprietary interests. In *Spencer* v *Marchington* [1988] IRLR 392 (Ch D) a non-competition clause for two years after employment in the contract of service of an employment agency's general manager extended for 25 miles from Banbury. Mowbray QC held that since all clients except one lived within 20 miles, 25 miles was too extensive: one with a radius of 20 miles would have succeeded. The judge suggested using a non-solicitation covenant. For a Scottish case see *Lux Traffic Controls Ltd* v *Healey*, 1994 SLT 1153.

The judicial limits on area mean that it is easier to justify a broad territory in a trade secrets case than in a trade connection one: *Caribonum Co Ltd* v *Le Couch* (1913) 109 LT 587 (Ch D), *Forster & Sons Ltd* v *Suggett* (1918) 35 TLR 87 (Ch D), and *Kerchiss* v *Colora Printing Inks Ltd* [1960] RPC 235 (Ch D). For example, the stipulated territory was 16 countries in the last case. While it is not impossible for a trade connection to extend so far, it will be rare. See also *Under Water Welders and Repairers Ltd* v *Street* [1968] RPC 498.

Generally speaking worldwide covenants will not be upheld for they go wider than is necessary for the protection of the employers' interests: *Vandervell Products Ltd* v *McLeod* (1957) 74 RPC 185, 191 (CA). Lord Evershed MR said *obiter* that the covenant was too wide because it was not restricted in area and an unlimited area was not necessary to protect the plaintiffs' interests. (For some unknown reason this issue was not argued in *Panayiotou* v *Sony Music Entertainment (UK) Ltd* [1994] EMLR 229.) It was thought at one time that the restraint doctrine did not apply to that part of the covenant which applied beyond the United Kingdom, but that approach was firmly rejected by the Court of Appeal in *Commercial Plastics Ltd* v *Vincent* [1965] 1 QB 623, 630–1 and 645. Nevertheless, covenants extending across the world may be upheld, especially ones made by vendors. In *Nordenfelt* v *Maxim Nordenfelt Guns and Ammunition Co* [1894] AC 535, the covenant was unlimited in area. The Lords exploded the previous orthodoxy first stated in *Mitchel* v *Reynolds* (1711) P Wms 181, 24 ER 347 (KB), that a covenant was unreasonable *per se* if it was in general restraint of trade (that is, if it was not restricted to a particular locality). Lord Herschell C said (at 547) that:

> regard must be had to the changed conditions of commerce and of the means of communication which have been developed in recent years . . . An order can be sent to Newcastle more quickly than it could then [a century ago] have been transmitted from one end of London to the other . . . Competition has assumed altogether different proportions in these altered circumstances, and that which would have been once merely a burden on the covenantor may now be essential if there is to be reasonable protection to the covenantee.

In *Mitchel* v *Reynolds* Parker CJ (later Lord Macclesfield) said (at 191, 350): "what does it signify to a tradesman in London, what another does at Newcastle?" By the late nineteenth century it did not matter for some trades and professions. On the facts Lord Herschell C held in *Nordenfelt* (at 549) that the covenant would be nugatory unless it extended at least to the whole of the United Kingdom. UK and foreign governments would not consider it material that business was carried on in one part of the United Kingdom rather than another. The business sold needed protection from the vendor by means of a covenant unlimited in space. The restraint was, therefore, reasonable on the facts. "The generality of time or space must always be an important factor in the consideration of reasonableness though not *per se* a decisive test" is how Lord Morris put it (at 575). A worldwide restraint was upheld in *White, Tomkins & Courage Ltd* v *Wilson* (1907) 23 TLR 469 (Ch D), but a clause permitted the employee to work for non-competing companies and trade secrets as well as trade connections were involved.

Where the employers seek to protect their client base through a covenant, they must show that the chosen area matches the places where the customers are. In *Office Angels Ltd* v *Rainer–Thomas* [1991] IRLR 214 (CA), Sir Christopher Slade said that a restriction on opening within six months of the termination of employment an employment agency within a radius of 1,000 metres of the branch where the defendant had worked for at least four weeks out of the previous six months was too wide. He said *obiter* (at 221) that there was no "real functional correspondence between the kilometre circle circumscribed and the area particularly associated with the defendant's branch". He referred to *Reed Executive plc* v *Somers*, 20 March 1986, LEXIS (CA), where Arnold P used the phrase "functional correspondence". On the facts of *Reed* there was no correspondence between a radius of half a mile and the coverage of the branch of the employment agency where the defendant worked. Accordingly, the area covenant was one purely against competition and on that basis unenforceable. Similarly, there must be a correspondence between the area and the activity of the former employee. For example, if the covenant's area extends from an office in which he never worked, it will be unenforceable: *Scorer* v *Seymour Jones* [1966] 1 WLR 1419 (CA). For more on this case, see Chapter 7 on "Severance", below. *Office Angels* was followed on the "functional and correspondence" point in the franchise case of *Kall-Kwik Printing (UK) Ltd* v *Rush* [1996] FSR 114.

Where there is a functional correspondence, there need not be a customer in every part of the prohibited area for the claim to be successful. In *Kerchiss* v *Colora Printing Inks Ltd*, above, Danckwerts J said (at 241) that: "though there must be substantial goodwill throughout the area as a whole, the Court does not require that the persons relying on the covenant should prove sales in every part of the area in question". There is, therefore, no requirement that the employers carry on business in every part of the territory: *Connors Bros Ltd* v *Connors* [1940] 4 All ER 179, 195 (PC, on appeal from Canada), a vendor case. Viscount Maugham *per curiam* stated that goodwill may not be adequately protected if the covenant was limited to places where there had been sales for otherwise the vendor would be "free to establish a business, which would almost certainly be competitive, in all the adjoining places".

Where no limit is placed on the covenant's area, it will normally be read as extending across the whole world. For example, in *Dowden & Pook Ltd* v *Pook* [1904] 1 KB 45 (CA) Collins MR held that a covenant that the defendant should not carry on the business of a cider merchant for five years after leaving the plaintiffs' service was unreasonable because it applied to the whole world, whereas their business was largely in England. Cozens-Hardy LJ (at 55) said that a worldwide covenant could not be read as one applying just to the United Kingdom. *Vandervell Products Ltd* v *McLeod*, above, and *Marshall* v *NM Financial Management Ltd* [1995] 1 WLR 1461 (Ch D) are similar cases. The most famous case on this point is *Commercial Plastics Ltd* v *Vincent* [1965] 1 QB 623 (CA). One reason for holding a covenant not to take up employment with any of the plaintiffs' competitors in the same field of operations for one year after leaving their employ to be enforceable was that the defendant was prevented from joining a competitor anywhere in the world. Therefore, since the covenant was not restricted in area, it was one which applied throughout the whole world. The defendant's counsel contended that the clause was limited because it applied only to competitors. However Pearson LJ *per curiam* (at 645) held that there was no evidence to show that the plaintiffs needed protection from competitors world-wide: indeed, the plaintiffs' principal witness had said that they did not require protection from foreign manufacturers, a rather disastrous case of being hoist with one's own petard.

One case, however, where a covenant which was not limited in area was read down to cover only operations in the United Kingdom was *Littlewoods Organisation Ltd* v *Harris* [1977] 1 WLR 1472 (CA). Lord Denning MR said that the Court of Appeal in *Commercial Plastics* would have come to a different conclusion if they had been referred to cases concerned with the construction of covenants, especially *Haynes* v *Doman* [1899] 2 Ch 13 (CA), where Lindley MR had said that a covenant was to be interpreted with respect to the object sought to be achieved. In *Littlewoods* protection was needed only for the plaintiffs' UK interests and in this way the clause was impliedly limited. Lord Denning MR thought that the same construction ought to have been taken of the clause in *Commercial Plastics*. Megaw LJ, impressed by the doctrine of precedent more than Lord Denning MR, said that it had not been argued in that case that the covenant should be restrictively construed in the light of the circumstances. The dissentient, Browne LJ, approved *Commercial Plastics* and held that, unlike in the cases on which the majority relied, there was no restriction in the present one. Leave to appeal was granted but unfortunately not taken up.

A covenant against solicitation need not be limited in area since it is limited by the addresses of the clients. A covenant against using or disclosing trade secrets may be upheld even though it is not limited to a certain area too. Sometimes, however, such a clause is restricted to a certain area. It is suggested that, if a secret were revealed in one country, continent or hemisphere without undermining the employers' competitive advantage, the area should be limited to districts where revelation would lead to harm.

The courts also closely investigate the type of area covered. For example, a wider area is allowed where the district is rural than if it is urban, all things being equal: see, for example *Routh* v *Jones* [1947] 1 All ER 179 (Evershed J). In *Scorer* v *Seymour Jones*, above, Danckwerts LJ (at 1425) said that "in present day conditions a radius of five miles is not a great distance, particularly in a district which is mainly rural". Similarly, a wide area is permissible where the customers live in scattered places: *Tallis* v *Tallis* (1853) 1 E & B 391, 118 ER 482 (KB) *per* Lord Campbell CJ *per curiam*. The effect of these propositions can be seen from *Office Angels*, above. The restriction on employment agents was for six months not to undertake the same work within 1,000 metres of branches at which they had been employed within the last six months of their employment. On the facts the covenant was over-broad because it covered most of the City of London in which there were some 400 agencies and thousands of job applicants and employers.

What is not permissible is that the covenants protect an area in which the plaintiffs have no interest at the time of the making of the agreement but might wish to move into at a later time. In *Beetham* v *Fraser* (1904) 21 TLR 8 (DC) the defendant had covenanted that he would not compete (etc) with the plaintiff's business in Weybridge, London or at any other address the plaintiff might have in the future. Lord Alverstone CJ (at 8) held that for this reason the covenant was unenforceable. An area into which the employers have a reasonable expectation of expanding is, however, protectable. The most recent case is the Canadian one of *Tank Lining Corp* v *Dunlop Industrial Pty Ltd* (1982) 140 DLR (3d) 659.

The courts thus investigate the businesses sought to be protected. In *Mason*, above, the covenant prevented the appellant, a canvasser, from *inter alia* being engaged by any person in a firm carrying on a business the same as or similar to his employers within 25 miles of London or within 25 miles of any of their places of business for three years after termination of his employment. The Lords held that the clause was unreasonable. Lord Haldane C (at 731) stated that "the character of the respondents' business does not appear . . . to be such as to entitle them to say that they had any right which justified them in excluding the appellant from exercising his talents . . . within a wide area". He said (at 734) that "in the case of a business which is local and which is carried on simply by canvassing, it is hardly possible for an employer to justify an area with a twenty five mile radius and I do not think it is justified here". He thought that a non-solicitation covenant would have been upheld. Lord Shaw expressed himself strongly (at 741): the covenant did not protect the employers but was "a means of coercing and punishing the workman and putting him under a tyrannous and, therefore, legally indefensible restraint". Lord Moulton (at 744) equated the restraint with one of 25 miles on a milkman. What was unreasonable for a milkman was unreasonable for the canvasser.

Among cases where wide covenants were upheld are the following. In *E Underwood & Son Ltd* v *Barker* [1899] 1 Ch 300 (CA) the defendant covenanted that he would not for 12 months after leaving the plaintiffs' employ work as a hay and straw merchant in the United Kingdom, France, Belgium, Holland or Canada. The majority held the restraint to be reasonable and said that if the covenant was unreasonable as to the foreign countries, they could be severed. In *Lamson Pneumatic Tube Co* v *Phillips* (1904) 91 LT 367 (CA) the defendant, managing director of the plaintiffs, covenanted that he would not for five years after termination of his contract engage or be employed in any business similar to that of the plaintiffs "within the limit of the Eastern Hemisphere". He left and joined a rival company. The majority held in unreserved judgments that the covenant was reasonably necessary for the protection of the former employers. The dissenting judge, Cozens-Hardy LJ (at 369–70), said that the covenant was unjustified because at no time did the former employers have a business outside Europe.

Relationship between Time and Area

Duration and space are inversely proportional. The smaller the area is, the lengthier is the permissible period of time. The time and area of the restraint are also related to the proof needed. Lord Shaw in *Herbert Morris Ltd* v *Saxelby* [1916] 1 AC 688, 715, stated that if the facts of the case were relevantly set out, "the onus of proof is upon the party averring them to satisfy the Court of their sufficiency to overcome the presumption [of unreasonableness]; while as the time of restriction lengthens, or the space of its operation extends, the weight of that onus grows".

Fitch v *Dewes*, above, illustrates the inverse proportionality proposition. Lord Birkenhead C (at 163) said that "guidance may be derived in dealing with a restriction relating to time from an examination of the restriction which is made in respect of space. And the converse remark is of course equally true. For instance, if the restriction in respect of space is extremely limited, it is evident that a very considerable restriction in respect of time may be more acceptable than would otherwise have been the case". On the facts a lifelong restraint was acceptable because it was balanced by an area restriction consisting of a seven mile radius from Tamworth Town Hall. It is, however, suggested that such a restraint is too long nowadays to be enforceable. Surely any trade connection a solicitor's clerk may have will fade away quickly. The principle, however, stands. Similarly, the shorter the duration is, the wider the permitted territory may be. In

Continental Tyre and Rubber Great Britain Co Ltd v *Heath* (1913) 29 TLR 308 (KBD) Scrutton LJ, after severing "Germany or France" from the defendant's covenant, gave judgment for the plaintiffs, holding that a stipulation that he would not carry on, manage, be concerned or interested in the sale, purchase, manufacture or other dealings in indiarubber goods "in any part of the UK, Germany or France" was reasonable in covering the whole of the United Kingdom and a one-year restraint was not unreasonable. Lifelong covenants such as that upheld in *Gilford Motor Co* v *Horne* [1933] 1 Ch 935 and worldwide ones are especially prone to being upset but may be valid where the space or duration respectively is short.

Reasonableness is a Question of Law

The issue of reasonableness is for the judge. Early cases which make this point include *Mitchel* v *Reynolds* (1711) 1 P Wms 181, 24 ER 347 (demurrer), *Chesman* v *Nainby* (1727) 2 Str 740, 93 ER 819, *Davies* v *Mason* (1793) 5 Term Rep 119, 101 ER 69, *Horner* v *Graves* (1831) 7 Bing 735, 131 ER 284, *Proctor* v *Sargent* (1840) 2 M & G 20, 133 ER 647, *Mallan* v *May*, above, and *Tallis* v *Tallis*, above. More up to date is the speech of Lord Hodson in *Esso Petroleum Co Ltd* v *Harper's Garage (Stourport) Ltd* [1968] AC 269, 319. If a judge were to sit with a jury, she must not invite them to determine reasonableness: *United Shoe Machinery Co of Canada* v *Brunet* [1909] AC 330, 341 (PC).

One effect of this rule is that evidence of reasonableness cannot be adduced, as was pointed out by *inter alios* Viscount Haldane in *Mason*, above (at 732). Therefore, evidence that the covenantee or others believe the covenant was reasonable may not be led: see, for example, *Haynes* v *Doman* [1899] 2 Ch 13, *Sir W C Leng & Co* v *Andrews* [1909] 1 Ch 763, and *Eastham* v *Newcastle United FC Ltd* [1964] Ch 413. However, the fact that a covenant is a usual one is evidence of reasonableness: see for example *Catt* v *Tourle* (1869) LR 4 Ch App 654, 662, *Cornwall* v *Hawkins* (1872) 41 LJ Ch 435, 436, *Leng* (unusual), *Mason* at 742, and *Heine Bros (Australia) Pty Ltd* v *Forrest* [1963] VR 383, 385. The Common Pleas of Ohio held in *ER Moore Co* v *Ochiltree*, 239 NE 2d 242 (1968) that counsel's advice is not conclusive but is evidence of reasonableness.

Reasonableness between the Parties: The Problem

Any attempt to fix clear rules on the reasonableness of covenants will come unstuck. There are cases not formally overruled which are contrary to modern authority. An analysis of the principles degenerates into a list of cases. The reader is invited to consider the quote from Hoover J in the preface. Certainly some older decisions are out of line with the modern approach. Ones from before the First World War are particularly suspect. Furthermore, "there is no inflexible formula for deciding the ubiquitous question of reasonableness. Each case must stand or fall on its own facts": *Allright Auto Parks Inc* v *Borg*, 409 SW 2d 361 (1966) (Tenn). The Court of Appeal has continued to say that first instance judges cannot use earlier decisions as precedents: *Dairy Crest Ltd* v *Pigott* [1989] ICR 90. Therefore, as Glidewell LJ said in *Rex Stewart Jeffries Parker Ginsberg Ltd* v *Parker* [1988] IRLR 483, 486, reasonableness is "in the end . . . a matter of impression". Judges have emphasised that each case turns on its own facts, for example Croom-Johnson LJ in *Horsell Graphic Industries Ltd* v *Slattery* 4 February 1988, LEXIS. Nevertheless, a few cases have been extracted to provide a flavour of judicial thinking about reasonableness.

Lists of cases appear in *Avery* v *Langford* (1854) Kay 663, 667, 69 ER 281, 283, *Halsbury's Laws of England*, 4th ed (Hailsham), vol 47 (Butterworths, 1986, as updated), and S Mehigan and D Griffiths, *Restraint of Trade and Business Secrets*, 2nd ed (Longman, 1991), among other places. In the last-mentioned book, there is a ready reckoner of cases since 1909 with columns for job, time, area, and outcome. If one looked only at the first three columns, one might more readily select whether the covenant was valid or not by spinning a coin than by knowing the law. For example, to take two cases from the same year: *Bowler* v *Lovegrove* [1921] 1 Ch D 642 and *Fitch* v *Dewes* [1921] AC 158 (HL), the reader is invited to predict the outcome on these facts:

– *Bowler:* estate agent's clerk, one year, Portsmouth and Gosport.
– *Fitch:* solicitor's clerk, no limit of time, seven miles from Tamworth Town Hall.

The covenant was struck down in *Bowler* but upheld in *Fitch*. One might have predicted the opposite outcome. One might explain the cases on several grounds such as in *Fitch* the lawyers were protecting their own, but such explanations do not aid practitioners. It is suggested that *Fitch* is incorrect: lifelong restraints on employees should not be upheld unless circumstances are exceptional. Even on the same facts, courts may differ. Predictability and certainty, essences of a good legal system, are lacking.

Hoover J in *Arthur Murray Dance Studios of Cleveland Inc* v *Witter*, 105 NE 2d 605 (1952) (Common Pleas, Cuyahoga County, Ohio) listed 41 questions which go to reasonableness. A sample cannot deal with all of these, but the cases below do exemplify this area of law.

Illustrations of Various Types of Covenants: Proprietary Interest, Area and Duration

A decision upon the question of reasonableness depends upon a judgment, the reasons for which do not admit of great elaboration (*Amoco Australia Pty Ltd* v *Rocca Motor Engineering Co Ltd* (1972–3) 113 CLR 288, 308, HCA, *per* Walsh J).

Non-solicitation and Non-dealing Covenants

Like area covenants these post-termination clauses must extend no further than is reasonably necessary to protect the employers' legitimate proprietary interests. Their success depends on whether the employee had influence over the clientele (see *Herbert Morris Ltd* v *Saxelby* [1916] AC 688 (HL)) or had confidential information relating to customers, and in both instances whether the employers relied on the employee's loyalty. For example, in *Stenhouse Australia Ltd* v *Phillips* [1974] AC 391 (PC) Lord Wilberforce said (at 401):

> the connection between an insurer or insurance broker and his client is not nearly so firm as, for example, that between a solicitor and his client. On the other hand its comparative fragility makes the risk of solicitation of clients by a former employee the more serious. A client is not easily detached from a solicitor who has been handling his affairs over a period of years: but a comparatively mild solicitation may deprive an insurance broker of valuable business ... These considerations make it appear that, in principle, a covenant against solicitation of clients may be entirely reasonable and necessary for the protection of the employer.

The emphasis on influence over customers explains why a non-solicitation or non-dealing covenant fails when customers do not seek out the employee. The Scottish case of *Douglas Llambias Associates Ltd* v *Napier* 31 October 1990, LEXIS (Outer House) illustrates the law. Lord Morton held that there was no legitimate proprietary interest which the plaintiffs – employment agents – could protect. There was no customer list which was confidential and there was no other possible trade secret. Customers were Edinburgh solicitors' firms, the names of which were readily accessible. These firms would contact all three recruitment agencies including both the defendant's former and present employers. The former employee, it was held, was not in a position to attract the firms to the new employers. Therefore, a covenant that the defendant would not for 12 months after termination of his contract solicit or deal with those clients who had used his services as a recruitment specialist for two years preceding termination was struck down. In such a case the covenant falls because the clients are not loyal to one firm. On the facts they used all three agencies. If the defendant had had influence over the clients, then a suitably drafted covenant would have succeeded.

An example of such a covenant is one where influence has developed even in a field where there are multiple suppliers. Take, for instance, companies which promise next-day delivery of goods. If an employee of a sending firm comes to use the services of a carrying company because of that company's friendly receptionist, a well-drafted covenant protecting the employers' trade connection with the sending firm will succeed and it would do so even though it is the receptionist who has built up the influence and even though he has done so through his own personality. The courts look on the receptionist as being the company: it is through him that it gains influence. In relation to an estate agent's clerk Salmon LJ said in *Scorer* v *Seymour Jones* [1966] 1 WLR 1419, 1426 (CA): "When the defendant was in the Kingsbridge office he *was* [his emphasis] in effect the Kingsbridge office. Every customer who came into that office dealt with him. He was in a position in which he would have every opportunity of gaining knowledge of the customers' business and influence over the customers". He quoted from the speech of Lord Parker in *Herbert Morris*, above (at 769):

"Wherever such covenants have been upheld it has been on the ground ... that [the servant or apprentice] might obtain such personal knowledge of and influence over the customers of his employer ... as would enable him, if competition were allowed, to take advantage of his employer's trade connection".

The validity of a covenant is judged at the date when the contract was entered into. Accordingly, if at that date the employee might acquire influence over customers or suppliers during his employment, the covenant protects a legitimate proprietary interest despite the fact that the employee never did work with all the possible customers. The principal authority is *G W Plowman & Son Ltd* v *Ash* [1964] 1 WLR 568 (CA). The defendant covenanted that he would not *inter alia* for two years after termination "canvass or solicit for himself or any other person or persons any farmer or market gardener who shall at any time during the employment of the employee ... have been a customer of the employers". Davies LJ (at 573) was like Harman LJ (at 572) somewhat doubtful on the point but held that "employers are entitled to retain the possibility that those who at one time during the employee's employment placed orders with them and have discontinued their custom might come back again". The clause was upheld by Russell LJ (at 574) because at the time when the contract was made the employers could have required him to work anywhere within the stipulated area and therefore he could have acquired influence over customers across the whole territory. Lord Denning MR in *Marley Tile Co Ltd* v *Johnson* [1982] IRLR 75, 77 (CA), restricted *Plowman* to cases where the reps might acquire influence over all the customers. There were in *Plowman* only five reps and their territories were small. On the facts of *Marley Tile*, however, there were some 2,500 customers, and the defendant could not have known or come into contact with more than a small percentage of them. It was unreasonable to prevent him from dealing with that number for a year. Eveleigh and Templeman LJJ briefly concurred.

Similarly it is thought that a covenant can apply to persons who already have contact with the employers in one aspect of their trade and who may buy from the department in which the covenantor worked. In *Business Seating (Renovations) Ltd* v *Broad* [1989] ICR 729 (Ch D), part of the covenant fell because the coverage of potential clients was unreasonable in that it included those belonging to associated companies. This part was severed. Millett J applied *Plowman* to that part of the clause which governed customers and held that it did not matter whether they had discontinued their custom or indeed whether the employee had "any actual contact with them".

The courts investigate the frequency of transactions between the employee and customers or suppliers to see whether there is a trade connection. It would appear that a "casual purchaser" is not a customer in the relevant sense: *Gilford Motor Co* v *Horne* [1933] Ch 935, 960 (CA), where the covenant was expressly limited to customers "or persons in the habit of dealing with the company". What was required in that case was a person's frequenting of a place of business "for the purpose of making purchases". Nowadays the phrase would have to be widened to cover, for example, placing orders over the phone or by fax.

Where it is impossible to state whether a person or firm is a customer or not the covenant will be struck down for uncertainty. In *Reed Executive plc* v *Somers*, 20 March 1986, LEXIS (CA) one covenant at issue forbade the defendant for one year from the termination of her contract from seeking to obtain orders from persons who at the date of termination were customers or "in the habit of dealing with" the plaintiffs, employment agents, and "with whom any of the employees in any offices of the Employer at which the Employee was employed shall have contracted or endeavoured to contract on behalf of the Employer whilst the Employee was employed at this office". Arnold P disagreed first with the plaintiffs' counsel's contention that a customer was on the facts either "someone who has been coming to the plaintiffs either to find staff, permanent or temporary, or to get employment themselves" or "a person who is on the books and has regularly and recently been using the plaintiffs' services". The judge considered that in some trades there is no difficulty in identifying customers, for example a milkman knows who are his customers. However, "where there are more sporadic types of business, such as employment agencies, different considerations apply". There was no easy definition in such businesses. Secondly, the clause distinguished between customers and those who were in the habit of dealing with the employers. The two concepts were separate ones: the latter term did not explain the former. Thirdly, the latter part of the definition ("with whom ... ") might cover a lengthy period or a short one. The employee herself did not, according to the covenant, have to deal with the customers. Fourthly, it was impossible to say whether a person who had used the employers' services before the termination of the contract was a customer or not. On all these grounds the covenant was unenforceable.

The law relating to customers who came with the employee when she joined the employers is revealing. In *M & S Drapers (a Firm)* v *Reynolds* [1957] 1 WLR 1295 the employee, a draper, brought with him a good number of customers who had traded with him during his previous employment. The Court of Appeal held that nevertheless the employers, who imposed the covenant, had a legitimate proprietary interest in those customers. However, the fact that the employee had brought those customers with him was a factor in assessing the reasonableness of the covenant. A non-solicitation clause for five years was struck down on this basis. The ruling opens up several difficulties. It is likely that an employee will be subject to one non-solicitation covenant, and not to two: one prohibiting the solicitation of customers she acquired during employment with the employers and one prohibiting solicitation of customers who came with her. That single covenant may have only one time period. The duration may be legitimate in respect of those she brought into the business but not those she acquired during employment, or vice versa. If so, the whole covenant falls. Accordingly, it is suggested that the duration is kept within tight bounds or that there are two separate covenants with different prohibited periods, one for each type of customer. The permissible time may depend on how long the employers will take to acquire customers of similar spending power, though the law is not certain. Perhaps the period is limited to that which it will take the employers to recoup the money they spent on servicing the customers the employee brought with her. This suggestion ensures that if one covenant falls, protection is not lost for the other type of customers. *M & S Drapers* should be contrasted with *Hanover Insurance Brokers Ltd* v *Schapiro* [1994] IRLR 82, where the Court of Appeal held that the defendant, chair of the plaintiffs, could not lawfully take with him clients which he had acquired before his employment with them. It is arguable that in relation to trade connections statements in *M & S Drapers* about existing customers are dicta, for the ratio is that the covenant was unreasonable in the light of its duration, five years: see Morris LJ (at 17). There are statements which are referable to the particular employee's situation: his contract could be determined with only two weeks' notice and in the words of Denning LJ (at 18), which were endorsed in *Schapiro*, "a Managing director can look after himself. A traveller is not so well placed to do so. The law must protect him". Similarly, a chair can protect himself. The other element which distinguishes *Schapiro* from *M & S Drapers* is that in the former the employee was recruited *in order to* widen the plaintiffs' clientele.

Another issue is that employers must be wary of recruiting staff who bring clients with them. There is the possibility of an action for the tort of inducing breach of contract against them by the previous employers. This is a difficult matter because the interest of the former employers in those customers has not been considered in the cases; if they have a legitimate proprietary interest in those customers, how can the present employers have one too? *M & S Drapers* leads to the conclusion that the current employers have an interest but the judges did not consider any interest the previous employers might have. The issue awaits resolution. Perhaps the second employers' claim ought to fail because they are second in time, unless the former employers' interest has evaporated. The court held that a firm or person cannot be a "customer" for the purposes of a restraint of trade covenant unless it or she was a customer at the date of the termination of the contract of employment. Therefore, if it was uncertain whether it or she was a customer on that date, the covenant fell. This outcome may be contrasted with that in *Gilford*, above, where the Court of Appeal arrived at the opposite conclusion: there was no need for specification of all customers. It is possible that the courts have become more stringent since the 1930s in this respect.

Non-solicitation and non-dealing covenants are unenforceable if they relate solely to suppliers or customers who were so before the employee took up her job: *Hinton & Higgs (UK) Ltd* v *Murphy*, 1989 SLT 450 (CS). Lord Dervaird (at 451) stated that employers cannot have protection against the employee working for those firms which had ceased to be clients 10 years ago but only when the firms were clients during the time that the employee worked for the employers. They have no legitimate proprietary interest. *Plowman* supports this approach. The Lord Ordinary was, however, willing to concede that there may be circumstances in which it was necessary to give protection to prior customers.

What of those customers or suppliers who during the currency of the employee's contract traded with the employers but were not doing business with them at the termination of employment? The present law is uncertain. One line of cases strikes down such clauses. In *Reed Executive*, above, the Court of Appeal as stated above held that the covenant must relate to customers who were clients at the date of termination. However, in *Gilford* this was not the case, yet the covenant was not held to be unenforceable. Similarly, in *Plowman* the Court of Appeal upheld a covenant which related to those who were customers at any time during the defendant's employment. As previously noted the court said that those who had been customers might become so again. Therefore, the employers had a legitimate proprietary interest. It is suggested that a covenant is unenforceable if it relates to customers with whom the former did not come into contact because she has not acquired influence over them.

A covenant will fall, of course, if it covers persons who became customers after the termination of the contract: *Konski* v *Peet* [1915] Ch 530 (Ch D). Neville J (at 539) said that coverage of future customers was not reasonable: "It appears to me to place the covenantor in an exceedingly awkward position, because he might at any time be quite innocently offending against the terms of the contract that he entered into".

If there is a legitimate proprietary interest, the covenant must also be reasonable in extent. A clause prohibiting an employee from soliciting clients of all the employers' branches was struck down by the first instance judge in *Office Angels Ltd* v *Rainer-Thomas* [1991] IRLR 214 (CA) because the defendants knew only customers who came to their branch. The plaintiffs had 6–7,000 clients but the defendants knew only some 100 of them. There was no appeal from that decision. Similar was *Marley Tile*, above. The covenants were unenforceable because they covered some 2,500 customers: the defendant did not have influence over so many. The territory ("any area in which you have been employed by the Employer at any time during the 12 months before termination") was also too wide. It covered the whole of Cornwall and most of Devon. This case is discussed in detail below.

It should be noted that there is no need in relation to a non-solicitation or non-dealing covenant to limit coverage to any particular area. If, however, an area restriction is inserted, it must be no wider than is reasonably necessary to protect the employers' interest. In *Hinton* v *Higgs*, above, the covenant extended beyond the employers' place of business – Scotland. Lord Dervaird said (at 452) that the covenant was a worldwide one but the plaintiffs' activities did not extend beyond the United Kingdom. Even if the covenant could be read as being restricted to the United Kingdom, the plaintiffs had no legitimate proprietary interest in preventing the defendants from working for clients in parts of the United Kingdom other than Scotland because their area of operations was only Scotland.

The duration of non-solicitation and non-dealing covenants is limited to a reasonable time: *Stenhouse*, above. As Lord Wilberforce put it (at 402), the covenant's reasonableness is not predicated on the length of time it might be expected that the defendant would have retained a "competitive edge" over his former employers: "It is, rather, what is a reasonable time during which the employer is entitled to protection against solicitation of clients with whom the employee had contact and influence during employment and who were not bound to the employer by contract or by stability of association". It has been said that there are no reported cases where such covenants (called "barring out" ones in the instant case) have been struck down on this ground alone: *Rex Stewart Jeffries Parker Ginsberg Ltd* v *Parker* [1988] IRLR 483 (CA) *per* Glidewell LJ (at 486), relying on the plaintiffs' counsel. On the facts the restraint occasioned by a covenant not to solicit for 18 months was upheld on the managing director of an advertising agency. Through his position he had the opportunity to obtain more influence over clients than had junior staff.

Non-Poaching Covenants

These are covenants designed to prevent an ex-employee from enticing away his former colleagues. As always the covenant must be no wider than is reasonably necessary for the protection of the employers' proprietary interest, which in this context is one in the stability of their workforce. Employers do not wish to lose valued members of staff or to have to recruit and train new workers for selection and supervision are expensive and time-consuming processes.

Trade Secrets

Once the employers have demonstrated that the covenant protects trade secrets or other like confidential information, it is easy to show that a covenant protecting them is reasonable. The covenant may extend worldwide and last for a lengthy period. It should be noted that the implied term of confidentiality is not restricted in area.

Further Illustrations of Time and Space Restrictions

Many judges are reported as saying simply that the limits are reasonable without explaining the reason for the decision. For example, in *Calvert, Hunt & Bardon* v *Elton* [1975] EG Dig 219 Graham J in dealing with the plaintiffs' claim for an injunction to restrain their former employee, an estate agent, seems to have held that on the facts a restraint extending to five miles from any branch of the plaintiffs for three years was reasonable without determining why the radius and the term were such. Some judges do however investigate such matters and two English cases from the early 1980s illustrate the approach.

In *Spafax Ltd* v *Harrison, Spafax Ltd* v *Taylor* [1980] IRLR 442, the plaintiffs sold motor parts wholesale. Harrison was a branch manager, in which capacity he trained salesmen for the Cumbria area. He also was a salesman in about a quarter of that area. Clause 8 of his service agreement stated:

> for a period of two years from the termination of his employment hereunder from whatever cause, the Manager shall not either on his own behalf or for any other person firm or company solicit or seek to obtain orders by way of trade in respect of any goods with which he shall have dealt on behalf of the company or goods of a substantially similar kind from any person firm or company to whom, during the period of 12 months prior to such termination of his employment, the Manager or to his knowledge any member of his staff shall have sold such goods on behalf of the company.

Mr Harrison left the plaintiffs and joined a competitor. Mr Taylor was a salesman in the Liverpool area and he covenanted:

> for a period of two years from the determination from any cause whatsoever of his employment hereunder the salesman shall not either on his own behalf or for any other person firm or company by way of trade solicit or seek to obtain orders for any goods which he shall have dealt in on behalf of the company or any similar goods from any person firm or company to whom during the period of six months prior to such determination of employment he shall have sold goods on behalf of the company.

He left and started work for the same rivals which Mr Harrison had joined. The Court of Appeal dismissed their consolidated appeals relating to these covenants. Stephenson LJ, with whom Geoffrey Lane LJ agreed, said (at 446):

> I do not find any of the voluminous authorities on this branch of the law anything but of the most general guidance. They all turn on their particular facts and though one can see roughly what sort of restrictions have been held to be too wide or too narrow, one really has to treat each case of a restrictive covenant on its own merits in the light of all the relevant facts and ... it very often comes down or comes back to a matter of first or it may be last impression.

He considered that a judge has to ignore whether the defendants had unfairly exploited their advantages, enabling them to damage their former employers' trade interests. He thought that the 12 and six months' time-limits as to previous customers were reasonable, especially in the light of the fact with regard to the 12 months' limit that Mr Harrison was a manager. He held that the two years' restraint on both defendants was reasonable, and he adopted the argument of leading counsel for the plaintiffs that the enforcement of the covenants was not unfair and still left the ex-employees with scope for employment. Mr Taylor "is free to act in any other part of the country than his small though densely populated Liverpool area in any capacity. He is free to act in the same district in any capacity, including that of salesman, subject only to this, that in that area he should not sell the same or similar type of goods to those particular persons or firms or companies to whom within a limited period of six months he had himself sold such goods" (at 448). Accordingly the appeal court enforced these covenants against solicitation. Neither the duration nor the customers to whom they applied was unreasonably designated.

A contrasting case, also involving a non-solicitation covenant, also in the Court of Appeal and also from the early 1980s, is *Marley Tile Co Ltd v Johnson* [1982] IRLR 75. The defendant had been the unit manager of the plaintiffs in Dorset when he left to become a director of a company which did the same work as the plaintiffs – tiling for roofs and floors. He had covenanted that he would not:

(a)   for a period of one year from the date of termination of your employment hereunder be employed by any other person, company or firm as manager, salesman or representative in the supply, sale or fixing of products made, sold or fixed by the employer (and with which you have been concerned during your employment hereunder) or of other person's products similar to such products within any area in which you have been employed by the employer at any time during the 12 months before such termination;

(b)   during the like period and within any such area as aforesaid, act as agent for or be concerned or interested either directly or indirectly (save as a holder of shares in a public company) in any business engaged in the supply, sale or fixing of products made, sold or fixed by the employer or other person's products similar to such products;

(c)   during the like period canvass, solicit or deal with in connection with products made, sold or fixed by the company or other person's products similar to such products any person, company or firm carrying on business within any such area as aforesaid who was during the 12 months before the termination of your employment a customer of the employer or accustomed to deal with the employer.

Lord Denning MR (at 77) held that the 12-month duration was reasonable, but that clauses (a) and (b) were too wide to be enforceable. In reality they were covenants against competition: the area was 200 miles long and 50 miles wide. He had some doubts about (c) – the covenant against solicitation – but the evidence was that in the area there were some 2,500 customers. The defendant had not come into contact with more than a few of them in one part of the area: "taking the size of the area, the number of customers, the class of products – because Marley may have many lines 'other than roofing and tiling' – it seems to be that the covenant is too wide to be reasonable". Eveleigh LJ (at 78) said that the restraint "prevents the defendant from dealing as a manager of a timber yard of a builders' merchant with products which might be used for purposes far removed from that of roofing – for example, aluminium rails … [I]f a green-grocer's shop had been re-roofed by the plaintiff, the defendant, or the manage-ment of a small 'do-it-yourself' shop, could not sell 25 mm by 50 mm timber to be used for vegetable and fruit racks in the greengrocer's shop". Templeman LJ (at 78) briefly pointed out that since the defendant had no substantial influence over most of the 2,500 customers, the covenant was one against competition *per se*.

A Northern Irish case also involving a non-solicitation clause illustrates how the English approach to space restrictions is used in another common law country. In *NIS Fertilisers Ltd* v *Neville*, 10 February 1986 the defendant worked as a salesman for the plaintiffs in County Down. He covenanted that he would not solicit customers for 12 months after the termination of his contract within his sales territory "and any area outside this territory which stands at a distance of less than 20 miles from the boundary of the same". The court held that the covenant doubled the area of the defendant's territory and was too wide.

As was stated above, the deployment of cases illustrative of time and space restrictions is likely to degenerate into a list of authorities barely if at all distinguishable one from another. One last reported case does however exem-plify what modern judges are doing in first instance courts. Since the issue of reasonableness is one of degree for the judge, the higher courts do not deal with or intervene in such cases. In *Spencer* v *Marchington* [1988] IRLR 392, the plaintiff owned an employment agency and she employed the defendant to run it. The agency was based in Banbury and there were negotiations to take over another agency in Leamington Spa. The contract of employment contained the following:

> [a]fter termination of this employment you shall not for a period of two years after such termination, either alone or in partnership with any other person or persons, or as servant or agent or officer of any person, concern or company, carry on or in any way be engaged or concerned or interested in the business of any Employment Agency within a radius of 25 miles of the office address, Banbury, Oxfordshire, and 10 miles from 47 The Parade, Leamington Spa.

After an altercation, the employee left and took with her the plaintiff's best customer and her second in command at the agency. The judge, Mowbray QC, held that the plaintiff had several legitimate interests to protect: lists of customers, trade discounts, close business relationships. However, the clause was too wide in area. It covered towns where the plaintiff had no customers and could prevent the defendant from setting up in those towns and attracting clients from outside the area. The maximum radius, the judge thought, was 20 miles. He suggested that the plaintiff should have adopted a non-solicitation covenant to cover existing customers. He said:

> [t]he object of the rule of public policy against too wide an area is not primarily to protect the employee ... it is to protect the market open [*sic*] to prospective customers, to maximise the number of, in the present case, Employment Agencies available to them and to promote competition among them. No authority was cited ... to justify extending the area of restriction beyond where actual customers are to where possible future customers might have been won, or to places from which they could have been reached.

Nevertheless, the judge expressed concern for the plaintiff who had sought fairly to protect the business's goodwill, whereas the employee was "in flagrant breach of both letter and spirit of an agreement which she freely entered into".

It should be noted that just as some employees do not have the sort of recurring contact which will permit the employers to safeguard a trade connection, so also may it occur that the permissible length of the restriction will vary with regard to the position which the employee occupies. For example, an 18-month restraint may be valid with regard to a joint managing director of an advertising agency when such a length would be unreasonable for a junior employee: *Rex Stewart Jeffries Parker Ginsberg Ltd* v *Parker*, above at 486.

There is truth in the statement of Harman LJ in *G W Plowman & Son Ltd* v *Ash*, above, that where there is a non-solicitation covenant, as opposed to a carrying-on-the-business covenant, area need not be mentioned. The same applies to a restraint forbidding the use or disclosure of a trade secret.

The measure of the length of time permissible for a restraint of trade clause might be: how long will it take the employer to train someone to the same standard of the departing employee? If it takes two years for an employer to train a salesperson, a covenant for two years or less would be upheld. Such a measurement, however, does not look to the employers' interest in protecting his or her trade secret, and should be rejected in such cases. Examples of confidential information covenants which were upheld include three years in *Under Water Welders and Repairers Ltd* v *Street* [1968] RPC 498 (the process was new and was used only by the plaintiffs) and 12 months in *Littlewood Organisation Ltd* v *Harris* [1977] 1 WLR 1472, where the Court of Appeal considered that in view of changes to women's fashions a longer term would not have been enforceable.

Time of Assessing Reasonableness

Most authorities state that reasonableness is judged at the time when the contract is entered into, not at the date of the alleged breach or of trial. Cases are numerous and and include *Rannie* v *Irvine* (1844) 7 Man & G 969, 976–7, 13 ER 393, 396 (followed in, for example *Aling* v *Olivier* [1967] 1 SA 215, 219 (TPD)); *Benwell* v *Inns* (1857) 24 Beav 307, 311, 53 ER 376, 378 (Rolls Court); *Townsend* v *Jarman* [1900] 2 Ch 698, 703 (partners); *Lamson Pneumatic Tube Co* v *Phillips* (1904) 91 LT 363, 370; *S V Nevanas & Co* v *Walker* [1914] 1 Ch 413, 422; *Burton Rowe & Viner Ltd* v *Brereton* (1946) 79 Ll LR 438, 444; *Marchon Products Ltd* v *Thomes* (1954) 71 RPC 445, 449; *Gledhow Autoparts Ltd* v *Delaney* [1965] 1 WLR 1366, 1377; *Texaco Ltd* v *Mulberry Filling Station Ltd* [1972] 1 All ER 513, 522 (solus tie); *Calvert Hunt & Bardon* v *Elton* [1975] EG Dig 219, 224; *Adavin Plastics Ltd* v *Norbury*, 15 November 1984, LEXIS; *Bridge* v *Deacons* [1984] AC 705, 718; *Rex Stewart Jeffries Parker Ginsberg Ltd* v *Parker* [1988] IRLR 483, 486; *Rockall Ltd* v *Murray*, 1 March 1988, LEXIS, *Watson* v *Prager* [1991] 1 WLR 726, 738, *Poly Lina Ltd* v *Finch* [1995] FSR 751, 763 and *Alliance Paper Group plc* v *Prestwich* [1996] IRLR 25, 27 (Ch D). The most authoritative statement remains that of Lord Reid in *Esso Petroleum Co Ltd* v *Harper's Garage (Stourport) Ltd* [1968] AC 269, 336: "The validity of the agreement must be determined as at the date when it was signed". One effect of the law is that the employee's motives for wishing to be free of the restraint are irrelevant. Commonwealth authorities include *Williams* v *Masters* [1912] NZLR 1148, 1154; *Attorney-General of the Commonwealth of Australia* v *Adelaide SS Co* [1913] AC 781, 797; *Pest Control (Central Africa) Ltd* v *Martin* [1955] 3 SA 609, 613 (S Rhodesia); *Marquett* v *Walsh* (1929) 29 SRNSW 298, 307; *Baldwin* v *McIver* [1937] NZLR 265, 272; *Lindner* v *Murdock's Garage* (1950) 83 CLR 628, 638; *Peters Ice Cream (Victoria) Ltd* v *Todd* [1961] VR 485, 489; *McAllister* v *Cardinal* (1964) 67 DLR (2d) 313, 320; *Green* v *Stanton* (1969) 6 DLR (3d) 680, 687 (BCCA); *Phillip M Levy Pty Ltd* v *Christopoulos* [1973] VR 673, 675; *Amoco Australia Pty Ltd* v *Rocca Motor Engineering Co Ltd* (1972–3) 133 CLR 288, 301 (but see Gibbs J at 318); *Geraghty* v *Minter* (1979) 142 CLR 177, 188; and *Tank Lining Corp* v *Dunlop Industrial Ltd* (1983) 140 DLR (3d) 659, 665. For a Scottish case see *PR Consultants Ltd* v *Mann*,

15 August 1995, LEXIS. The construction of the covenant is judged at the time of contracting: *Rockall*, above. An illustrative case is *S W Strange Ltd* v *Mann* [1965] 1 WLR 629. At the time of contracting betting shops were illegal. The plaintiffs' business was one of credit betting over the telephone. By the time of the alleged breach of covenant betting shops had been legalised and the employers had established one. Protection for trade at that bookmaker's could not be granted, for it did not exist at the time of entering into the contract. The case may be seen as an instructive one: covenants should be revised in the light of developments.

However, it was said (in a Scottish case) that what is confidential need not be determined at the commencement of the contract: *SOS Bureau Ltd* v *Payne*, 1982 SLT 22 (Sh Ct); and the time for determining who are the employer's competitors is the trial date: *Commercial Plastics Ltd* v *Vincent* [1965] 1 QB 623, 641–2. Lord Denning MR exceptionally did take later events into account in *Shell UK Ltd* v *Lostock Garage Ltd* [1976] 1 WLR 1187, 1198. The majority disagreed.

The rule is open to the criticism that a covenant may be held to be valid in the light of circumstances existing at the time of contracting but those may have changed by the time of trial. The court must not look at actual events but at possible ones, which may never occur. For instance, in *Elves* v *Crofts* (1850) 10 Ch 241, 138 ER 98, the covenantor was bound even though the covenantee and assigns had never traded at the shop. The effect is to put a premium on drafting carefully. As Diplock LJ said in *Gledhow Autoparts Ltd* v *Delaney*, above at 1377, "[a] covenant of this kind is invalid *ab initio* or valid *ab initio*. There cannot come a moment at which it passes from the class of invalid into that of valid covenants".

Position in the Hierarchy

It may be that senior employees will have greater access to confidential information than junior ones, and they may have greater influence than persons of lower rank. This difference may be taken into account by the court in determining whether a covenant was reasonable or not: *Herbert Morris Ltd* v *Saxelby* [1915] 2 Ch 57, 90 (CA). In *Sir W C Leng & Co Ltd* v *Andrews* [1909] 1 Ch 763, 771, Fletcher Moulton LJ said that on the facts of the case the defendant, a junior reporter, did not occupy a position which "would to any exceptional extent inform him of any secrets connected with the business. His duties would be those which naturally attach to reporting and . . . very little more". There are several similar cases. In *Rex Stewart Jeffries Parker Ginsberg Ltd* v *Parker* [1988] IRLR 483 (CA) an 18-month non-solicitation covenant was upheld on the defendant, the joint managing director of an advertising agency, whereas the first instance judge considered that one of the same length was inept in relation to a more junior employee. Glidewell LJ (at 486) rejected criticism of that approach. The defendant presumably had oversight over all business transactions and therefore he had, through his position, opportunities to develop relationships with clients which a junior employee would not have had. An older case involving a managing director is *Welstead* v *Hadley* (1904) 21 TLR 165.

It is partly for this reason that the courts in England do not like what US jurists call "boilerplate" covenants, that is ones which are not framed for each individual or at least not for each category of employee.

Notice Period

Viscount Haldane C noted in *Mason* v *Provident Clothing & Supply Co* [1913] AC 726, 732, that the defendant's employment may have lasted for a fortnight, yet he was under the covenant bound for three years within 25 miles of London or any of the plaintiffs' branches and seemed to think that this was an important factor in denouncing the covenant. Lord Shaw spoke to the same effect (at 741). Accordingly, the duration of the period of notice to be given to the employee is a factor to be considered when determining the reasonableness of the covenant. It is unlikely that a lengthy covenant will be upheld where the employee is provided with only a short period of notice in her contract. This law provides a good opportunity for employers to demonstrate the reasonableness of the covenant. They can insert a clause stipulating that the period of notice will lengthen, the longer the employee remains in employment. In effect as she becomes more experienced in her job, she presumably acquires more influence over customers, greater access to confidential information and so on; in this way the reasonableness of the covenant's duration becomes increasingly more evident as time elapses.

There is a statement of Hodson LJ in *M & S Drapers (a Firm)* v *Reynolds* [1957] 1 WLR 9, 11, to the contrary. He said that if the court took the length of notice into account, it would be investigating the adequacy of the consideration, which it cannot do. The statement is incorrect in the light of the House of Lords' authority, quoted above and indeed it conflicts with his own view in *Esso Petroleum Co Ltd* v *Harper's Garage (Stourport) Ltd* [1968] AC 269 (HL) at 318 that consideration need not be adequate but the adequacy or otherwise affects the covenant's reasonableness. In *Esso* he quoted from Lord Macnaghten in *Nordenfelt* v *Maxim Nordenfelt Guns and Ammunition Co* [1894] AC 535, 565: " ... in time it was found that the parties themselves were better judges of that matter than the Court, and it was held to be sufficient if there was a legal consideration of value, though of course the quantum of consideration may enter into the question of the reasonableness of the covenant".

A case illustrative of this area of law is *Gledhow Autoparts Ltd* v *Delaney*, above. Diplock LJ said *obiter* that the employee could have been dismissed with a fortnight's notice at any time including two weeks after he had started work. The covenant was for three years. Therefore, the employee would have been bound even though he had contacted only a small number of customers. He thought that the covenant could have been invalidated on this ground because a short notice period reflected the unimportance of his services to the employers.

Compare, however, the Jamaican decision in *National Chemsearch Corp Caribbean* v *Davidson* (1966) 10 WIR 36, 43: if the period of employment was short, the defendant would obtain fewer customers than otherwise, and therefore the covenant was not affected by the short duration. It is suggested that if the length of the notice period were to be considered in all cases, very many covenants would fail, but as yet few covenants have been invalidated for this reason.

Public Interest

Covenants in employment contracts rarely fail on the ground that, though they are reasonable between the parties, they are unreasonable in the interests of the public. Lord Parker said in *Attorney-General of the Commonwealth of Australia* v *Adelaide SS Co Ltd* [1913] AC 781, 795 (PC), that he was not "aware of any case in which a restraint, though reasonable in the interests of the parties, has been held unenforceable because it involves some injury to the public". Nevertheless, cases over the last 30 years have emphasised that the public interest hurdle remains important. Recent authorities continue this emphasis. Lord Wilberforce in *Esso Petroleum Co Ltd* v *Harper's Garage (Stourport) Ltd* [1968] AC 269, 341, said: "I venture to think it important that the vitality of the second limb [of reasonableness], or as I would prefer to put it of the wider aspects of a single public policy rule, should continue to be recognised". His phrasing was chosen because, as he noted (at 340), the first limb is also imbued with public policy, for otherwise persons who had voluntarily submitted to a contract would not be released from their obligations. Therefore, both the public interest aspect and the parties' viewpoint are based on a policy wider than the private interest of the parties. The fact remains that a covenant may be struck down on public policy grounds no matter how reasonable it is in the interests of the parties: see *Tank Lining Corp* v *Dunlop Industrial Pty Ltd* (1982) 140 DLR (3d) 659 for a Canadian illustration.

The public policy aspects of the restraint of trade doctrine were aptly summarised by Lord Macnaghten in an oft-quoted passage in *Nordenfelt* v *Maxim Nordenfelt Guns and Ammunition Co* [1894] AC 535, 565: "the public have an interest in every person's carrying on his trade freely; so has the individual. All interference with individual liberty of action in trading, and all restraints of trade of themselves, if there is nothing more, are contrary to public policy, and therefore void". His Lordship was clearly of the view that the two issues of reasonableness were separate. For cases where public policy has been discussed in the context of pensions and post-termination commission, see below. In the general run, however, of employment cases the public interest plays little or no part, being subsumed into the issue of reasonableness between the parties. Certainly no effort is made to assess the impact of the restraint empirically. The approach of Lord Macnaghten continues to apply. In *Texaco Ltd* v *Mulberry Filling Station Ltd* [1972] 1 WLR 814, 828, the judge stated that he preferred to decide that the relevant covenants "are reasonable in the interests of the public, not on balance of existing or possible economic advantages and disadvantages to the public but because there is . . . no unreasonable limitation of liberty to trade".

While one may posit that there are public policy factors at issue in restraint cases between former employers and former employees, such as that the doctrine is useful because it allows employers to reveal techniques to their workforce without the employees being able to utilise them for their own purposes, the courts have tended to avoid considering the public interest but have subsumed the interests of society into the interests of the parties. Furthermore, there are several aspects of public policy in the doctrine of restraint of trade which are not concerned with reasonableness in the public interest. Is the whole doctrine based on public interest? Is the clause one which falls within the doctrine? Will the employee not be able to work if the covenant is enforced? And the remedy may be determined on policy grounds. In *S W Strange Ltd* v *Mann* [1965] 1 WLR 629, 638, Stamp J stated that skill and knowledge was not the employers' property "and it is contrary to public policy to restrain its use in any degree". See also pp 63–5.

Burden of Proof

It is normally said that employers bear the onus of proving that the covenant is reasonable between the parties. In *Herbert Morris Ltd* v *Saxelby* [1916] AC 688, 700, Lord Atkinson said that the burden of proving reasonableness between the parties lies on the party alleging reasonableness, who will normally be the employers, but the onus of proving injury to the public rests on the alleger. Lord Parker (at 707) stated that the onus of proving the "special circumstances" that the covenant was not void was on the party alleging them. The standard of proof increases as the territory and duration lengthen: Lord Shaw (at 715). If, however, all the facts are before the courts Lords Atkinson (at 699) and Parker (at 706) stated that the burden of proof was irrelevant for reasonableness is to be inferred by the judge.

In a normal case once the former employers have shown that the covenant is reasonable between the parties, the onus shifts to the former employee to demonstrate that the covenant does not accord with the public interest. Lord Atkinson in *Herbert Morris* said that the burden was on the party alleging that the covenant was injurious to the public. Canadian authority is to like effect: *Tank Lining Corp* v *Dunlop Industrial Pty Ltd* (1982) 140 DLR (3d) 659, 665, and *Western Inventory Service Ltd* v *Sagar* (1983) 148 DLR (3d) 434, 440. There is, however, authority for placing the burden on the employers: *Technograph Printed Circuits Ltd* v *Chalwyn Ltd* [1967] RPC 379. See also *Poly Lina Ltd* v *Finch* [1995] FSR 751, 761, where Judge Phelan appears to place the onus on the employers, but the judgment was unreserved. It might be argued that once the employers have demonstrated that the covenant is reasonable between the parties, the policy that *pacta sunt servanda* reasserts itself and the employee must disprove that the clause is unreasonable in the interests of the public. Alternatively, it may be said that the restraint doctrine, which encompasses both of the reasonableness tests, has to be proved to be disapplied; in other words the burden lies on the employers. There is no prioritisation between the two principles. It is suggested, however, that the second argument constitutes the stronger argument of the two. Be that as it may, it is surprising that their Lordships, in *Herbert Morris*, did not strive to justify placing the burdens on different parties, and English judges have not always been consistent: *cf. Triplex Safety Glass Co* v *Scorah* [1938] Ch 211. The law as to standard of proof was laid down by the Privy Council in a case where the defendants who were otherwise in breach were asserting unenforceability, a fact which may have affected the advice: *Attorney-General of the Commonwealth of Australia* v *Adelaide SS Co Ltd* [1913] AC 701. Lord Parker said (at 706–7) that the onus was "no light one". A strong case is needed to show that the clause is contrary to the public interest: *Kerchiss* v *Colora Printing Inks Ltd* [1960] RPC 235, 239.

It has been stated that the different burdens are no longer of importance. Lord Hodson in *Esso Petroleum Co Ltd* v *Harper's Garage (Stourport) Ltd* [1968] AC 269, 319, stated that, though the position of the burden of proof had been settled authoritatively in *Herbert Morris*, its effect will rarely be significant because the court can look at all the circumstances surrounding the covenant and the issue of reasonableness is one of law. It was said by Lord Reid that the burden lay on the professional body when a code of conduct was at issue, but the majority held otherwise: *Pharmaceutical Society of Great Britain* v *Dickson* [1970] AC 403 (HL).

Defences

Affirmation

At common law an unequivocal election to treat the allegedly restrictive covenant as continuing is a defence to a claim that the clause is unenforceable: *Panayiotou* v *Sony Music Entertainments (UK) Ltd*, above (at 386). A request for an advance on royalties constituted affirmation (and did so despite the fact that it was repaid).

Acquiescence

In equity "waiver, or laches or estoppel or whatever", as Dillon L J put it in *Zang Tumb Tuum Records Ltd* v *Johnson* [1993] EMLR 61, 76, is a defence. Parker J in *Panayiotou* explained the jurisdiction thus (at 385): "the court will examine all the circumstances of the case in order to determine whether it would be unjust or unconscionable to allow the claim to be made: the mere fact that the claim is not made at 'the earliest possible moment' will not suffice to establish injustice or unconscionableness for this purpose". On the facts though *obiter* the defendants had a defence of acquiescence. It was unfair and unconscionable for the plaintiff to assert that a contract was unreasonable as being in restraint of trade on the facts. There may be "counter-equities" which demolish this defence, though on the facts of *Panayiotou* there were none.

For criticism of Parker J see Coulthard (1995) 58 MLR 731, 741–3.

Distinctions between Covenants given by Employees and by Vendors

If vendors of businesses were free on the sale to set up in the adjoining shop, purchasers would not obtain what they had bargained for: *Trego* v *Hunt* [1896] AC 7 (HL), a case on the dissolution of a partnership which has been taken to represent the law relating to vendors. There is no implied term not to compete, but a term not to solicit customers is implied, as was held in *Trego* v *Hunt*. There is no authority on the implication of a non-dealing covenant but one can be expressly incorporated, and an express non-solicitation clause can be included *ex abundanti cautela*. Such implied and express clauses are obviously in the interests of the purchasers, for they protect what has been bought. It may also be asserted that the clauses are in the sellers' interests, since without such clauses purchasers would not buy the business. As James V-C put it in *Leather Couch Co* v *Lorsont* (1869) LR 9 Eq 345, 354 (the case is also known as *Leather Cloth*): "public policy requires that when a man has by skill or by any other means obtained something which he wants to sell, he should be at liberty to sell it in the most advantageous way in the market; and in order to enable him to sell it advantageously in the market it is necessary that he should be able to preclude himself from entering into competition with the purchaser". Without a covenant the Lords held in *Trego* v *Hunt* that vendors (as in the case) could set up in business immediately in competition with the purchasers and could even use the name of their former business (this ruling is doubtful after the partnership cases of *Curl Bros Ltd* v *Webster* [1904] 1 Ch 685 and *Boorne* v *Wicker* [1927] Ch 667), to the great prejudice of the goodwill bought by the purchasers from the vendors. Covenants thus can protect the purchasers from their greatest potential trade rivals – the vendors.

It has been held that a covenant by the vendors not to use a name is not in restraint of trade: *Vernon* v *Hallam* (1886) 34 Ch D 748. Other vendor covenants are subject to the restraint doctrine, as *Nordenfelt* v *Maxim Nordenfelt Guns and Ammunition Co* [1894] AC 535 (HL) demonstrates. The defendant sold his armaments business to the plaintiffs and covenanted that he would not compete for 25 years. There was no restriction as to territory. The House held that his appeal should be dismissed. A general covenant could be enforced. The covenant afforded reasonable protection for the covenantees in the circumstances. The legitimate proprietary interest to be protected will normally be the expectation that customers will return to the business, but trade secrets may be involved as in *Hagg* v *Darley* (1878) 47 LJ Ch 567 (Ch D). The defendant, a vendor, covenanted that he would not make or sell disinfectants for 14 years. Bacon V-C (at 569) held that covenant to be reasonable in that it indirectly protected a trade secret. An area covenant will be unreasonable if, for instance, it extends to the whole of England and Wales when the business operated in central Birmingham only.

British Reinforced Concrete Engineering Co Ltd v *Schelff* [1921] 2 Ch 563 illustrates a covenant unreasonable for the protection of the sold business. The defendants sold their business to the plaintiffs and contracted that they would not compete with them in the manufacture of road reinforcements. The covenant was unenforceable because it extended beyond the covenantors' business, selling "loop" road reinforcements. (Perhaps nowadays the clause would be read to cover only loop road reinforcements, rendering the clause reasonable.) The clause therefore must not extend beyond protecting the business sold; it cannot protect the purchasers' business as it was before the purchase of the vendors' business. The interest – goodwill – was defined by Lord Macnaghten in *Trego* v *Hunt*, above, at 24, as: "the whole advantage ... of the reputation and connection of the firm which may have been built up by years of honest work or gained by lavish expenditure of money".

The vendors' covenant increases the value of the sale. Lord Atkinson in *Herbert Morris Ltd* v *Saxelby* [1916] 1 AC 688, 701, stated that a vendor:

> would in the absence of some restrictive covenant be entitled to set up in the same line of business as he sold in competition with the purchaser ... The possibility of such competition would necessarily depreciate the value of the goodwill. The covenant excluding it necessarily evidences that value, and presumably the price demanded and paid, and, therefore, all those restrictions on trading are permissible which are necessary at once to secure that the vendor shall get the highest price for what he has to sell and that the purchaser shall get all he has paid for ...

Lord Parker (at 709) said that without a covenant the vendor would not be giving what he had contracted to sell and the purchaser would not obtain what he had contracted to buy. For this reason the covenant is reasonable if confined to the area within which the vendor's competition "would in all probability enure to the injury of the purchaser". Lord Herschell C in *Nordenfelt*, above (at 548) stated that "a covenant entered into in connection of the sale of the goodwill of a business must be valid where the full benefit of the purchase price cannot be otherwise secured to the purchaser ... [T]here are no grounds of public policy which countervail the disadvantage which could arise if the goodwill were in such cases rendered unsaleable".

The courts scrutinise restraint of trade covenants more laxly on a sale than ones contained in a contract of employment. Lord Macnaghten in *Nordenfelt*, above (at 566), proposed a basis for this distinction. Employees had less freedom of contract than did purchasers of business. For example, purchasers may well have access to legal advice but employees may not, and there is usually little negotiation between employers and employees whereas there might be between vendors and purchasers. As Millett J said in *Allied Dunbar (Frank Weisinger) Ltd* v *Weisinger* [1988] IRLR 60, 64, vendors and purchasers are best able to judge what is reasonable (whereas the same may not be true of employers and employees).

There is also a difference between the rules on severance. The courts are more ready to blue-pencil in a vendor case than in an employee one. For example, in *Goldsoll* v *Goldman* [1915] 1 Ch 292 (CA) "real or" was severed in a business sale agreement, whereas in *Attwood* v *Lamont* [1920] 3 KB 571 severance of all jobs except "tailor" was not allowed on the grounds that the clause constituted one covenant, not a series of independent covenants. The courts are more likely to construe a list of prohibited activities as separate covenants in sale cases than in employment ones, with the result that severance is easier in the former than in the latter.

Commentary

The acceptance of a distinction in the United Kingdom and the Commonwealth between employees and vendors does not mean that the dichotomy was not open to criticism from judges and others.

Historically the difference is novel. As Younger LJ pointed out in *Attwood* v *Lamont* [1920] 3 KB 410, while the difference was not presented by the House of Lords as a radical departure from previous law, it *was* such. He quoted cases from the nineteenth century to show that the language of the judgments in both types was interchangeable. Nevertheless, law does develop and in the light of changed circumstances the distinction may be acceptable for sound policy reasons.

Rather than contrasting employees and vendors, one should perhaps think of a spectrum. One might have a spectrum ranging from manual worker to vendor like *Nordenfelt*, above. On such a view a person such as the director and manager of the employers' firm is more assimilable to a vendor than to an ordinary employee, as Luxmoore J saw in *Spink (Bournemouth) Ltd* v *Spink* [1936] Ch 544, 547. There is an added difficulty with workers other than employees: are partners to be treated as employees? (see below). What about cases where the employee has bargaining power? In *Garbutt Business College Ltd* v *Henderson* [1939] 4 DLR 151 Ford JA in the Alberta Appellate Division thought that a case involving the principal of a business school was to be likened to a partnership and, when judging the reasonableness of the covenant, took into account the equality of the parties, applying *Spink*. As Denning LJ put it in a case involving a director, distinguishing *Gilford Motor Co Ltd* v *Horne* [1933] Ch 935, "A managing director can look after himself. A traveller is not so well placed to do so": *M & S Drapers* v *Reynolds*, above (at 19). Lord Denning MR put a licensee into a position intermediate between employees and vendors in *Office Overload Ltd* v *Gunn*, above. English law has not dealt with licensees enough to have developed a well-settled rule.

Despite such criticisms the distinction holds sway. It was utilised or mentioned in, for example *Gledhow Autoparts Ltd* v *Delaney*, above. It is suggested however, that a spectrum approach is more suitable than a strict employee/vendor one.

The distinction between vendors and employees is said to be marked by the policy in relation to the former that they have to sell their property at the best price and in order to do so they have to be precluded from competing. See, for example, Joyce J in *Herbert Morris Ltd* v *Saxelby* [1915] 2 Ch 57, 77. That argument, it is said, does not apply to employees: they must be allowed to use their skills to the full. However, the latter statement is not true, for covenants are permitted, if reasonable. Even if the argument is modified to take this rule into effect, one might say that employees can earn higher pay during employment because they are subject to covenants after leaving, though there is not empirical evidence of such. They sell what they have at the best price, and in order to do so, have to be precluded from competing. This way of thinking is not advanced to destroy the distinction, but it does show that the usual public policy reasons for the difference are not to be uncritically accepted. There may, for instance, be much more bargaining in a vendor case than in an employee one, and so a vendor may be able to extract a better price for what he or she has built up than can an employee offered a standard-form contract.

There are similarities between vendors and employees in relation to trade secrets. Both can covenant not to use or disclose trade secrets. There is, however, a difference in relation to information. Where there is a non-competition covenant in a vendor case, such a clause will protect goodwill. A covenant not to solicit would not be effective because customers could come to the vendor without there being a breach of covenant. In a non-competition covenant the court is not interested in the incidental restraint on skill and experience, that is information which the vendor has gained. In an employee case, however, the courts seek to strike down restraints on skill and experience. The protection of goodwill can therefore lead to a more extensive covenant in a vendor case than in an employee one. So a covenant not to deal in the same business may be upheld when one would not be upheld with regard to employees. In *Nordenfelt*, above, a worldwide restraint for 25 years was upheld, even though the effect was to stop the vendor from working in the same line of business, that is from using his skill and experience, such as the names of clients, who being largely governments, were well-known. Such a covenant, it seems probable, would not survive investigation in an employee case.

The effect is that a non-competition covenant in a vendor case may survive (see J Bell, *Policy Arguments in Judicial Decisions* (Clarendon, 1983) 166), whereas one against competition *per se* by an employee would not, as indeed Younger LJ said in *Attwood* v *Lamont*, above (at 589). The consequence is that a vendor may co-incidentally not be entitled to use skill and knowledge, whereas an employee will be.

Another similarity between employees and vendors is that the public is not deprived of services. The employers and the purchasers continue to trade, though it may happen that the purchasers buy the business to close it down to prevent competition. Therefore, from the viewpoint of the public interest the public is not injured. This argument is one which underlies the insignificance of the public interest in these types of restraint categories although it looms larger in cartel cases.

Where the vendor is not selling goodwill, but a trade secret, presumably the same judicial attitude as is taken in employment cases should be adopted (see A Turner, *The Law of Trade Secrets* (Sweet & Maxwell, 1962) 117), for the same matter is being sold and the distinction is not relevant.

Employees who are also Vendors

What happens when a person sells her business to a firm and at the same time joins it as an employee or perhaps as a self-employed consultant? There are as it were two contracts: one of sale, one of employment (or for services, or perhaps of partnership). Both contracts no doubt will contain covenants against solicitation and competition. Are these covenants judged as if they were in a contract of sale or in a contract of employment? Recent authority is to the effect that they are to be assimilated to vendor covenants, the reason being that the parties are in a more even bargaining position than is usually the case in employment contracts. The contract is a commercial one and should be enforced.

Systems Reliability Holdings plc v *Smith* [1990] IRLR 377 has been criticised on the ground that the facts do not relate more closely to a vendor covenant. A former employee of the plaintiffs had during employment acquired 1.6% of their shares. He sold them to the plaintiffs for £247,000. In the agreement there were covenants *inter alia* against competing with the company throughout the world for some 17 months. Harman J said that on the facts the case was one of vendor and purchaser, even though the ex-employee had only a small amount in percentage terms of the shares, because he received a sum of money which was the same as another seller of shares would have received. One problem with *Systems Reliability* is that with the growth of employees' shareholdings in privatised utilities in the 1980s and continued government support for employees to purchase shares in their own companies many more employees than before will be classed as "vendors" when in truth they have extremely little control over their firm. A second difficulty is that Harman J enunciated a new definition of confidential information. He distinguished *Faccenda Chicken Ltd* v *Fowler* [1987] Ch 117 (CA) as being a case concerned with implied terms, not with express covenants. He also distinguished the definition provided by Cross J in *Printers & Finishers Ltd* v *Holloway* [1965] RPC 239 as being also concerned with implied terms and as being given in a true master and servant case. He held that the express covenant was intended to protect information relating to the business. The employee/vendor knew that the information was confidential. Accordingly, Harman J held that the restraint was reasonable. That information, which could be called "know-how", is not protectable in an employment case even by an express covenant because it does not amount to a trade secret or other highly confidential information. There is, therefore, a distinction between the vendor and the employee categories on this point. Even if *Faccenda* is incorrect on this issue, the "vendor definition" of trade secrets is wider than that used in employment cases. It is uncertain whether *Systems Reliability* will be followed. Even if Harman J were correct as to vendor and shareholder agreements, it is suggested that his definition should not influence restraints on employees, for their skill and experience are not lightly to be shackled, whereas by selling a business the vendor submits to a restraint on her skill and experience and she receives consideration, perhaps a substantial sum of money, for agreeing not to compete.

A second case is *Allied Dunbar (Frank Weisinger) Ltd* v *Weisinger*, above. Frank Weisinger sold his financial consultancy including goodwill to the plaintiffs for £386,000. He agreed to work for them as a consultant and not *inter alia* to compete for two years after termination of his consultancy. Millett J held that the covenant was to protect the business acquired by the plaintiffs from the defendant: it did not protect the plaintiffs' business as the defendant's employers. Therefore, the covenant was to be adjudged by the law applying to covenants on sales of businesses and not by the law governing employment contracts. *Cf. Alliance Paper Group plc* v *Prestwich*, above at 27 and 28.

The Special Position of Directors

A director who is an employee is subject to the same implied terms as is an ordinary employee, and special rules apply to directors, whether they are also employees or not.

Directors may, through their positions, acquire a greater knowledge of corporate trade secrets and connections than many ordinary employees. They may well have shares in the company, and they may be in a more favourable bargaining position than non-director employees. For these reasons the courts have accepted that well-drafted restraint clauses can apply to directors to prevent them from exploiting their company's legitimate proprietary interests, and that directors' covenants are to be treated more like covenants taken from vendors on the sale of a business than from employees.

An early case was *Gilford Motor Co Ltd* v *Horne* [1933] Ch 935 (CA). The managing director of the plaintiffs agreed in his contract of employment that he would not solicit customers at any time after the end of the contract. The covenant was restricted to his soliciting customers personally. On leaving the plaintiffs he set up a company, which solicited their customers. The court held that he was liable for the solicitation. The corporate form was a smokescreen which hid the true situation.

Implied Duties: Corporate Opportunities

When a director takes advantage of her position to secure a contract for herself rather than for the company she is liable to account for the benefit. In *Cook* v *Deeks* [1916] 1 AC 554 (PC) three out of four directors who were negotiating for a contract established a company to exploit the contract. The fourth director sued them and recovered the benefit of the contract for the company of which they were directors. The rule in *Cook* v *Deeks* applies even though the firm which contracted with the defendant, the director, would not have entered into a contract with his employers. In *Industrial Development Consultants Ltd* v *Cooley* [1972] 1 WLR 443, Roskill J held that the director must disgorge the profit he had made to the company, even though it had failed to win the contract. See also *Thomas Marshall Ltd* v *Guinle* [1979] Ch 227, 245.

These cases have sometimes been explained on the basis of *mala fides*. However, the rule applies even though the directors acted in good faith as is demonstrated by the celebrated authority of *Regal (Hastings) Ltd* v *Gulliver* (1942) [1967] 1 AC 134 (HL). The directors had to disgorge their profits made on leasing two cinemas, even though the lessors would not have contracted with their company because they believed it to suffer from under-capitalisation, and even though the directors had used their own money to acquire the leases. Unfortunately for the directors their original company was under new management and accordingly the profits went to a company which no longer had them at the helm.

In *Industrial Development Consultants Ltd* v *Cooley*, above, the defendant resigned to take advantage of a contract for which he had been negotiating. If, however, when the director left the company, it was not actively seeking the contract and she then secured it, she is not liable: *Island Export Finance Ltd* v *Umunna* [1986] BCLC 460 (QBD), where there was no corporate opportunity, no "maturing business opportunity".

A case summarising much of the law is *Balston Ltd* v *Headline Filters Ltd* [1990] FSR 385, an authority which should warn companies to insert express terms. The parties agreed that the restraint of trade covenants were too wide to be enforceable. The judge held that the director was not liable for breach of fiduciary duty as a director because there was no corporate opportunity for him to acquire. The director was liable for breach of the duty of good faith during employment by offering an employee of the plaintiffs a job with the firm he had set up while a director of them and by competing with them while still an employee. He was not, however, in breach of his obligation of confidentiality because, although the processes for making the product at issue, glass tubes, were trade secrets, he had the skill and experience to manufacture the products.

A director is like other employees bound by the implied duties of faithful service and confidentiality during employment. There is, however, no additional implied duty not to compete on directors, though they may be subject to express terms such as exclusive services clauses.

Partners

Partners are akin to directors in some respects. They are in a better bargaining position than are ordinary employees just as directors are. Like directors they may have easier access to trade connections and secrets than such employees. Furthermore, they share in the goodwill of the firm.

During the partnership a partner owes an implied duty of good faith to the other partners. There may also be express terms. The implied duty terminates when she leaves. Therefore, without an express covenant the ex-partner can compete, deal with former clients and advertise that she used to be a partner in the firm which she left, see for example *Macfarlane* v *Kent* [1965] 1 WLR 1019 (Ch D). She must not, however, solicit the clients of the firm or use the old name, see for example *Curl Bros Ltd* v *Webster*, above.

Former partners like ex-directors may be bound by covenants. The partnership seeks to protect its legitimate proprietary interests and, if the clause is reasonable, it will be upheld. For example, in *Whitehill* v *Bradford* [1952] 1 Ch 236 (CA) there was in a partnership agreement a covenant that a retiring partner would not practise as a general medical practitioner within 10 miles of the parish church of Atherstone, Warwickshire. The court held that the clause protected the partnership's goodwill and was reasonable in territorial extent and duration. In *Kerr* v *Morris* [1986] 3 All ER 217 (CA) an agreement provided that an ex-partner should not compete as a GP within two miles for a period of two years from expulsion from the partnership. One partner was expelled after a disagreement. He determined to set up as a GP a few doors away from the practice. The court granted an interlocutory injunction restricting him from doing so. The court held that such a covenant was not inconsistent with the National Health Service. In *Bridge* v *Deacons* [1984] AC 705 the Privy Council held that a covenant in a partnership agreement was not analogous either to one given by an employee or one provided by the vendor of a business. Their Lordships considered that a covenant in a partnership agreement should not be placed in the most closely analogous category but should be determined by the general principle laid down by Lord Reid in *Esso Petroleum Co Ltd* v *Harper's Garage (Stourport) Ltd* [1968] AC 269, 301 (HL): what were the legitimate interests of the partners? Was the covenant too wide to protect those interests? The Committee stressed the element of mutuality: all partners were restricted. Lord Fraser (at 717) added: "some weight should be given to the fact that the restriction is found in a partnership agreement which has evidently been carefully drafted and which must be taken to represent the views of experienced solicitors, who could be well aware that an unduly severe restriction would be unenforceable".

The implied duty of confidentiality continues after the defendant has left the partnership, and it is suggested that the same law which applies to ex-employees governs former partners. One possible difference is that when the partnership dissolves on a partner's leaving, she can take with her trade secrets because as a partner she was part-owner of the information; therefore, she cannot misappropriate it from the partnership. One possibility is that the defendant ceased to be owner on dissolution, the information remaining with the others, who may therefore sue the former partner for using or disclosing the confidential information in breach of the implied duty of confidentiality. An express clause would solve this conundrum.

Bridge v *Deacons* is nowadays the most important authority. The facts related to Hong Kong where the plaintiff was a large firm of solicitors. The firm was divided into departments. The defendant worked in the intellectual property department and dealt only with clients who came to that department. As a salaried partner he received 5% of the partnership business, including a nominal amount for goodwill. He covenanted that if he ceased to be a partner, he would not work for five years for any firm or person who had been a client of the firm within the three years preceding his departure. He resigned and was paid a substantial amount for his share plus a nominal amount for the goodwill. He then practised in Hong

Kong on his own account, working for his former clients. The plaintiff sought an injunction. The defendant contended that, first, he worked during the partnership only for the clients of his department, not for other clients of the firm; therefore, the covenant was too wide; secondly, that since the firm had given him only a nominal sum for the goodwill, it could not protect the whole of its goodwill; and, thirdly, the five-year duration was too long. Lord Fraser, giving the advice of the board, said that the partners owned the whole assets of the firm including its goodwill and the firm was one practice in which each partner had an interest. There was no separation of their interests. The nominal sum for goodwill was justifiable: it was difficult to put a value on the goodwill each time a partner joined or left and few partners-to-be had the finance to enable them to pay for the true value of the goodwill at the start of the partnership. The five-year period was reasonable, having regard to the fact that the covenant was drafted by competent lawyers and that there is no case in which a covenant was struck down on the grounds of time alone. Their Lordships felt that the covenant was justified in the public interest because without it young persons would not join firms and it encouraged continuity within the firm. In criticism it may be said that, first, the defendant did not acquire influence over clients who did not come into his department; secondly, the justifications for the five-year period look thin; and, thirdly, lawyers do make mistakes as to law including the width of covenants; and the lack of precedent ought not to prevent a court from acting for there is nothing to prohibit a judge from rendering invalid a covenant purely on the ground of time just as occurs with regard to territory.

The Privy Council disagreed with the statement of Lord Denning MR in *Oswald Hickson Collier & Co* v *Carter-Ruck* [1984] 2 All ER 15 (CA) that a lawyer could not bind himself not to act for a client for whom he had worked in his previous job. Lord Denning MR also thought that, because a solicitor received confidential information from clients, he was in a fiduciary position. The dicta had already been treated as incorrect by the Court of Appeal in *Edwards* v *Warboys* [1984] AC 724. In *Bridge* v *Deacons* Lord Fraser said that the proposition was:

> unsupported by authority, and . . . was directly contrary to a considerable volume of authority including a decision of the House of Lords in *Fitch* v *Dewes* [1921] 2 AC 158. It also seems to be unjustified in principle. For one thing a solicitor is always (except to some extent in legal aid cases) entitled to refuse to act for a particular person, and it is difficult to see any reason why he should not be entitled to bind himself by contract not to act in future for a particular group of persons. For another thing, the relationship of solicitor and client is not unique as being confidential; the relationship of medical men with their patients and of many other professional persons with their clients are also confidential.

Doctors as Partners

The National Health Service Act 1946, section 35, states "Where the name of any medical practitioner is . . . entered on any list of medical practitioners undertaking to provide general medical services, it shall be unlawful subsequently to sell the goodwill ... of the medical practice ... ". In *Macfarlane* v *Kent*, above, Stamp J was faced with the following clause: "the outgoing partner shall not within a period of 3 years thereafter within the area comprised within a radius of one-and-a-half miles from any premises at which the parties shall have carried on at the date of such determination (a) directly or indirectly set up in practice ... (b) professionally advise attend prescribe for or treat any person who is or has during the subsistence of this partnership been a patient". He severed clause (a). It was too broad in that a covenant not to attend on patients would have sufficed. However, the covenant in (b) was "clearly valid", though the judge did not (in his reserved judgment) give any reason in support of his conclusion. He would not be drawn on the question whether section 35 made the covenant illegal. On the facts there was no sale of the goodwill because the outgoing partner did not receive a payment on leaving for his share of the goodwill.

A second problem is that since a doctor works for the NHS the practice for which he works has no goodwill; in other words, there is no legitimate proprietary interest to protect. Stamp J in *Macfarlane* v *Kent* (at 1024) doubted whether an area covenant could ever be reasonable when it was designed to protect goodwill, which "cannot be sold ... ", but then he said that he thought that the goodwill could be protected by a covenant not to attend the patients of the partnership. This statement seems to be based on the proposition that goodwill exists even though it is not a saleable asset of the partnership.

The Restrictive Trade Practices Act 1976 and Article 85 of the Treaty of Rome

This statute renders unenforceable agreements which are not registered under it when restrictions are imposed on two or more parties to the contract. Covenants in restraint of trade are, however, usually employed only on one side, the employee. Therefore, the Act does not normally affect such covenants. The reader is referred to the standard works on competition law, which treat of this topic in detail. Scottish cases, *Donald Storrie Estate Agency Ltd* v *Adams*, 1989 SLT 305 and *Sterling Financial Services Ltd* v *Johnston*, 1990 SLT 111, where the Act was applied on the sale of businesses, were reversed by the Restrictive Trade Practices (Services) (Amendment) Order 1989 (SI No 1082).

Article 85 of the EC Treaty is inapplicable to employees because they are not "undertakings" within Article 85 (1). If, however, the employee provides her services through service companies, the law is potentially applicable: see *Panayiotou* v *Sony Music Entertainment (UK) Ltd* [1994] EMLR 229, 412. The reader is referred to specialist works such as Bellamy and Child, *Common Market Law of Competition*, 4th ed (Sweet & Maxwell 1993). If the clause is invalid, as a matter of EC law the rest of the contract is valid (in English terms severance is possible): whether the rest then is invalid depends on national law.

Contents of Chapter Six

CONSTRUCTION

Chapter Six

CONSTRUCTION

It is cautiously considered, carefully scrutinized, looked upon with disfavor, strictly interpreted ... (*per* Hoover J in *Arthur Murray Dance Studios of Cleveland Inc* v *Witter*, 105 NE 2d 685 (1952)).

A court, if it wishes to uphold a covenant, may construe it in such a way that it is read as not being in restraint of trade. The technique of severance may be seen in a similar light. Both are means of upholding clauses which *ex facie* are void or unenforceable. If one method is successful there is no need to discuss the other, except *ex abundante cautela*. The two techniques are also linked because if the clause cannot be interpreted as two or more covenants the judge cannot utilise the doctrine of severance. An illustration was provided by C J W Farwell (1918) 44 LQR 66, 70:

> if the employee is required to covenant against being engaged in a series of trades for the same time and over the same area in each case, the covenant will be treated as one single covenant, notwithstanding that the document is drawn as though there was a separate covenant for each trade and it will stand or fall as a whole. On the other hand, if there are in fact separate covenants, if for example an employee covenants against being engaged in one trade for a particular time and over a particular area and against being engaged in another trade for a different period or over a different area, the fact that one covenant is too wide will not necessarily vitiate the other.

The two techniques are linked in another way. If one construes a covenant in a narrow fashion so as to uphold its validity, there is no need for severance; however, if one construes the covenant broadly, one can fall back on severance to preserve validity: Heydon, *The Restraint of Trade Doctrine*, (Butterworths, 1971) 122.

The rules of construction of covenant may be stated straightforwardly, and in many cases there will be no problem. Difficulties may arise, however, should a court try to use all the rules together. Courts have not always been consistent. There is no prioritisation of the rules, and they may conflict in particular instances. Moreover, the rules were not settled until towards the end of the nineteenth century and they have for the last few years been in a state of flux, partly as a result of Lord Denning MR. To call the rules of construction "rules" is something of a misnomer in the light of the potential conflict among the rules and of the fact that they are not always applied, but the term is often used. Perhaps a better term than rules would be principles, that is norms which have weight according to the circumstances. Since, however, the weight attached to these norms seems to vary with the period and with the judge, perhaps a more helpful term than either rules or principles would be guidelines.

Construction as Contract

"The first duty of the court is to construe ... " said Evershed MR in *Whitehill* v *Bradford* [1952] 1 Ch 236, 248. But how is the court to fulfil that duty? Since covenants form part of contract, the court has to construe the covenant as it would construe any other contractual term; that is, that "the clause must be construed according to the ordinary use of language" (*Perls* v *Saalfeld* [1892] 2 Ch 149). Kay LJ expressed the mode of thought in these terms in that case (at 154–5):

> [a]greements of this kind are to be read without any bias either one way or the other, and to be construed, like all other agreements, fairly, according to their general intention, and with reference to the state of circumstances existing at the time which must be taken into consideration in construing any written document.

This statement remains the basic stance of the courts. However, in the event of ambiguity it is sometimes said that "[t]he words ... are to be construed in their ordinary sense, bearing in mind that such is [the parties'] object" (*per* Blackburn J in *Mouflet* v *Cole* (1872) LR 8 Ex 32 (Ex Ch)). This guideline has been called by R N Gooderson, "Restraint of Trade in the Field Code" (1963) 79 LQR 410, 423, 425 the "rule in *Mills* v *Dunham*" [1891] 1 Ch 576: " ... the duty of the Court is first to interpret the covenant or agreement itself and to ascertain according to the rules of construction what is the fair meaning of the parties". (The object of the agreement is investigated: that object is the protection of the employers. This is the rule in *Haynes* v *Doman* [1899] 2 Ch 13, 25.) In *Mills* v *Dunham* in the Court of Appeal Kay LJ added (at 589) in an oft-approved sentence a third approach, one of strict construction (or the *contra proferentem* approach): "if there is any ambiguity in a stipulation between employer and employed imposing a restriction on the latter, it ought to receive the narrower construction, rather than the wider – the employed ought to have the benefit of the doubt". (He then stated the contrary policy of upholding contracts in the event of ambiguity.) The policy, therefore, behind the strict construction of covenants is to prevent employers from overreaching: *Hudson Foam Latex Products Inc* v *Aiken*, 198 A 2d 136 (1964) (NJ Super). The strict construction and *contra proferentem* approach may not always be the same. If the employee is a senior manager, she may be involved in the drafting of the covenant. There may be no single *proferens*. It is suggested that the *contra proferentem* approach does not apply to this situation but the strict construction one might. Accordingly there is inconsistency in the jurisprudence. At present the general approach is that the "true object", as Lord Dunedin put it in the partners case of *Hadsley* v *Dayer-Smith* [1914] AC 979, 982–3, of the parties has to be divined, and then the words read in their context. If there is no ambiguity, one cannot construe the phrase according to the intended meaning: *Perls* v *Saalfield* [1892] 2 Ch 149. The covenant must not be read so as to create ambiguity: *Gale* v *Reed* (1806) 8 East 86, 87, 103 ER 274, 277. Judges may disagree whether there is an ambiguity: *Rogers* v *Maddocks* [1892] 3 Ch 346, 354. Lopes LJ (at 356) adopted a "literal and grammatical reading", whereas the trial judge read the clause with reference to its object.

Many examples might be given of these approaches, but a selection will give the flavour. In *Electric Transmission Ltd* v *Dannenberg* (1949) 66 RPC 193 the employee gave the plaintiffs certain rights to his inventions. He left and joined a company which manufactured equipment similar to that produced by the plaintiffs. They sought a declaration that improvements made by the employee were the joint property of the plaintiffs and the defendant. Evershed MR said (at 188) that when a court was faced with covenants potentially in restraint of trade, it did not interpret the provisions in "a restricted meaning so as to save them from invalidity, if upon a natural reading of the language it appears that the employer has sought to extract unreasonably wide covenants". The employee would be restricted from freely acting in his own interests unless the clause about joint property could be construed as being restricted to the employee's period of service with the plaintiffs. He held, however, (at 189) that the clause was intended to apply indefinitely, and so fell. Wynn-Parry J said (at 192) that the phrase "any invention" covered those made by the employee after the end of his employment. Since it extended to the rest of the employee's life, it was unreasonably wide. It should be noted, however, that a court wishing to uphold a covenant might have said that the clause's true object was to protect the employers during the time of service, but such an interpretation would not have given the employers what they desired. But the legal position is not always totally clear, as may be seen from the fact that the third judge dissented.

Mills v *Dunham*, above, itself is an excellent illustration of how the rule in *Mills* v *Dunham* may be used to save a covenant which read in another way would be invalid. The employee covenanted that he would not "in any way deal or transact business with" any person who had been a customer of the employers during the currency of the contract of service. The employee contended that the covenant was unreasonable: he was a salesman of antiseptic products, but the clause prohibited him from calling on his former clients on behalf of a watchmaker or umbrella maker. The employers argued that the clause had to be read so that it was limited to businesses like their own. Lindley LJ said (at 586–7):

the first thing we have to do is to ascertain the real meaning of the parties by construing the agreement without leaning either way . . . The object of the plaintiffs was to prevent the defendant from being allowed to do anything which would be detrimental to their business; and I think that "transact business" ought to be construed as confined to businesses similar to that of the plaintiffs.

Accordingly, the covenant was valid.

Mills v *Dunham* was a case in which general words were cut down because after construing them the court found that the words did not bear a literal but a limited meaning. There are many other instances. A reasonably full list occurs in *Halsbury's Laws of England*, 4th ed (Butterworths, 1984), Vol 47, Trade & Labour, para 51. Other cases include: *Kavanagh* v *Dallaston* (1894) 38 SJ 216 (mentioned by Heydon, *supra* at 124 and see the quote at 132); *Stride* v *Martin* (1898) 77 LT 600, 601 (in milkroundsman's covenant "neighbourhood" meant immediate neighbourhood or the area in which competition would occur); *E Underwood & Son Ltd* v *Barker* [1899] 1 Ch 300, 306 (employee working for a hay and straw merchant to be read as covering only competing business); *Vandervell Products Ltd* v *MacLeod* (1957) 74 RPC 186, 193 (CA); *G W Plowman & Son Ltd* v *Ash* [1964] 1 WLR 568 (followed in *Business Seating (Renovations) Ltd* v *Broad* [1989] ICR 729, though wording of interlocutory injunction made the matter free from doubt); and *Marion White Ltd* v *Francis* [1972] 1 WLR 1423 (CA). The most recent authority is *Poly Lina Ltd* v *Finch* [1995] FSR 751, 763–4. The NICA read down the general words in *Norbrook Laboratories Ltd* v *Smith* IRLIB 335, 17, 18 August 1987. Gooderson, above (at 426), wrote that the rule in *Mills* v *Dunham* first occurred in *Avery* v *Langford* (1854) Kay 663, 666, 69 ER 281, 282 (a vendor case), but *Gale* v *Reed*, above, is earlier and illustrates the rule well. Three ropemakers dissolved their partnership. In the indenture two parties agreed that they would pay the other for all business they received as a result of his recommendations to friends and connections. However, the two were not to be compelled to provide rope "to any connections" of the third ex-partner "whom they might be disinclined to trust or give credit to". The ex-partner agreed that he would not make rope again. Could he work for those of his friends whom the other two refused to trust? Lord Ellenborough CJ in the King's Bench said (at 278) that general words were to be read in a restricted way so as to accord with "the intention of the deed" so that the parties received what they had stipulated for. *Rannie* v *Irvine* (1844) 7 Man & G 969, 135 ER 393 (a vendor case) is also pre-*Avery* v *Langford*. The case concerned a clause in the assignment of a lease that the defendant would not solicit or supply customers who were customers at that time of the baker's business. Maule J in the Common Pleas said (at 978, 397) that the covenant "must receive a reasonable construction. For instance, it cannot be held to apply to a dealing in any other trade than that of a baker . . . Such construction could probably exclude the case that has been put of the baker and some of his old customers going to some distant spot where bread would be provisable only from him". *Mills* v *Dunham* confirmed that this rule applied to employees. A modern illustration is *Home Counties Dairies Ltd* v *Skilton* [1970] 1 WLR 511 where the Court of Appeal considered the clause "serve or sell milk or dairy produce" as "act as a milkman". It was not read to cover "serve in a grocer's": if it had been, it would have been too wide. Cross LJ stated that since it was difficult to frame covenants without covering non-harmful behaviour, clauses carefully drafted for a legitimate purpose should not be struck down on the basis of the defendant's contention.

Illustrations of Construction

Construction by reference to the object of the contract is the generally accepted modern approach. Four cases from the last four decades have been selected to illustrate this proposition. Earlier cases include *Hayne* v *Burchell* (1890) 7 TLR 116 and *Lewis* v *Durnford* (1907) 24 TLR 64.

(1)   In *G W Plowman & Son Ltd* v *Ash*, above, the Court of Appeal interpreted a covenant not to canvass persons who were or had been customers of the plaintiffs during the defendant's employment as one restricted to goods he had sold. The plaintiffs were corn and agricultural merchants. There was no express restriction to such goods. Indeed, the covenant could be read as preventing the defendant from selling any type of goods. The court's ruling is supported by a reference in the covenant itself to "the business of a corn and agricultural merchant or animal feeding stuffs manufacturer". For a similar case from the same era see *Clark* v *Electronic Applications (Commercial) Ltd* [1963] RPC 234, where "designs" was read as "secret designs".

(2)   In *Marion White Ltd* v *Francis*, above, the plaintiffs sought an injunction to restrain the defendant from acting in breach of her covenant not to work in any capacity for a ladies' hairdresser within half a mile of their establishment for 12 months after termination. The defendant contended that the clause was too wide because it prevented her working as a receptionist or book-keeper. Buckley LJ in an unreserved judgment said (at 1430): "I do not think it was within the contemplation of the parties ... that the employee would either be likely to be employed as a bookkeeper in another hair-dressing establishment or as a cleaner or in any other capacity that one can think of that has nothing to do with dressing hair. As was pointed out in *Home Counties Dairies Ltd* v *Skilton*, an agreement of this kind ... must be read in the context of the business in relation to which the covenant is entered into". The clause was read to exclude non-hairdressing jobs and was upheld. The other judges did not deal with this point but spoke briefly about the remedy. The court managed to construe the covenant with the object of protecting the interest that the plaintiffs sought to safeguard.

(3)   In *Business Seating (Renovations) Ltd* v *Broad*, above, (Ch D) a covenant not to canvass, solicit or entice away "the business of any customers or clients of the employer" was construed by Millett J as one preventing the employee from doing so in respect of the repairing or renovating of office furniture and commercial seating – his job with the plaintiffs. The defendant's contention was that the covenant prevented him, if he became a milkman,

from soliciting orders for milk from persons who were the plaintiffs' customers. The judge quoted from *Plowman*, above (at 572): " ... the articles in which he may not canvass are the very articles in respect of which his employer employed him". In other words, the restraint was one as to the business the company undertook, and was not to be read in a broader fashion. For a second case from the same decade see *Normalec Ltd* v *Britton* [1983] FSR 18.

(4)   In *Clarke* v *Newland* [1991] 1 All ER 397 (CA) the covenant read: "In the event of the partnership being ... determined the salaried partner undertakes not to practice [*sic*] within the practice area ... within a period of three years from such determination". The defendant, the salaried partner, intended to set up as a GP 100 yards away. The plaintiffs sought damages and an injunction. Neill LJ (at 400) summarised the law: "(1) that the question of construction should be approached in the first instance without regard to the question of legality or illegality; (2) that the clause should be construed with reference to the object sought to be attained; (3) that in a restraint of trade case the object is the protection of one of the parties against rivalry in trade; (4) that the clause should be construed in the light of the factual matrix at the time when the agreement was made". Point (1) derives from *Mills* v *Dunham*, above; (2) from *Littlewoods Organisation Ltd* v *Harris* [1977] 1 WLR 1472, 1481, *per* Lord Denning MR; (3) from *Haynes* v *Doman* quoted below; and (4) from the non-covenant House of Lords case of *Prenn* v *Simmonds* [1971] 1 WLR 1381, 1383, *per* Lord Wilberforce. The clause was read as one covering only practice as a GP. It was not to prevent all work as a doctor such as acting as a consultant. The case of *Lyne-Pirkis* v *Jones* [1969] 1 WLR 1293 (CA) was distinguished because in the contract there was an antithesis between "as general medical practitioners" in the recital and "as a medical practitioner" in the covenants. The verb "practice" in the present case was to be interpreted as covering only practising as a GP. Thus the clause was not too wide. The rules in this case, which involved a partner who was salaried, apply even more strongly when the defendant is an employee.

For a Scottish case see *PR Consultants Scotland Ltd* v *Mann*, 15 August 1995, LEXIS. One issue for discussion is whether the type of construction seen above may save a clause which is expressed to cover "confidential information" without further specification. Injunctions, trial or otherwise, will not be granted in such terms because the employee does not know exactly what he may not do. It is, however, suggested that such language may be clarified by reference to the other terms of the contract. *Cf. Pioneer Concrete Services Ltd* v *Galli* [1985] VR 675.

Evidence

Concomitants of the rule in *Mills* v *Dunham* are the admittance of parole evidence to explain the meaning of words and the exclusion of extravagant contingencies.

The admission of oral evidence is exemplified by *Mumford* v *Gething* (1859) 7 CBNS 305, 141 ER 834. One clause in a traveller's contract stated that he would pay the plaintiffs – lace merchants – if he should travel "for any other house in the same trade on any part of the same ground". The Common Pleas *obiter* admitted the parole evidence that the parties intended to restrict the employee to the "Midland district" where he had worked. Similarly, evidence is admissible to determine the meaning of words. A good illustration is *Lovell & Christmas Ltd* v *Wall* (1911) 104 LT 85. The defendant agreed that he would not act as a "provision merchant" in London, Manchester or Liverpool at any time after he had left the plaintiff's employ. He left and intended to start a business of manufacturing and selling margarine. The Court of Appeal held that a manufacturer was not a merchant and that evidence was admissible to reach that conclusion. Of course since the contract has to be construed at the time when it was made, evidence as to how it was performed cannot affect its construction: *Elves* v *Crofts* (1850) 10 CB 241, 138 ER 98, *Jacoby* v *Whitmore* (1883) 49 LT 335, and *Perls* v *Saalfeld*, above. Evidence may not be adduced in order to show that a certain clause is a usual one in contracts of a particular type of worker: see for example *Mason* v *Provident Clothing Co* [1913] AC 724, 732.

Extravagant Contingencies

The point about extravagant contingencies was made by Tindal CJ in *Rannie* v *Irvine*, above. He said (at 976–7, 396): "[i]f the contract is a reasonable one ... we are not bound to look for improbable and extravagant consequences in order to make it void". An illustration of the application of this approach is *E Underwood & Son* v *Barker*, above. The plaintiffs sought to enforce a covenant that the defendant would not, for 12 months after leaving their employ, work as a hay and straw merchant in the United Kingdom, France, Belgium, Holland or Canada. Lindley MR said that the defendant's counsel had asked the Court of Appeal to put "a very far-fetched ... construction on this contract. He contended that if the defendant in any part of the world acted for any hay merchant carrying on business in any of the enumerated countries, the defendant would be guilty of a breach of his contract ... But ... the contract must be construed with reference to the business of the plaintiffs". The principle in *Rannie* v *Irvine* received approval by the highest court: see Lord Macnaghten in *Nordenfelt* v *Maxim Nordenfelt Guns and Ammunition Co Ltd* [1894] AC 534, 574. The approach remains applicable in modern times: *Commercial Plastics Ltd* v *Vincent* [1965] 1 WLR 623, 644; *Home Counties Dairies Ltd* v *Skilton* [1970] 1 WLR 526, 533, 534, 537; *Office Overload Ltd* v *Gunn* [1977] FSR 39, 42; *Greer* v *Sketchley Ltd* [1979] IRLR 445, 446; *Rockall Ltd* v *Murray*, 1 March 1988, LEXIS; *Office International (London) Ltd* v *Palm Contract Furniture Ltd*, 2 December 1985, LEXIS. It may be argued that there is nothing extravagant about employers wanting to prevent employees acting as grocer's assistants, which was the extravagant contingency mentioned by the Court of

Appeal in *Home Counties*. Nowadays a shop selling cheese may well be in competition with a dairy farm; in other words, the contingency is likely. Rivalry was less keen in the 1960s but it still existed, and there is nothing extravagant about the plaintiffs' wish to forbid competition by other sellers of dairy produce. In that event the clause should have been held to be too wide and thus unenforceable. A second criticism of *Home Counties* is that the court determined the validity of the clause at the date of breach, not at the time of entering into the covenant. The defendant left and joined a rival firm. He operated in the same area as he had done before. This fact was seized upon by the court. Both Harman LJ (at 530) and Cross LJ (at 536) spoke of the breach as "flagrant". Therefore, they excluded from the scope of the covenant the sale of butter or cheese in a grocer's. But it is doubtful that they would have so held, had he actually served butter in a grocer's. Literally the clause covers such an event. It does not do so only after construing the forbidden trades in the light of the plaintiffs' business. Moreover, as Parker put it in *Panayiotou* v *Sony Music Entertainment (UK) Ltd* [1994] EMLR 229, 317, the test used to judge whether a covenant is enforceable is one of reasonableness: "the court does not have to be satisfied that the defendant behaved in a morally reprehensible way".

To sum up so far, the courts will disregard extravagant contingencies put forward by an employee to strike down a covenant as being unreasonably wide, and they will interpret a clause in the light of the surrounding circumstances (as the British Columbia Court of Appeal put it in *Betz Laboratories Ltd* v *Klyn* (1969) 70 WWR 742, 743) including parole evidence which clarifies the terms of the covenant.

Lord Denning MR and Construction

As stated in the introduction to this section, the law is in a state of flux because of the judgments of Lord Denning MR and Megaw LJ in *Littlewoods Organisation Ltd* v *Harris*, above. They purported to follow the proposition of Lindley MR in *Haynes* v *Doman*, above (at 25): "agreements in restraint of trade, like other agreements, must be construed with reference to the object sought to be attained by them". Other cases have approved this phase, for example *Clark* v *Electronic Applications (Commercial) Ltd* (1963) 66 RPC 234, 235, *Anscombe & Ringland Ltd* v *Butchoff* (1986) 134 NLJ 37; and *Cash Orders (Amalgamated) Ltd* v *Haynes* (1937) 37 SRNSW 157, 176–7. Neill LJ in *Clarke* v *Newland* [1991] 1 All ER 397, 401, called this "a purposive construction". At issue in *Littlewoods* was a clause which prohibited the defendant, divisional director of women's fashions in a mail order business, for 12 months from the termination of his contract of employment from entering the service of, or being directly or indirectly engaged, concerned or interested in, the trading of the plaintiffs' main rival or its subsidiaries. On its face, the clause applied to all activities of the rival throughout the world. The majority of the Appeal Court, however, managed to limit the clause to mail order businesses in the United Kingdom. This outcome certainly seems to be contrary to that in, for example *Dannenberg*, above, on the phrase "any inventions". How did the Court of Appeal purport to justify its conclusion? It stated that the parties must have intended to limit the clause to the UK mail order business because that was the sole business in which the firms were competing. On that ground, the covenant was not unreasonably wide.

This approach has been strongly criticised by J Phillips, "The Construction of Covenants in Restraint of Trade" (1978) 13 IJ 254. His main point is this (at 256–7):

> The mode of construction adopted by the Court takes no account of the ambiguous nature of the word "construction" in Sir Nathaniel Lindley's statement: which of two acts does it refer to, the construction of the words of the restraining clause so as to give it a meaning, or the construction of the entire contract in the light of the restraining clause so as to decide whether that entire contract is in all the circumstances a reasonable justification for the restraints contained in it? . . . It is inconceivable that both could be construed in the light of the object toward which the work of the restraining clause are directed, for then the effect of the two steps would be, first, the fixing of the meaning of the word by relation to the object to be attained and, second, the assessment of those words so construed in the light of the same objects . . . [T]he dictum . . . refers to a construction of the second version . . . In *Haynes* itself there were no ambiguities . . . There is certainly nothing in the ratio of that case which suggests that one may interpret the plain meanings of unambiguous words by reference to implications to the contrary.

Yet precisely that is what the majority did. The cases which Lord Denning MR used (*Moenich* v *Fenestre* (1892) 67 LT 602, *Underwood*, above, *Plowman*, above, and *Home Counties*, above) were ones involving the first type of construction: ambiguous words were construed in the light of other matters. These cases did not relate to whether the restraint was reasonable. They merely said that the literal interpretation of the clause could not be supported because of other words or evidence.

The court managed to avoid the normal construction that a clause without a territorial restriction is read as a worldwide one; that protection for subsidiaries is not possible; and that according to *Commercial Plastics Ltd* v *Vincent* [1965] 1 QB 623, also a Court of Appeal decision, clauses should not be read in the employers' favour. In *Littlewoods* the court suited their arguments to the preferred result, legality. Another criticism of *Littlewoods* is that the court really construed the covenant by reference to what the defendant did – he had already broken the agreement – and not by reference to the circumstances existing at the moment of entering into it. By considering his activities, the court took into account irrelevant factors. There is a dictum of Cross J in *Printers & Finishers Ltd* v *Holloway* [1965] 1 WLR 1, 5, which makes this point wonderfully: "one naturally approaches the problem in this case with some bias in favour of the plaintiffs because Holloway has shown himself unworthy of their trust: but to test their argument fairly one must take the case of an employee who has been guilty of no breach of contract". Lord Denning MR in fact interpreted a covenant in favour of those who drafted them. It is hard, if not impossible, to find a reported case where the employee had any input into the drafting of the clause. Since the employers or their advisers drafted the clause, any ambiguity should be construed against them, as with exemption clauses. Furthermore, it is possible that the employer did intend to protect more than the law allows. If so, why should judges reduce the ambit of the covenant to save it? The Denning analysis is inconsistent with the restraint of trade doctrine. If the covenant has been negligently drawn up, the employers may sue the draftsperson, as occurred in *Moore & Co* v *Ferrier* [1988] 1 WLR 267 (CA). On the facts of *Littlewoods* there were authorities against construing a clause without territorial restriction as being limited to the United Kingdom, and legal advice should have demonstrated that the clause should not have been inserted into the contract in the form it was. Either the advice was defective or it was not sought. In either event to visit the consequences on the former employee looks perverse.

Indeed, in the next case which came before Lord Denning MR, he seems to have resiled from his position in *Littlewoods Organisation Ltd* v *Harris*, though he did give that case his approval. In *Greer* v *Sketchley Ltd*, above, the plaintiff, the defendants' managing director, covenanted that he would not for 12 months after the end of his employment with them "engage in any part of the UK in any business which is similar to any business involving ... trade secrets and/or processes carried on by the Company". He sought a declaration that the clause was invalid. Shaw LJ (at 448) said that "*Littlewoods* was a very special case". He would not extend it to apply to a geographical restriction. He seemed to want *Littlewoods* restricted to clauses which specify a competing firm. Waller LJ (*ibid*) took the view that the area "could not be cut down without substantial alteration in the whole clause". Lord Denning MR (at 447) held that the possible expansion of the defendants into all the parts of the United Kingdom where they did not have shops was too vague a possibility to justify a restraint covering all parts of the United Kingdom.

One is faced with the problem that one does not know when the type of construction which was adopted in *Littlewoods* might rear its head again. The other judges were less sanguine than Lord Denning MR. Megaw LJ (at 1489) distinguished *Commercial Plastics* by holding that the covenant was not argued to be other than intended to be worldwide, whereas that in *Littlewoods* was intended to be restricted to the United Kingdom. He applied the usual authorities including *Moenich*, *Plowman* and *Home Counties* to hold that the defendant was prohibited only from being involved in the sort of being he had conducted when employed by the plaintiffs.

Littlewoods was followed in, for example *Normalec Ltd* v *Britton* [1983] FSR 318 (unlimited restriction read as Yorkshire: rather surprisingly the officious by-stander made an appearance) and *SKK (UK) Ltd* v *Willis*, 15 May 1985, LEXIS: computer software industry cut down to firms in competition with plaintiffs: approved in Scotland in *SOS Bureau* v *Payne*, 1982 SLT (Sh Ct) 33. In *Horsell Graphic Industries Ltd* v *Slattery*, 4 February 1981, LEXIS, *Littlewoods* was restricted by Staughton LJ *obiter* to home-made covenants: "I do not see that the professional lawyer, employed by the employer, would be entitled to draft the contract widely in the knowledge that the court will save it from him by limiting the apparent meaning of the wording, whilst the employee, who may not have access to legal advice, could well be intimidated by the thought that the words to which he has put his signature meant what they said". In *J A Mont (UK) Ltd* v *Mills* [1993] IRLR 172 (CA) Simon Brown LJ (at 176) held that employers has to focus in the contract on the relevant proprietory interest before that *Haynes* v *Doman* approach could be used. Impliedly he restricted *Littlewoods* to this situation. Leave to appeal was refused.

If the courts wish to uphold the covenant, they will find an ambiguity. As Gurry points out, *Breach of Confidence* (Clarendon 1984) 207, n 44:

> it is difficult to find any ambiguity in the words "milk or dairy produce", which were confined to milk produce in *Home Counties Dairies Ltd* v *Skilton*, or in the words "the trading or business of ... Great Universal Stores Ltd or any company subsidiary thereto" which were confined to the mail order section of the business of such companies in *Littlewoods Organisation Ltd* v *Harris*.

Littlewoods has led to uncertainty where certainty is a virtue. It is no help to legal advisers. After all, the construction adopted in these cases is not always used. Gurry (at 209–10) suggests that the approach in cases such as *Home Counties*, *Littlewoods* and *Moenich* v *Fenestre* is that in those cases the employee deliberately did "what he had plainly agreed not to do" (*per* Lindley MR in *Haynes* v *Doman*, above at 27). If, however, the employee has not so acted, the covenant may be struck down. Gurry's view would not however seem to explain all the cases where clauses have been read literally, for example *S V Nevanas & Co* v *Walker* [1914] 1 Ch 413, 424, *Vancouver Malt & Sake Brewing Co* v *Vancouver Breweries Ltd* [1936] 2 DLR 310, 316 (PC), *Spafax (1965) Ltd* v *Dommett* (1972) 116 SJ 711 and perhaps most famous of all *Commercial Plastics Ltd* v *Vincent*, above.

In *Commercial Plastics* the defendant was employed as a plastics technologist on co-ordinating research and development in the production of polyvinyl chloride (PVC) calendered (that is rolled) sheeting for adhesive tape. He covenanted "not to seek employment with any of our competitors in the PVC calendering field for at least one year after leaving our employ". Pearson LJ *per curiam* adjudged the clause to be invalid. It was too wide in that it covered the whole of the calendering field, not just the field in which the defendant worked – PVC calendered tape for adhesive tape. The covenant was not limited by place. Therefore, it could have applied throughout the world. Since the employers traded solely in the United Kingdom, the clause was unreasonable, applying *Dowden & Pook Ltd* v *Pook* [1904] 1 KB 45 (CA) and *Vandervell Products Ltd* v *McLeod* [1957] RPC 185 (CA). The limitation in the clause to competitors was not sufficient to validate it, for "competitors" could be worldwide and the plaintiff did not require global protection. Lord Denning MR in *Littlewoods*, above (at 1481–2) criticised *Commercial Plastics* on the basis of the law previously mentioned that a covenant must not be rendered unenforceable because the former employee could point to "unlikely or improbable contingencies" which fell within the scope. There does not, however, seem much that is unlikely or improbable about the contingency in the case. The defendant would have been obliged to seek work outside the United Kingdom. If Lord Denning MR were correct about *Commercial Plastics*, the law would be that covenants were to be construed in favour of employers, a contention which is inconsistent with the rest of the restraint doctrine and the *contra proferentem* rule. Furthermore, covenants by vendors would presumably have to be construed in favour of vendors. It is at odds with the differences between employee and vendor cases that a liberal approach should be taken in employment cases and a narrow one in vendor cases. If anything, the law should be the other way round.

Criticism of *Littlewoods* ought not to allow one to believe that a literal interpretation is correct – even though a literal construction is more in accord with the policy of striking down clauses in restraint of trade in the interests of free competition and employee mobility than is an approach of construing covenants so as to uphold them as the *Littlewoods* approach does. An illustration of the harshness of the literal view is *Jenkins* v *Reid* [1948] 1 All ER 471. The plaintiff, a doctor, was prohibited after the termination of the partnership to which her husband was a party from practising "at any time . . . as a physician, surgeon or apothecary" within five miles of two named post offices. She never worked as a specialist or consultant, and the area covered certain parts of Bristol with which the practice had never dealt. Romer J held the covenant to be bad, because it prevented the plaintiff from acting as a consultant. It could not be construed as covering the jobs which the plaintiff actually did, since the words were not ambiguous. This approach seems to defeat the intention of the parties, which was not to include occupations which did not compete with the practice. The approach of Romer J is supported by other cases, such as *Lyne-Pirkis* v *Jones*, above, and as Romer J said (at 481): "I do not feel inclined to guess at some narrow meaning which would save it [a covenant] from defeat, especially having regard to the fact that these covenants are construed contra proferentes". Perhaps cases involving doctors, in which the literal rule has been applied, are exceptional. Alternatively, nowadays they would be decided differently.

In view of *Littlewoods* it is nowadays hard to see that covenants are to be construed *contra proferentes*. Prior to *Littlewoods* the rule in *Mills* v *Dunham* seems to have been rarely applied. Moreover, there is support for the view that "where a clause is ambiguous a construction which will make it valid is to be preferred to one which will make it void" (*per* Kay LJ in *Mills* v *Dunham*, above at 592; there are similar statements, for example in *Millers Ltd* v *Steedman* (1915) 84 LJKB 2057, 2065, and *Whitmore* v *King* (1918) LJ Ch 647, 649) but that attitude does not take the public policy against covenants in restraint into account. The same may also be said of phrases in which judges have sought to uphold covenants drafted by lay people (see Pearson LJ in *Commercial Plastics*, above at 647).

A lot therefore depends upon the desire of the judge to consider a phrase to be ambiguous. Take for example *Gilford Motor Co* v *Horne* [1933] Ch 935, which turned on "persons in the habit of dealing with the company". The words are vague, in that one might not be able to say whether a propositus was in that habit, but the words do not mean two different things, it might be argued. But if one says that since one cannot tell whether the propositus is included in the group, the phrase bears no certain meaning and is therefore ambiguous, one can "create" ambiguity, and so give oneself free rein to read down the phrase in order to save the covenant.

This issue is very well put by Heydon, above, at 124–5:

> [t]he problem is that the courts prefer to apply a single rule, or group of rules, to construe covenants in restraint of trade. They say that the meaning of the parties must be discovered without reference to issues of illegality unless there is ambiguity, in which case the maxim *ut res magis valeat quam pereat* will apply . . . If this is the rule, and the judges state it again and again, why are different results reached in seemingly similar cases? Largely because "ambiguity" is a vague and ambivalent word, a cloak behind which judges can reach the decisions they desire depending on their sympathies.

No apter epithet could be applied to *Littlewoods*. One might want to compare the result reached in *Littlewoods* with that in *Morris & Co v Ryle* (1910) 103 LT 545, 548. The plaintiff, hop merchants, employed the defendant as a trader. He covenanted that he would not, for five years after the end of his contract of service, solicit orders for anything from any persons whom he had asked for orders while in the plaintiffs' employ. He proposed to enter into the service of maltsters. The Court of Appeal thought it "in the highest degree unreasonable" to prevent the employee from trading with hop merchants if he went into the hardware business or acted as a licensed victualler. While it is difficult to enter into the minds of the parties, if one had asked the plaintiffs whether they wished to prohibit the defendant from trading with hop merchants in some instances, they might have replied that they wished only to prevent the defendant's soliciting orders. The covenant could be read down in this way if the clause in *Littlewoods* could be so construed. The words of Heydon (at 132) are again apposite. "Why should the court waste its time and the State's money in straightening out the affairs of the powerful in their attempts to oppress the weak, or keeping within the letter of the law those who seek to infringe its spirit?" Contrariwise, a strict constructionist approach may strike down covenants where there is a trade secret to protect.

Summary

To say that the courts always adopt a literal or a liberal view is far too inclusive. It is probably time to say today that the judiciary usually adopts the rule in *Mills* v *Dunham*, also known as the rule in *Haynes* v *Doman*, both of which are quoted above.

In the light of the different approaches, employers would be well-advised to have covenants drafted tightly in the knowledge that both parties and the courts can clearly recognise what they are seeking to prohibit. It is a case of "half a loaf is better than none". If employers try to grab the whole loaf, they may finish up with none. If the covenant is well-drafted, the case may well not come to court, and if it does the judge will not need to resort to rules of construction.

Interpretation Guidelines

Two further principles in the area of construction deserve notice:

First, the courts will not construct a contract for the parties. If there is an agreement, the judge is not empowered to rewrite the contract to cover what the employer desired in order to save the covenant: see, for example, *Marshall & Murray Ltd* v *Jones* (1913) 29 TLR 351. The court will not read in a limitation that the employers will not refuse consent to a transfer to competing employers if an employee, who could work for only those two employers, could not fairly be expected to work for the first employers: *Kores Manufacturing Co Ltd* v *Kolok Manufacturing Co Ltd* [1957] 3 All ER 158, 163 (first instance). Similarly, employers cannot voluntarily contract the area of restriction: *Gordon* v *Ferguson* (1962) 30 DLR (2d) 420 (NSSC).

In *Mason* v *Provident Clothing & Supply Co Ltd* [1913] AC 724, 745, Lord Moulton rejected the contention that the court would enforce restrictions which it considered to be reasonable but which were not written into the covenant. Severance was permissible but not a reconstruction of the clause. He added that:

> the real sanction at the back of these covenants is the terror and expense of litigation, in which the servant is usually at a great disadvantage, in view of the larger purse of his master ... [T]he hardship imposed by the exaction of unreasonable covenants by employers would be greatly increased if they could continue the practice with the expectation that ... the court would in the end enable them to obtain everything which they could have obtained by acting reasonably

A recent example is *WAC Ltd* v *Whillock* [1990] IRLR 23 (CS). The covenant prevented the defendant from carrying on any business in competition with his former employers. The court held (at 25) that the covenant did not prohibit him from being a director or employee of a competitor: it was limited to his carrying on a rival business himself: "a clear distinction falls to be drawn between an individual carrying on business and a company carrying on business". The court noted *Taylor* v *Campbell*, 1926 SLT 260, where a clause not to become an employee did not prevent his setting up in business on his own account. The court approved a statement of Lord Constable in that case: "The duty of a court of law in construing contracts is to give effect to them as they are expressed and not to correct their language or to supply their omissions". If the covenant had been expressed to cover acting as a director or employee, the defendant would have been prohibited from so acting.

The refusal to construct a covenant represents orthodoxy. This is not to say that the rule has not come under attack. In *Commercial Plastics Ltd* v *Vincent* the Court of Appeal said, above (at 642): "[i]t is unfortunate that a home-made provision, offered and accepted in good faith between commercial men and not in the least intended to be oppressive, has to be ruled out and declared void in a court of law for lack of the necessary limiting words". Stamp J said in *S W Strange Ltd* v *Mann* [1965] 1 WLR 629, 642, that "[i]t is no doubt a defect in the law that the court has no power to reframe such a covenant so as to make it no more than adequate to afford legitimate protection". These two cases show that courts sometimes think themselves constrained to decide in a certain way, but *Littlewoods* demonstrates that if a court is determined to find in a certain way it will do so. If one adopts the *Commercial Plastics* approach, one strikes down covenants. The expressions of regret might by some be seen as class sympathy. The problem with a class sympathy approach is that the doctrine of restraint of trade acts against the interests of employers and so against class solidarity between judges and ex-ploiters. Parliament has not taken up the hint to permit the judiciary to redefine the covenant's duration and territory.

Lord Denning MR in *Littlewoods* (at 1481) picked up the point in *Commercial Plastics* about the covenant being home-made. He said that "the Court should have upheld the clause because it was a just and honest agreement made in good faith ... ". He also said that "the provision was quite reasonable and sensible for the protection of the plaintiffs ... ". Nevertheless, if the company did not obtain legal advice, there seems little to be gained by penalising the former employee by holding her to a covenant which without the court-imposed limitation would be invalid. The consequences of failing to obtain legal advice should lie on the employers. The dissentient in *Littlewoods*, Browne LJ (at 1493), thought that the judgments of the majority went beyond construction into rewriting the covenant. In those cases such as *Moenich* and *Home Counties* (both above) the restrictive way in which the covenants were read derived support from parts of the contract other than the covenant. For example, in *Moenich* the employers' business was de-scribed as "an agent or commission merchant" and therefore the term "trade or business" could be read as being limited to such work. In *Littlewoods* there was nothing elsewhere which limited the covenant to employment with a firm concerned in the mail order business.

Secondly, if, as a result of construction, the agreement is too vague, it will not be enforced. Examples include the Irish case of *Coleborne* v *Kearns* (1912) 46 ILT 305 (CA) where the phrase "shall we leave your employment" was held to be too vague, and *Beetham* v *Fraser* (1904) 21 TLR 8 (DC). The most interesting of the cases is the well known authority of *Davies* v *Davies* (1887) 36 Ch D 359, a partnership case, where the covenant was to apply "so far as the law allows". The Court of Appeal had no doubt that the covenant could not be enforced. The parties had to fix the limits. It should be noted that the presumption of validity, which has been used in several authorities noted above applies only where the covenant is not void for uncertainty. The doctrine of *ut res magis valeat* would therefore not have saved the covenant in *Davies* v *Davies*. It is arguable that the maxim *ut res magis valeat* comes into effect only where the words used did not express what the parties intended and not simply where there is an ambiguity. This was the view of Neville J in *Konski* v *Peet*, above. If the maxim applied with full force to covenants, surely the burden of proof is on the wrong party. A similar but more recent authority is the unreported Northern Irish case of *NIS Fertilisers Ltd* v *Neville*, 10 February 1986, where the judge refused to accede to the plaintiffs' counsel's invitation to cut down an area restraint of 20 miles to cover only the areas actively covered by the defendant.

The Outer House in Scotland did not advert to this principle in *Hinton & Higgs (UK) Ltd* v *Murphy*, 1989 SLT 450 where Lord Dervaird said that the phrase "at least" in a covenant to last "at least 18 months" had no validity. Presumably the phrase was too vague to be enforced. Nevertheless, he struck out those words and held 18 months to be reasonable.

There are only a few cases where a court has refused to uphold a covenant because it was uncertain in scope. One example is *Gledhow Autoparts Ltd* v *Delaney* [1965] 1 WLR 1366 (CA). Danckwerts LJ (at 1376) held that "districts to which the traveller had operated" was too vague because there was no satisfactory evidence of the area. He said: "An employer who is seeking to enforce a restrictive clause of this kind is under an obligation to make the conditions to which the clause is to apply clear". In both *Spafax (1965) Ltd* v *Dommett* (1972) 116 SJ 711 *per* Phillimore LJ and *Reed Executive plc* v *Somers*, 20 March 1986, LEXIS (CA) the term "customer" was held to be too vague to be enforced. In the latter case Arnold P said: "[t]here are some trades or businesses, for instance a milk roundsman is the obvious one, where there is no difficulty in identifying customers. Where there are more sporadic type [*sic*] of businesses, such as employment agencies, different considerations apply . . . [The clause] is wholly uncertain in its effect", for in such a job it was not possible to say whether a person was a customer or not. Moreover, the class was to be determined at the date of the expiry of the contract. One could not say at that moment whether a person who had previously used the agency was a customer for one could not know whether her resorting to the office had finished. The clause used the terms "customer" and "person in the habit of dealing" disjunctively. The latter concept did not define the former. It was accordingly impossible to say who was a customer.

Particular Words

For the interpretation of specific phrases, such as "carry on", "engage in", "be interested or concerned in", see W Sanderson, *Restraint of Trade in English Law* (Sweet & Maxwell, 1926) 79–84, G H L Fridman, *The Modern Law of Employment*, (Stevens, 1963) 59–60, D D Prentice in *Chitty on Contracts*, 27th ed, (Sweet & Maxwell, 1993) ch 16, and *Halsbury's Laws of England*, above, paragraphs 54–9, among others. These meanings are well settled. One American case may however be taken to illustrate a difficulty. In *Dunn* v *Frank Miller Associates Inc*, 227 SE 2d 263 (1976) the Supreme Court of Georgia was faced with a covenant that the defendant would not, for one year after employment, engage in the employment agency business "in any capacity" within 25 miles of the plaintiff's office. The court held the clause unenforceable because on the authorities, that is as a matter of law, a covenant not to serve "in any capacity" was unreasonable. The dissenting judge, Jordan J (who incidentally often dissented in Georgia covenant cases), saved the clause by construing "in any capacity" closely with the business. The defendant was not prevented from working "in any capacity" at all – no doubt she could be a cleaner. Soliciting custom includes advertising for orders: *Sweeney* v *Astle* [1923] NZLR 1198 (SC by a majority). "Soliciting" also covers sending letters to clients residing within the prohibited area.

The well-settled nature of such phrases in English law is illustrated by *Peyton* v *Mindham* [1971] 3 All ER 1215 where Plowman J was faced with a covenant between partners, who were general medical practitioners, that the partner who received notice of termination of the partnership would not for five years "professionally advise ... any person who is or has ... been a patient" within a prescribed area. In *Routh* v *Jones*, above, "practise medicine" was held to cover practise as a consultant. In *Lyne-Pirkis* v *Jones*, above, the Court of Appeal reached the same result with the phrase "practise as a medical practitioner". Though *Macfarlane* v *Kent* [1965] 1 WLR 1059 might be seen as a contrary authority, Plowman J did not follow it because *Lyne-Pirkis* had not been cited to the judge. Accordingly, since the covenant in *Peyton* covered practising as a consultant, which the defendant had never done, the covenant was invalid and an injunction to enforce it was refused. In these cases phrases were not read in the light of the business of the parties. In *Lyne-Pirkis* the decision was supported by two facts. First, the parties were of equal standing: "The defendant is not an employee" is how Russell LJ put it (at 1299). Secondly, in the agreement the parties had referred to "general medical practitioners", thereby demonstrating that they meant something different by "medical practitioner". This approach is decidedly one of strict construction. In another medical case, *Robertson* v *Buchanan* (1904) 73 LJ Ch 408, "set up in practice" was held not to cover attending on some patients in the prohibited area.

Another illustration is *Bowers* v *Whittle*, 63 NH 147, 148 (1884). A covenant not to practise dentistry "on his own account or by any agent" was held not to cover practice as an employee. The court said that restraints "are not to be extended by construction beyond the fair and natural import of the language". A contrasting case from New Hampshire, and one in which *Bowers* was cited, is *Moore* v *Dover Veterinary Hospital Inc*, 367 A 2d 1044 (1975). The Supreme Court was faced with a covenant which prevented the employee from competing "in his own name or in association with any other person, either directly or indirectly, in the practice or business of veterinary medicine ... ". The clause was held to cover practising under a trade name, even though that was not expressly prohibited: "the covenant clearly precludes either a sole or joint venture by which the plaintiff would directly or indirectly compete with his former employer. The fair and natural import of the language is that practice under a trade name is prohibited". The construction is rather wide, but looking at the case as a whole, the court seems to have striven to hold the covenant valid, and this ruling is an instance of that inclination.

A similar type of construction to that adopted in *Bowers* v *Whittle* was adopted by Learned Hand Cir J in the Court of Appeals for the Second Circuit's case of *Ream* v *Callahan*, 136 F 2d 194 (1943) which indeed also involved dentists. The judge said that if the employee was bound he would be ruined, for the application of the covenant would mean that for three years he could not practise where he had worked. Moreover, the other party drafted the clause's language: "we start with a strong bias against the plaintiff's interpretation". Since the law "does not look with an auspicious eye" on covenants and "doubts are to be resolved against a latitudinarian construction", the court was able to construe the covenant to cover only the period when the defendant was in employment. It did not cover the period when the parties had entered into a co-operative equal association.

A more up-to-date illustration is the Court of Session authority of *WAC Ltd* v *Whillock*, above, where a shareholder in the plaintiffs was subject to a covenant that he would not "carry on" a competing business. The court held that being a director or employee of a competing company did not fall within the phrase. The outcome would have been different if the clause had been phrased as "carry on a competing business as owner, partner, employee or consultant". The court noted the contrasting case of *Group 4 Total Security Ltd* v *Ferrier*, 1985 SC 70, where the clause was expressed to cover being the owner of a competing business. A covenant in a contract to provide consultancy services which stipulated that Sir Terence Conran would not engage directly in a competing business was breached by his working as a non-executive director of a rival firm: *Euro RSCG SA* v Conran, *The Times*, 2 November 1992. A last illustration is *Farrand* v *Armstrong* (1911) 11 SRNSW 193, 197, where Simpson CJ in Eq held that a former partner carried on the business of an auctioneer by distributing circulars within the forbidden area.

Breach of Covenant

Whether the employee is in breach of covenant may depend on the covenant's width. A good illustration is the celebrated House of Lords case of *Herbert Morris Ltd* v *Saxelby* [1916] AC 688. The employers sought to prevent the employee from divulging or communicating information. They were unsuccessful because he was using it. Such an authority shows the premium placed on draftsmanship and is somewhat at variance with *Littlewoods*, above. Similarly, there is no breach of a non-solicitation covenant if customers approach the ex-employee: the covenant is broken only where the former employee approaches the customers. Solicitation may occur orally (as by telephone), in writing or by modern methods such as fax and e-mail. It may not always be obvious whether the defendant solicited her former clients. For example, if a former customer phones the ex-employee and discovers that she has left her employers and set up in business on her own account, is she soliciting when she tells the client that she would be grateful if he placed orders her way? It is suggested that solicitation occurs when the former employee intentionally attempts to exert or does exert some kind of pressure, using that term in a non-pejorative sense, over a possible customer. The mere provision of information does not, it is thought, constitute solicitation. For example, if in response to an inquiry the former employee tells people who in her previous job have ordered material from her that she has moved to new premises from where she is working for new employers and she is still engaged in the same line of business, she is not soliciting. The line between soliciting and providing information occurs also in the tort of inducing a breach of contract. It is also probable that there is no breach when soliciting occurs fortuitously. If the propositus worked only for customers in London, moved to Birmingham and advertised in the local press, it is most likely that the court will not hold him to be in breach when a London ex-customer goes to Birmingham for a conference and sees the advertisement while relaxing over a drink in the hotel bar, and puts in an order. In *Hanover Insurance Brokers Ltd* v *Schapiro* [1994] IRLR 92 the Court of Appeal held that "endeavour to take away" meant the same as "solicit". It too did not extend to a former client's approaching a broker.

"Competition" is not always easy to define. For instance, is a former employee acting in competition with his former employers when a client has stated that he will no longer trade with them? The issue arose in *John Michael Design plc* v *Cooke* [1987] 2 All ER 332 (CA). The clause read thus: "At no time within two years of the termination of this contract shall the employee directly or indirectly canvass, or accept from any client who is or was in the four years prior to the termination of this employment, a client of John Michael any business in competition to [*sic*] or similar to that of John Michael". It is arguable that by soliciting a firm which no longer intends to deal with the employers, the employee is not breaking the contract. However, O'Connor LJ (at 334) held that employers do have a legitimate proprietary interest over such customers. A covenant is irrelevant in respect of customers who will not be attracted to the former employee; it is very relevant in respect of customers who might be enticed away. Nicholls LJ (at 335) stated:

> With a non-dealing covenant, in practice the plaintiff will often only need protection when a customer of his has decided to change horses and go with the defendants. To regard that change of allegiance by a customer as *per se* a sufficient reason for refining an injunction would be tantamount to refusing the court's assistance in giving a plaintiff protection in precisely the circumstances where that assistance is needed and for which the covenant was designed.

Nevertheless, it is suggested that employers do not have an interest to protect. They have no trade connection with clients who will not do business with them. The employee can hardly be said to compete with her former employer when they have no chance of securing continuing business.

Courts will pierce the veil of incorporation if the former employee has established a company to compete with her former employers: *Gilford Motor Co* v *Horne* [1933] Ch 935. See also *Alliance Paper Group plc* v *Prestwich* [1996] IRLR 25, 28.

Brief Comparison with US Law

One may like to compare the English approach to construction exemplified in *Littlewoods* with the attitude adopted by the Court of Appeals for the Fourth Circuit applying Virginian law in *Grant* v *Carotek Inc*, 737 F 2d 410 (1984). The respondent was a former employee of the appellants, a company which distributed chemical processing equipment. He was dismissed and he established his own distribution company. In the contract of employment, a clause read: "the EMPLOYEE agrees not to contract with any of the principles [*sic*] or manufacturers with which the EMPLOYER has contracts for a period of five (5) years after termination of his employment ... ". The court held that the clause was unreasonable because it prohibited the ex-employee from entering into contracts with any of the appellants' clients, even those who were not involved with the distribution of chemical equipment. For example, the clause would prevent the defendant from supplying office equipment. Virginian law required that covenants were to be strictly construed against the employers. The appellants' argument that the clause, which was headed "NON-COMPETITION CLAUSE" must be read down to mean direct competition in the area of chemical processing equipment distribution was rejected. The "plain meaning" of the provision could not be altered by the heading. The court also rejected the appellants' second contention that the "plain language" had to be read in the light of an independent assessment of what the parties actually intended. It decided that the meaning of the clause was not to be gathered from extrinsic material such as an affidavit by the appellants' president, where the clause was *ex facie* unambiguous.

One may also like to compare the English rule about vagueness with the jurisprudence in Georgia, which requires that the nature of the business activities in which the employee is forbidden to engage must be "specified with particularity" in the covenant. Therefore, covenants which forbade the employee from engaging in "any business or activity competitive with" the employers' business were struck down for lack of definition: *Uni-Worth Enterprises Inc* v *Wilson*, 261 SE 2d 572 (1979), relying on earlier cases.

Contents of Chapter Seven

SEVERANCE

Chapter Seven

SEVERANCE

Introduction

Lord Moulton in *Mason* v *Provident Clothing & Supply Co Ltd* [1913] AC 724, 745, expressed the courts' policy as to the doctrine of severance in these ringing words: "It would ... be *pessimi exempli* if, when an employer had exacted a covenant deliberately framed in unreasonably wide terms, the Courts were to come to his assistance and, by applying their ingenuity and knowledge of the law, carve out of this void covenant the maximum of what he might validly have required". The courts are willing in some situations to strike out parts of covenants. The effect is that the part saved is enforceable, whereas if the unacceptable part had not been excised, the whole covenant would have been unenforceable. The issue of severance agreements is considered in Chapter 5.

The Law

The rules were stated by P J Crawford QC in *Sadler* v *Imperial Life Assurance Co of Canada* [1988] IRLR 388, 392. The unenforceable part must be severable without altering the words of the new enforceable part; the remaining, enforceable, part must be one that is still recognisable as being the same covenant on which the parties agreed; and the enforceable part must be supported by adequate consideration. The last issue is rarely a problem, for consideration will normally be provided by employment or continuing employment. It should be noted that the effect of severance is not to render the remaining covenant or the whole contract void but to render enforceable part of a previously non-enforceable clause. On the facts of the case a clause prohibiting the former employee from working during the rest of his life for any insurance company other than his former employers was severable with the result that he was still entitled to commission after termination of employment. The judge held that the proviso about cessation of commission was "grammatically self-contained and can be removed without any modification of or addition to what remains, which continues to make perfect sense". Consideration was provided by the plaintiff completing employment for a certain time before the stipulation as to commission came into force. He rejected the contention that if the offending words were excised, the clause as to commission would be fundamentally altered: "The only alteration to the contract is the removal of the unenforceable restraint of trade. This is no more fundamental than the variation which inevitably takes place in any contract when a provision assented to by the parties is excised by the court in consequence of the operation of a rule of law". Therefore the provision was severed and the former employee obtained the post-termination commission. The tests in *Sadler* were applied to an independent contractor in *Marshall* v *NM Financial Management Ltd* [1995] 1 WLR 1461 (Ch D), where Sumption QC followed employment cases and did not refer to precedents dealing with vendors or partners, on which see below.

The first rule stated in *Sadler* is known as the "blue-pencil" test. If the terms of the covenant after severance would not make grammatical sense, severance is not possible. Blue pencilling or the striking out of the unenforceable part is not allowed when the remaining words would have to be changed. For example, a covenant not to act as a sales representative in "Croydon, Gatwick or Heathrow" may be severed as to "Gatwick" to leave "Croydon or Heathrow" as the prohibited territory. Accordingly "Gatwick" may be severed. However, a covenant not to solicit orders in Kent when the employee worked only in Dover cannot be severed to remove the rest of Kent while preserving the restriction as to Dover. This type of modification, known in the United States as partial enforcement, is not permissible in English law. English courts see the US approach as an illegitimate rewriting of the contract. The English approach is mechanical and formalistic, in strange contrast to the doctrine of restraint of trade, which relies on the open-ended notion of reasonableness.

Deletion of words in covenants in employment contracts is quite common. In *Bromley* v *Smith* [1909] 2 KB 235 the defendant, employed to go round Clacton-on-Sea selling bread, covenanted that he would not for three years after leaving his master's service be engaged "in any of the business of miller baker straw and corn merchant etc or be engaged in the manufacture of flour meal bread or confectionery restaurant keeper or assistant to such either wholesale or retail within a radius of ten miles from Great Clacton". Channell J severed the words so that only the supply of bread was restrained, and he granted the plaintiff an injunction to enforce the revised covenant. In *Scorer* v *Seymour Jones* [1966] 1 WLR 1419 (CA) the defendant covenanted that he would not *inter alia* for three years after determination of his contract of employment carry on "in the business of an auctioneer surveyor or estate agent or in any ancillary business carried on by [the plaintiff] at 85 Fore Street Kingsbridge or Duke Street Dartmouth ... within a radius of five miles thereof ... ". The defendant had never been employed in Dartmouth and the court severed that restriction. Dartmouth "was sufficiently remote from the interests of Kingsbridge as to make that a separate concern" is how Sellers LJ in an unreserved judgment put it (at 1421). The covenant was a separate one from the Kingsbridge one and was therefore severable. A more recent but still simple case is *Business Seating (Renovations) Ltd* v *Broad* [1989] IRLR 729 (Ch D). The defendant covenanted that he would not canvass, solicit or endeavour to take away customers or clients of the defendants or any associated company who have been customers or clients of the company or any associated company during the period of one year immediately preceding termination. Millett J (at 734–5) severed the words concerning associated employers with the result that the clause was lawful. Applying *Attwood* v *Lamont* [1920] 3 KB 571 (CA), he blue-pencilled the phrase. The part severed was independent of that remaining. On the facts there were two companies, each with a distinct business and different customers. In effect there were two covenants, one of which could be severed, leaving the remainder grammatically unaffected.

A slightly more complex authority factually is *Rex Stewart Jeffries Parker Ginsberg Ltd* v *Parker* [1988] IRLR 483 (CA). The defendant covenanted that he would not for 18 months after termination *inter alia* be concerned in a business of any firm or person "who to your knowledge is or has been during the period of your employment a customer of the company or an associated company or associated companies so as to harm the goodwill of the company". The court quoted from the speech of Lord Moulton in *Mason*, above (at 745): "I do not doubt that the court may . . . enforce a part of a covenant in restraint of trade, even though taken as a whole the covenant exceeds what is reasonable. But . . . that ought to be done in cases where the part so enforceable is clearly severable, and even so only in cases where the excess is of trivial importance, or merely technical, and not a part of the main purport and substance of the clause". Glidewell LJ held that there were three independent covenants. The covenant not to solicit persons who became customers after the defendant had left employment and the covenant not to solicit customers of associated companies were unenforceable, but the words "is or" and "an associated company or associated companies" were excised, leaving a valid covenant not to solicit those who were customers during his employment. The parts severed were "trivial" within *Mason*. This point about triviality is sometimes seen as a separate rule. However, the Court of Appeal in *T Lucas & Co Ltd* v *Mitchell* [1974] Ch 129 would have none of this. They said (at 137) that: "if you find two restraints which as a matter of construction are to be regarded as intended by the parties to be separate and severable, and the excision of the unenforceable restraint being capable of being made without other addition or modification, there is no third question, even in master and servant cases". In *Anscombe & Ringland Ltd* v *Butchoff* (1983) 134 NLJ 37 (QBD), transcript available on LEXIS, Cantley J noted that a different result might have been obtained pre-*Lucas* when Lord Moulton's words were applied. He said that under the influence of *Scorer* v *Seymour Jones*, above, the law had changed and he could now delete "auctioneer" and "surveyor" from a covenant that the employee would not compete "in the business of an auctioneer, valuer, surveyor or estate agent within a radius of one mile" from a certain address.

The blue-pencil test also applies to partners and vendors. More is said below but two illustrations may be given here. An early exemplar is *Price* v *Green* (1847) 16 M & W 346, 153 ER 1222 (Ex Ch), a case involving partners. Price covenanted with a deceased person, of whom Green was the executor, that he would not carry on the trade of a parfumier, etc, within London or Westminster or 600 miles of the same. Patteson J *per curiam* (at 353, 1225) held that the phrase as to 600 miles was to be severed, and the rest of the covenant was upheld. A covenant involving a vendor is the famous one in *Nordenfelt* v *Maxim Nordenfelt Guns and Ammunition Co* [1894] AC 535, where there was no appeal from the decision of the Court of Appeal [1893] 1 Ch 630 that the phrase "or in any business competing or liable to compete in any way with that for the time being carried on by the company" could be severed, leaving a covenant which was enforced by injunction. *Price* v *Green* is a case emphasising that it is a matter of construction whether the clause is divisible into two or more separate covenants. So also said Salter J in *Putsman* v *Taylor* [1927] 1 KB 637, 640 (DC).

The second rule about severance is that, after blue-pencilling, the remaining covenant must have consideration. In modern guise this requirement is the old rule that each clause must form a separate independent promise. The principal authority and illustration is the celebrated case of *Attwood* v *Lamont*, above. The defendant had been an assistant in the plaintiff's tailoring department. He covenanted that he would not at any time within a 10 mile radius of Kidderminster be involved in "the trade or business of a tailor, dressmaker, general draper, milliner, hatter, haberdasher, gentlemen's, ladies or children's outfitters". The court held that no severance was possible. The whole covenant constituted one promise; that promise was to protect the plaintiff's whole business, not just the tailoring business; and, therefore, the entire covenant was unenforceable. It should be noted that it was possible to "blue-pencil" the words after "tailor". This second rule is thus separate from and in addition to the blue-pencil test. Therefore, there must be two separate interests before one is severed. Glidewell LJ in *Rex Stewart*, above (at 487) spoke of "separate prohibitions".

The ruling in *Attwood* v *Lamont* is still the law, as the Northern Irish case of *NIS Fertilisers Ltd* v *Neville*, 10 February 1986, LEXIS (Ch D) demonstrates. The defendant covenanted that he would not solicit customers "in an area which covers the territory within which you represented the company and any area outside the territory which stands at a distance of 20 miles from the boundary of it". It was possible grammatically to blue-pencil the words after "company" but the court held that the covenant was a single promise and therefore could not be severed. The effect was that the whole clause was unreasonable. Sumption QC in *Marshall* v *NM Financial Management Ltd*, above (at 1466) considered that the second and third rules in *Sadler* replaced the rule on independent covenants. It is, however, suggested that the rules are the same but differently formulated. Scottish law is the same as English: see, for example *Mulvein* v *Murray*, 1908 SC 528 and *Rentokil Ltd* v *Hampton*, 1982 SLT 422. *Hall* v *Moore* [1928] 1 DLR 1028 (BC), *Garbutt Business College Ltd* v *Henderson* (1931) 4 DLR 151 (Alta) and *E P Chester Ltd* v *Masterkis* (1968) 70 DLR (2d) 133 (NS) demonstrate the vitality of *Attwood* v

Lamont in Canada. After the offending words are excised, the covenant is tested in the usual way.

In *Marshall* the judge thought that "there should be added a fourth [rule], namely that the severance must be consistent with the public policy underlying the avoidance of the offending part". Unless this condition is a rephrasing of Lord Moulton's speech in *Mason*, quoted above, it is novel and not supported by the authorities.

The Effect of the Deleted Words on the Surviving Covenant

The part severed is not totally discarded. The severed words may be used to interpret the portion remaining.

One authority is *T Lucas & Co Ltd* v *Mitchell*, above. The defendant covenanted that he would not for one year after the termination of his employment deal in any goods similar to those sold in his area or solicit orders for or supply any such goods within that area. The court severed the covenant not to "deal" in the goods. By doing so it severed the type of goods to which the other, non-blue-pencilled, covenants related. Nevertheless, the remaining covenants were restricted to those goods by reference to the severed covenant.

Severance and Similar Clauses

A practice has grown up of including in a contract of employment an express term permitting severance of independent covenants. Such clauses have not often been the subject of judicial comment but the thinking is that they simply express what is otherwise implicit; namely, that there is a doctrine of severance. In *Hinton & Higgs (UK) Ltd* v *Murphy* [1989] IRLR 519 (CS, Outer House) Lord Dervaird considered that a clause stating that the restrictions "are considered reasonable between the parties" was "probably an illegitimate attempt to oust the jurisdiction of the court" (at 520). The clause went on to permit the court to delete words. His Lordship used the clause to sever words in the covenant. The clause did not in this respect go further than the general law. The clause did, however, permit a reduction in the period of application, which was stated to be 18 months. Lord Dervaird did not comment on this part.

Lord Dervaird (at 520) said that "the parties have agreed in advance they will accept as continuing to bind them such part of the arrangements which they have made or the court finds by deletion only to be alterations which permit the restriction to be regarded as reasonable. I do not see why the court should refuse to perform that role, not being one of rewriting the contract but of selecting that version of it which the parties have *inter alia* made with each other and enabling the bargain as so modified to stand". If read literally these words could go very far, but they must be construed in the context in which they were issued. The restraint clause prevented the defenders from "providing . . . the services of consultancy in health and safety to any such previous or present client . . . ". The court severed the words "previous or" to limit the clause to present clients. The severance clause permitted the court to modify the clause *by deletion*. It did not permit the court to reduce the area, the time, or the scope of the business to be protected. The statement must be read in this context. The court was not faced with a type of clause, which has been used in the Commonwealth, which consists of a term enabling the court to select among several expressly stated areas or durations or both. An example is a covenant not to compete in a certain line of business with her former company for (3), (6), (12) months within a radius of (1), (3), (5), (10), (20) miles of her former office. In England the law is not yet laid down. It is suggested that since at the commencement of employment (or at any other time when the clause was inserted) the employee does not know the time or the area or both, the covenant is void for uncertainty.

The principal Commonwealth authority, though one which deals with the sale of a business, is *Austra Tanks Pty Ltd* v *Running* [1982] 2 NSWLR 840 (Eq D). A covenant provided for various areas and times. No priority was attached to any specific area or time. The number of possible covenants was 82,152. Wootten J said that uncertainty includes words which have more than one meaning; however, *id certum est quod certum reddi potest*, which the judge translated as "a contract is good if the inquiry for which the words call is one which will lead to a sufficiently certain result". Applying *Davies* v *Davies* (1887) 36 Ch D 389, the judge held (at 844) that there was no definite answer to the question: what was the covenantor forbidden to do in terms of area and time? He approved Heydon, *The Restraint of Trade Doctrine* (Butterworths, 1971): "there is much to be said for the doctrine in *Davies* v *Davies*; its reversal would certainly result in more litigation and might increase an employer's power of oppressing his employees" (at 164). The judge approved the statement of Lord Moulton in *Mason*, above (at 725–7), that employees should not be put to "the terror and expense" of a trial to determine whether a covenant is valid.

The contrasting case to *Austra Tanks* is the little-known authority of *Lloyd's Ships Holdings Pty Ltd* v *Davros Pty Ltd* (1987) 72 ALR 643, a decision of Spender J in the Federal Court of Australia, General Division. The judgment was unreserved and also involved vendors. As the judge noted, the covenant was negotiated at arm's length by the businessmen, both having commercial and legal advice. The judgment, therefore, may not apply to employment. Spender J distinguished *Austra Tanks* as being a case in which the clause contemplates "a single covenant, being the widest restraint that is enforceable". Not only was the clause uncertain, but it might also be void on the grounds that the parties had left the width of the covenant to be determined by the court. "If, however, the clause contemplates all the combinations applying with severance of those found to be an unreasonable restraint of trade, then no uncertainty exists. The clause operates cumulatively" (at 658). On the facts, the restraint expressly stated that it was to apply as if it was composed of several separate covenants consisting of combinations: "The intention of the parties was for all the combinations to apply, subject to the severance of any of them which became invalid or unenforceable for any reason" (at 658). As the judge noted, the difference would not always be obvious, being a question of degree. The question was whether there was a "genuine attempt" to protect the covenantee, or whether it was merely an exercise in leaving it to the court to make the agreement for the parties: "One might think the more numerous the variables, and the more mechanical and indiscriminate the combination of variables, the more likely would be a conclusion that the exercise is of the latter kind". The covenant read that it was to apply for 10, 9, 8, . . . 1 years and within the United States, Canada, Australia and New Zealand, or Australia, or the East Coast of Australia. Ten years was thought to be reasonable in view of the small size of the market for shipbuilding. Canada was severed, and the rest of the territory was held to be valid. However, the covenant covered "shipbuilding of any description". Since the clause covered aspects which the plaintiffs had not engaged in, for example oil tankers, and could not be construed as covering only such matters as the plaintiffs had traded in, the clause was unreasonable. English courts may take the view that what Spender J did was a rewriting of the contract, which is impermissible. Lord Shaw in *Mason*, above at 742, spoke of the need for "separate and clearly-defined divisions", a concept not present in *Lloyd's Ships*. For a similar authority see *JQAT Ltd* v *Storm* [1987] 2 Qd R 162, where the judge again held that this type of clause was not void for uncertainty.

Severance in Covenants given by Partners and Vendors

Case law emphasises that it is more difficult to sever in employment contracts than in ones involving the sale of businesses and partners. In *Ronbar Enterprises Ltd* v *Green* [1954] 1 WLR 815 (CA) the facts were that the plaintiffs sought to enforce a covenant against a former partner that he would not "carry on or be engaged or interested in any business similar to or competing with the business of the partnership" for five years after he had left. The defendants had begun to write articles for *Sport and Show News*, a magazine very much like the one he had worked for during the partnership, *Weekly Sporting Review and Show Business*. Jenkins LJ (at 201) distinguished *Attwood* v *Lamont*, above, on the grounds that it was concerned with masters and servants, whereas *Goldsoll* v *Goldman* [1915] 1 Ch 292 and *British Reinforced Concrete Co Ltd* v *Schelff* [1921] 2 Ch 563 (Ch D) were both vendor cases. He agreed with the trial judge that there were in reality two covenants: (1) carrying on, etc, a similar business, and (2) carrying on, etc, a competing business. The first in a vendor case could be severed, leaving a valid covenant. Hodson LJ and Harman J concurred without mentioning the point.

Younger LJ in *Attwood* v *Lamont*, above (at 593–4), said that covenants given by vendors may be governed simply by the blue-pencil rule. If the restraint of trade doctrine is founded on protecting the weaker party, a policy of doing so would allow stricter rules on severance to apply to employees than to vendors. Employees are likely to be in a weaker position than vendors and so more deserving of protection. Younger LJ said that the striking down of standard-form covenants was done to obtain fair play between the parties. There is no need to ensure fair play when the parties are at arm's length. The contrary view, that *Goldsoll* v *Goldman* and *Attwood* v *Lamont* are simply inconsistent, has however also been advanced: see Maugham LJ in *Lambournes Ltd* v *Cascelloid* (1934), mentioned in (1937) 77 LJ 75 and by Gare, *The Law relating to Covenants in Restraint of Trade* (Solicitors' Law Stationery Society 1935) 83.

As stated above, the judge in *Marshall* v *NM Financial Management Ltd*, above, applied the employment doctrine of severance and not the vendor one to an independent contractor. It seems, however, that he was not directed to the issue. It is suggested that the law remains unsettled, but that at least with regard to persons like the plaintiff in this case the position ought to be that the law applicable to employees applies for they are very much subject to the direction of their "employers". Generally speaking, they do not have the same contractual freedom as vendors. For franchises see *Kall-Kwik Printing (UK) Ltd* v *Rush* [1996] FSR 114 (Ch D).

Policy of Severance

If the majority in *Littlewoods Organisation Ltd* v *Harris* [1977] 1 WLR 1472 (CA) were correct, there would be little scope for severance. Employers could draft wide clauses in the knowledge that courts would lick them into shape to fit the individual employee. In that event, employers ought not to draft clauses in the nineteenth century fashion of great particularity (see, for example the covenant in *Attwood* v *Lamont*, cited above). Construction with regard to the object of the covenant would achieve the employers' desire, and former employees would lose. Moreover, as Bryan pointed out "Restraint of Trade: Back to a Basic Approach" [1980] JBL 326, 332, the majority's construction will lead to a reduction in the "predictive value" of restraint clauses but the main point about *Littlewoods* was written seven years before the case. Heydon in his book at 290 wrote that English law " ... is internally inconsistent. It has a narrow severance doctrine, but some courts act on a broad liberal school of construction. Any court wishing to evade the doctrine of severance can construe the covenant in such a way that it is not illegal in the first place, so that the severance issue never arises". It is uncertain whether the majority in *Littlewoods* realised just what they were doing. Other considerations mentioned above support the approach of Browne LJ: the task of drafting contracts is for the parties, not for the courts; and the law of restraint of trade exists to protect employees. The majority redrafted the contract and they did so to uphold it contrary to the interest of the employee.

Heydon's attempts (at 288–9) to widen severance are unconvincing. He stated that nowadays employees can get legal aid; they are backed by the negotiating power of trade unions; and employees may ultimately suffer because they may be bound by covenants. None of these arguments is adumbrated at greater length. The last one apparently means that if the courts hold that severance is inapplicable, the clause may be upheld because they wish to protect employers. Be that as it may, the first two arguments are inconclusive. Not all employees can get legal aid, and it is unknown at present for unions to negotiate on covenants in restraint of trade. Even if they did so, would they really wish to negotiate about the specific terminology in one contract? After all in England the courts frown upon what Americans such as Wise, *Trade Secrets and Know-how throughout the World* (Clark Boardman & Co Ltd, 1974) vol 2, 450 call "boiler plate" covenants; that is, standard-form restraint clauses: see Lord Sterndale MR in *Attwood* v *Lamont*, above (at 579). And public policy is on the side of the employee, or so the courts say. Certainly not all employees are under the heel of the employers and standard-form covenants have the advantage of administrative convenience, but neither argument bears much weight in relation to the interest in the free mobility of labour, to be discussed later.

Heydon suggested (at 290) that the courts should engage in a balancing act, weighing up "the drawbacks, in terms of time and effort, of having the courts re-draft covenants, against the advantages of not striking down *bona fide* bargains tainted by accidental illegality". But this proposal does not deal with non-*bona fide* agreements or, better put, agreements between non-equals; and it does not meet the point of Lord Moulton mentioned above that: why should a court redraft a contract which was too wide when that covenant has an *in terrorem* effect and puts an ex-employee to litigation which she is bound to lose?: either the covenant is valid or is redrafted to be valid. His proposal furthermore does not meet the criticism that public policy is on the former employee's side. That is why one must reject his comparison (at 291) with other instances of remoulding agreements (and of giving compensation for the redraft). Certainly the blue-pencil test is partial enforcement of the covenant as originally drafted just as the redrafting on the unenforceable covenant to make it enforceable is, but the blue-pencil test gives the courts much less latitude to intervene in favour of employers than rewriting the term would do: if the term could be redrafted, then provided that there was a proprietary interest, the employers would always win. That outcome might well in some cases be contrary to the public interest.

In restraint cases, the courts are thus told by the law that it is legitimate to sever but illegitimate to redraw the contract. (For example, in *Marshall* v *NM Financial Management Ltd*, above, the judge (at 1466) noted that "judicial rewriting of the agreement" was not available as part of severance.) Yet the techniques are similar in form – the term is rewritten – and in substance – the term is made valid. Why is one permissible and one not? After all, the courts have the years of practice in implying terms. The answer may lie in the courts' desire not to be seen to be altering the words of the agreement of the parties. It is an easier task to excise words held to be irrelevant than to remould the words to fit the mischief (though the courts have the canons of construction to help them do that anyway).

Harman J in *Systems Reliability Holdings plc* v *Smith* [1990] IRLR 377, 385, rapidly summarised this topic. Excision of "or products of" from a clause was proper where the company did not supply products and such deletion is "one well within the classic blue pencil test, leaving the clause fully grammatical, having full effect in its other parts and not in any way so radically altering it so as to make it a different covenant from that entered into".

Five Final Points

Severance appears to be possible with regard to covenants in restraint of trade during employment. In *Marco Productions Ltd* v *Pagola* [1945] 1 All ER 155, the "Four Pagolas" agreed *inter alia* that they would not "during the engagement or any time prior, appear in any other entertainment". Hallett J said that the phrase "at any time prior" was severable. The issue was not discussed, but there seems to be no doubt that the doctrine is applicable to such covenants. The *Pagola* case illustrates how some judges have disregarded the exhortation of Lord Moulton in *Mason* only to excise trivial restraints and of Lord Sterndale MR in *Attwood* v *Lamont* that the blue-pencil test was not sufficient in itself.

Secondly, no case has recently reached the House of Lords on severance. Their Lordships could usefully review the Court of Appeal judgments since the 1920s to provide authoritative guidelines to that area.

Thirdly, an unenforceable covenant cannot be made valid by restricting the width of the injunction, for example *Agma Chemical Co Ltd* v *Hart*, 1985 SLT 246. Nevertheless, Lord Emslie, Lord President, thought that the company's desire not to enforce the covenant outside the area of the employee's agency was a factor in refusing to disturb the Outer House's grant of an interlocutory injunction. To English eyes the judgment appears suspect: it appears the employers are getting indirectly what they cannot have directly.

Fourthly, severance cannot be used to construct a covenant: *Vincents of Reading Ltd* v *Fogden* (1932) 48 TLR 613, 614.

Fifthly, employers cannot voluntarily reduce the area of restriction: *Gordon* v *Ferguson* (1962) 30 DLR (2d) 420 (NSSC), approving *Achen Manufacturing Co* v *Murphy* (1911) 23 Ont 467, 475. This issue has not been raised in England, but it is thought that the same rule would govern.

Antipodean Legislation

One or two members of the Commonwealth have statutes which provide for the partial enforcement of covenants. Perhaps the most litigated statute is the New South Wales Restraints of Trade Act 1974. By section 4(1) "a restraint of trade is valid to the extent to which it is not against public policy, whether it is in severable terms or not". By section 4(2), "Sub-s (1) does not affect the invalidity of a restraint of trade by reason of any matter other than public policy". Accordingly as Rath J said in *Iraf Pty Ltd* v *Graham* (1982) 41 ALR 209, 214, Supreme Court, Equity Division, subsection (2) does not impinge upon, for example voidness for uncertainty. Section 2 defines public policy for the purposes of the Act as "public policy in respect of restraint of trade", a none too helpful phrase, but one which covers the public policy of reasonableness between the parties. Section 4(3) states that the Court is not to use its power to modify if there is "a manifest failure by a person who created or joined in creating the restraint to make the restraint a reasonable restraint".

In the light of the words of section 4(1) ("whether it is in severable terms or not") and the legislative history, the statute being based on the report (No 9) of the Law Reform Commission on Covenants in Restraint of Trade, the original interpretation was to permit severance only where blue-pencilling was possible: *Davis* v *Wood*, 14 October 1977, unreported, and *Magna Alloys & Research Pty Ltd* v *Bradshaw* (1977) 3 TPC 71, 73, both decisions of Powell J. McLelland J put the law on the right footing in *Orton* v *Melman* [1981] 1 NSWLR 583, 586–7. A similar case is *Beeton* v *Humphreys*, 3 April 1980, unreported. A simple illustration of the application of the Act is a case involving the sale of a hairdressing business, but the same principle applies to employment. In *Iraf* the defendant covenanted not to engage, etc, in a business of the same nature as the one sold for three years within a radius of one kilometre. The court held that the area was reasonable, but time was not. The clause was limited to 12 months (at 219).

The Restraints of Trade Act is interesting for another reason. While there have been doubts voiced as to the principle, the doctrine is that the reasonableness of a covenant is judged at the time of the agreement. This rule was accepted in *Orton* v *Melman* but McLelland J said that one should look at the particular case, not at every conceivable circumstance (at 58). Accordingly, one looks at the actual breach. One then determines the reasonableness of the covenant in the light of the breach. It may, therefore, be difficult to grant a declaratory judgment, but the emphasis on the breach does allow the court to deal with non-hypothetical situations and without recourse to rules of construction such as the one in *Rannie* v *Irvine* (1844) 7 Man & G 969, 135 ER 393.

New Zealand has an Illegal Contracts Act 1970. Section 8 of that statute was used by the Supreme Court to reduce a covenant not to compete for five years to one lasting for three years in *H & R Block* v *Sanott* [1976] 1 NZLR 213, 219.

These statutes do not appear to have created problems for the judges in those countries. Whether they should be imported in England to replace the present technical rules of severance should be judged by policy. They are contrary to the policies of:

(1) not to have *in terrorem* covenants (though there is a provision in New South Wales not to enforce manifestly unreasonable restraints, which is similar to the law found in some US states not to enforce covenants where the employers have acted unfairly):

(2) construing covenants *contra proferentem*, because it is employers and their advisers who draft covenants.

Conclusion

If by means of construction of the covenant and severance of any offending term Courts permitted employers to enforce wide constraints on employee mobility, there would seem to be no control over managerial discretion. Allowing severance contradicts the judicial policy of prohibiting unreasonable restraints. The law appears two-faced. Blake argued "Employee Agreements not to Compete" (1960) 73 Harv LR 625, 682–3:

> "[f]or every covenant that finds its way to court, there are thousands which will exercise an *in terrorem* effect on employees who respect their contractual obligations and on competitors who fear legal complications if they employ a covenantor, or who are anxious to maintain gentlemanly relations with their competitors. Thus, the mobility of untold numbers of employees is restricted by the intimidation of restrictions whose severity no court would sanction. If severance is generally applied, employers can fashion truly ominous covenants with confidence that they will be pared down and enforced when the facts of a particular case are not unreasonable. This smacks of having one's cake and eating it too.

The statement of Sumption QC in *Marshall v NM Financial Management Ltd*, above, that there is "perhaps" a requirement that severance is consistent with public policy may be a harbinger of the developments which take Blake's comments into account.

The restraint of trade doctrine is either contrary to freedom of contract or in truth a fulfilment of it working in favour of employees; the doctrine of severance is contrary to freedom of contract and works in favour of employers.

It should be noted that if the employers fear that the covenants will not survive, there is nothing to prevent the parties agreeing in the usual fashion to vary the term, as occurred in *Bryson v Whitehead* (1822) 1 Sim & St 72, 57 ER 29 (V-C). See Chapter 8.

Contents of Chapter Eight

VARYING COVENANTS, THE TRANSFER REGULATIONS AND ASSIGNMENTS

Chapter Eight

VARYING COVENANTS, THE TRANSFER REGULATIONS AND ASSIGNMENTS

Varying Covenants

This section deals with changes to covenants during the contract's existence. Since the covenant forms part of the contract, it cannot be altered unilaterally. Bilateral agreement is needed. If the employee agrees expressly or impliedly to the variation, there is no problem. The legality of the new or revised covenant is determined as at the time of its insertion. Where the employee does not agree, a covenant may be imposed by the employers if the contract allows such a procedure. For example, where a staff handbook states that the contract may be varied at any time by the employers, the sole difficulty may be thought to be whether or not the relevant part of the book is contractual in nature. However, in the unreported authority of *United Association for the Protection of Trade Ltd* v *Kilburn*, 17 September 1985, the EAT held that the clause permitted only slight changes to an employee's contract. The addition of a restraint is a major change. It is also possible that a covenant may be incorporated in the normal ways from a collective agreement.

The issue of consent to a variation is much debated. The courts and tribunals are reluctant to hold that an employee has consented to any variation (see especially *Jones* v *Associated Tunnelling Co Ltd* [1981] IRLR 477 (EAT), where it was decided that an employee could not be deemed to have consented to a change until at the earliest it affected him). In *Sheet Metal Components Ltd* v *Plumridge* [1974] ICR 373 (NIRC) the court stated that implied consent to a variation will not be easily assumed when the change was contrary to the employee's interests. For a Scottish case applying *Jones* see *James C Watson & Co Ltd* v *Jacobson*, 12 January 1995, LEXIS. In the event of a covenant forming part of a package of changes the employee may face a particular problem. If she accepts the remainder of the changes such as increased pay, she may be held to be bound by the covenant when she repudiates that clause within a reasonable time. Employees would be well-advised to reject it immediately and in writing.

If an employee refuses the revised covenant (or the insertion of one into her existing contract), one option for employers is to dismiss her, preferably with notice, or to dismiss her with an offer of re-employment with the revised or new covenant. If the dismissal is with the correct notice period the employee has no wrongful dismissal claim. There is, however, the possibility of a qualified employee claiming a remedy for being unfairly dismissed. This topic falls outwith the scope of this book except that a refusal to agree to a covenant may amount to "some other substantial reason" within section 57(1)(b) of the Employment Protection (Consolidation) Act 1978 as occurred in *R S Components Ltd* v *Irwin* [1974] 1 All ER 41 (NIRC). The court further held on the facts that the employee had been treated reasonably within section 57(3). The court was particularly concerned that only four out of 92 staff had refused to agree to the covenant and that there had been some opportunity for consultation of the employees. In other words, it would be inefficient if four employees had contracts different from the others, and the employers had acted in a procedurally fair manner. It was stressed that a change to covenants may sometimes be essential for employers. An example occurs when new technology is introduced and the nature of the confidential information changes, necessitating a variation of the covenant. Sir John Brightman said (at 45): "it would be unfortunate for the development of industry if an employer was unable to meet such a situation without infringing the law of unfair dismissal".

Employers should beware of attempting to introduce covenants. An employee may take the opportunity to leave and set up a competing business – just what the employers sought to prevent by the covenant! If only for this reason it is better for employers to insist on a covenant at the commencement of employment. A possible alternative device is a collateral contract, but that requires consideration, which for a well-regarded employee may be substantial.

The Transfer of Undertakings (Protection of Employment) Regulations 1981

These Regulations (SI 1794) effect what is sometimes known as a statutory novation of contracts of employment where as a result of a relevant transfer as defined in the Regulations one economic entity is transferred to another. Rights and duties under the contract are transferred to the new employers with one or two exceptions such as criminal liability and old age, invalidity, and survivors' benefits. It is as if the contract made with the transferors had been made with the transferees. The employees must have been employed "immediately before" the transfer, subject to the law laid down by the House of Lords in *Litster* v *Forth Dry Dock and Engineering Co Ltd* [1990] 1 AC 546.

What if the new employers seek to change the contracts of employees they have acquired in order to put in a covenant which already exists in the contracts of their existing employees? One possibility is that the attempt will amount to a constructive dismissal, and any dismissal connected with the transfer is automatically unfair, unless the dismissal was for an economic, technical or organisational ("ETO") reason entailing changes in the workforce (regulation 8(2)). The insertion of new covenants does not involve a change in the workforce even if it was done for an ETO reason. In *Delabole State Ltd v Berriman* [1985] ICR 545 the Court of Appeal held an attempt to reduce pay to transferred workers in order to standardise terms and conditions did not entail a change in the workforce, which meant that the numbers of staff employed had to change or their functions did. In *Crawford v Swinton Insurance Brokers Ltd* [1990] ICR 85 the EAT held that there could be a change in the workforce if the persons employed remained at work but their functions changed ("entirely different jobs" according to Knox J at 92): there need be no change in the identity of the workforce.

There have been two cases in which the courts have referred to the effect of transfer on the transfer of covenants in restraint of trade. In *Initial Supplies Ltd v McCall* (1990) IRLIB 411, 7, the Court of Session opined without totally committing itself that the benefit of covenants was transferred. The court's reasoning seems to have been that the substitution of the new employers for the old in an employee's contract of service would mean that, for example, with regard to a non-solicitation covenant an employee would be prevented from soliciting orders from the transferees' customers, whom he had never even met. The covenant would be different in scope from that made between the original parties. Lord Coulsfield accepted (for the purposes of the Scottish law of interim interdicts) that the plaintiffs had a *prima facie* case but in the light of the company's acquiescence and the balance of convenience an interim interdict was refused, relegating the plaintiffs to their remedy in damages. The English Court of Appeal, however, ruled differently in *Morris Angel & Son Ltd v Hollande* [1993] ICR 71. The defendant, the managing director of a company, was dismissed when its business was transferred to the plaintiffs. He began competition with them. The plaintiffs sought to enforce the covenant he had given to his former employers. Dillon LJ said that the Regulations' effect was not to substitute the plaintiffs' customers for the transferors' ones in the covenant. The clause after the transfer still referred to the previous business's customers. What they did was to substitute the transferees for the transferors with the result that the plaintiffs could seek an injunction to restrain the defendant from soliciting customers covered by the agreement he had made with the transferors. The approach of the first instance judge, with whom Dillon LJ disagreed, "turns the obligation on the employee . . . into a quite different and possibly much wider obligation not to do business with the persons who had done business in the relevant year with the plaintiffs, not the company. Such an obligation was not remotely in contemplation when the service agreement was entered into, and I can see no reason why the regulation should have sought to change the burden on the employee" (at 78). In sum, the Regulations give the transferees a standing to enforce the covenant made between the transferors and their employee.

If the transferees wish to protect their business, individual negotiation with employees is strictly needed. If the employee does not consent, the issue of variation of contract discussed above is reached.

It should be noted that the reasonableness of a covenant is judged at the moment it was entered into. The transfer does not affect reasonableness: the change of employers does not enter into this question. It is just that the covenant may not cover what the transferees may wish it to do. There is a dictum of Lord Denning MR in *Shell UK Ltd* v *Lostock Garage Ltd* [1976] 1 WLR 1187, 1198, that later events may be taken into account when changed circumstances make the covenant work unfairly. Though the statement has not been applied in England, and it is inconsistent with authority, perhaps later judges might use it to strike down some covenants which have been transferred by the Regulations.

Assignment

The benefit of covenants may be assigned in the normal way. After assignment the new owners of a firm are able to enforce covenants in restraint of trade against an employee. In *Home Counties Dairies Ltd* v *Skilton* [1970] 1 WLR 521 (CA) the employers sold the goodwill of their dairy business to the plaintiffs, who agreed to employ all the employees. The benefit of the contracts of employment was assigned (that is in equity) to the plaintiffs, but, there was no (legal) assignment document. The defendant left their employ and started work for a rival business in the same area. Although judgments were reserved, only Harman LJ mentioned the assignment, and even he did not deal with the relevant law, which presumably the court regarded as settled.

The purchasers of a firm which bought out the vendors, who undertook not to compete on the sale, may sue the sellers for breach of covenant. In *Elves* v *Croft* (1850) 10 CB 241, 138 ER 98, a butcher, the defendant, sold the lease remaining on his premises and his goodwill to the plaintiff and covenanted that he would not carry on the trade of a butcher within five miles of the premises. Wilde CJ *per curiam* (at 260, 105) held that the covenant continued to be binding even though the covenantee no longer carried on the business. *Elves* v *Crofts* has been applied since. For example, in *Jacoby* v *Whitmore* (1883) 49 LT 335 (CA) the defendant entered into a covenant when he commenced employment with an Italian warehouseman that he would not carry on a similar business within one mile of the shop. The business was sold to the plaintiff. The defendant established a similar business within one mile. Brett MR held that the covenant passed either as "goodwill" in the sale document or under the term "beneficial interest".

It should be noted that a covenantee cannot assign the benefit of a covenant for personal services. *Davies* v *Davies* (1887) 36 Ch D 359 is an example.

Contents of Chapter Nine

JUDICIAL POLICIES IN CASES OF RESTRAINT OF TRADE AFTER CESSATION OF EMPLOYMENT

Chapter Nine

JUDICIAL POLICIES IN CASES OF RESTRAINT OF TRADE AFTER CESSATION OF EMPLOYMENT

Of course the equitable doctrine of restrictive covenants is the law's reflex to the needs of the businessman and the commercial world. Consequently it is the business judgment on the value of the relationship, the nature of acquired trade confidences, the uniqueness of skills and the like which counts for much ... But in the final analysis a court has to evaluate the competing factors to determine whether the legal sanction sought unduly interferes with personal economic freedom of individuals ... Consequently, the court must inescapably ... weigh these practical factors. (*Per* Brown Cir J in *Budget Rent-A-Car Corp of America* v *Fein*, 342 F 2d 509 (CA–5 (1965)).

Post-employment covenants present an effective method of preventing unscrupulous competition by employees who may attempt to appropriate valuable trade information and to take advantage of customer relationships for their own unfair personal gain. On the other hand, these covenants restrict the economic mobility of employees and their personal freedom. There are certainly policy considerations which necessitate looking with disfavour upon approving the loss of a man's ability to earn a living ... (*Per* Goldman P J in *Service Systems Corp* v *Harris*, 41 AD 20 (1973 (spelling anglicised)).

We do not mean to suggest that all of our decisions can easily be related one to the other. These cases turn on their facts. Some of our older cases seem to rest in part on the assumption that a former employee should be held to the dimensions of his bargain, however uneven the bargaining power of the parties, without a substantial analysis of the employer's need for protection. See, *e.g. Becker College of Business Administration & Secretarial Science* v *Gross* 281 Mass 355, 356 (1933). ("The defendant, a man of full age, married and a father, contends that he is not bound ... ".) Other decisions may be explained in relation to each other by the economic circumstances prevailing at the time of the exercise of the courts' equity power. Compare a wartime decision imposing a broad restraint (*Saltman* v *Smith* 313 Mass 135 (1943)) with decisions during an economic depression where the restraint was imposed (*Economic Grocery Stores Corp* v *McMenamy* 290 Mass 549 ... (1935)). These

latter decisions reflect the effect of considerations of the public interest ... (*Per*
Wilkins J in *All Stainless Inc* v *Colby*, 308 NE 2d 481 (1974)).

In attempting to balance the policies of "freedom of contract, freedom of trade,
sanctity of contract, individual liberty, protection of business, right to work, making
of training available to employee, earning of livelihood for one's self and family,
utilization of one's skill and talent, continued productivity, betterment of one's
status, avoidance of one's becoming a public charge, encouragement of competition
and discouragement of monopoly", *Arthur Murray Dance Studios Inc* v *Witter* 105 NE
2d 685, 692 (1952), the decisions not surprisingly have produced something less
than a seamless web (*Per curiam* in *Moore* v *Dover Veterinary Hospital Inc* 367 A 2d 1044,
NH (1976)).

A determination of the reasonableness of territorial restraints upon noncompetition
covenants requires a balance of the interests of the employer, the employee, and the
public while being "mindful of the basic policies of individual liberty, freedom of
contract, freedom of trade, protection of business, encouragement of competition
and discouragement of monopoly". (*Per* Jack Pope J in *Matlock* v *Data Processing Inc*,
618 SW 2d 327 (1981), Tex, quoting from *Fidelity Union Life Ins Co* v *Protective Life Ins
Co*, 356 F Supp 1199, 1203 (1972), ND Tex, affirmed without opinion 477 F 2d 574
(1973), CA-5).

Because courts will perennially be involved in settling disputes over anticompetitive
covenants, it is important that further inquiry be pursued. This is not an inquiry that
can be pursued in pure and abstract legal terms, however. One must first consider
the social and economic landscape that is the natural habitat of the restrictive
covenant. (*Per* Neely J in *Reddy* v *Community Health Foundation of Man*, 298 SE 2d 906
(CA WVa) (1982)).

Circumstances may change and make a commercial practice expedient which
formerly was mischievous to commerce. (*Per* Bowen LJ in *Maxim Nordenfelt Guns and
Ammunition Co* v *Nordenfelt* [1893] 1 Ch 630, 661 (CA)).

In periods when the law is settled, judges need not explain why they are ruling
in favour or against a certain legal proposition. The rule or principle is given and
the judicial task is seen largely as one of applying it to the facts, a sometimes
difficult process but not an insurmountable problem. In restraint of trade cases
this process may be seen at work subject to the caveat that in the early authorities
there is some slight (as reported) discussion of settled law, which perhaps reflects
a perception that law and morality were more closely linked in the immediate
post-medieval period than is thought to be the case nowadays according to the
prevalent Western legal theories. The judges often state that the law on covenants
in restraint of trade between employers and employees is settled and accordingly
not open for debate, though there is much more scope outside that area for
policy-making. This section focuses on the protection of the confidentiality of
information after the termination of the employment relationship but in order
not to present an ill-balanced account other interests and policies are noted.

Attention may be drawn to the Dicey's aphorism in *Lectures on the Relation between Law and Public Opinion in England*, 2nd ed (1913) 367 (Macmillan reprint 1963): "if a statute ... is apt to reproduce the public opinion not so much of today as of yesterday, judge-made law occasionally represents the opinion of the day before yesterday". As Winfield ("Public Policy in English Common Law" (1929), 42 Harv LR 76, 94), said: "Many decisions in the field of restraint of trade barely fifty years old are now museums of fossil economic theories". If Kessler, "Contracts of Adhesion–Some Thoughts about Freedom of Contract" (1943) 43 Col LR, 643, 649, was correct and *laissez-faire* lasted in Parliament for only 22 years (1825–47) the theory continued to dominate the thinking of judges for a much longer period. Cf. Atiyah, *The Rise and Fall of Freedom of Contract* (Clarendon 1979) *passim.*

Early References to Policy

The doctrine of restraint of trade is said to be based on public policy. Therefore, one would expect judges to refer to policy from earliest times, but not to mention confidential information if its protection was not being sought or if it was not a protectable interest. Unfortunately to twentieth century eyes the cases are ill-reported and one has to reconstruct the argumentation. The authority which is generally accepted as being the first on the doctrine is *Anon* (1414) YB 2 Hen 5, fol 5b, pl 126, usually called *The Dyer's Case.* The court was called upon to rule on the validity of a condition in a bond which prohibited the defendant from acting as a dyer within the plaintiff's town for six months. The response of Hull J (or Hall J) was emphatic: "By God, if the plaintiff were here, he would be sent to prison, until he paid a fine to the King" (author's translation). While one should properly not rely too much on the dictum of one judge, there would seem to be much force in Blake's comment "Employee Agreements not to Compete" (1960) 73 Harv LR 625, 637, that cases such as *The Dyer's Case:*

> represent reactions by the judges against erosions in the customs of the guilds by aggressive craftsmen ... They show judicial support of the customary concepts of "fair" commercial activity of the late medieval period ... It was the "unethical" master craftsman, seeking to increase his scale of operations and making use of contracts to alter customary practices, who was moving in the direction of modern enterprise capitalism.

Until the early seventeenth century the law remained static. Carpenter wrote "Validity of Covenants not to Compete" (1928) 76 U Pa LR 244, 244–5 (spelling anglicised):

> The reasons for holding contracts not to engage in a trade or employment void were not stated in the early cases, but the objections to such covenants are not difficult to

surmise when it is remembered that at the time there were few trades a man could follow without having been duly apprenticed, and that there were perhaps no other trades in which he was competent; and when it is remembered that following the Great Plague, which carried off so many workmen and servants, the Statute of Labourers was passed in 1349, requiring every able-bodied person under sixty years of age "not living in merchandise nor exercising any craft, nor having of his own whereof he may live, nor proper land about whose tillage he may himself occupy and not serving any other", to serve him that required it, under penalty of being committed to gaol. Under these conditions it is apparent that an agreement not to carry on a trade or to refrain from competing with the covenantee might have greatly injured the covenantor by divesting him of his only means of earning a livelihood; and it might have been in effect an agreement to violate the Statute of Labourers.

This seems an apt summary of the position, even with 70 years' more knowledge of the economy of the times of the Wars of the Roses. The law once decided by force of such doctrine of precedent as existed at that time and of such matters as the reputation of the judge and inertia remained static throughout the period of the Tudors. In *Claygate* v *Batchelor* (43 & 44 Eliz) Owen 143, 74 ER 961, all the Queen's Bench judges said (at 143, 962), in relation to an action of debt for £20 on a conditioned bond by which the defendant's son promised not to enter into the trade of haberdasher as journeyman, servant, apprentice or master in Kent within four years, that "the condition was against the law, ... for it is against the liberty of a free man, and against the Statute of Magna Carta Cap. 20 and is against the Commonwealth, 2 H5 & 5" (that is *The Dyer's Case*). The Croke report (*sub nom Colgate* v *Bacheler*, Cro Eliz 872, 78 ER 1097) presents a picture of the judges on the demurrer giving judgment for the defendant because if the action of debt on the obligation were successful, he would lose his trade and living: it did not matter that the restriction was limited to one trade in one place. These justifications for striking down all covenants in restraint of trade were put in more "picturesque" language (as Parry put it in *The Sanctity of Contracts in English Law* (Stevens & Sons 1959) 57) in *The Tailors of Ipswich Case* (1615) 11 Co Rep 53a, 53b, 77 ER 1218, 1219, "at the common law no man could be prohibited from working in any lawful trade, for the law abhors idleness, the mother of all evil ... and especially as young men who ought in their youth ... to learn sciences and trades which are profitable to the Commonwealth, and whereof they might reap the fruit in their old age". The topic of general and partial restraints is discussed in the section on history.

A change in the law was signalled in *Rogers* v *Parry* (1614) 2 Bulst 136, 80 ER 1012, in which the court stated that a person could not bind himself generally but that "for a time certain and in a place certain, a man may be well bound and restrained from using his trade". The acceptance of this doctrine in *Mitchel* v *Reynolds* (1711) 1 P Wms 181, 193, 24 ER 347, 351, which also destroyed the distinction between promises and bonds replacing it with the law that there had to be adequate and sufficient consideration, was moulded by the judges' conception of the demands of policy. A general covenant was void because it was "of no benefit to either party, and only oppressive" (at 182, 348). Parker CJ noted the elements of policy which led to the upholding of particular restraints:

- *volenti non fit injuria* (at 186, 349)
- there was no monopoly (at 187, 349)
- there was no loss of livelihood (at 190, 350)
- the public was not deprived of a person's labour (*ibid*)
- the covenant may be useful in that it stops one town from being "over-stocked with any particular trade" (at 191, 350).

A similar list of policies was stated in the early US case, *Alger* v *Thacher*, 19 Pick 51, 54 (1857) (Mass): covenants diminish livelihoods, deprive the public of services, discourage enterprise, raise prices, and lead to monopoly. In this context "oppressive" means "unreasonable": *Horner* v *Graves* (1831) 7 Bing 725, 743, 131 ER 284, 287. Furthermore, the fact that a covenant may be used oppressively is a reason for nullifying it: *Mineral Water and Bottle Exchange and Trade Protection Society* v *Booth* (1887) 36 Ch D 465, 471.

To these may be added the point that if one employee is restrained from practising in one place, other persons are free to take that employee's place: *Davis* v *Mason* (1793) 5 Term Rep 118, 120, 101 ER 69, 70 (Lord Kenyon CJKB). Blake wrote (above, at 630) of *Mitchel* v *Reynolds* that it was "a remarkable opinion for its method of balancing the social utility of certain types of restraints against their possible undesirable effects upon the covenantor and the public ... ". There have been no large changes in the policies judges nowadays take into account.

One can also see in Parker CJ's judgment the starting point for the development of the modern doctrine: general restraints "can be of no use to the obligee ... ; for what does it signify to a tradesman in London, what another does at Newcastle? and surely it would be unreasonable to fix a certain loss on one side, without any benefit to the other" (above, at 190–1, 350). Putting the point another way, Parker CJ's acknowledgement of policy factors proved too much: some of the arguments could be utilised to support general covenants in restraint of trade, the very mischief he was concerned to repel. Lord Macnaghten put it this way in *Nordenfelt* v *Maxim Nordenfelt Guns and Ammunition Co* [1894] AC 535, 571:

> it is no wonder that judges of former times did not foresee that the discoveries of science and the practical results of those discoveries might in time prove general restraints in some cases to be perfectly reasonable. When that time came it was only a legitimate development – it was hardly even an extension - of the principle on which exceptions were allowed to admit unlimited restraints into the class of allowable exceptions to the general rule.

Lord Macnaghten phrased his speech thus to refute Bowen LJ's judgment, as to which see Chapter 1, pp 13–14.

A summary of the legal history was outlined by Cohen J in *Morgan's Home Equipment Corp* v *Martucci*, 390 Pa 618, 627 (1957) (footnotes omitted).

> The earliest cases were decided against the economic background of a chronic shortage of skilled workers in England, the result of the virulent epidemics of the Black Death during the fourteenth century. It was not surprising, then, that all covenants to refrain from practising a trade were held to be void as against public policy. This policy carried over into the early seventeenth century when the grants of exclusive trading privileges by the Sovereign caused widespread public indignation which broadened into a dislike for all restraints upon the free exercise of trade. However, by the eighteenth century England found itself in the midst of a new commercial era, and adjusting to changed economic conditions, the courts upheld at common law contracts in partial restraint of trade.

The Nineteenth Century

The first discussion of confidential information in restraint of trade cases occurs in *Homer* v *Ashford* (1825) 3 Bing 322, 130 ER 537. The plaintiff, who traded as a saddler's ironmonger, engaged the defendant as clerk, bookkeeper and traveller. The latter covenanted in his indenture that he would not breach various restraints. Best CJCP said (at 326–7):

> The law will not permit anyone to restrain a person from doing what the public welfare and his own interest requires that he should do. Any deed, therefore, by which a person binds himself not to employ his talents, his industry, or his capital, in any useful undertaking in the kingdom, would be void, because no good reason can be imagined for any person's imposing such a restraint on himself. But it may often happen (and the present case is a strong instance of it) that individual interest, and general convenience, render engagements not to carry on trade or to act in a profession in a particular place, proper. Manufactures or dealings cannot be carried on to any great extent without the assistance of agents and servants. These must soon acquire a knowledge of the manufactures or dealings of their employers. A merchant or manufacturer would soon find a rival in every one of his servants, if he could not prevent them from using to his prejudice the knowledge acquired in his employ. Engagements of this sort between masters and servants are not injurious restraints of trade, but securities necessary for those who are engaged in it. The effect of such contracts is to encourage rather than cramp the employment of capital in trade, and the promotion of industry.

Part of this quote was approved by Erle CJ in *Mumford* v *Gething* (1859) 7 CB (NS) 305, 320, 141 ER 834, 840.

A statement of policy is also to be found in *Mallan* v *May* (1843) 11 M & W 653, 152 ER 967. Parke B in the Exchequer said (at 665, 972): "the public derives an advantage in the unrestrained choice which such a stipulation gives to the employer of able assistants, and the security it affords that the master will not withhold from the servant instruction in the secrets of his trade, and the communication of his own skill and experience, from the fear of his afterwards having a rival in the same business". Applying this approach, Parke B, after severing an independent part of the covenant, enforced the agreement that the defendant would not act in London for an unlimited time and he said that it did not matter that London contained at that time a million inhabitants. In *Sainter* v *Ferguson* (1849) 7 CB 716, 137 ER 283, Wilde CJCP remarked (at 726, 287) that the employee, an assistant surgeon, had been given the opportunity by his employer "of worming himself into his employer's connexion", and in that situation it was reasonable for the plaintiff to protect himself from a rival. In *Mumford* v *Gething*, above, Erle CJ (at 319, 840) stressed that "if the law discouraged such agreements as those [that is covenants in partial restraint of trade], employers would be extremely scrupulous as to engaging servants in a confidential capacity, seeing that they would incur the risk of their taking advantage of the knowledge they acquired of their customers and their mode of conducting business, and then transferring their services to a rival trader". Similar comments occur in, for example, *Howard* v *Woodward* (1864) 34 LJ Ch 47, 48.

The enforcement of the covenant was in that case also partly justified on the basis that the defendant, a traveller in lace in the plaintiff's Midland District, was "perfectly competent to judge whether or not it will be to his interest to enter into such a contract" (at 320, 840).

In the later nineteenth century judicial struggles were concerned with matters other than the potential disclosure of confidential information by ex-employers – adequacy or otherwise of consideration, general and partial covenants, the distinction between vendors and employees. The ground rules for the conflict which developed around the turn of the century were being laid down in mid-century. In *Leather Couch Co* v *Lorsont* (1869) LR 9 Eq 345 James V-C put forward the two arguments which were later seen as typifying this area of law (at 354):

> public policy requires that every man shall be at liberty to work for himself, and shall not be at liberty to deprive himself or the state of his labour, skill or talent, by any contract that he enters into. On the other hand, public policy requires that when a man has by skill or by any other means obtained something which he wants to sell, he should be at liberty to sell it in the most advantageous way in the market: and in order to enable him to sell it advantageously in the market it is necessary that he should be able to preclude himself from entering into competition with the purchaser ... provided that restriction in the judgment of the Court is not unreasonable, having regard to the subject matter of the contract.

This clash of policy was said by J L Bryenton "Validity and Enforceability of Restrictive Covenants not to Compete" (1964) 16 W Res LR 161 at 161 and 189 to be unresolvable.

The Big Three Cases and Others: 1892 to the End of World War I

Blake wrote in "Employee Agreements not to Compete" (1960) 73 Harv LR 625, 638, that with the breakdown of the apprenticeship system, contractual provisions were necessary to protect employers from loss of customers and trade secrets, while "employees were willing or had no better alternative than to restrict their future freedom of action in order to obtain present employment and such training and experience as came with it".

Putting aside most non-employment cases such as *English Hop Growers Ltd v Dering* [1928] 2 KB 174, 180, one can distinguish several strands of arguments in the speeches in *Nordenfelt*, above, *Mason v Provident Clothing & Supply Co Ltd* [1913] AC 724, and *Herbert Morris Ltd v Saxelby* [1916] 1 AC 688, all House of Lords authorities. In the period under discussion the courts of that time largely (for exceptions see Bowen and A L Smith LJJ in *Nordenfelt* (CA), above (at 667 and 674), and Lords Macnaghten, Herschell and Watson in *Nordenfelt* (HL), above (at 576, 550 and 556)) assumed that the interests of the parties were not separate from those of the public (see for example *Lamson Pneumatic Tube Co v Phillips* (1904) 91 LT 373 and *Mouchel v William Cubitt & Co* (1907) 24 RPC 194, 200) or rather if the covenant was reasonable between the parties it was not easily to be struck down on the ground of public policy. See *Attorney-General of the Commonwealth of Australia v Adelaide SS Co Ltd* [1913] AC 981 (PC) (cartel), *North Western Salt Co v Electrolytic Alkali Co Ltd* [1914] AC 461 (HL), *Fitch v Dewes* [1921] 2 AC 158 (HL), *Connors Bros Ltd v Connors* [1940] 4 All ER 179 (PC), *Kerchiss v Colora Printing Inks Ltd* [1960] RPC 235 (no poaching of employees), *Dickson v PSGB* [1967] Ch 708 (society's rules), and the cases on forfeiture of pensions discussed above. There was seen to be a conflict between freedoms of trade and contract. Both liberties were of interest to the community, even though it did not have a separate voice in determining reasonableness. One classification of the arguments is that adopted here, namely between policies which favour employees and those which favour employers.

Pro-employees

The interest most often mentioned in restraint of trade cases is the promotion of competition and the related interest of the encouragement of trade. The best-known phrase is that of Lord Macnaghten in *Nordenfelt*, above (at 565): "the public have an interest in every person's carrying on his trade freely: so has the individual. All interference with individual liberty of action in trading and all restraints of trade themselves, if there is nothing more, are contrary to public policy, and therefore void". It is thought that Lord Macnaghten was not postulating a new test but rephrasing terminology used in mid-nineteenth century authorities. The phrases have often been approved and in *Rockall Ltd v Murray*,

1 March 1988, LEXIS, these lines and the ones following were called "the basic principle".

A more explicit dictum occurs in the judgment of Neville J in *Dottridge Bros* v *Crook* (1904) 23 TLR 644, 645: "in a competitive country the public are concerned in the free competition of these [*sic*] engaged in business and, prima facie, everything that tends to restrict competition, however advantageous it may be to the individual, is subversive of the public generally". A similar statement occurs in the speech of Lord Shaw in *Herbert Morris*, above (at 718): "under modern conditions, both of society and of trade, it would appear to be in accord with the public interest to open and not to shut the markets of these islands to the skilled and industrial abilities of its inhabitants, and to further and not to obstruct for these *les carrières ouvertes*". Such sentiments were even bolstered by reference to God: the plaintiffs – cake makers – were refused an injunction to restrain the defendant partly on the ground that to grant it would restrict "unduly the right to earn and the duty to toil – in pursuance of the Divine command": *per* Meredith CJCP in *George Weston Ltd* v *Baird* (1916) 31 DLR 730, 739 (Ont App Div).

Freedom to compete was buttressed by subsidiary arguments. To stop competition meant that the former employee was "in ... bondage": *per* Lord Shaw in *Herbert Morris*, above at 718. He or she was to be granted the "fullest liberty of action consistent with all reasonably necessary precautions consented to for the adequate protection of the covenantee", as Isaacs J put it in *Brightman* v *Lamson Paragon Ltd* (1914) 18 CLR 331, 337 (HCA). And "the general policy of the law is opposed to all restraints upon liberty of individual action which are injurious to the interests of the State or community" in the words of Lord Watson in *Nordenfelt*, above (at 552). Freedom of competition meant that there were no monopolies (see Lindley LJ in *Nordenfelt* (CA), above) and that the public had a free choice (see Buckley LJ in *Morris & Co* v *Ryle* (1910) 103 LT 545, 549). Moreover, the state had an interest in promoting production, according to A L Smith LJ in *Nordenfelt* (CA), above (at 674) and it was contrary to public policy to deprive a person of his or her trade: see, for example *Nordenfelt* (CA) (at 641, 665 and 676). In promoting freedom of competition, the courts were also encouraging an employee to develop his or her "ability and industry", per Buckley LJ in *Morris & Co* v *Ryle*, above (at 549). Through the deterrence of potential rivals, covenants also inhibited the dissemination of new ideas and processes.

Pro-employers

The courts, as would be expected from *a priori* reasoning, emphasised that a valid covenant was one which protects employers' interests. If those interests were not safeguarded, the business of employers would suffer. As Lindley MR put it in *E Underwood & Son Ltd* v *Barker* [1899] 1 Ch 300, 307: "the defendant was engaged as their clerk and foreman and would, whilst acting as such, obtain information [which ...] would, if imparted to a rival in trade, greatly benefit him and proportionately injure the plaintiffs".

Protected by the covenant, employers were free to engage in competition with rival firms. In this sense, freedom of competition was a two-edged sword. The employee's interest was in freedom of competition – to compete against his or her former employers. The employers' interest was also in freedom of competition – to compete against rivals.

The courts at times stressed that the enforcement of covenants in restraint of trade did not mean that an employee was destitute. He or she could work elsewhere, his or her job given to someone else, and indeed a person might have been engaged without submitting to the covenant: see, for example Lord Macnaghten in *Nordenfelt*, above (at 56). If the employers wanted a new person in the former post of the defendant, they did not want the latter to compete: *Ballachulish Slate Quarries Ltd* v *Grant* (1903) 5 Sess Cas (5th Series) 1105, 1112.

Also to be expected from English judges in the era at the turn of the century is a devotion to freedom of contract. Sometimes this policy is couched in terms of freedom of contract *per se* (for example Channell LJ, *arguendo* in *Phillips* v *Stevens* (1899) 15 TLR 325, 325), sometimes in terms of common honesty and fair dealing (see Lord Watson in *Nordenfelt*, above at 552), and sometimes in an amalgam of the two, good faith adherence to contract: see Bowen LJ in *Nordenfelt*, above (at 668). In *Attwood* v *Lamont* [1920] 3 KB 571, 581, doctrinal developments were said to be "under the shadow of the '*laissez faire*' school of economics".

While the judges do see that in terms of power and wealth the relationship of employers and employee is more likely to be one of superordination and subordination than that between vendors and purchasers (*Nordenfelt* is the best example), and for that reason covenants are often said to be construed against employers (though not always: at the time the construction was to be done "fairly"), there is little appreciation that, to take the job, the employee may have to accept the covenant; and to continue in it, he or she may have to agree to a variation in the covenant: continued employment was seen as good consideration for variation. Accordingly, covenants were seen as embodying two conflicting policies, freedom of competition and freedom of contract. The conflict was to be resolved by applying the rules that employers could not protect themselves against competition *per se* but they could protect their trade secrets and customer connection.

The interests of the public were the same as those of the employers *and* the employee: they too wanted free competition and they too wanted the parties to adhere to the express terms of the contract of employment. That is why the public interest, prominent in the judgments but not in the outcomes, was hidden behind the interests of the parties. There was no public policy in favour of the underprivileged: "the fact that the person restricted is out of work, and is seeking employment, and is therefore at a disadvantage in making a bargain, cannot be a ground for holding his bargain invalid ... " (*E Underwood & Son Ltd* v *Barker*, above at 306). Except for fraud, duress, undue influence, and "any other recognised ground of invalidity", (*ibid* at 305): "if there is one thing more than another

which is essential to the trade and commerce of this country, it is the inviolability
of contracts deliberately entered into".

Conclusion: 1892 to the End of World War I

From the above outline of judicial policy one can see that judges tended to
consider the rules relating to covenants in restraint of trade as incorporating two
opposing principles – freedom of contract and freedom of competition. Such is
not the sole possible analysis of the state of the law (see Lord Diplock in *Macaulay*
v *A Schroeder Publishing Co Ltd* [1974] 1 WLR 1308 (HL), trenchantly criticised by
M J Trebilcock "The Doctrine of Inequality of Bargaining Power" (1976) 26 U To
LJ 359), but it represents the way in which judges saw their role and justified their
refusal to enforce covenants which did not protect a recognised interest of the
employers, a refusal which stood in stark contrast to their normal upholding of
contracts, no matter how unreasonable or unequal the bargain was. If the cases of
this period were minor ones scattered thinly across the reports, this breach in
laissez-faire would not have mattered so much. The law could have been seen as a
fossil, a survivor of an earlier period when conditions were different. However,
such a picture is falsified first of all by the plethora of cases reported from the mid-
1820s to the present, both in England and the Commonwealth. Law reporters
thought the cases interesting enough to be preserved, and they presumably had
assessed what the market could take. Secondly, it is falsified by the importance of
the cases, and thirdly by the vigour with which the principles were expounded, of
which the titanic clashes in *Nordenfelt* constitute the best illustration.

Certainly the judges in this period considered that "the history, indeed, of the
entire doctrine as to restraint of trade is itself nothing but a narrative of the
continual efforts of the English law, amidst all the changing conditions of English
industry and commerce, to adjust and harmonise their two opposite points of
view" (*per* Bowen LJ in *Nordenfelt*, above at 666), freedom of contract and freedom
of trade. These considerations continue to be voiced in the modern era. In
Panayiotou v *Sony Music Entertainment (UK) Ltd* [1994] EMLR 229, 317, Parker J
said that "in the case of the common law jurisdiction to declare a contract
unenforceable as a restraint of trade, the particular public policy consideration is
that of free trade". At 374 he declared that in the event of conflict, "freedom of
contract should prevail". A solution of the conflict was put by Lord Shaw in
Mason, above (at 739–40):

> I have referred, My Lords, to the apparent antagonism between the right to bargain
> and the right to work. The extreme of the one destroys the other. But the public
> interest reconciles these two, and removes all antagonism by the establishment of a
> principle and a limit of general application. It may be that bargains have been
> entered into with the eyes open, which restrict the field of liberty and of labour, and
> the law answers the public interest by refusing to enforce such bargains in every case
> where the right to contract has been used so as to afford more than a reasonable
> protection to the covenantee. In every case in which it exceeds that protection, the

public interest, which is always upon the side of liberty, including the liberty to exercise one's powers or to earn a livelihood, stands invaded and can accordingly be invoked to justify the non-enforcement of the restraint.

Lord Pearce in *Esso Petroleum Co Ltd* v *Harper's Garage (Stourport) Ltd* [1968] AC 269, 324, pointed out the effect: "since the rule must be a compromise, it is difficult to define its limits on any logical basis".

This suggested reconciliation would seem dubious in terms of logic if the public interest was always on the side of liberty. Why was it always on the side of liberty to trade and not on the side of liberty to contract? And why did liberty come into play only when the employers' interests had been safeguarded? Beyond logic there were other difficulties such as when does a covenant afford more than reasonable protection? Beyond logic and difficulties of applying the law, the analysis is defective in other respects (leaving aside the Hohfeldian point that if there is a right to work, should there not also be a duty to employ, though Lord Shaw seems to be using "right to work" in terms of a Dworkinian principle and not a Hohfeldian claim-right; *cf.* B Hepple, "The Right to Work at One's Job" (1974) 37 MLR 681). The statement does not reflect the social facts of employment. There is no "right to bargain" in times of unemployment as there was in 1913 or where the employers issue standard-form contracts. The power relationship between employer and employees meant that the interests of the former were advanced to the detriment of the latter.

Appreciation of the difference in wealth and power is nevertheless shown in the distinction drawn by the courts between covenants in restraint of trade between vendors and purchasers of business and between employers and employees, a distinction which was not really strongly drawn until *Attwood* v *Lamont* [1920] 3 KB 571. Younger LJ noted (at 581–2) that:

> we are here dealing with a branch of the law which has at all times been particularly susceptible to influence from current views of public policy. Its modern developments have grown up under the shadow of the "laissez-faire" school of economics, and, until recently, have, in consequence, been uniformly in the direction of extending the principle of freedom of contract in relation to such bargains, a tendency that has not yet ceased to be operative when the covenant in question is one exacted from a vendor in the sale of the goodwill of his business. But current opinion on the relations between employers and employed has moved rapidly in recent years, and thus it is that the House of Lords ... took the opportunity in 1913 [that is in *Mason*, above] ... to examine the problem afresh, with the result that the supreme tribunal ... has now placed upon the permissibility of such covenants a limit which the general interest ... had not previously seemed to require.

The covenant to stand had to attain a "legitimate purpose" (at 597) of the employers. Younger LJ also criticised standard-form terms (at 596) and what he saw as a "mischievous tendency" at that time to make covenants penal rather than protective (at 597).

The Modern Approach to the Protection of Confidential Information in Restraint of Trade Cases

The higher tribunals [have wrought] a practical revolution in previously current judicial views (Younger LJ in *Dewes* v *Fitch* [1920] 2 Ch 159, 185).

With the establishment of the present law on covenants in restraint of trade in the early twentieth century, the courts were free to concentrate on the nature of the interests to be protected, and sometimes they gave reasons why that protection was afforded. Between employers and employees there were two interests, both of which could be used to safeguard secret information.)"Masters are to be protected against the abuse by their ex-servants of the confidential information or of the relationships which servants have had with customers of the master while they were in his service": *Kerridge* v *Rotorua Theatres Ltd* [1937] NZLR 156, 179. Similar dicta abound in Commonwealth cases.

Customer Connection

The need for there to be an interest to be protected before the covenant is valid is not a twentieth century phenomenon. *Nordenfelt, Mason,* and *Herbert Morris* (all above) did not totally break with the past. In *Cornwall* v *Hawkins* (1872) 41 LJ Ch 435 the plaintiff sought an injunction and damages against his former employee, a milkman, who had breached a covenant that he would not carry on the same trade within two miles of Brixton Dairy for two years after leaving the plaintiff. Wickens V-C, in granting the injunction, said (at 436) that the defendant as a milkman was in constant communication with the customers while the employer never saw them. Accordingly, the defendant had broken the covenant by enticing the customers away, so reducing the employer's trade connection. The flexibility of *Nordenfelt* coupled with the courts' predilection for deciding cases in this area in a manner dependent on circumstances not on precedent, with the result that the judges have increased freedom of action, means that the courts are sometimes obliged to argue out their reasons for deciding one way or another but need not do so.

After *Herbert Morris* the courts did investigate whether or not there was a customer connection. In *Ropeways Ltd* v *Hoyle* (1919) 88 LJ Ch 446, 447, for example, Peterson J could not find that the defendant, an assistant draftsman of aerial ropeways, "had, or was likely to have, any such communication with the plaintiffs' customers, during his employment, as would render it possible for him, on the termination of his employment, to take away the plaintiffs' customers from them". A contrasting case is *McPherson* v *Moiler* (1920) 20 SRNSW 535. The defendant covenanted that he would not *inter alia* carry on the business of auctioneer or commission agent in a certain town for five years after the termination of his contract of employment. Harvey J, as he then was, held (at 542) that by coming into contact with customers, the defendant had not merely increased his skill, but had gained a connection with the plaintiffs' customers. The new emphasis on trade connections did not lead to totally new arguments in favour of or against covenants in restraint of trade.

Pro-employee

> These factors are easy to list. The difficulty arises when one tries to apply these factors to specific circumstances. (M Gunter, "Restraints on Trade" (1971) 49 NCLR 393, 401).

The courts continued to note that an ex-employee had to earn her living (for example *Whitehill* v *Bradford* [1952] 1 Ch 236, 246), a rationale which does not apply to covenants during employment, and that the ex-employee may have been in an unequal bargaining position (for example *Dewes* v *Fitch* [1920] 2 Ch 159, 187 (CA) and at "some disadvantage" (*Whitehill* v *Bradford*, at 246), or oppressed (*Campbell Imrie & Shankland* v *Park* [1954] 2 DLR 170, 176 (BC)), so that she had little choice in the matter. A former employee should also be able to exercise her talents, whether inborn or self-made, to the full (*Stenhouse Australia Ltd* v *Phillips* [1974] AC 391, 400 (PC)); to do so she needed to have freedom of mobility. Enforcing a covenant may have the effect that the worker loses her sole source of income. The employee may have to uproot her family to go beyond the area of restriction, which will be harder than usual to do because she has lost the main source of income, or she may be forced out of the industry. It has been stated in, for instance, *Lindner* v *Murdock's Garage* (1950) 83 CLR 628, 633 (HCA) that the public interest is that the public should have as wide a choice as possible. Such arguments are strengthened in times of labour shortage, where the skill is in short supply, or where the covenant obliges the employee to stay on or give up her skill. The enforcement of the covenant may be such that the ex-employee has difficulty in getting a new job.

American cases explore in more depth than English authorities the relevant authorities. In *Kellogg* v *Larkin* (cited by A M Kales "Contracts to Refrain from doing Business" (1917) 31 Harv LR 193, 194) the court said:

> [t]he capacity of an individual to produce . . . constitutes his value to the public. That branch of industry in which a man has been educated, and to which he is accustomed, and for the abandonment of which he demands compensation, is supposed to be the one in which he can render the greatest profit . . . The actual profit belongs immediately to him who employs him, but mediately to the State and goes to swell the aggregate of public wealth. Therefore the law says to each and every tradesman: You [*sic*] shall not, for a present sum in hand, alien your right to pursue that calling by which you can produce the most. . . .

As the Appellate Court of Illinois said in *Disher* v *Fulgoni*, 464 NE 2d 639 (1984) summarising earlier cases:

Illinois courts have sought to encourage fair competition in the business sector in order to avoid restriction of an employee's freedom to pursue a particular occupation ... Since our free economy is based upon competition, one who has worked in a particular field cannot be compelled to erase from his mind all of the skills, knowledge, acquaintances and overall expertise acquired during his tenure with the former employer ... [W]here an employer seeks to enforce a palpably unfair and unconscionable agreement, there is no entitlement to equitable remedies. ...

Since information flow is necessary for business, confidentiality clauses must be strictly construed. Such interpretation accords also with "every individual's fundamental right to pursue that vocation in which he is most proficient ... ". In that case the agreement was held to be palpably unfair. The employee had liquidated his business interests and moved home to get a job with the employers; the confidentiality clause was said to be non-negotiable; and the clause had no time or space limitation. In *Data Communication Inc* v *Dirmeyer*, 514 F Supp 26 (1981) the District Court for the Eastern District of New York stressed that a total restraint would oblige an employee to leave the business field even though the employers would suffer no harm by his remaining.

Pro-employers

The courts have continued to say that with a correctly drafted covenant employers can protect their trade connections without harming employees who can work elsewhere (for example *Spence* v *Mercantile Bank of India* (1925) 37 TLR 745, 748 (CA)). However, as Goodhart said as early as 1933 in an untitled case comment at 49 LQR 465, 467, such rationale breaks down in an age of high unemployment. The courts have also been ready to uphold a covenant where the ex-employee accepted it "with his eyes open" *per* Luxmoore J in *Spink (Bournemouth) Ltd* v *Spink* [1936] Ch 544, 548). New reasons for upholding covenants have sometimes been adduced. In *Fitch* v *Dewes*, above, Lord Birkenhead C said (at 165): "it is in the public interest that a proper restrictive agreement of this kind between an established solicitor, possibly an elderly man, and a younger man should be allowed. It is in the public interest because otherwise solicitors carrying on their business without a partner would be extremely chary of admitting competent young men to their offices and to the confidential knowledge to be derived by frequenting those offices". To the same effect is *Bridge* v *Deacons* [1984] AC 705 (PC). Courts have been willing to encourage professionalism (*Under Water Welders & Repairers Ltd* v *Street* (1968) 85 RPC 498, 504) and to protect a company's market leadership (*Scorer* v *Seymour Jones* [1966] 1 WLR 1419, 1423). And the granting of remedies may favour employers. In *Curson & Poole (Suing as a Firm)* v *Rash* [1982] EG Dig 404 the judge granted an interlocutory injunction to stop the defendant, an estate agent formerly with the plaintiffs, opening a shop in breach of a covenant. Vinelott J held that the grant would not irreparably harm the defendant and that because he had acted provocatively in setting up his business very close to the plaintiffs' place of business, "it lies ill in [his] mouth to complain that enforcement of the covenant might mortally injure this business" (at 411–2).

Some shift in the attitude of the judges is visible. In *Kerridge* v *Rotorua Theatres Ltd*, above, Callan J could say (at 184) that the common law allows employers "to be harsh and selfish, and contents itself with requiring that they be honest. It is not the business of the courts to import into the common law ethical principles that are not already enshrined there, or to adjudge between conflicting theories of political economy". "The common law has nothing to say" about the imposition of covenants. Sixty years later, partly as a result of legislative and judicial developments in other fields (see the list in *Consumers Distributing Co Ltd* v *Seiko Time Canada Ltd* (1984) 10 DLR (4th) 161, 171 (CSC), a passing-off action) the courts are more sophisticated in their grasp of the public interest in covenant cases despite the occasional *cri de coeur* for other values, such as that of Hughes J in *Nelson Burns & Co Ltd* v *Gratham Industries Ltd* (1983) 150 DLR (3d) 692 (Ont): "the principle of the market place, the laws of supply and demand, freedom of competition and freedom of action generally are always in retreat before measures taken and doctrines developed in the name of social justice".

Lord Diplock put his finger on this development in *Macaulay* v *A Schroeder Publishing Co Ltd*, above, an exclusive service case, when he said that the courts struck down contracts in restraint of trade not because of "some nineteenth century economic theory about the benefit to the general public of freedom of trade" but because the courts wished to protect "those whose bargaining power is weak" (at 1315). One does not need to accept all that Lord Diplock said in *Schroeder* to see that there is some truth in this dictum, especially because freedom to trade is a two-edged sword: an ex-employee has freedom to trade if he or she is not contractually bound; a firm has freedom to trade if one of its potential rivals is restrained by covenant. *Cf. Allied Dunbar (Frank Weisinger) Ltd* v *Weisinger* [1988] IRLR 60, 65.

The clash between the principles which work in favour of employers and those which do not is seen in *Evans Laboratories Inc* v *Melder*, 562 SW 2d 62 (1978). The Supreme Court of Arkansas, In Banc, was faced with a covenant which prohibited ex-employees from "accepting, soliciting, diverting or appropriating or continuing to service" any former customers who had been serviced by the employees during their employment. The majority struck down the covenant. Customers had not defected from the employers because they had been solicited by the ex-employees, but because they were satisfied by the service they had received from them. Fogleman J dissented, rather intemperately: "The court's reluctance to uphold a contract having negative covenants with reference to future employment has led it up a one-way alley from which it cannot see the basic purpose for these covenants and the legitimate right of an employer to protect himself against unfair competition. By doing so, employers are deprived of their right to contract to protect themselves from business piracy". He continued by stating that "the most important of the legitimate interests of the employer which are entitled to protection is the stock of customers he has been able to develop". He stated that the majority did not take into account the personal relationship between the employee and customers. That relationship means that customers may follow the employee to pastures new. The majority's ruling that the customers followed the employee because of their relationship shows the importance of customer connection to the employers. The majority also held that the covenant was an "undue interference with the interests of the public's right to the availability of a serviceman it prefers to use". Fogleman J's response would seem to be that the restraint applied only to a small section of the public, and even those persons would use the competing firm provided they were not solicited. Accordingly, the restraint ought to be upheld. Fogleman J's view commands respect. The employees alone could create the relationship by which clients would return to the employers. If the employers could not protect that interest in recurring business, their assets would be substantially reduced. It does indeed look like business piracy. And, since the employers had no monopoly, the public was not deprived of its right to choose.

Another illustrative case is *Ruhl* v *F A Bartlett Tree Expert Co Inc*, 225 A 2d 288 (1967). The Court of Appeals of Maryland was faced with a covenant which restricted a former area manager of a tree-care business from engaging in a competing business for two years after termination within an area of six counties. Before investigating the time and space limits (which were held to be reasonable), the court ruled that a covenant, to be valid, must cause no injury to society. The tree-care business was highly competitive, and there was no danger of monopoly. Accordingly, the covenant was not injurious to the public interest. The court supported its investigation of the public interest by reference to *Operations Research Inc* v *Davidson*, 217 A 2d 375 (1966):

> There are interests of public policy as well as of private rights to be balanced in the category of cases in which this litigation falls. It is important to our economic system as well as to employers that proprietary interests of businesses be properly protected; it is important to the free competition basic to our national development as well as to the individual rights of employees who want to go into business for themselves that their spirit of enterprise be not unduly hampered.

The manager had received training and experience from his former employers. His personal contact with the customers would be useful to him after he left: indeed, most of his business came from former clients of the employers. Therefore, the covenant was reasonable.

The interests of employees in desiring to work at the usual job when and where they will are weak interests because they are overridden by the legitimate proprietary interests of employers in customer connections and trade secrets, to which I now turn.

Trade Secrets

Even Bowen LJ in *Nordenfelt* (CA), above (at 665) admitted that trade secrets were an exception to the rule that general covenants in restraint of trade were void. He also stated (at 666):

Before the manufacturer or trader sells his trade secret he is the sole possessor of it. If he is to sell it to advantage, he must of necessity be able to undertake not to retain the right to use it or to communicate it to others. A covenant that he will not destroy the value of that which he is handing over causes, in such a case, no discrimination in the supply of commodities to the world, but tends, in nine cases out of ten, to stimulate it. There is no tendency in such a transaction to create a monopoly, for the monopoly existed *ex hypothesi* already. Trade cannot suffer by the substitution of one possessor of a secret for another.

These words, spoken in the context of the sale of a business, can be applied to employment. If employers are to be able to trade, they have to divulge their trade secrets to employees to produce the machinery, etc. The covenant protects such confidential information. As long as the information remains confidential, it can be protected: the period may be for the life of the former employee and the secret may need to be protected by a clause not limited in space.

After *Herbert Morris*, above, the courts have looked for trade secrets before giving protection to the employees. Although the law was taken to be settled, some judges did advance arguments other than those based on precedent, for example the encouragement of business and the promotion of economic activity. The arguments about freedom of contract and freedom of work continue to be put forward (for example *Kores Manufacturing Co Ltd* v *Kolok Manufacturing Co Ltd* [1957] 3 All ER 158, 162), as are the arguments about not throwing a person out of work) for example *Taxation Services of Australia Ltd* v *Townsend* (1936) 37 SRNSW 98, 101) and not restricting ex-employees totally.

While the judges have borne in mind the injunction of Lord Davey in *Janson* v *Driefontein Consolidated Mines Ltd* [1902] AC 484, 500, that "public policy is always an unsafe and treacherous ground for legal decision", the judges outside the area of covenants between employees and employers have stated that, where there is not equal bargaining power, the court has "greater freedom and looks more jealously" (*per* Lord Reid in *Esso Petroleum Co Ltd* v *Harper's Garage (Stourport) Ltd* [1968] AC 269, 300) at the clause than where the bargain is made between equals.

Most judges would probably agree with the speech of Lord Diplock in *Macaulay* v *Schroeder*, quoted above (at 1315–16), which has been approved several times. But not all judges would concur. In *Spencer* v *Marchington* [1988] IRLR 392 the High Court was faced with a covenant which prohibited the employee from being involved with any other employment agency within a radius *inter alia* of 25 miles from Banbury for two years after the end of her covenant. The judge held that the covenant was too wide in point of space in that a 20 mile radius would have been sufficient. The covenant would also prevent customers from outside the area coming to towns within the area which had an employment agency. A non-solicitation clause would have sufficed. The judge, noting that the doctrine of restraint of trade was based on public policy, did not assent to the proposition that its purpose was to protect employees. Instead, he said that the aim was to keep the market open to prospective customers, *in casu* to promote competition and to maximise the potential of employment agencies. Whether this case marks a turning point remains to be seen. Perhaps the judge was influenced by the Thatcherite 1980s.

The possibility of a doctrine of inequality of bargaining power in English law has been doubted recently by several including Lord Scarman speaking for the House of Lords in *National Westminster Bank plc* v *Morgan* [1985] AC 686, 708, a case on undue influence. He criticised the (minority) view of Lord Denning MR in *Lloyds Bank Ltd* v *Bundy* [1975] QB 326, 334 that undue influence was one example of a general doctrine of inequality of bargaining power. Lord Scarman's dictum reads:

> I question whether there is any need in the modern law to erect a general principle of relief against inequality of bargaining power. Parliament has undertaken the task – and it is essentially a legislative task – of erecting such restrictions against the mischief ... I doubt whether the courts should assume the burden of formulating further restrictions.

Parker J in *Panayiotou* v *Sony Music Entertainment (UK) Ltd*, above (at 316–319) was concerned to distinguish the common law restraint of trade doctrine from "the equitable jurisdiction to grant relief ... against unfair and unconscionable bargains". He adjudged Lord Diplock to be referring to the latter with the result that there was no attempt to upset well-established restraint rules. The public policy behind restraint of trade was freedom to trade, whereas the equitable jurisdiction was founded on "the public policy of protecting the weak against being forced by the strong to enter into unconscionable bargains". The two could overlap as where the unconscionable bargain is in the form of a covenant imposed on the plaintiff. In that event the restraint of trade doctrine is to be applied, as occurred in *Macaulay* v *A Schroeder Music Publishing Co Ltd*. However, there is no necessary link between the doctrines.

Summary

Much sense comes from the following passage written by an anonymous hand as long ago as 1928 "Enforceability of covenants not to Compete" (1928) 28 Col LR 81, 85. Courts:

> seem at first to have entirely overlooked the fact that the industrial revolution had, in many instances, so changed the economic structure as to remove the very factor which justified the enforcement of any contract not to compete, regardless of its territorial limitations, namely, the necessity of enforcement to secure for the employee technical training. The growth of large businesses rendered the competition offered by a single skilled employee so negligible a factor that it would hardly affect the giving of employment by the employer. Moreover, due to the increased use of machines for the operation of which no real skill was necessary, employment in many trades gave no technical training at all ... Lastly, the more modern growth

of technical schools makes it no longer necessary in many cases for an apprentice or employee to go to an employer to obtain training ...

Consequently, in modern times there seems to be no valid reason for enforcing generally a contract not to compete after a term of employment ... In modern times the threat of the individual arises only from his knowledge of trade secrets learned during his employment or from his personal hold on customers with whom, but for his employment, he would not have come into contact.

The argument is overdrawn, and there may be exceptional cases, but the contention holds true for the 1990s. Courts must investigate closely the basis on which businesses seek to rely on covenants in restraint of trade. As R D Lewis put it "Contracts in Restraint of Trade" (1967) 21 Ark LR 214, 215, it "seems unfair to compel individuals to a servitude merely because they are too talented or know too much". However, without "protection of trade secrets, businessmen could not afford to stimulate research and improvement of business methods to a desirable level, nor could they achieve the degree of freedom of competition within a company that is necessary for efficient operation". As Parker J noted in *Panayiotou* v *Sony Music Entertainment (UK) Ltd*, above at 320, "the doctrine of restraint of trade is not an absolute doctrine. As public policy has changed and developed over time, so has the doctrine itself and the approach of the court in applying it".

Other Elements in Restraint Cases and US Analyses

Judges may be not conversant with modern economic doctrines and may fail to refer to relevant factors when considering covenants in restraint of trade. To say this is not to criticise judges: they have to work under constraints such as precedent and the narrowness of counsel's arguments. Moreover, they are faced with a doctrine which is said to be both based on policy and has "public policy" as a constituent. For example, the judiciary, in formulating the rules, either expressly or *sub silentio*, regarded covenants as:

perhaps the only effective method of preventing unscrupulous competitors or employees from appropriating valuable trade information and customer relationships for their own benefit. Without the protection afforded by such covenants, it is argued, business men could not afford to stimulate research and improvement of business methods to a desirably high level, nor could they achieve the degree of freedom of communication within a company that is necessary for efficient operation (H M Blake "Employee Agreements not to Compete" (1960) 73 Harv LR 625, 627).

On the other hand, covenants reduce economic mobility and personal freedom: they inhibit the free exchange of ideas and they deter competition in the market: "They unfairly weaken the individual employee's bargaining position *vis-à-vis* his employer and, from the social point of view, clog the market's channelling of manpower to employments in which productivity is greatest'' (*ibid*). And, if the employers really want a certain person, they may waive the clause, so losing express protection, or be obliged to grant concessions on other issues. Such judicial assumptions are based on hypotheses which are rarely founded on empirical evidence.

The quotes above are based on anecdotal evidence, and most judges do not wish to become involved in disputes about political economy. Nevertheless, the doctrine of restraint of trade is ripe for re-analysis in the light of current developments both in market theory and in the literature.

Arguments in Favour of Covenants

In highly competitive industries there may be economic advantages in preventing more rivals entering the field. There is no problem of monopoly, but the addition of another competitor may lead to undercutting, bankruptcies, and so on. Take, for example, the employee, not subject to a covenant, who leaves the employment of a company manufacturing computers. Assuming that he or she is not subject to any implied obligation of fidelity, he or she may use the confidential information acquired during employment either personally or in the employ of others. He or she will have saved costs on research and development, and gained skills and experience (which could be said to have been bought at the expense of a covenant). He or she will have a competitive edge over the ex-employers. If the employers cannot buy off competition the result in market terms is obvious. The firm may suffer serious losses and the success or failure of a product may depend on comparatively small differences in prices. It seems hard if employers are obliged to train competitors. The regulation of trade through the denial of employee mobility is, accordingly, one effect of covenants. A firm may wish to save on research and development costs by hiring employees who possess trade secrets: covenants inhibit this unfair competition.

Use of covenants may also protect new forms of business and production. Results of product testing will be kept within the organisation and not revealed to outsiders; expenditure on advertising will not be wasted; and so new technology will be encouraged through the prevention of loss of time, money and effort. What would be the use of research and development if the results were immediately available to rivals?

Covenants may also help companies to know where they stand. If their trade secrets are protected from disclosure, they can co-operate with others on a sound footing. Employees also know what they can and cannot do. They know where their loyalty to their old firm ends and their loyalty to the new one begins. Moreover, if covenants were not legally enforceable, employers might have to go in for other methods of preventing the loss of confidential information, for example phone-tapping, obliging employees to live within compounds; and such restrictions may not necessarily be as effective as covenants. An enforceable covenant may furthermore lead to employment stability, and so the costs of training will not be so readily lost as in a system which lacked unenforceable covenants. Indeed, the present law may not go far enough in protecting employers' investments in training because the employee is entitled to use the general skills and knowledge acquired during training.

Against Covenants

Covenants sometimes have the effect of reducing employee mobility. He or she cannot go to another firm because of the restriction. Such a restraint affects personal freedoms, such as freedom to associate with whom one wants, and freedom to communicate ideas. If the employee wants the job, he or she must submit to the covenant if bargaining power is unequal; if bargaining power favours the employee, he or she may be able when submitting to gain concessions elsewhere.

> Public policy favouring agent mobility and free competition is evident in the near-unanimous judicial acknowledgement of the covenant's disfavoured status as a restraint of trade. Courts also perceive the covenant as inherently unfair because the principal's bargaining power is usually superior to the agent's ...
>
> The agent, eager for the job opportunity, is not likely to seriously consider the potentially devastating impact of such a covenant on a career (P J Closius and H M Schaffer "Involuntary Nonservitude" (1984) 57 S Cal LR 531, 540–1) (spelling anglicised).

The covenant will have a grave effect on an employee who is specially skilled or experienced. An illustration might be a computer programmer who is obliged to stay with one company throughout his or her inventive period.

The striking down of a covenant may work in favour of competition. "By preventing an ex-employee from working within the industry or using information obtained during employment, the employer may remove a potential competitor from the market, or deprive an existing competitor of a valuable resource" (M B Callahan "Post-Employment Restraint Agreements" (1985) 52 U Chi LR 703, 718–9, footnote omitted). However, economic theory challenges this supposition.

> The employer cannot affect competition unless he has a dominant position in the product market. ... Moreover, even a firm with market dominance cannot use such agreements to increase its market power or to charge a higher price in a given period. Post-employment restraint agreements merely protect valuable information – they do not produce it, or prevent a competitor from producing its equivalent. By lowering the cost of producing information, these agreements would, if anything, decrease the price charged in the product market. An employer with market dominance, however, may be able to use post-employment restraints to prolong that position by reducing the dissemination of knowledge that would allow others to

compete effectively with the employer or by restricting the number of potential competitors ... That a post-employment restraint agreement may preserve an employer's market power by restricting the spread of information does not, however, imply that the agreement is anti-competitive. While competition by way of product imitation and improvement requires the free flow of information, an unlimited flow of information would allow imitators to share in the benefits from information without incurring the costs necessary to produce the information. To the extent that inventors are prevented from reaping the benefits of the information they develop, they are discouraged from engaging in costly research and development, and competition will suffer because few products will be produced (*ibid*, footnote omitted).

Nevertheless, from the viewpoint of the employee, there may be hardship and, although the economic cost to society may be exaggerated according to Blake, above (at 685–6), there may be losses other than economic ones which do affect individuals and therefore society.

The arguments deployed so far would support the application of covenants in restraint of trade in a somewhat different form than the present law. If covenants are an incentive to technological development and are not anti-competitive in effect (though they may be in intention), covenants should always be enforced to protect trade secrets in the absence of any sustainable counter-policy. However, there are counter-balancing arguments to this Chicagoan approach: the United Nations Covenant on Economic, Social and Cultural Rights declares that everyone has the right to earn one's living through freely chosen employment. The ILO's Declaration of Philadelphia speaks of the right to pursue one's own material well-being. Moreover, as Cuvillier wrote "Non-competition and Non-disclosure Obligations" (1977) 115 ILR 193, 209:

> the information and know-how that the enterprise regards as weapons with which to capture new markets are for him part of his professional "capital" and this goes too for his personal and professional relationships and contacts, since at a certain level of responsibility these are also among a good candidate's employment qualifications ... in order to control this asset longer in the former employee's head, it is necessary to exercise a degree of domination over him which amounts to serfdom ... it would be much simpler for enterprises to agree directly among themselves – without involving their employees – to refrain from using the information they wish to protect.

In this situation, the fight is not the employee's, but that of employers.

English courts have, however, eschewed such formulations of policy. The judicial view was epitomised in *Texaco Ltd v Mulberry Filling Station Ltd* [1972] 1 All ER 513, 526, a decision of Ungoed-Thomas J. Having determined that the public policy of freedom to trade was matched against the policy of freedom to contract, he moved on to discuss what was meant by saying that a covenant had to be reasonable in the interests of the public. He held that this aspect of the doctrine of restraint of trade was based on common law, not economics. Therefore, the court could refer only to the interests recognised by law. If the doctrine were to refer to the non-legal interests of the public:

> it might not only involve balancing a mass of conflicting economic, social and other interests which a court of law might be ill-adapted to achieve; but, more important, interests of the public at large would lack sufficiently specific formulation to be capable of judicial as contrasted with unregulated personal decision and application
> . . .

He held that general economic considerations were irrelevant.

Certainly there may be difficulty at first in a judge determining economic questions, but the judiciary have not been afraid of policy arguments in other areas of law such as torts, and in time a body of precedent would build up in the usual manner so that a judge would not always be applying first principles. Economic decisions, moreover, cannot be equated with unregulated personal decisions. Counsel would in the short term have to adapt.

North American Analyses of the Economic Basis of Covenants in Restraint of Trade and other Forms of Protecting Confidential Information

English readers may be unfamiliar with the development of critical appraisals of the law of restrictive covenants both by followers of free market economics (such as L J Harris and I H Kiegel, "Trade Secrets in the Context of Positive Competition" [1967] IDEA 297) and by disciples of the Critical Legal Studies Movement. Here is not the place for an exegesis of either school, but certain of their apercus will be assessed in the relevant contexts. This section opens by examining two articles treating the theory of human capital originated by Becker in *Human Capital: a Theoretical and Empirical Analysis*, 3rd ed (University of Chicago Press, 1993).

The Influence of Gary Becker

Becker's work postulates that a firm has "human capital" in its jobs. That capital is of two types, general and specific. General human capital is that capital of value to many firms, not merely a single firm. An employee will gain this sort of capital by working at any of the firms. He or she will, Becker says, acquire this capital at the expense of accepting a reduction in pay or through paying to accumulate it (for example tuition fees). As a result, there is no need to restrict the free movement of employees so as to create incentives for the training which provides this sort of human capital. Specific human capital is that capital which is of value to only one employer. Since the capital is such, that employer will pay for the employee to acquire it; and the capital will not be used for any other employer. This being so, there is no need to restrict an employee's freedom of movement with regard to human capital. Since human capital includes information which is protectable under a covenant in restraint of trade, Becker's analysis is important.

E W Kitch, "The Law and Economics of Rights in Valuable Information" (1980) 9 JLS 683

Kitch's contention is that there is "a coherent functional framework" (at 683) to the law of trade secrets, covenants in restraint of trade, corporate opportunity, fraud and restitution. He notes that the present Anglo-American law is hostile to covenants in restraint of trade. Yet, there are economic reasons why such clauses are desirable (at 685):

> [i]n the case of general human capital, an employee may be unable to finance training that enhances his capital unless he is able to borrow against the promise of his future services. The employer would loan the employee funds during the training period by paying his wages above his marginal productivity and collect the loan in a later period by paying wages under marginal productivity. But if the employee is free to leave at any time he will be attracted to other employers by wages equal to his marginal productivity during the "pay-back" period, and the employer will have no incentive to make the loan. In the case of specific human capital, training costs will be reduced if the employer can use contractual devices that reduce turnover.

Accordingly, it would seem that for economic reasons courts should uphold covenants.

Why, then, do they not? Kitch relies on Blake's influential article "Employee Agreements not to Compete" (1960) 73 Harv LR 625 to explain the courts' reaction. Blake's answer is to say that, first, employees lack capacity to accept the legal duties in a covenant, and, secondly, covenants in restraint of trade hinder competition. Both responses are based on tradition, though neither completely explains the legal position. The reason of lack of capacity is inconsistent with the courts' approach to covenants dealing with trade secrets and customer connections. This inconsistency cannot be explained by contending that such covenants affect only high-level employees who possess the ability to comprehend their economic effects, because low-level employees are bound where there is reasonable protection of trade secrets and high-level employees are not bound if there is no trade secret. Kitch continues (at 686: footnote omitted, spelling anglicised):

> [t]he view is sometimes expressed that if such clauses were generally permitted they would be routinely exacted from employees. This view assumes either that such clauses are usually in the interest of the employer, or that employees would not value, and hence not charge for, the right to future freedom of choice. Such clauses are not in the interest of the employer unless he makes significant investment in the employee's human capital. If the employee offers general skills that can be provided

by others in the labour market, the employer is indifferent to who provides these skills since he will have to pay the market wage anyway.

The second reason – the promotion of competition – also fails to explain the non-enforcement covenants. The argument confuses spot-markets with competition and errs in considering contracts for an indefinite period with monopoly: "The question is not whether there will be competition for labour and vice versa, but whether that competition will take the form of a spot market for hours of labour ... " (at 688). Furthermore, the assumption that covenants restrain competition is fallacious. If employees of a firm possess skills and information not possessed by others, then if the firm invested to create those aptitudes and knowledge, "the question is not whether there will be competition, but whether such contracts would serve a useful purpose in permitting firms to capture the returns from investments in human capital and, thus, create the appropriate incentives to make such investments" (ibid).

Without covenants against the use or disclosure of information employers may be put to wasteful expenditure, for example through artificial internal barriers in the firm, and they may not invest in new products unless their processes can be protected. If firms cannot control information their profits will disappear and employees will leave the firm to exploit that information.

This lack of incentive to invest in information is compounded by another problem: "Once information is produced it is socially wasteful to create a situation in which other firms have an incentive to produce that information again unless production is cheaper than transmission. But information transactions are difficult" (at 709); for example if one firm sells to another, how can the second firm monitor whether the seller is selling to a third firm? Logically, firms should be preoccupied with secrecy. However, as Kitch points out, that is not the way employers act in the real world. He argues that information is difficult to steal and that no one has an interest in stealing information because: (1) information depreciates quickly; (2) markets for stolen information are difficult to organise; (3) the value of the information self-destructs through there being two firms in possession of the process after the theft, with the result that its value decreases; and (4) some information is protected by the law of intellectual property.

Kitch concludes (at 723) by saying that human capital creates inappropriate incentives to use restrictive covenants, the effect of which on the market is an external cost not borne by the contracting parties. The courts then step in to limit those costs external to the transaction by policing the permissible scope of the transaction. Thus, Kitch argues that Becker's theory of human capital is an exploratory framework for covenants in restraint of trade.

P H Rubin and P Shedd, "Human Capital and Covenants not to Compete" (1981) 10 JLS 93

This article opens by stating that the courts' attitude to covenants in restraint of trade was shaped by their attitude to monopoly. Rubin and Shedd argue, however, that such covenants in fact serve other purposes and are at times necessary in order to lead to the efficient amount of investment in human capital. Covenants, they say, enable the parties to contract on a long-term basis and they give the example of a basket-weaver to explain this phenomenon (at 95): if the employee has signed an enforceable agreement promising not to engage in basket-weaving for five years after leaving the employment of Firm A, the employee has effectively agreed to work for Firm A or cease weaving baskets for five years. If he is more valuable as a basket-weaver than in any other trade, he will continue to work for Firm A. In this way, covenants contribute a method of enabling employers and employees to continue a contractual relationship.

Becker's analysis, however, undermines such reasons for the enforceability of covenants in restraint of trade. If the training is one which provides specific human capital, the employee will have to continue working for the employers because he or she cannot sell his or her skill in any other market, and so a covenant is unnecessary. If, however, general human capital is provided, the employee will realise that he or she can recoup the loss from paying for training by going to work for other employers: a long-term covenant has no value to either the employee or the employers.

Yet covenants are routinely exacted from employees in the real world – why? Rubin and Shedd argue that Becker's theory is defective. Contrary to Becker, they argue (at 96–7):

> there are some types of general training for which the worker will not pay. Assume, for example, that it takes a firm one day to teach a worker the details of a trade secret valuable to many other firms and worth 100,000 dollars. The value of the information is so great that the worker cannot pay for it by accepting reduced wages. In this circumstance, the firm would want the worker to sign a non-competition clause, for such a clause would indicate that the worker could not use the training acquired elsewhere.

However, as soon as the employee has acquired the general human capital:

> [t]he worker has an incentive to violate the contract and profit from his training – either by going to work for himself or by going to work for another firm, which will pay him a premium because of the value of his training. In that situation, the worker is attempting to appropriate for himself the value of training for which he did not pay. If workers were able to do this, the incentive for firms to invest in acquiring valuable information would be greatly reduced, for firms would not be able to protect valuable information (at 97).

Furthermore, economic inefficiency would be increased because, if trade secrets could not be protected by covenants, employers would have to seek other, more costly, methods. Therefore, at least some covenants should be enforced, the aim being to reduce the incentive to employees to behave opportunistically by seizing the value of the information for themselves.

Contrariwise:

> [t]he employer may have an incentive to behave opportunistically and underpay the
> worker relative to the value of that part of the general training financed by the
> worker if the employer believes that the covenant will reduce the worker's mobility.
> It would therefore be inefficient to enforce all restrictive covenants, just as it would
> be inefficient to enforce none of them. In such circumstances, the courts, in
> enforcing covenants not to compete, may serve a useful function (at 98).

The courts' purpose is, in the area of covenants in restraint of trade, to stop
employers and employees behaving opportunistically, and they can do this by
enforcing only those covenants which protect trade secrets: only such covenants
relate to specific human capital.

Accordingly, in Rubin and Shedd's view, covenants in restraint of trade are
necessary because they lead to an efficient level of investment in training when an
employee cannot pay for the human capital by accepting a reduced salary. Does
the legal approach to covenants reflect economic doctrine?

Standard legal terminology is inconsistent with economic analysis. It speaks of
the enforcement of covenants when they are not "unduly harsh" and so on, a
consideration which is irrelevant to the economic theory of contracts. That theory
states in this context that if employers include covenants, they reduce the supply
of potential employees and so pay more to those who do work for them.
Employers, therefore, will not use covenants unless the gain is greater than the
cost in higher wages. The rationale of unequal bargaining power accordingly
does not fit in with economic analysis.

Rubin and Shedd, however, go on to say that the failure by the courts to use
economic terminology is not *per se* inconsistent with the hidden use of economic
logic (at 102) and courts can reach conclusions which are economically desirable
without knowledge of economics. At present, Rubin and Shedd say, protection is
afforded to customer lists and trade secrets. If a list is not protected, employers
will not devote sufficient resources to compiling it. Therefore, the rule which
protects lists is economically efficient. Similarly with regard to trade secrets.

Rubin and Shedd, therefore, contend that Becker's analysis is incomplete.
There are, they say, two types of general human capital:

> In some cases, the value of general training is sufficiently high so that the trainee is
> unable to pay for such training, especially by accepting reduced wages during the
> training period. When this is the case, a firm will commonly have the employee sign
> an agreement not to use this training in a competing business. If it were not for the
> possibility of signing such agreements, firms would find their incentives for invest-
> ment in valuable information reduced. However, with such constraints, there are
> incentives for both parties to the agreement to behave opportunistically. Employees
> have an incentive to violate the agreement by using the information in competing
> business: firms have an incentive to underpay employees who have acquired in-
> formation for which the employers have themselves obtained, by claiming that all

information is covered by the covenant. The courts have been successful in determining which types of contracts should be enforced (at 109–110).

Rubin and Shedd, therefore, conclude that the courts have acted in the correct
manner when determining which covenants should be enforced. They add that
their article shows that an economic analysis is useful in understanding the law.

Rubin and Shedd's article has been cited in cases. In *American Hardware Mutual
Insurance Co* v *Moran*, 705 F 2d 219 (1983) the Court of Appeals for the Seventh
Circuit applied Illinois law to hold that the former employers had no legitimate
interest in recouping the money it spent on the defendant's training. Cummings
Ch J said that the plaintiffs could recoup their expenditure by paying a lesser
salary or by requiring their employees to pay for their training – if it did not
already do so. There was no secret in the skills.

First, American claims that it expended considerable resources training Moran
when it first hired him and that it has a legitimate interest in recouping those
resources. American argues that the only way it can do this is to prevent Moran from
taking some of its customers with him upon his leaving its employ. We doubt that this
is so. American could probably recoup whatever it spends to train its salesmen – if it
does not already do so – simply by paying them a lower base salary or rate of
commission or by requiring that they pay out of pocket for the cost of their training.
It appears that there is nothing secret about the skills American teaches its novice
salesmen. That salesmen do not covenant not to compete with American until after
all of their classroom training is complete is some indication of this. The skills taught
are commonly possessed by experienced salesmen throughout the industry so that
there is no reason to suppose that employees could not afford to pay for their
training out of the income they earn while employed by American. See P Rubin & P
Shedd, "Human Capital and Covenants Not to Compete," 10 J Legal Stud 93
(1981). But American might not want to recoup its investment in its employees by
paying them a lower salary or a lower rate of commission. Salesmen might prefer
foregoing the chance to do business with American's insureds on their own or for
another Insurer sometime in the future rather than receiving a lower salary or
commission, perhaps because a dollar in the hand is worth more to them than the
chance to earn more than a dollar sometime in the future. And American might
prefer to pay its salesmen higher salaries and commission rates than to run the risk
of losing business when salesmen quit ... Thus American might be paying its
salesmen more if it can prevent them from competing for its customers.

This suggests that American's professed interest in recouping its training costs
derives from its interest in hiring good salesmen. The amount of goodwill between
purchasers and salesmen, or the cost of training salesmen, might be less in other
markets than in the market for package insurance plans. If no-compete covenants by
American's employees are not enforced, American might be forced to pay its
salesmen less than other firms pay their salesmen. If so, the quality of salesmen
American is able to hire might decrease.

It would seem to follow that a firm should be free to compete with other firms for
good employees by preventing its former employees from competing with it,
provided that the firm, as here, is not a monopolist in the market in which the
employee is prohibited from competing. Only when a firm enjoys monopoly power

is there any danger that enforcing an employee's covenant not to compete will injure the public by requiring it to pay more for the firm's product. The market in northern Illinois for package insurance plans for automobile, truck and motorcycle dealers is apparently very competitive – in fact, American's market share appears to be dwindling, so that there is probably no danger that enforcing Moran's covenant will have any effect upon the market price of the package insurance plans American sells. Thus, one might suppose that American should not be required to pay Moran more than it agreed to when it hired him, that is, it should not be required to pay him the value in insurance premiums of the goodwill he built up with his customers while employed by American.

Unfortunately, Illinois law requires otherwise. A firm's interest in attracting well-qualified employees is not a "legitimate business interest" entitled to protection under Illinois law.

In *Reddy v Community Health Foundation of Man*, 298 SE 2d 906 (1982) Neely J in the Supreme Court of Appeals of West Virginia also referred to Rubin and Shedd. He analysed their article as being based on whether the employee has paid for the asset he or she seeks to use in a competitive market. Trade secrets are unlikely to have been paid for by the employees. Therefore, courts protect them. With regard to customer lists, the position depends on the relationship between the employers and employee, while courts are reluctant to enjoin valuable skills the employee has learned on the job. Neely J, however, cited Becker's book to say that economic analysis stipulates that covenants preventing the use of skills should be expressed as a matter of efficient investment in human capital, whereas legal analysis, for example *Club Aluminium Co v Young*, 160 NE 804 (Mass 1928) held that restraint clauses will not be enforced to prevent the employee using skills acquired through instruction in employment. Neely J cited a Louisiana case where under statute the court held that training expense could validate a covenant.

> Once the worker has received this training an incentive for opportunist behaviour is created. The worker has an incentive to violate the contract and profit from his training ... An enforceable restrictive covenant ... would protect the employer against the employee's violating his contract, and would augment the incentive to train workers ...

Neely J continued: "the covenant not to compete provides a mechanism consistent with the economic rationale of contract law". But, as the judge immediately noted, at some point the employer will have recouped the investment through payment of reduced wages to trainees but the covenant may remain effective. He then discussed whether partial enforcement resolves the situation. One effect of Rubin and Shedd's analysis is that hardship to the employee, previously part of the legal approach to covenants, is irrelevant. If the covenant "operates purposely as a hardship in order to encourage the employee to remain with his employer until his investment is recouped, a court should review the extent of the covenant limitations only with the greatest reluctance ... ".

A Criticism of Micro-economics from the Viewpoint of Covenants in Restraint of Trade: S D Shadowen and K Voytek's "Economic and Critical Analyses of the Law of Covenants not to Compete" (1984) 72 Georgetown LJ 1425

Chicagoan free market economics have had an effect on the thinking of the UK Government. In the United States the influence of micro-economics has been significant (Richard Posner is a California judge), and it looked at one time as if academic lawyers had to write something on its application to law for professional advancement. In recent years, however, criticisms of micro-economic theory have been voiced especially by followers of the Critical Legal Studies Movement – they decry the appellation of "School". They say, *inter alia*, that micro-economic theory fails to deal with the problems raised by the non-existence or malfunctioning of markets, by the inefficient provision or non-provision of services, for example national defence and pollution control, if left to market forces, by externalities (that is where the customer's choice is affected by non-market factors). A law based solely on micro-economics does not take notions of fairness (or indeed the distribution of wealth or process values) into account and so does not produce a "socially optimal result" (A M Polinsky, "Economic Analysis as a Potentially Defective Product" (1973–4) 87 Harv LR 1655, 1681, though there is surely some truth in Coase's view that legal intervention is expensive: "Problem of Social Cost" (1963) 3 JL & E 1.

Shadowen and Voytek, noting that adherents to the micro-economic cause believe that their theory provides definitive answers to legal problems, commenced their analysis by drawing attention to the defects of micro-economics as applied to law: it fails to consider the just allocation of resources, the present inequalities of resources, and the ongoing nature of social relations. They contended that contrary to the adherents' view micro-economics does incorporate values, one of which is "faith in competitive markets" as W Gramm wrote in *The Chicago School of Political Economy* (ed W J Samuels, Association of Evolutionary Economics, 1976 (2nd ed, 1992) 176, 178. Contrary to the view of Rubin and Shedd, outlined above, they contended that there is a lack of fit between micro-economic theory and legal decisions in the area of covenants in restraint of trade. They said that the analysis of Rubin and Shedd is defective because it does not deal with the remedies for breach, above (at 1430). As they put it (*ibid*, footnote omitted),

> Rubin's and Shedd's analysis assumes that the promisee has paid for something of value and that economic inefficiency results when the promisor can appropriate it without paying full value. Rubin and Shedd contend that courts enforce the covenants only if, and to the extent that, the promise has paid for something of value. Therefore, the substantive doctrine regarding covenants not to compete promotes economic efficiency. Even if one accepts Rubin's and Shedd's argument, no conclusion regarding the overall efficiency of enforcement of restrictive covenants can be drawn until the remedies available for breach are analysed. That is, if the only remedy for breach of a covenant not to compete is one dollar, one cannot say that courts efficiently enforce restrictive covenants.

Shadowen and Voytek's argument is based on there being no market price for the measurement of the employers' damage when an employee has broken a covenant in restraint of trade. The gain to the employee is not a good measure because the employers may be undercompensated or overcompensated. The decrease in the employers' profits is not an appropriate measure because of the difficulty of attributing that loss to the employee's behaviour. Because of the problems in assessing damages, an injunction is to be preferred (at 1434). It is more efficient that a monetary award. Therefore, injunctions should be used to prohibit the continuing breach of a covenant in restraint of trade.

What, however, of the period after the expiry of the contractual term? An injunction for this period, equal to the length of the breach, Shadowen and Voytek call a "compensatory injunction". Their argument is complex and may best be taken in stages.

(1) (a) If demand for the product or service is greater during the period when the employee was in breach than during the period of the compensatory injunction, that injunction will undercompensate the employers because they will receive less than the value of the non-competition for which they bargained.

     (b) If demand is greater in the compensatory period than at the time of the breach, the employers will be overcompensated.

(2) Because the result of a "compensatory injunction" is dependent on the state of the market, such injunction is no more efficient than an award of damages.

(3) However, that conclusion will not stand because the potentiality of the award of the injunction may affect the employee's decision on whether or not to breach the covenant.

(4) Shadowen and Voytek argue (at 1435):

> [a]reasonable promisor faced only with the possibility of having to pay money damages for the period of the breach will breach whenever she believes that the profit she can earn by competing is greater than the profit the plaintiff can *prove* that he lost due to the competition. The unavailability of a compensatory injunction therefore is likely to lead to economic inefficiency because the probability of an under-compensatory money judgment encourages the defendant to gamble on whether a court will award an under-compensatory money judgment rather than on whether demand for the good [*sic*] or service will rise over time.

If, however, a compensatory injunction were to be awarded, the employee will breach the covenant only if the demand is less during the period of the injunction than in the period of the envisaged breach. The employee will therefore base the decision on the market and not on the possibility of the court's failure to compensate the employers adequately. This outcome is economically efficient.

(5)   The authors then compare the giving of a compensatory injunction in four
      possible scenarios, relating to an award of damages, where the employee
      believes the demand will fall or rise and where the damages either under- or
      overcompensate the employers. They conclude (at 1439) that a compensa-
      tory injunction will increase the number of logically possible efficient
      results. They add (*ibid*):

> in the absence of evidence to the contrary, it is reasonable to assume that a
> compensatory injunction rule also will increase the number of actual occasions
> on which the court will effect an efficient outcome. This increased efficiency is
> achieved by shifting the focus of the defendant's decision on whether to breach
> from speculation about the size of potential damages to interpretation of market
> factors, thus reducing both the frequency of breach and the likelihood of under-
> compensation.

Accordingly, the compensatory injunction is more efficient than damages.
Here comes the problem for micro-economics. Courts have not awarded compensatory injunctions. Injunctions are not granted for more than the contractual
term. Courts have emphasised that covenants in restraint of trade impede
employees' freedom to find work and constitute an onerous burden on them.
This discontinuity between judicial attitudes and micro-economic theorising,
Shadowen and Voytek say, comes about through the failure of micro-economics
to take account of the concern of the courts for parties who are coerced. "The
proponents of microeconomics espouse the theory that neither party would
assent to a contract unless it were to her benefit to do so; thus, relative economic
status is not a valid consideration in deciding whether contracts should be
enforced" (at 1442). The courts' benevolence to employees leads them to reach
results contrary to those dictated by micro-economic theory. Moreover, the courts
look at the interests of the public and not just those of the parties, again in breach
of a tenet of micro-economics. As Shadowen and Voytek cogently put it (at 1443,
footnotes omitted):

> Microeconomic analysis typically falls solely on the economic effect on the parties to
> the contract. For the microeconomic theorist the individual bargain is the building
> block for the whole economic system and the market is a mere aggregation of
> individual contracts. The microeconomic theorist leaves unstated that the analytic
> viability of microeconomics requires the existence of an established economic
> system in which individual bargains are mere incremental changes in a preexisting
> order.

To sum up, the courts take into account the social need for competition in the
market. The result is contrary to micro-economics which is concerned with the
economic consequences to individuals. The courts therefore look at the effect of
covenants on society and at the relative bargaining powers of the employers and
employees. They do not in this area enforce freedom of contract, preferring

instead to promote commerce. Micro-economics does not adequately account for the law. Since it cannot describe the law, it certainly cannot prescribe it.

The Replacement of Micro-economics by Critical Analysis

If micro-economic theory is defective, what can replace it? Shadowen and Voytek argued that critical analysis correctly describes the present law. This is not the place to examine the general approach of the Critical Legal Studies Movement with its methodology of critical analysis. Two critiques of contract law by followers of Critical Legal Studies do seem applicable to covenants in restraint of trade. Feinman, "Critical Approaches to Contract Law" (1983) 30 UCLALR 829 held that contract law has two aspects which he called "individualist" and "collectivist". The individualist approach is reflected in the doctrine of freedom of contract. The enforcement of covenants is a facet of the individualistic concept, which pays no attention to the power of the parties. The "collectivist" viewpoint opines that persons are social beings, with behaviour that is not solely selfish, and that unregulated choice does not maximise the functioning of the market in an advanced society (for example individual contracts may impede commerce). This collectivist attitude allows the courts not to enforce covenants where they deprive an employee of income or where they adversely affect the market.

Unger, "The Critical Legal Studies Movement" (1983) 95 Harv LR 653 adopted a similar approach. The market's function is inappropriate where there is inequality of resources. If the courts did, however, intervene to correct such inequality, the market theory would break down. Unger suggested that what the courts then do is to deal only with the most serious problems or they hide behind "vague slogans" (at 626) which enable them to strike down bargains on an *ad hoc* basis. No doubt the law on covenants in restraint of trade is a reflection through a glass darkly of these ideas.

In the context of covenants it would seem from looking at judicial policies as expressed in judgments that the judiciary do not adopt the law-and-economics theory explicitly and this ideology can be explained in terms other than those of micro-economics. The judges do refer to normative matters such as freedom of contract and the protection of the party who is the weaker in a bargain, and their outlook does seem to be based on their perceptions of the demands of the times widely stated, rather than on non-normative assumptions as to the economic restrictions on human appetites.

The intervention of the judiciary in restraint of trade covenants even in times of *laissez-faire* is difficult to reconcile both with freedom of contract as private ordering and with economic freedom. Unlike full-blooded contractarian theory, judicial interventionism did, perhaps haphazardly, embody values which took into account the economic patterns of society, though the judges did not expressly declare those values in the era of classical contract. The law was never totally based on individualism: see J N Adams and R Brownsword, "The Ideologies of Contracts" (1987) 7 LS 205 and their later work. If modern contract law is based on nineteenth century precedents and values, one would expect micro-economics to predict correctly the form of the law: both are informed by the same thinking about *laissez-faire* and the ability of the market to value an efficient result.

I suggest, therefore, that the position presently adopted by the judiciary does not totally reflect either the Chicago approach or the doctrines of the Critical Legal Studies Movement.

Criticism by M J Trebilcock

In his book, *The Common Law of Restraint of Trade*, (Carswell, 1986), Professor Trebilcock asked: "Is the common law of restraint of trade efficient?" There are several variants of the school which contends that the common law is economic-ally efficient. One variant centres on that of Richard Posner, who in his book *Economic Analysis of Law*, 4th ed (Little, Brown, 1992) contended that since judges do not have constituencies to pacify, they are free to adopt rules which conform to the public interest; in comparison, legislators have to bend to political interests and so do not always enact laws which promote economic matters. Another variant is based on the perception that cases laying down inefficient rules will be appealed more than cases establishing efficient ones, and so the law will tend towards efficiency see, for example, P J Rubin, "Why is the Common Law Efficient?" (1977) 6 JL & S 51: Both variants purport to describe the law, and not prescribe how judges should act.

The Posner view is open to criticism, as Trebilcock puts it (at 392):

> even though judges do not face the same incentives in their lawmaking as politicians, it is not clear why, *a priori*, they would be any more minded to adopt efficiency-determined conceptions of the social welfare rather than, for example, particular notions of distributive justice as among sub-groups of the community or narrower notions of corrective or commutative justice or between the actual parties in conflict in the litigation before the court, or any of a number of other possible objectives.

Trebilcock wrote (at 55): " ... the doctrine has never reflected a coherent *economic* theory of when restraints are or are not justifiable" (emphasis in original). Moreover, it is not true to say that legislators always promote sectional interests.

The other approach is liable to criticism because there may be litigation to get rid of the inefficient rule. The incentive to litigate may be small in comparison with the cost, and appealing is even more costly than litigating.

How does the view of those adopting the position that the common law is efficient match up to covenants in restraint of trade? It would seem that this area of law is an ideal test-ground for the thesis – the law has been in place for five centuries and the judges have recognised that the rules have a connection with economic objectives. Accordingly, if the theory were correct, the law would have worked itself pure. This, indeed, is the claim of Rubin and Shedd, above.

If, however, one looks at the stages in the development of the law, one can distinguish three periods. First, in the era of the guilds, there was no notion of competitive markets and mobility was not encouraged. Secondly, in the *laissez-faire* era, the judges emphasised freedom of contract, a concept which did not always promote freedom of competition. Thirdly, nowadays, the courts have become concerned with inequality of bargaining power but have not enunciated a coherent doctrine and so have invalidated efficient restraints. Trebilcock's contention (at 395) is that the courts find difficulty identifying and applying efficient rules. Accordingly it cannot be said that the common law of restraint of trade exhibits efficiency: at best there is a tendency over the centuries towards the economists' ideals.

Some of Trebilcock's critique relates to cartels and vertical restraint cases, but one can tease out points which apply to employment:

1. The public has no cause of action to upset covenants, even though the covenant may affect public welfare.
2. The parties may both have economists supporting their viewpoints, and the court, being ill-equipped to choose, may decide to reject the economic evidence. See, for example Ungoed-Thomas J in *Texaco Ltd* v *Mulberry Filling Station Ltd*, above. However, where the courts have taken public policy into account, they have emphasised that economic conditions alter. Even when the courts do investigate economic matters, they find difficulty in identifying relevant material. In Trebilcock's view (at 401):

   > the substantial consensus that exists at any point in time in the economics profession on matters of microeconomic analysis will be systematically obscured from the courts by the nature of the adversary process and their lack of specialised capacity to impose a discerning discipline on what economic viewpoints will be treated seriously . . . .

3. Two-party litigation is unlikely to lead to evidence being led as to long-term economic impact. Evidence will be *ad hoc*, and not general. In Trebilcock's words (at 403): "the inability of courts to evaluate accurately the impacts of contracts or other institutional arrangements on non-participating third parties renders it less likely that their decisions will satisfy any general economic welfare criterion".
4. The courts see themselves as involved with distributive justice between the parties and not with longer-term economic impact, for example they look at the effect on this doctor, and not on the provision of health care.
5. The remedy may be inefficient, for example it may not strike down covenants for the future. Take the invalidation of covenants affecting a doctor. The effect may be that the medical practice does not take on young doctors. Restraint of trade powers do not permit the courts to order the practice to take on the young doctor or to subsidise the practice for doing so.
6. The ritualistic adherence to the need for reasonableness between the parties and in the public interest does not help judges to decide cases.

From these reasons Trebilcock concluded that the restraint of trade doctrine does not lead to economic efficiency.

Trebilcock's approach is useful. It is almost axiomatic to say that in the employment situation once the covenant has been held to be reasonable between the parties, it is most unlikely that it was unreasonable in the public interest. The value of competition in promoting efficiency was not considered when the common law rules were being created. Statute has not intervened so no official, such as the Director-General of Fair Trading, has responsibility as he has in the restrictive trade practices legislation to safeguard the interests of the public. Many employment clauses are hidden away and enforcement would be difficult, but, perhaps to a lesser extent, the same can be said about trade practices which constrain competition. If vendor covenants fall within the scope of the statute as being between two companies carrying on business, there is room for an official similar to that of the Director-General of Fair Trading in employment law.

Even within the common law, we may be seeing a shift in attitudes. As stated above, in employment cases judges have normally focused on the issue of reasonableness between the parties and disregarded the public interest. The public interest notion has, however, always been available to act as an extra hoop through which, as it were, covenants must jump. It has never been abrogated. The Privy Council case of *Bridge* v *Deacons* [1984] AC 705 is a straw in the wind as to how the law might develop. The case was a partnership one but that fact was not relevant to the point at issue. A partner in a firm of solicitors in Hong Kong covenanted that he would not work as a solicitor for any of the firm's clients for five years after termination of the partnership. The Judicial Committee said that the clause was reasonable between partners. It did, however, go on to hold that the stipulation was reasonable in the public interest. The covenant encouraged firms of solicitors to take on quite young people as partners, and clients gained a benefit through continuity of service. The case is not, perhaps, a strong one. It is not one where the clause was reasonable between the parties, but unreasonable from the public's viewpoint. The case is one involving lawyers, and different principles sometimes inhabit that sphere, for example the American Bar Association prohibits covenants between attorneys (see also legal professional privilege and immunity from suit). Nevertheless, *Bridge* v *Deacons* could be used in the future to strike down covenants which are against the public interest.

Colophon

It is no doubt apparent to the reader at this point that we have not cleared up the swampy morass of conflicting interests and policies into which a court may eventually need to plunge to resolve the problems these covenants present. *Per* Neely J in *Reddy* v *Community Health Foundation of Man*, above.

Until *Faccenda Chicken Ltd* v *Fowler* [1987] Ch 117 it might have been said the law of restraint of trade was easy to state, hard to apply. The distinction in that case, however, between trade secrets and other confidential information – the former being protectable, the latter not – by the action for breach of confidence, in the vernacular threw a spanner in the works. It was thought that the decision affected covenants in restraint of trade. However, the Court of Appeal in *Lansing Linde Ltd v Kerr* [1991] 1 WLR 251 reaffirmed that covenants protect any confidential information which, if disclosed, would cause real (or significant) harm to the employers. Since such information would cover non-technical trade secrets such as customer lists, the court seems to have reasserted *status quo ante Faccenda*.

The next part of this book considers implied duties including confidentiality.

Part 2

THE IMPLIED DUTIES OF FIDELITY
AND CONFIDENTIALITY

Contents of Chapter Ten

IMPLIED OBLIGATIONS DURING EMPLOYMENT

Chapter Ten

IMPLIED OBLIGATIONS DURING EMPLOYMENT

The courts have distinguished between situations where a person is an employee and where she is not. The implied duty of fidelity terminates when the contract does; the duty not to use or disclose trade secrets or similar confidential information continues after employment ceases. This duty of confidentiality remains but with diminished width. The effect is that subject to an express restraint of trade covenant and the implied obligation of confidentiality the ex-employee is free to compete once the contract of employment has been determined. Employers are, therefore, well-advised to take covenants if they wish to avoid competition from their former employees. As Hawkins J put it at first instance in *Robb* v *Green* [1895] 2 QB 1, 14, "the dividing line between owing his master a duty and owing him none is that imperceptible period of time between the termination of his service and the moment he acquires freedom of action after his service has terminated". In *Stenhouse Australia Ltd* v *Phillips* [1974] AC 391, 400, Lord Wilberforce advised that an employee can build up his expertise during employment and must "develop and improve his employer's business for the benefit of his employer", but afterwards, while the employee is free to use his expertise, he must not take with him "some advantage or asset inherent in the business which can properly be regarded as, in a general sense, [the employer's] property, and which it would be unjust to allow the employee to appropriate for his own purposes, even though he, the employee, may have contributed to its creation". Simon Brown LJ summarised the law in *J A Mont (UK) Ltd* v *Mills* [1993] IRLR 172, 177: "Once the employment relationship ceases there is no occasion for loyalty. All that is left is a residual duty of confidentiality in respect of the employer's trade secrets".

The termination of an employee's duty of faithful service on completion of the contract of employment should be contrasted with fiduciary duties, which extend beyond removal or resignation from office. For example, in *Island Exports Finance Ltd* v *Umunna* [1986] BCLC 460 Hutchison J said (at 481) that immediately on termination of office an agent or trustee is not completely unfettered in the use of information acquired when in office. If the director is also an employee, she is subject both to the duty of fidelity as an ordinary employee is and thus is subject to the duty to preserve confidentiality and to fiduciary obligations. In Canada fiduciary duties affecting directors have been extended to senior employees. The principal authority is *Canadian Aero Service Ltd* v *O'Malley* (1973) 40 DLR (3d) 371 (CSC), a case often called "*Canaero*". Attempts have been made to apply that doctrine to English employees but as yet without success. Hutchison J in *Island Export* stated (at 483) that *Canaero* "is not supported by authority, conflicts with the rules of public policy as to restraint of trade, and does not represent English law" insofar as it laid down the proposition that a director or senior employee was liable simply through becoming acquainted with a possible corporate opportunity, *in casu* the existence of a market for postal caller boxes in the Cameroons. The doctrine was also rejected by Falconer J in *Flexiveyor Products Ltd* v *Owens*, 4 May 1982, LEXIS, partly because the rule would lead to a managing director after termination owing for all time a duty not to solicit clients. No express restraint would stretch that far. In other words an express clause would have been struck down as being in unreasonable restraint of trade.

During employment any express non-competition clause is supplemented by the implied term of faithful service or fidelity. This implied term is best seen as an incident of employment or, differently put, as a term implied in law in all contracts of employment: see *Robb* v *Green* [1895] 2 QB 315 (CA), and *Faccenda Chicken Ltd* v *Fowler* [1987] Ch 117, 135 (CA), where Neill LJ *per curiam* stated "[w]hile the employee remains in the employment of the employer the obligations [of confidentiality] are included in the implied term which imposes a duty of good faith or fidelity on the employee". Neill LJ in this passage equates "good faith" and "fidelity", as Whitford J did in *Electrolux Ltd* v *Hudson* [1977] FSR 312, 326, a patents case. The present author uses the terms "faithful service" and "fidelity" interchangeably. Whether this implied term restricts an employee is dependent on the facts. Among matters which may be considered is the status of the employee in the hierarchy.

It has been said that the duty of fidelity is "rather vague" (*per* Lord Greene M R in *Hivac Ltd* v *Park Royal Scientific Instruments Ltd* [1946] Ch 169, 174). The uncertainty in its ambit may be reduced by envisaging it as consisting of several sub-duties.

Confidential Information

Perhaps the most important aspect of the duty of fidelity for the purposes of this book is the implied obligation not to use or disclose the employers' trade secrets or other information of a similar nature. As with the law concerning permissible and impermissible preparations for competition discussed below there is no bright line separating information which is confidential before the termination of employment and information which is not. This section summarises the principal issues. They are treated in more depth below.

In *Universal Thermosensors Ltd* v *Hibben* [1992] 1 WLR 840 (Ch D) the employees were not entitled to steal their employers' documents which contained confidential information or to copy it out. Nicholls V-C said (at 855) that: "by misappropriating and misusing confidential information, the defendants sought to save themselves the trouble and expense of making a tedious trawl through directories". He awarded damages. There are several similar cases such as *Louis* v *Smellie* (1895) 73 LT 226 (CA). The most famous is *Robb* v *Green* (CA), above. The defendant in breach of the implied term copied a list of clients of pheasant buyers manually. The prohibition extends to photocopying.

In *Roger Bullivant Ltd* v *Ellis* [1987] ICR 464 (CA) the first defendant resigned as managing director of the second plaintiffs, taking with him a card index of the names and addresses of the plaintiffs' clients. He established a competing business. On the facts there existed strong evidence that he had used the index to contact those clients in order to provide the same services as the plaintiffs, who were specialist engineers. The trial judge granted an interlocutory injunction to prevent the employee from using or disclosing the plaintiffs' trade secrets. Applying *Faccenda Chicken Ltd* v *Fowler*, above, Nourse LJ said (at 473) that trade secrets or their equivalent "may not in any circumstances be used by the employee, either during or after the employment, except for the benefit of the employer", in respect of information not of this class, it "must nevertheless be treated as confidential by the employee in the discharge of his general implied duty of good faith to his employer. Such information may not be used by the employee during the employment except for the benefit of the employer but if and only to the extent that it is inevitably carried away in the employee's head after the employment has ended, it may then be freely used for the benefit either of himself or of others". The information in the card index fell within the second category. Nourse LJ stated (at 474): "if it is a breach of the duty of good faith for the employee to make or copy a list of the employer's customers, the removal of a card index is an *a fortiori* case". He emphasised that "it is of the highest importance that the principle of *Robb* v *Green*, which . . . is one of no more than fair and honourable dealing, should be steadfastly maintained". May LJ concurred. For a case applying *Roger Bullivant* see *Mainmet Holdings plc* v *Austin* [1991] FSR 538 (QBD). For a Scottish case applying *Faccenda* see *Harben Pumps (Scotland) Ltd* v *Lafferty*, 1989 SLT 752 (Outer House).

The prohibition extends to the deliberate memorisation of information. This issue is discussed in the section on the memory rule in Chapter 11 on the confidentiality of the information in the action for breach of confidence.

An employee does not breach this sub-duty if she does not memorise the information but recalls it. In *Coral Index Ltd* v *Regent Index Ltd* [1970] RPC 147 (Ch D) Stamp J said (at 149) on motions for interlocutory injunctions that, through his employment as office manager for five years with the plaintiffs, a company which accepted bets on the movement of the *Financial Times* index, the second defendant could not fail to remember a considerable number of names and perhaps addresses of the plaintiffs' customers. He remembered without making any conscious effort to memorise a list when he joined a rival firm. The judge

refused, for the purposes of the motions, to infer that the defendant made off
with a list or consciously memorised customers' names.

Where the information has become part of the employee's skill and knowledge,
she is not in breach of the duty of faithful service if she uses or discloses it. The
rule was applied by Nicholls V-C in *Universal Thermosensors*, above (at 850), in this
way. The relevant employees "were entitled to use for their own purposes any
information they carried in their heads regarding the identity of the plaintiff's
customers, or customer contacts, or the nature of the customers' product requirements, or the plaintiff's pricing policies, provided that they had acquired that
information honestly in the course of their employment, and had not, for
instance, deliberately sought to memorise lists of names for the purposes of their
own business".

The duty of confidentiality is sometimes seen as an obligation separate from the
duty of fidelity and sometimes as an instance of it. In *Faccenda Chicken Ltd* v *Fowler*
[1984] IRLR 61, Goulding J in a confidential information case referred to
authorities on the duty of faithful service, and Hazel Carty described the duty of
confidentiality as arising from "the notion of faithful service": "Employment
Confidentiality" [1985] 7 EIPR 195. In *Spafax Ltd* v *Harrison* [1980] IRLR 442,
446, Stephenson L J said: "a promise not to divulge trade secrets or confidential
information may express little more than the duty of fidelity". He referred to
authorities on the duty of fidelity. The quote emphasises that the implied duty
may cover the same ground as an express term.

Competition in Working Time: the Servant of Two Masters (Act 1)

An employee must not use the time she works for her employers to engage in
work for a rival. An example is *Thomas Marshall (Exports) Ltd* v *Guinle* [1979] Ch
227. The defendant was the managing director of the plaintiffs. By contract he
was not to engage in any other business without their consent while he was
employed by them. He, however, traded on his own behalf and on behalf of his
two companies. Megarry V-C (at 244) said that the defendant was "guilty of gross
and repeated breaches of his implied obligation to be faithful" to his employers
by placing orders for himself and his companies with the plaintiffs' suppliers. His
"prolonged duplicity" was deplored, and an interlocutory injunction was granted. As Greer LJ stated in *Wessex Dairies Ltd* v *Smith* [1935] 2 KB 80, 84, " . . . during
the continuance of his employment [the servant] will act in his employers'
interests and not use the time for which he is paid by the employers in furthering
his own interests". Cases are rare but the principle is firm.

Employers may release the employee from this sub-duty by giving consent to
competitive work. Presumably consent need not be expressly given but may be
implied. Consent might, therefore, derive from custom and practice. It is,
however, suggested that a court will be loath to reach the conclusion that the

employers did permit their employee to work for their rival or perform other competing activities at a time when she was contractually obliged to work for them.

The line between not working for others in one's contracted hours or in one's free time and preparing for competition is a fine one. In *Laughton* v *Bapp Industrial Supplies Ltd* [1986] ICR 248 (EAT), the EAT distinguish *Guinle* on three grounds:

(1)   in *Guinle* there was an express term prohibiting working for another;
(2)   in *Guinle* orders had been placed; and
(3)   *Guinle* involved a managing director, whereas the employees in *Bapp* were low-paid warehousemen.

Preparing to place orders and actually ordering is a fine line on which to base liability.

Spare-time Work: the Servant of Two Masters (Act 2)

In some situations an employee must not work for a competitor of her employers even in her spare time. The duty to serve faithfully is not restricted to the hours when the employee works for her employers. However, not all activities are prohibited. To be forbidden the work must occasion detriment to the employers.

The principal authority is *Hivac Ltd* v *Park Royal Scientific Instruments Ltd*, above, an unreserved Court of Appeal decision. The employers sought interlocutory injunctions to prevent their employees working in their spare time in the same sphere of business for their sole competitor. The workers had gone to work for the first defendants, which were also making midget valves for hearing aids. Indeed, until the corporate defendants were established, the plaintiffs held a monopoly. The court granted relief. In Lord Greene MR's words (at 178): "it would be deplorable if ... a workman could consistently with his duty to his employer knowingly, deliberately and secretly set himself to do in his spare time something which would inflict great harm on his employer's business". The court held that no trade secrets or other confidential information had been revealed by the employers to their spare-time employers but that such data would inevitably be revealed in the future to them by the very nature of the job. Morton LJ (at 182) said: "it is difficult to conceive that if the plaintiffs were showing the employees a new and improved way of making midget valves there would be no mention and no demonstration of that to the defendant company". (Whitford J in *Electrolux Ltd* v *Hudson*, above (at 329), used this ground to distinguish *Hivac*. See also *Ansell Rubber Co Pty Ltd* v *Allied Rubber Industries Ltd* [1967] VR 37 and *United Sterling Corp* v *Felton* [1974] RPC 162.) The remedy would forestall any such disclosure. The option of dismissing the employees was not available because of the wartime Essential Work Order and had they left, they would have gone to the rivals.

The court in *Hivac* emphasised that it would not lightly impose restrictions on spare-time activities. It distinguished between ordinary manual workers, who could work for others, and those whose employment meant that they could not do so even in their "free" time: a solicitors' clerk was instanced as an employee who was forbidden from working for others because of the harm which would be caused to his firm. An illustration of the former class of employee is the odd job man in *Nova Plastics Ltd* v *Froggatt* [1982] IRLR 146 (EAT). To perform the same job for a rival in his spare time did not seriously increase the other employers' competitiveness *vis-à-vis* his normal employers. For a similar case, see *EEPTU* v *Parnham*, EAT 378/78, 21 January 1979. For cases where the employee was forbidden to work for another see *Bartlett* v *Shoe & Leather Record, The Times*, 29 March 1960, *Gibson* v *NUDBTW* (1972) 13 KIR 143, and *Gray* v *CP Pembroke Ltd*, COIT 1350/72. *Bartlett*, however, does not seem to have facts where "great harm" was caused to the employers. For more recent cases see *Golden Cross Hire Co Ltd* v *Lovell* [1979] IRLR 267, *Fraser* v *Tuller Business Services Ltd* (1988) IRLIB 354, 13 (EAT), *Connor* v *Comet Radiovision Services* (1981) EAT mentioned in IDS Brief 420, 10 (1990), and *Heron* v *Scaffolding (GB) Ltd*, COIT 1011/78. The stress on "great harm" remains: see for example *Hawkins* v *Prickett* [1976] IRLR 52.

There may be an express term that the employee shall devote her whole time and attention to her employer's business. Nevertheless, it is suggested that there is still room for an implied term of fidelity. It would be absurd if the employee had to devote her dining and sleeping hours solely to the company: in other words, "whole time" excludes some time for leisure and other activities. If the employee were to work in that free time for a competitor, the implied duty would be breached. It may, however, be easier for the court to rely on the express term, the words and width of which are stated, than on an implied term, the boundaries of which may be uncertain. As an alternative to this approach a court may be ready to read the express term as prohibiting only competing work. Whichever approach is adopted, there is scope for spare-time activities which do not compete.

Whether the employee is in breach of the duty not to work for others in her spare time when it causes great harm to the principal employers may depend on the custom of the trade or any permission impliedly granted by the employers. In *Frame* v *McKean & Graham Ltd* [1974] IRLR 179 the claimant did some work for a former customer of the employers in his spare time. His dismissal was unfair because previously they had allowed such work.

Criticism of the requirement of "great harm" has come from Professor Rideout (*Principles of Labour Law*, 4th ed (Butterworths, 1983) 92; not in 5th ed). In *Philip Kunick Ltd* v *Smith*, unreported, 1973 (NIRC) the court held that the basis of *Hivac* was the risk that confidential information might be divulged to a competitor, causing the employers to suffer loss. The court stated that an employee may work for herself or others if there is not conflict of interest or harm to the employers. Rideout wrote that "[t]he conflict of interest which undoubtedly existed in *Hivac* was not the basis of the decision and it is not correct to suppose that where there is a conflict of interests there will inevitably be a risk to confidentiality ... The degree of detriment may affect the decision whether to grant an injunction but it cannot possibly have any relevance to the existence of a breach of contract".

Garden Leave Clauses and Working for Rivals

When the employers or the employee give notice of the termination of the contract of employment, the employers may invite or require the employee not to come to work during the notice period. The aim is to prevent the employee from contacting suppliers, customers, and colleagues before her contract ends and taking them with her into her new job. The employee is paid during this period and may perform non-competitive work such as cultivating her garden.

Scott J in *Balston Ltd* v *Headline Filters Ltd* [1987] FSR 330, 340, said *obiter* that the duty of faithful service does not apply with full force to persons working out garden leave. The duty was of lesser width than that which applied to an employee working normally. He suggested that the employee could set up a company which would compete after termination of contract, rent premises for that company and order materials. He even stated that she could approach colleagues with a view to enticing them to join her enterprise after termination. These matters are discussed next. Scott J thought that an employee on garden leave could lawfully solicit orders, those orders to be fulfilled after termination, whereas an employee working normally in the notice period could not. In the author's view there is no distinction between those on garden leave and others. Both are subject to the full weight of the duty of faithful service until the moment of termination. In fact at trial ([1990] FSR 385, 416) Falconer J said that what the defendant employee had done was in breach of his duty of faithful service despite the fact that he was on garden leave.

Ilegitimate Competition

During employment an employee must not establish a business which will compete with that of her employers after employment. She may, however, make preparations before leaving in order to acquire customers after termination. It would be disastrous for her if she left a safe job for one which might quickly lead to bankruptcy without being able to make various preparations. Accordingly, a line is drawn between legitimate and illegitimate preparations.

Many of the cases falling within this subheading are ones in which the employee has solicited her employers' customers with the intention of enticing them away from them to her new firm. A simple illustration is *Wessex Dairies Ltd* v *Smith*, above. The defendant, a milkman, told his customers during employment that he was going to set up in business for himself. He did so and some customers transferred their custom to himself. The Court of Appeal awarded damages to the employers – they did not seek an injunction – because he had not broken his duty of faithful service. In *Marshall* v *Industrial Systems and Control Ltd* [1992] IRLR 294 the plaintiff, the managing director of the defendants, sought a remedy for unfair dismissal when he was dismissed for making preparations to set up a company which would take away the best customer of the defendants, a distribution company. He and another employee had drafted a business plan and had *inter alia* approached the best customer. The Scottish EAT held that he was in breach of his duty of faithful service by making such preparations. He had gone beyond merely intending to compete, as was the case in *Laughton* v *Bapp Industrial Supplies Ltd*, above: see below. In *Adamson* v *B & L Cleaning Services Ltd* [1995] IRLR 197 putting in a tender for a contract which his employers held was a breach of the implied term. Preparing to bid would not have been a breach.

In *Wessex Dairies* the breach of duty occurred during the roundsman's contracted hours. However, the principle is not so restricted but applies to spare-time work too: *Hivac*, above. In the latter case Lord Greene MR said (at 178) that nothing in the reasoning of Maugham LJ in *Wessex Dairies* was restricted to doing "certain things in his employer's time. I cannot read the judgment as meaning that if the roundsman had on a Saturday afternoon, when his work was over, gone round to all those customers and canvassed them, he would have been doing something he was entitled to do". Morton LJ spoke similarly (at 182). Bucknill LJ simply agreed with both judgments.

It is immaterial that the employee is to leave that very day to establish her own business or join a rival. In *Wessex Dairies* the solicitation took place on the last day of the defendant's job. Nevertheless, he was liable.

The line between permissible and impermissible activities is not a clear one. One reason for the lack of clarity is that judges are faced by two sometimes irreconcilable policies. They do not wish to be seen as approving of dishonourable conduct by employees, but they also want to encourage competition, the lifeblood of capitalism. It is not always easy to weigh these interests and thus draw the line. Therefore, the law is not always predictable on facts which fall on one side of the line or another. Until the case is heard and a precedent set there is uncertainty. In these unclear cases judges' sympathies may be engaged differently on quite similar fact situations. If the employee steals away in the night with her employers' list of customers, the likelihood is that an interlocutory injunction will be granted; if, however, she is under threat of redundancy and she makes preparations which are not egregious, she may find that the court holds that she has not broken the duty to serve faithfully. It is, of course, not solely the facts which count but also the presentation of those facts.

The result is that there are exceptions to the rule that an employee must not during employment do anything to set up a business which after employment will compete with her employers' trade. The main one is that an employee may approach firms which are rivals of her employers. In *Harris & Russell Ltd* v *Slingsby* [1973] 3 All ER 31 (NIRC) the court determined that the employers had unfairly dismissed the employee. They had sacked him peremptorily when their managing director had heard that he was seeking employment with a competitor. Sir Hugh Griffiths said (at 34) that only when the employers had "reasonably solid grounds for believing that he abused his confidential position and information with his present employer" would there be sufficient grounds to dismiss him fairly. In *Laughton* v *Bapp Industrial Supplies Ltd*, above, two employees, warehouse and deputy warehouse managers of a firm involved in supplying nuts and bolts, wrote to their employers' suppliers inquiring about the best terms they could offer them when they left to set up a rival business. It was held that there was no breach of the obligation of faithful service. There was merely an intent to compete. The English EAT stated that the employees had not crossed the Rubicon into impermissible behaviour. They would have done so, had they solicited orders from the suppliers.

Hawkins J at first instance in *Robb* v *Green* [1895] 2 QB 1, 15, said that among acceptable practices were issuing circulars, renting a place for business and hiring employees. His actual words were that an employee could "for instance, ... legitimately canvass, issue his circulars, have his place of business in readiness, hire his servants etc". The wording, which was given in an *extempore* judgment, has been severely criticised. In *Wessex Dairies*, above, Maugham LJ said (at 87) that the meaning of "legitimately canvass" was obscure: "if he meant that the servant while going his rounds [*sic*] or while he was employed ... is entitled to use the opportunity to canvass his customers for himself ..., I doubt whether that view is correct, and I observe that when that case went to the Court of Appeal nothing to that effect is to be found in the judgments". At trial in *Balston Ltd* v *Headline Filters Ltd* [1990] FSR 385 Falconer J stated that Hawkins J meant that the employee could approach firms which were not customers of her present employers. It is suggested that the word "legitimately" qualifies all the activities, not just "canvass". For example, the employee is possibly not permitted during employment to hire servants who are employees of her employers or to issue circulars to her employers' clients. The law on this point remains uncertain, and it is for the court to determine in unclear cases whether the employee is merely at the stage of intending to compete (as in *Laughton* v *Bapp Industrial Supplies Ltd*) or has reached a state of preparation which is impermissible (as in *Marshall* v *Industrial Systems and Control Ltd*).

A specialised aspect of impermissible activities during employment is that the employee must not recruit a colleague to work in her competing business after employment. In *Sanders* v *Parry* [1967] 1 WLR 753 an assistant solicitor, the defendant, was on the point of leaving to establish his own practice when one of his employer's other employees, a secretary, told him that she was no longer satisfied with her job. The defendant offered her employment in the firm he was about to set up. The judge held that he was in breach of his duty of faithful service. A more recent authority, though a Scottish one, is *Marshall* v *Industrial Systems & Control Ltd*, above. The managing director of a company and the manager of software sales sought to induce the senior engineer to join a new company they were establishing to replace their employers as distributors of Boeing software products. The EAT held that the managing director was in breach of his duty of faithful service, his breach was gross, and he had not been unfairly dismissed. Lord Mayfield distinguished *Laughton v Bapp Industrial Supplies Ltd* as a case where the employees had merely intended to compete and therefore were not in breach of the duty of loyalty, whereas on the present facts the employee had sought to recruit a colleague with the intention of depriving the company of their best client, and indeed the director and the manager had already approached that client.

A mere intimation to other workers that the employee is to leave and set up a rival business is not a breach of the duty of faithful service. In *Tithebarn Ltd v Hubbard* (1992) IRLIB 449, 6 (EAT) the employee, a senior sales trainer, asked a salesman if he was interested in joining a company he intended to establish. This venture would compete with the business of his present employers. The EAT decided that the employee was simply discussing plans and those plans might lead to an offer of employment to the salesman in the future. The employee was held to have been unfairly dismissed. One point of concern to all parties, employers, employees and advisors is that the EAT stated that the industrial tribunal might have come to the opposite conclusion on the facts, but whichever way it decided, the EAT could not intervene.

Cumming Bruce LJ said in *G D Searle & Co Ltd v Celltech Ltd* [1982] FSR 92, 101–2, that a group of employees could band together to leave their employers and set up a rival firm. This statement is *obiter* and is inconsistent with the law concerning not recruiting colleagues during employment to work for a rival firm after employment ceases. An employee, it should be noted, is under a duty to disclose misdeeds of her colleagues (see below) and she must not leave with her employer's confidential information.

For other authorities see *Betts v D Beresford* [1974] IRLR 271 (suspicion of soliciting customers does not justify dismissal), *Hawkins v R B Prickett* [1976] IRLR 52 (dismissal was unfair if it was impossible to say that the employee would compete even though customers had been solicited), *Coltman v Multilite (Rooflights) Ltd*, EAT 565/179, *Rowe v Radio Rentals Ltd* [1982] IRLR 177, *Hutchinson v Seigar TPA Ltd*, 4 March 1988, LEXIS, and *Sandiford v George Smith of Avery Row Ltd* (1988) IRLIB 353, 12. In the last case it was held not to be unfair to dismiss directors who had solicited business from a client and had arranged for the purchase of office equipment and notepaper. For a case from Victoria see *Independent Management Resources Pty Ltd v Brown* [1987] VR 605, 612.

Business Opportunities

Employees must not obtain for themselves corporate opportunities which properly belong to the employers. An illustration is *Sanders v Parry*, above. The defendant, an employed solicitor, was informed that if he established his own practice, a major client would leave his present firm and join his. Havers J held that the employee was under an obligation to retain the client for his employers, the plaintiff. *Sanders* v *Parry* demonstrates that the rule applies even though the opportunity was not sought by the employee.

In relation to directors, it is a breach of fiduciary duty to appropriate for themselves contracts which they have been negotiating for their company: *Cook* v *Deeks* [1916] 1 AC 554 (PC). Three directors, who together owned three-quarters of the capital of a company, obtained for themselves a contract to build the continuation of a railway line in Ontario. They deliberately withheld the information from the company. Lord Buckmaster advised that the defendants had acted to exclude "the company whose interest it was their first duty to protect" (at 562): "men who assume the complete control of a company's business must remember that they are not at liberty to sacrifice the interests which they are bound to protect, and, while ostensibly acting for the company, divert in their own favour business which should properly belong to the company they represent" (at 563). Therefore, the defendants held the benefit of the contract for their company; in other words, the contract belonged in equity to the company. The Judicial Committee held further that the position could not be regularised by ratification by means of a company resolution. Otherwise the majority would oppress the minority.

The profit belongs to the company: *Regal (Hastings) Ltd* v *Gulliver (1942)* [1967] 2 AC 134n. Viscount Sankey said (at 137) that a fiduciary who entered into engagements in which he had a personal interest conflicting with his duty to protect the interests of others held the property on trust and was under an obligation to account to the beneficiary for the profits. Lord Russell spoke to similar effect (at 143).

There is no need for fraud or lack of good faith (see Lord Russell at 144), nor need the plaintiffs have been damaged (same). The celebrated authority of *Boardman* v *Phipps* [1967] 2 AC 46 (HL) demonstrates that directors are liable even though they do not act in an underhand or covert fashion, and they remain liable even if they have acted mistakenly. Lord Cohen said (at 104) that the appellants "acted with complete honesty throughout and the respondent is a fortunate man in that the rigour of equity enables him to participate in the profits which have accrued as a result of . . . the appellants . . . purchasing the shares at their own risk". The House supported the views of the trial judge, Wilberforce J, that the appellants should receive a liberal amount of money for their work and skills in acquiring the relevant shares.

Directors are subject to a fiduciary duty not to exploit opportunities which belong to the company even after resignation. *Industrial Development Consultants Ltd* v *Cooley* [1972] 1 WLR 443 has fascinating facts. The managing director of the plaintiffs had been negotiating with the Eastern Gas Board in order to obtain contracts for them. The negotiations, however, were unsuccessful. The new deputy chair of the Gas Board contacted the managing director privately and told him that he would stand a good chance of obtaining the contract if he did the work privately. He added that the Board did not want any trouble with the plaintiffs. The director lied about his health, and the company released him. Shortly afterwards the deputy chair offered him work as project manager. Roskill

J at Birmingham Assizes applied *Regal* and *Boardman* v *Phipps* and held that the director's duty to his former company and his self-interest conflicted. Therefore, he was in breach of his fiduciary duty, and he was under a duty to account for the benefits he would receive under his contract with the Gas Board. He would not have been liable had he informed the plaintiffs of the true facts. It should be noted that the defendant was liable despite the fact that it was the deputy chair who had contacted him, and not vice versa. If was also irrelevant, as Roskill J said (at 453), that the company could not obtain the business because the Gas Board was unwilling to trade with it. Other cases include *Cranleigh Precision Engineering Ltd* v *Bryant* [1966] RPC 81 and *Industrial Furnaces Ltd* v *Reaves* [1970] RPC 605.

A case where the corporate opportunity doctrine was held not to apply is *Island Export Finance Ltd* v *Umunna*, above. At first instance the judge, Hutchison J, held that any expectation by the company of fresh orders was not likely to be fulfilled because it was not seeking orders. Though the fiduciary duty of a director did not terminate on her ceasing to be a director, there was no "maturing business opportunity" (at 482) within *Canaero*, above. Therefore, the defendant was not in a position where his duty and interest conflicted. Provided the defendant did not resign in order to take up the opportunity, he can, subject to *Faccenda Chicken Ltd* v *Fowler* [1987] Ch 117, exploit the market he has come to know during employment. The case was reversed on appeal (8 January 1989, unreported) on the production of fresh evidence, but the principle stands.

It is thought that the obligation does not apply when the corporate opportunity comes to the director purely in her private capacity, though the line may be difficult to draw. It is suggested that an express clause could make the director liable, and companies should consider incorporating such a term into the contracts of their directors.

One case which causes problems is *Horcal Ltd* v *Gatland* [1984] IRLR 288 (CA). The plaintiffs sought to recover back money they had paid to the defendant, their former managing director, under the terms of a severance agreement on the grounds that they believed him to be faithfully serving the company whereas he had pocketed money from a customer. The court held that he did intend to keep the money but had not in fact done so by the time of the agreement. Therefore, he had not broken his contract. Goff J (at 290) stated that it would be "extravagant" law if a managing director had to confess to his misdeeds before obtaining payment under a termination arrangement. However, Dr Honeyball has correctly contended that a director is under a fiduciary duty to give relevant information to the company (see *Industrial Development Consultants Ltd* v *Cooley*, above) and she must by statute declare an interest in a contract in which she is interested. These contentions, which were not put to the court, were stated in (1984) 13 ILJ 257.

This area of law is sometimes seen as an example of the prohibition on a director placing herself in a position where her duty to the company and to self-interest conflict: see *Aberdeen Railway Co* v *Blaikie Bros* (1854) 1 Macq 461. A Commonwealth case is *Clayton* v *Chambers* (1913) 32 NZLR 65, 91. *Worthington Pumping Engine Co* v *Moore* (1902) 19 TLR 84 involved an employee but one who was the alter ego of the company. For a case on partners see *Aas* v *Benham* [1891] 2 Ch 244 (CA).

Non-directors

While there is a Canadian doctrine which applies the corporate opportunity doctrine to senior employees, English law does not apply fiduciary duties to those who are not directors (see above). In *Ixora Trading Inc* v *Jones* [1990] FSR 251 Mummery J held that information in a feasibility study did not constitute a trade secret, use of which could be enjoined post-employment by the employers. If the corporate opportunity had amounted to a trade secret, it could have been protected. The judge said that the "maturing business opportunity" was "both too obvious and too vague and unspecific to be caught by any fiduciary duty … ".

It is a breach of the duty of faithful service if the employee has an interest in a firm which is dealing with her employers without disclosing that interest: *Hardisty* v *Lowton Construction Group Ltd* (1973) 8 ITR 719. See also *Mansard Precision Engineering Ltd* v *Taylor* [1978] ICR 44. In *Severn* v *Filler and Pepper* (1988) IRLIB 363, 8, a legal executive in a solicitors' conveyancing department qualified as a licensed conveyancer. He informed his employers that he was leaving to establish a rival business and was sacked as a result. The industrial tribunal held that the dismissal was fair. The employers had a reasonable belief that the employee would abuse the trust they reposed in him, had he continued in employment. There was a real risk that he might use confidential client information. Dismissal would have been unfair, had he been dismissed simply because of his intention to leave and compete. A contrasting case is *Southwick* v *Linvar Ltd* (1988) IDS Brief 364, 5 (EAT). The employee was dismissed when her boyfriend departed to join a rival firm. Dismissal was unfair because the employers did not conduct an adequate investigation. Had they done so, they would have realised that the relationship was breaking down. Popplewell J said that the company would have been able fairly to dismiss, if they had believed on reasonable grounds after reasonable investigation that there was a risk that confidential information was changing hands.

Secret Profit

The duty not to make a secret profit from employment may be seen as one part of the duty of faithful service or as a separate incident of employment attaching to all service agreements.

The most celebrated authority is one involving a director: *Boston Deep Sea Fishing and Ice Co* v *Ansell* (1888) 39 Ch D 339 (CA). The plaintiffs' managing director contracted to buy fishing smacks from a firm in which he held shares. He was made liable to account for the commission (secret profit) he received from the firm. He had broken the condition in his contract of employment that "he will faithfully and truly discharge his duty towards his master". The commission belonged to the plaintiffs. The court granted an order inquiring into the sum which the defendant had received.

The House of Lords extended the law to bribes received by a sergeant serving in the British Army in Egypt, who was not an employee, in *Reading* v *Attorney-General* [1951] AC 507. Their Lordships differed among themselves. Lord Porter applied the *Boston Deep Sea* case (at 516). He said that there need be no implied promise to pay, as Lord Oaksey (at 517) thought, nor need there be a fiduciary relationship, as Lord Normand (*ibid*) had thought. *Boston Deep Sea* has been applied in several other cases, for example *Federal Supply & Coal Storage Co of South Africa* v *Angehrn* (1910) 80 LJMPC 1, 8, and *Attorney-General* v *Goddard* [1929] LJKB 743, 745. For a case involving an agent, see *Powell* v *Evan Jones & Co* [1905] 1 KB 11 (CA), where the defendant was held to be a debtor, not a trustee (*cf. Lister & Co* v *Stubbs* (1890) 45 Ch D 1 (CA). *Fawcett* v *Whitehouse* (1829) 1 Russ & M 132, 39 ER 51, is an old case involving partners.

The employee is in breach of the duty of fidelity whether or not the gift influenced her behaviour, as the facts of *Boston Deep Sea Fishing & Ice Co Ltd* v *Ansell* demonstrate. Bias is also unnecessary: *Burrell* v *Mossop* (1888) 4 TLR 270 (CA) and *Swale* v *Ipswich Tannery Ltd* (1906) 11 Comm Cas 88, 98 (Kennedy J). Bowen LJ (at 72) in a classic judgment (see Sachs LJ in *Sinclair* v *Neighbour* [1967] 2 QB 279, 289) said in *Boston Deep Sea* that there was a condition in every employment contract that the employee "will faithfully and truly discharge his duty towards his employer". If he is dismissed, he has no claim for wrongful dismissal, and this rule applies even though the facts were not discovered until after dismissal. The court gave his employers the restitutionary remedy of an account. An agreement to pay a bribe is not legally enforceable: *Harrington* (1878) 3 QBD 549.

The importance of the discussion of secret bribes in the context of the present work is that by the use of them rivals may be able to obtain information from employees to destroy any competitive edge the employers may have.

The most recent decision in this area is *Islamic Republic of Iran Shipping Lines* v *Denby* [1987] 1 Ll LR 367. The plaintiffs were in dispute with various shipowners, one of whom paid the defendant, the plaintiffs' solicitor, a commission. The plaintiffs alleged that the commission was a bribe. The defendant did not appear. Leggatt J in the Commercial Court held that the payment was indeed a bribe, and therefore the plaintiffs could recover it as money had and received. He rejected, however, the plaintiffs' claim that they could claim the profits earned on the bribe and an account of all payments made including the profits, because the defendant was in a fiduciary position. He held that there was no misapplication of trust property, applying *Metropolitan Bank* v *Heiron* (1880) 15 Ch D 369, and that the relationship between the parties was that of the creditor and debtor, not of *cestui que trust* and trustee, applying *Lister & Co* v *Stubbs* (1890) 45 Ch D 1 (CA). He distinguished *Boardman* v *Phipps* [1967] 2 AC 46, the well-known case involving a solicitor, and *Industrial Development Consultants Ltd* v *Cooley*, above, as being ones where fiduciaries had abused their position with the result that a constructive trust was imposed. The judge considered that *Lister & Co* v *Stubbs* was binding on him, though potentially distinguishable at the Court of Appeal level. Certainly there does appear to be an unfortunate mismatch in the law. In *Boardman* v *Phipps* the honest solicitor was held liable to account, whereas in the instant case the dishonest solicitor was not so liable. See L J Anderson (1987) 8 Co Law 220. Leggatt J thought that the two streams of authority were not necessarily in conflict but he did not attempt to reconcile them. Certainly if one were to conclude from the speeches in *Boardman* v *Phipps* that the solicitor was accountable because he acquired the chance to buy the shares as a result of his purporting to represent the trust, the same can be said of the agent in *Lister & Co* v *Stubbs* and the solicitor in the present case. As Anderson (at 221) points out, if Sergeant Reading was a fiduciary, why was not Denby? It may well be that *Lister & Co* v *Stubbs* requires reconsideration at the highest level. Peter Birks [1988] LMCLQ 128, 133, answers this criticism in this way:

> There is nothing in *Boardman* v *Phipps* itself to indicate that the shares acquired by Boardman in breach of duty . . . were caught by any adverse equitable proprietary interest. He was made personally accountable for the profits of his dealings . . . The addition in description of the liability of the words "as a constructive trustee" add nothing. Neither Boardman's circumstances – he was not insolvent – nor the words of the court's order contain the least indication of a proprietary liability.

Leggatt J in *Denby* (at 371) thought that *Boardman* v *Phipps* was a case where a fiduciary was regarded as holding any profits made from the use of the confidential information on constructive trust for the beneficiary, but there was no proprietary claim in *Boardman* v *Phipps*, solely a right *in personam*. The same may be said of *Industrial Development Consultants Ltd* v *Cooley*, which simply followed *Boardman* v *Phipps*, though the order did say that the defendant held his profit on trust.

Whether money paid to an employee is a bribe or is legitimate would seem to depend on the custom of the trade. In *Bartram & Son* v *Lloyd* (1903) 88 LT 286, an agency case, Bruce J held that there was a custom to pay a sum to the purchaser's broker. On the facts, however, the party who introduced the plaintiffs and defendants on the sale of a steamer acted beyond a mere broker and breached his duty as an agent to act in his principal's best interests. The judge said that even if the alleged custom covered what the broker did, it was too wide to be enforced. No doubt also matters of social intercourse such as handing over a cigarette are not to be regarded as breaking the duty of fidelity. Many of such problems may be resolved by the employer laying down guidelines on acceptable behaviour, for example not more than one bottle of whisky at Christmas from each supplier.

Disclosure of Misconduct

The duty of faithful service is sometimes considered to extend to the situation where an employee fails to disclose other employees' wrongdoing.

Whether the defendant is under a duty to disclose others' wrongdoing depends on the facts. In *Swain* v *West (Butchers) Ltd* [1936] 3 All ER 261 (CA) the employers' general manager was under an obligation to disclose unlawful orders given by the managing director. Greene LJ (at 264) said that there was no general duty on servants to reveal the improper conduct of fellow servants; rather the duty arose from the circumstances. The present plaintiff was under an express contractual term to promote the company. "The plaintiff was responsible for the management of the business and was responsible for seeing that the business was conducted honestly and efficiently by all who came under his control. If the dishonesty of a fellow-servant came within his notice he should tell the board" (at 265).

A more recent example of facts giving rise to the duty to reveal her fellow employees' misdeeds is *Sybron Corp* v *Rochem Ltd* [1984] Ch 112 (CA). The employee was the controller of the European zone for the plaintiffs. Several of his colleagues had banded together to set up in competition with their present employers. Stephenson LJ (at 126) said that whether the employee is under a duty to disclose "depends on the contract and on the terms of employment of the particular servant", applying *Swain*. In *Sybron* the duty was to reveal the misconduct of those lower in the corporate hierarchy. In *Swain* it was to reveal the misconduct of a higher placed individual. On the facts of *Sybron* there was a contractual duty to disclose the misdeeds of colleagues. His failure to report led to the company exercising its right not to pay him their part of a pension because he had acted fraudulently and had seriously misconducted himself.

The duty to reveal colleagues' misdeeds applies even though disclosure uncovers wrongdoing by the employee herself, as *Swain* and *Sybron* both demonstrate.

The well-known case of *Bell* v *Lever Bros Ltd* [1932] AC 161 (HL) exemplifies the rule that an employee is not under a duty to reveal her own misdeeds. Lord Atkin (at 228) stated that "to imply such a duty would be a departure from the well-established usage of mankind and would create obligations entirely outside the normal contemplation of the parties concerned. If a man agrees to raise his butler's wages, must the butler disclose that two years ago he received a secret commission from the wine merchant ...?" He said (at 227) that a contract of employment is not a contract of *uberrimae fidei*. There is therefore no duty to disclose that one is working for a rival in one's spare time causing great harm to one's employers. Finlay J held in *Hands* v *Simpson Fawcett & Co Ltd* (1928) 72 SJ 138 that a contract of employment is not like an insurance contract. Therefore, a driver before employment does not have to reveal all material facts such as that he had been convicted of motoring offences. Similar cases are *Fletcher* v *Krell* (1873) 42 LJQB 55 (QB) and *Healey* v *SA Française Rubastic* [1917] 1 KB 946 (Avory J).

The principle in *Bell* v *Lever Bros Ltd* is limited by the principle enunciated by Kerr LJ in *Sybron Corp* v *Rochem Ltd* that an employee must reveal her misconduct when she has fraudulently concealed her misdeeds (at 130). Fox LJ (at 128) distinguished *Bell* on the basis that it involved past breaches, whereas *Sybron* involved continuing breaches. It may be suggested that the distinction is absurd. Why, for example, should a successful fraudster not be subject to the duty but one who has just started be so liable?

The implied duty may be supplemented by an express term. In *Swain* there was a contractual term that the employee would "do all in his power to promote, extend and develop the interests of the company". The term was interpreted as one which obliged him to report any activities which were contrary to the interests of the company. This express term extended beyond the implied one by placing the employee under an obligation to reveal not only his colleagues' wrongdoing but also anything they did which did not accord with the company's interests. Greer LJ (*arguendo* at 263) said that the employee would not be in breach of this duty by refusing to answer questions about the fraud.

Intellectual Property

Patents, copyright and design rights fall outside the scope of this book. They are dealt with in this section as an example of situations where the duty of faithful service obliges the employee to disclose inventions to her employers.

In *Triplex Safety Glass Co* v *Scorah* [1938] Ch 211 an employee was under a duty to disclose discoveries or inventions made during working hours and in the course of employment. The duty arose out of an implied term. Farwell J (at 215) stated: "whether restrained by express contract or not, no employee is entitled to filch his employer's property in whatsoever form that property may be, whether it is in the form of a secret process or in some other form". The employee becomes a trustee of the invention for the employers. He is entitled to be indemnified for any expense incurred in protecting the property. The judge said that the obligation could be negatived by a release (at 218). The position is different when the employee is employed to perform a task. The facts of *British Syphon Co Ltd* v *Homewood* [1956] 1 WLR 1190 explain this principle. The employee was the employers' technical adviser. Part of his job was providing advice about manufacturing soda siphons. He made an invention, a new type of soda siphon. Roxburgh J (at 1192) held that he had broken his duty of faithful service. The invention belonged in equity to his employers. By not revealing the product to his employers he had placed himself in a position where he could not give correct advice to them. It was irrelevant whether or not the siphon was made during his contractual hours or was derived from the employers' confidential information or was made from their materials; it was also immaterial that he would try to exploit his invention only after he had left employment.

In relation to patents the rule is that inventions made during an employee's normal duties or when she is specifically assigned to duties falling outside the usual scope of her employment belong to the employers, provided that they might reasonably have been expected to result from those duties: Patents Act 1977, section 39(1)(a). Where the employee has "a special obligation to further the interests" of her employers' undertaking arising from her responsibilities in the firm, an invention made in the course of her employment belongs to the employer: section 39(1)(b). Paragraph (b) applies with particular force to employees high in the corporate hierarchy as well as directors. Outside of the situations mentioned in section 39(1) inventions belong to the employee: section 39(2). Employees' rights in inventions may not be diminished by contract: section 42(3). If the patent is "of outstanding benefit" to the employer the court or comptroller may award compensation: section 40(1). The sum is calculated in accordance with section 41(5), (6). Terms to the contrary except in collective agreements do not override the provisions for compensation: section 40(4).

The Copyright, Designs and Patents Act 1988 applies to employees. By section 11(2) if the employee makes a literary, dramatic, musical or artistic work in the course of employment, the employers are the first owners of the copyright, subject to any arrangement to the contrary. The copyright work must have been made in the course of employment. If the propositus is an employee but the employers give her extra-contractual work, the product belongs to the employee. *Byrne* v *Statist Co* [1914] 1 KB 622 (KBD) explains this rule. The employee worked for the *Financial Times* as a staff member. His employers asked him to translate, for a fee, a speech made by the Governor of a Brazilian State from Portuguese to English. The translation was to appear in the newspaper. He translated the speech in his own time. It was held that the work fell outside the scope of his contractual duties. Therefore, he owned the copyright. If the worker is an independent contractor, copyright belongs to her: see *Stevenson Jordan & Harrison Ltd* v *MacDonald & Evans* [1952] 1 TLR 101 (CA). In relation to such independent contractors the parties may agree that copyright will belong to the "employers". Practitioners would be well-advised to insert such clauses.

Unregistered designs, which were established by the 1988 Act, belong to the designer, if a freelance (section 215(1)), unless the design was commissioned: section 215(2). If the designer was an employee and the design was made in the course of employment, the right belongs to the employers: section 215(3). Registered design rights are treated in the same way.

Conclusion

The delineation of the sub-duties of the obligation of faithful service is not intended to be exhaustive of such duties but it does give a flavour of the implied terms in a contract of employment which actually or potentially restrain the employee from acting in a manner which undermines the employers' competitive advantage. These implied terms may also be supplemented and extended by express clauses. As Lord Esher MR stated in *Pearce* v *Foster* (1886) 17 QBD 536, 539: "what circumstances will put a servant into the position of not being able to perform his duty in a faithful manner, it is impossible to enumerate". The advantages of express terms over implied ones are noted in Chapter 3.

Contents of Chapter Eleven

CONFIDENTIALITY OF THE INFORMATION

Chapter Eleven

CONFIDENTIALITY OF THE INFORMATION

This section examines when information is to be classified as confidential for the purposes of the implied duty of confidentiality.

The *fons et origo* of this branch of the law in the modern era is the judgment of Lord Greene MR in *Saltman Engineering Co Ltd* v *Campbell Engineering Co Ltd* (1948) 65 RPC 203 (CA), a case not reported in a mainstream series until [1963] 2 All ER 413. He stated (at 213) in a case involving independent contractors: "if a defendant is proved to have used confidential information directly or indirectly obtained from a plaintiff, without the consent, express or implied, of the plaintiff, he would be guilty of an infringement of the plaintiff's rights". The definition applies only where the parties were in a confidential relationship. As Megarry J put it in *Coco* v *A N Clark (Engineers) Ltd* [1969] RPC 41, 47: "the information must have been imparted in circumstances imparting an obligation of confidence". Because of the requirement of a confidential relationship the action for breach of confidence does not cover industrial espionage or accidental acquisition of the information through the employers' carelessness.

The implied duty of confidentiality extends beyond the contractual relationship of employer and employee to, for example, government secrets, secrets of the marriage bed, and concrete literary ideas. Megarry J in *Coco* above said (at 48):

if the circumstances are such that any reasonable person standing in the shoes of the recipient of the information would have realised that upon reasonable grounds the information was being given to him in confidence, then this should suffice to impose upon him the equitable obligation of confidence. In particular, where information of commercial or industrial value is given on a business-like basis and with some avowed common object in mind ... I would regard the recipient as carrying a heavy burden if he seeks to repel a contention that he was bound by an obligation of confidence ...

In *Coco* the fact that the two mopeds were virtually identical did not prove that the defendants had used confidential information for their purposes. The plaintiff had to show that the similarity of the designs derived from the defendants' use of information given to them by him.

Later cases in the Commonwealth continue to apply the *Coco* test, for example in England *Haarhaus & Co GmbH* v *Law Debenture Trust Corp plc* [1988] BCLC 640, 645 (Comm Court); in Australia *Fractionated Cane Technology Ltd* v *Ruiz-Avila* [1988] 1 Qd 51, 62 (Sup Court); in Canada *Lac Minerals Ltd* v *International Corona Resources Ltd* (1989) 61 DLR (4th) 14, 24–5 (Sup Court); and in New Zealand *D* v *Hall* [1984] NZLR 727, 734–5 (High Court). In *Printers & Finishers Ltd* v *Holloway* [1965] RPC 239, 256, Cross J utilised the "man of average intelligence and honesty". Whitford J in *Yates Circuit Foil Co* v *Electrofoils* [1982] FSR 345, 348, spoke of "a man of ordinary honesty and intelligence". Both formulations are those of the reasonable person as used by Megarry J in *Coco*. Earlier cases had been more pragmatic. For example, Astbury J in *Amber Size & Chemical Co Ltd* v *Menzel* [1913] 2 Ch 239, 245, said that he had to answer four questions of fact: "(1) Did the Plaintiffs in fact possess and exercise a secret process? (2) Did the Defendant during the course of his employment know that such process was secret? (3) Did the Defendant acquire knowledge during his employment … ? … (4) Has he since leaving the Plaintiffs' employ made an improper use of the knowledge so acquired by him?"

The test in *Coco* looks at the views of the recipient of the information, the employee. Megarry V-C formulated a different test, which is dependent on the beliefs of the owners, the employers. Unfortunately Sir Robert did not attempt to synthesise the two tests or to state in a later one which test was correct. In *Thomas Marshall (Exports) Ltd* v *Guinle* [1979] Ch 227 the plaintiffs sought to restrain the defendant, their managing director, from trading on his own account in competition with the plaintiffs. The case involved an express clause, but nothing seems to turn on that fact. Megarry V–C noted that "it is far from easy to state in general terms what is confidential information or a trade secret" (at 248). He was not prepared to lay down a definitive statement, but for the purposes of that case he essayed a definition containing four elements (*ibid*), all of which relate to the owner's belief viewed objectively:

(1)   the information must be information the release of which the owner believes would be injurious to him or of advantage to his rivals or others;

(2)   the owner must believe that the information is confidential or secret *i.e.* that it is not already in the public domain. It may be that some or all of his rivals already have the information; but as long as the owner believes it to be confidential I think he is entitled to try and protect it;

(3)   the owner's belief under the two previous heads must be reasonable;

(4)   the information must be judged in the light of the usage and practices of the particular industry or trade concerned.

This test goes wider than others. Megarry V-C stated that his test was a maximum not a minimum: for example the belief perhaps need not be based on reasonable grounds. He thought that if the information passed all these tests it was entitled to protection, and that information which did not satisfy all the requirements might still be protected. As will be seen below, this adumbration of the factors does not resolve all contentious issues such as when information is in the public domain, and when the information is reasonably to be regarded as part of the employers' business. The test does not look at the *defendant's* mental element, on which see the excellent discussion in Peter North, "Breach of confidence: is there a new tort?" (1972) 15 JSPTL (NS) 149, 158–65.

The requirement in (1) was not mentioned by the Court of Appeal in *Faccenda Chicken Ltd* v *Fowler* [1987] Ch 117 where Neill LJ went further than Megarry V–C in attaching importance to the question of whether the employee habitually handled confidential material.

The *Guinle* definition has received judicial approval in, for example, *Norbrook Laboratories Ltd* v *King* [1984] IRLR 200 (NICA) and *Fractionated Cane Technology Ltd* v *Ruiz–Avila* above, on appeal [1988] 2 Qd 610.

The confidential information need not be in tangible form, and while the application of the law to the facts may be difficult, the next sections give an account of the requirements for the action of breach of confidence.

The Necessary Quality of Confidence

Can the law properly attribute the "necessary quality of confidence" to the information is the question to be asked. Lord Greene MR in *Saltman Engineering Co Ltd* v *Campbell Engineering Co Ltd*, above (at 215) said, "What makes it confidential is the fact that the maker of the document has used his brain and thus produced a result which can only be produced by somebody who goes through the same process". This test has been used in England, for example *Under Water Welders and Repairers Ltd* v *Street* [1968] RPC 498 (Ch D) and abroad for example *Harvey Tiling Co (Pty) Ltd* v *Rodomac Pty Ltd* [1977] RPC 399 (Sup Ct, SA, TPD), *Moorgate Tobacco Co Ltd* v *Philip Morris Ltd* [1985] RPC 219 (HCA) and *Attorney-General (UK)* v *Heinemann Publishers Australia Pty Ltd* (1987) 75 ALR 353 (Sup Ct NSW). In *Industrial Furnaces Ltd* v *Reaves* [1970] RPC 605, 613, the mark of a trade secret was that the employers had gone to "considerable labour and expense" (*per* Graham J). The "brain" test is what marks out confidential information from public knowledge.

Another approach was taken in *Suhner & Co AG* v *Transradio Ltd* [1967] RPC 329, 333. Plowman J said: "the confidential nature of the document is not dependent on whether the information which it contains is available elsewhere, but on the question of whether it contains useful information which has been compiled by the plaintiffs for a particular purpose and handed over to the defendants for a particular purpose".

Both the *Saltman* and *Suhner* approaches mean that two (or more) employers may have confidential information in the same matter (*cf.* patents): the first discoverer has no right to prohibit the second from using it. See, for example,

Chadwick v *Covell*, 23 NE 1068, 1068–9 (1899) (SJC Mass), applied by the same court in *Laughlin Filter Corp* v *Bird Machine Corp*, 65 NE 2d 545, 546 (1946).

One problem is that what is confidential in one case is not necessarily so in another. In English, Commonwealth and US law there is no agreed meaning for the term "trade secrets" and there is therefore no simple definition which encompasses and explains all the cases. "The concept of trade secrets is a chimerical, unanalysed concept ... ": *Vekamaf Holland BV* v *Pipe Benders Inc*, 211 USPQ (BNA) 955, 978 (1981) (D Minn), affirmed 217 USPQ 32 (1982) (CA 8). As the Seventh Circuit put it in *Smith* v *Dravo Corp*, 203 F 2d 369, 373 (1953), applying Pennsylvanian law, "almost any knowledge or information" may be a trade secret. In *ILG Industries* v *Scott*, 273 NE 2d 393, 398 (Ill) it was said: "the question whether a specific matter is a trade secret is an extremely close one, often not readily predictable until a court has announced its ruling". In *Argyll* v *Argyll* [1967] Ch 302, 330, certain communications within marriage were confidential because they fell within the mischief of the law but Ungoed-Thomas J refused to clarify further "the scope and limits of the jurisdiction". One has to agree with Gowans J in *Ansell Rubber Co Pty Ltd* v *Allied Rubber Industries Pty Ltd* (1967) [1972] RPC 811, 825, in the Supreme Court of Victoria:

> there is very little in [the] English cases to enable one to identify a "trade secret". But some collation of the characteristics may be attempted, without trying to make it an exhaustive statement. Its subject-matter may not be a process in common use, or something which is public property and public knowledge, but if it is the result of work done by the maker upon materials which may be available for the use of anybody, so as to achieve a result which can only be produced by somebody who goes through the same process, it will be sufficient ... There is no suggestion of the need for invention.

(See also the test in *Canadian Aero Service* v *O'Malley* (1973) 40 DLR (3d) 371 (CSC), applied in *Chevron Standard Ltd* v *Home Oil Co* [1980] 5 WWR 626.) As well as there being no need for invention Gowans J stressed that novelty was not required. In *Guinle's* case, above Megarry V-C held that the plaintiff company reasonably regarded as confidential several categories of information. These were: names and telex addresses of their suppliers and customers; prices paid for goods by the plaintiffs and their customers; names of overseas agents; new ranges; information regarding customers' requirements such as styles; information about negotiations; the company's samples; and details of their "fast-moving" lines. In accordance with the classification used in the restraint of trade doctrine both customer connection and trade secret may enjoy the protection afforded by an implied term as to confidentiality.

Other cases exemplify and flesh out what matters may be held to be the subject of confidentiality. In *Cranleigh Precision Engineering Ltd* v *Bryant* [1965] 1 WLR 1293 the employers manufactured swimming pools. The defendant, an employee, developed two inventions, a clamping strip, which held the inner and outer walls together, and an overlapping interfit of the metal plates which constituted the outer wall. He resigned and joined a rival firm. The plaintiffs sought an injunction to restrain the former employee and the rival company from using or disclosing these confidential features. The court held that the strip and the interfit were trade secrets. Roskill J said (at 1310) that:

> the knowledge that the particular clamping strip was the right type of clamping strip to use for this particular purpose, coupled with the knowledge of how to define to a plastics manufacturer what was required for this particular purpose and that a plastics manufacturer could readily supply this particular form of strip, is and was a trade secret ... Accordingly it follows that if Bryant acquired this knowledge in confidence as the plaintiffs' managing director, he is not entitled to make use of it in breach of his obligations of confidence to the plaintiffs.

Here then physical objects and the ideas behind those objects were treated as confidential.

Cases from the United States sometimes say that an exact definition of trade secrets is impossible. See, for example, *Lear Siegler Inc* v *Ark-Ell Springs Inc*, 569 F 2d 286, 288–9 (1978) (CA 5), *Anaconda Co* v *Metal Tool & Die Co*, 483 F Supp 410, 421 (1980) (ED Pa), and *American Can Co* v *Mansukhani*, 216 USPQ (BNA) 1094, 1099 (1984) (ED Wis). Francis Gurry, *Breach of Confidence* (Clarendon, 1984) 70, stated: "in general, the courts have approached the question of confidentiality in a pragmatic way. They have been reluctant to develop rigid definitions of what suffices to confer confidentiality on any item of information, but have preferred to adopt a 'recognition' approach in which the particular information in question is assessed in the context of the facts of the case in hand". Some of these cases are noted below. It is suggested that the same law applies in Scotland and Ireland. In both jurisdictions cases are few but English authorities are used. For example, in *Chill Foods (Scotland) Ltd* v *Cool Foods Ltd* [1977] RPC 522 the Court of Session seemed to accept English authorities as determinative, and in *House of Spring Gardens Ltd* v *Point Blank Ltd* [1983] FSR 213 Costello J in the Irish Supreme Court followed English authorities such as *Saltman* above, and his using them was not queried on appeal. Before examples are provided, the English case of *Faccenda Chicken Ltd* v *Fowler* [1987] Ch 117 (CA) must be considered.

The Facts of *Faccenda* and First Instance Judgment

The plaintiffs were a company which sold chickens to the trade. The chickens were transported fresh in refrigerated vans, and each van driver came to know customers on the route. The company had built up a large network of customers. The defendant was employed as a sales manager. There was no restraint of trade clause in his contract of service. He resigned and set up a competing firm. Eight of his former workmates joined him in the venture. The plaintiffs contended that they were entitled to protection for the names and addresses of customers, the routes driven, the customers' requirements (such as the number of chickens they normally ordered), delivery times, and the chickens' prices including discounts.

They sought, *inter alia*, damages for breach of the implied term in the contracts that the nine former employees "would not use confidential information and/or trade secrets gained by them and each of them whilst in the plaintiffs' employment to the disadvantage or detriment of the plaintiffs, whether during the currency of [their] employment or after its cessation".

Goulding J at first instance [1984] ICR 589 dismissed the plaintiffs' claim. He said at 598–9 that:

> information acquired by an employee in the course of his service, and not the subject of any relevant express agreement, may fall as regards confidence into any of three classes. First there is information which, because of its trivial character or its easy accessibility from public sources of information, cannot be regarded by reasonable persons or by the law as confidential at all. The servant is at liberty to impart it during his service or afterwards to anyone he pleases, even his master's competitor. An example might be a published patent specification well known to people in the industry concerned ... Secondly, there is information which the servant must treat as confidential (either because he is expressly told it is confidential, or because from its character it obviously is so) but which once learned necessarily remains in the servant's head and becomes part of his own skill and knowledge applied in the course of his master's business. So long as the employment continues, he cannot otherwise use or disclose such information without infidelity and therefore breach of contract. But when he is no longer in the same service, the law allows him to use his full skill and knowledge for his own benefit in competition with his former master; and ... there seems to be no established distinction between the use of such information where its possessor trades as a principal, and where he enters the employment of a new master, even though the latter case involves disclosure and not mere personal use of the information. If an employer wants to protect information of this kind, he can do so by an express stipulation restraining the servant from competing with him (within reasonable limits of time and space) after the termination of his employment.

Goulding J continued thus (at 600):

> Thirdly, however, there are, to my mind, specific trade secrets so confidential that, even though they may necessarily have been learned by heart and even though the servant may have left the service, they cannot lawfully be used for anyone's benefit but the master's. An example is the secret process which was the subject matter of *Amber Size and Chemical Co Ltd* v *Menzel* [1913] 2 Ch 239.

The judge gave as illustrations of the second category the information about a process of manufacture which came to court in *United Indigo Chemical Co Ltd* v *Robinson* (1931) 49 RPC 178. The plaintiffs manufactured a boiler disincrustant. They alleged that the defendant, their former works manager, was using the information he had gained during employment to manufacture a competitive product. Bennett J held that he could use the information in his new job. Goulding J also instanced the information in *E Worsley & Co Ltd* v *Cooper* [1939] 1

All ER 290 as falling within his second category. Morton J held that the source of paper was not "in the nature of a secret process" (at 310). "The information which he acquired during his [the defendant's] service with the plaintiffs he has used in advancing his own business and in damaging the plaintiff's business ... It was the use of his knowledge, skill and expertise ... " (at 310). The fact that he had gained that information during employment with the plaintiffs was irrelevant.

Goulding J held (at 600) that the information in *Faccenda* fell within his second category. Therefore in the absence of a restraint covenant it could be used by the ex-employees. It was protected during employment by the implied duty of faithful service but it was not protected after employment except by an express term.

The Court of Appeal

The Court of Appeal dismissed the plaintiffs' appeal. The court decided that the information sought to be protected was of the kind which became during employment part of an employee's memory, part of skill and knowledge. During that time he could not use or disclose it except for the benefit of his employers. After employment he could use it for himself or for others. The court went out of its way to disapprove of Goulding J's categorisation.

The court held in relation to the implied term of confidentiality that former employers could have protection only for trade secrets and "other information which is of a sufficiently high degree of confidentiality as to amount to a trade secret" (*per* Neill LJ *per curiam* at 136). Such information was protected by the implied term. Neill LJ gave the following examples of trade secrets: "secret processes of manufacture such as chemical formulae ... or designs or special methods of construction". The class of information which was of a high degree of confidentiality comprised data which was something more than information which during employment it would have been a breach of the implied duty of good faith to disclose. An example of less than highly confidential knowledge was given by Cross J in *Printers & Finishers Ltd* v *Holloway* [1965] RPC 239, 253 (not reported on this point in [1965] 1 WLR 1). "For example, the printing instructions were handed to Holloway to be used by him during his employment exclusively for the plaintiffs' benefit. It would have been a breach of duty on his part to divulge any of the contents to a stranger while he was employed, but many of these instructions are not really 'trade secrets' at all. Holloway was not, indeed, entitled to take the instructions away with him; but in so far as the instructions cannot be called 'trade secrets' and he carried them in his head, he is entitled to use them for his own benefit or for the benefit of any future employer." Neill LJ also referred (at 137) to *E Worsley & Co Ltd* v *Cooper*, above. The source of paper was confidential during employment in that the employee would have been in breach of his duty of fidelity if he had divulged it but after cessation of employment he could utilise it. For a Scottish case following *Faccenda* on this difference see *Malden Timber Ltd* v *McLeish*, 1992 SLT 727, 734.

The court, when it drew the distinction between protected (highly) confidential information and non-protected (merely) confidential information, stated that the difference was one of degree. In other words, a line had to be drawn but where it was drawn was not always clear. Litigation in the post-*Faccenda* era supports this approach. In *PSM International plc* v *Whitehouse* [1992] IRLR 279 (CA) Lloyd LJ said so (at 282), referring to *Faccenda*. On interlocutory appeal he considered that the design of the machine which made plastic bumpers for Rover cars and quotes for the machines were, if not trade secrets *stricto sensu*, highly confidential information. Neill LJ, the principal judge in *Faccenda*, just expressed his agreement with Lloyd LJ. Similar is *Roger Bullivant Ltd* v *Ellis* [1987] ICR 464, 473 (CA).

The Court of Appeal in distinguishing between trade secrets and highly confidential information on the one hand and (merely) confidential information after the termination of the contract of employment held that several factors were relevant to the drawing of the line (at 137–8).

Nature of the Employment

If the employee worked in a capacity in which he was accustomed to dealing with confidential information, his job "may impose a high obligation of confidentiality because the employee can be expected to realise its sensitive nature to a greater extent than if he were employed in a capacity where such material reaches him only occasionally or incidentally". A non-executive director of a contract cleaning firm may receive such information but a cleaner himself may not.

The first factor, that the nature of employment may give rise to a higher duty of confidentiality where confidential information is handled as part of the job than where it is not, is adeptly criticised by Rideout, *Principles of Labour Law*, 5th ed, (Sweet & Maxwell, 1989) 98–9:

> [t]his test would appear to be circular unless the Court of Appeal is intending to recognise two categories of confidential information, one of which is not protected by an enforceable obligation to respect that confidentiality. This . . . is exactly what the Court has in mind since it had earlier referred to information confidential in the sense only that its disclosure would be a breach of the duty of fidelity. This is to confuse what it had been at pains to distinguish. The duty of fidelity has no connection with confidentiality. What the Court probably means, therefore, is that where the nature of employment requires a high level of fidelity and the habitual handling of information is a characteristic of that employment there will be an indication that the information would be protected but only by the restricted implication of confidentiality as applicable to "trade secrets".

Nature of the Information

The information must be protectable by a restraint of trade covenant. Goulding J [1984] ICR 589, 599, was incorrect in the view of Neill LJ to state that employers can protect information in his second category (that is not a trade secret or highly confidential) by a covenant. The restricted circulation of the information within the firm is an indicator that it is highly confidential.

Impressing on the Employee the Nature of the Information

The employers' attitude towards the allegedly highly confidential information is material. If the employers do not warn the employee that the information is highly confidential, it is likely that the court will hold it not to be so, as happened in *Worsley*, above (at 307).

Isolation

Separability is not conclusive but it is important. In the words of the court, "the fact that the alleged 'confidential' information is part of a package and that the remainder of the package is not confidential is likely to throw light on whether the information in question is really a trade secret". The ability to isolate the data was also noted by Cross J in *Printers & Finishers Ltd* v *Holloway*, above (at 256). He inquired whether the information "can fairly be regarded as a separate part of the employee's stock of knowledge which a man of ordinary honesty and intelligence would recognise to be the property of his old employer".

It should be noted that the above four headings are merely factors and not requirements for protection post-employment. Presumably the absence of one factor could be outweighed by strength elsewhere. The list of factors is not closed.

The distinction between trade secrets (and similar highly confidential information) and (merely) confidential information is fundamental. The former is protected by law after employment through the implied duty of confidentiality but the latter is not. However, drawing the line may be difficult, as indeed may be gauged from the facts of *Faccenda* itself. The discounts offered to customers potentially fell within the former category. If one applies the factors, the essence of the van salespersons' jobs was the sale of fresh chickens to customers. These purchasers were obtained and retained partly through the giving of discounts. The extent of the discounts gave the employers an advantage over competitors, who did not know the amount (though it must be said that they could in normal situations easily gain access to the details by asking traders). The employers could have informed their employees that the discounts were not to be disclosed to third parties; and the discounts could be readily separated from other information. If the plaintiffs had taken more effort than they did to protect the information which they did consider to be confidential and which gave them an advantage over rival businesses, they would have been successful. Legal advisers should also take care to suggest a covenant in restraint of trade which might afford protection without recourse to the difficulties of interpretation in *Faccenda*.

On the facts of *Faccenda* the information was not of a sufficiently high degree of confidentiality that it merited protection. No one in authority in the company told the van drivers that the information was confidential. The information about sales contained some matters which were not confidential. The pricing information was not separable from the sales information. None was obviously of a secret nature. The information was needed by the van salespersons when doing their jobs, and it became part of their memory. It was known to others in the organisation including secretaries. Accordingly, neither the information as to customers nor that as to prices was confidential despite the fact that both classes of information would be of value to rival firms: if such firms knew the information, they could undercut the plaintiffs and thereby reduce their market share. The court said *obiter* that some pricing information could be protected. Neill LJ (at 140) instanced prices in tender documents, the price which would be charged for the new model of a car or some other product, and prices for various grades of oil in a competitive market. *Faccenda* was followed as to this type of pricing information in the restraint of trade case of *Poly Lina Ltd* v *Finch* [1995] FSR 751 (QBD). For a Scottish case so holding, see *Malden Timber Ltd* v *McLeish*, 1992 SLT 727.

Criticism of *Faccenda*

The Court of Appeal distinguished trade secrets (and other highly confidential information) and mere confidential information. Information which was not "of a sufficiently high degree of confidentiality as to amount to a trade secret" (at 136) was not protected after the employee's contract was terminated, even though it was confidential and did receive protection during employment. If that data were revealed during employment, the disclosure would constitute a breach of the duty of good faith, but after employment it was not subject to the continuing breach of confidentiality. Here, then, is one difficulty: to distinguish between highly confidential information and other confidential information. The court provided guidelines and said that the difference was one of degree. Accordingly, there is no hard and fast line between the two categories. As we have seen, sometimes pricing details are highly confidential, sometimes they are not.

A second criticism is the distinction between confidential information and the employee's skill and knowledge. Using mere confidential information is a breach of the implied duty of good faith, but so might the use of skill and knowledge, as when the employee works for another firm during her spare time and thereby causes grave harm to her main employers. After employment she can use both merely confidential information and her skill and experience without being in breach of any duty. On this analysis there is no distinction in legal effect between those two concepts. It is impossible to suppose that this outcome was in the mind of Neill LJ.

Thirdly, there is difficulty in accepting what the Court of Appeal said in relation to the first instance judgment. Goulding J ([1984] ICR 589, 599) stated that the employers could prevent the employee from using or disclosing information (such as the sales information at issue in the case) which is confidential after employment by means of a covenant in restraint of trade. The Court of Appeal disagreed. Neill LJ (at 137) said that a covenant protected only a "trade secret or its equivalent", the equivalent being highly confidential information. Merely confidential information is not protectable after employment by a covenant. This proposition is *obiter*. Before *Faccenda* it was settled law that express covenants in restraint of trade could be utilised to prevent former employees from using or disclosing merely confidential information. If the Court of Appeal's remarks were correct, they would upset well-established law as in *Printers & Finishers* where the information which was not protected by the implied term would have been by a restraint clause. For example, a clause in a service agreement that the employee will not "work for a rival in trade" may be upheld "if limited to a short period", as Lord Denning MR put it in *Littlewoods Organisation Ltd* v *Harris* [1977] 1 WLR 1472, 1479. Such a covenant strikes at an employee's freedom to work for another after termination of her contract of employment and prevents her from using merely confidential information for herself. Nevertheless, such covenants are routinely held to be reasonable if narrowly limited in time and space.

After *Faccenda* first instance judges have given their approval to Goulding J's approach. Scott J in *Balston Ltd* v *Headline Filters Ltd* [1987] FSR 330, 347, stated that the Court of Appeal could not have intended to exclude all merely confidential information from protection through covenants. He argued that since trade secrets and information of a sufficiently high degree of confidentiality were protected post-employment by the implied term, there was no need for any express term. In other words, a covenant was otiose. Such an outcome was unacceptable. Therefore, the covenant must protect some other matter. That matter had to be merely confidential information. These reservations were supported by Harman J in *Systems Reliability Holdings plc* v *Smith* [1990] IRLR 377. The judge held that on a true analysis the facts disclosed a relationship of vendor and purchaser and therefore anything he said about employees was *obiter*; nevertheless, he opined that the Court of Appeal in *Faccenda* was incorrect in positing the view that mere confidential information could not be protected by covenants. He said (at 384) that the court's approach was "improbable".

The Court of Appeal has not directly taken the opportunity to comment on this part of the ruling. The analysis here provided is not controverted by *Lansing Linde Ltd* v *Kerr* [1991] 1 All ER 418, 425, where Staughton LJ in a covenant case thought that the issue depended purely on the definition of trade secrets. Goulding J's second category, "information which the servant must treat as confidential but once learned necessarily remains in the servant's head and becomes part of his skill and knowledge", could receive protection from a covenant. Staughton LJ (at 426) instanced the names of customers and the goods they bought. Such data is easily learned, at least where the client base is small and in this way it becomes part of the employee's skill and knowledge. The other two judges did not mention *Faccenda*, but Butler-Sloss LJ (at 434) said that she agreed with Staughton LJ's judgment. If protection is not available through the restraint of trade doctrine, nevertheless a springboard injunction may be granted: *PSM International plc* v *Whitehouse* [1992] 1 WLR 279 (CA).

If the contention advanced here is correct, namely, that merely confidential information can be protected by an express covenant, the difficulty becomes one of distinguishing between that type of information and the employee's own skill and knowledge. It is suggested that part of the difficulty arises from the terminology of Goulding J. He spoke (at 589) of full skill and knowledge. What he meant was to distinguish confidential information which comprises a legitimate proprietary interest in the restraint of trade doctrine (a trade secret or a trade connection). This analysis is supported by his illustrations: manufacturing processes and customer lists. These examples are both ones of confidential information (even if they do not constitute trade secrets for the purposes of the implied duty of confidentiality after employment). Such information is protectable by a well-drafted clause. What Goulding J was not saying was that the employee's skill and knowledge cannot be used after employment by her. Neither an express covenant nor the implied duty stretches that far. The employee is free to use or disclose this category of information.

A fourth criticism of *Faccenda* is that there is a troubling dictum by Neill LJ (at 138–9): "We would wish to leave open, however, for further examination on some other occasion the question whether additional protection should be afforded to an employer where the former employee is not seeking to earn his living by making use of the body of skill, knowledge and experience which he has acquired in the course of his career, but is merely selling to a third party information which he acquired in confidence in the course of his former employment". It is suggested that there is no legal difference between the two situations. In both the former employee is seeking to realise his economic worth; in both the former employers' profitability may be cut. It is, therefore, not arguable that employers should receive protection in one situation (sale) but not in another (some other use). This analysis draws some support from the decision of Lionel Swift QC sitting as a deputy High Court judge in *Mainmet Holdings plc v Austin* [1991] FSR 538 (QBD). The plaintiffs contended that their former managing director was disclosing information to present customers. The information consisted of allegations of defective equipment. They contended that the defendant was revealing the information out of spite because he had resigned when the company had been taken over. The judge held that this information was not to be protected because it was merely confidential. In other words the plaintiffs lost even though the former employee was using the information for a purpose other than establishing a rival business. If information cannot be protected when it is maliciously revealed by a former employee, it does not seem possible to safeguard it legally when she is selling it to a third party. If motive is irrelevant when the ex-employee is divulging the information out of spite, it should also be irrelevant that he is exchanging the information for cash. Any distinction in this context ought to depend on the categorisation of the information, not on what the former employee intends to do with it. It is postulated that the dictum in *Faccenda* may be a remnant of the campaign of Lord Denning MR to deprive people of the protection of the law of confidentiality when they, for example, sold their story to the press but that theory is no longer espoused. He advanced the proposition in *Woodward* v *Hutchins* [1977] 1 WLR 760 (CA) and *Lennon* v *News Group Newspapers Ltd* [1978] FSR 573, 574 (CA), though in *Kashoggi* v *Smith* [1980] LSG 130, transcript on LEXIS, it was noted *obiter* that the plaintiff would not be denied protection just because she was negotiating for the sale of her memoirs. The criticism of *Woodward* v *Hutchins* by Raymond Wacks in "Pop goes Privacy" (1980) 41 MLR 67 repays study. These cases may be best viewed as "truth in publicity" ones or distinguished as being authoritative solely in the area of personal secrets and not concerned with confidential information about trading matters, and indeed some of the information which the Court of Appeal allowed to be published was tittle-tattle, which is not protected by the action for breach of confidence. Certainly if the true *ratio* of these cases is that the law intervenes to permit the revelation of information which adversely affects persons who have sought through the media to portray themselves favourably, the *ratio* does not affect confidential trade information law and thus does not affect whether the employee used or sold that data. *Woodward* v *Hutchins* itself may be supported on the grounds of Lawton LJ, that no injunction is awarded to restrain a libel if the defendant is relying on justification. It is suggested that these cases were not properly argued and that the cases are inconsistent with earlier ones, such as *Argyll* v *Argyll* [1967] Ch 302, where the Duchess had already published articles for gain. Since Lord Denning MR left the bench, the law in *Woodward* v *Hutchins* has not been resurrected. The dictum in *Faccenda* should also be quietly interred.

The Continuing Debate Over Information Protected Post-employment

Faccenda created difficulties for employers seeking to retain a competitive edge in a difficult market-place. The information which they could not protect was very much of use to rivals, who could use it to undercut the plaintiffs and drive them out of business. It is not surprising that the courts have returned to the issue of the protection afforded to information by the implied term of confidentiality after employment. In *Lansing Linde Ltd* v *Kerr*, above, Staughton LJ (at 425) defined trade secrets as "information which, if disclosed to a competitor, would be liable to cause real (or significant) harm to the owner of the secret ... [I]t must be information used in a trade or business, and ... the owner must limit the dissemination of it or at least not encourage or permit widespread publication". He said (at 426) that there may be no difference between trade secrets and confidential information, but unfortunately he did not state whether he was referring to (merely) confidential information or to highly confidential information, which in *Faccenda* terms is the equivalent to trade secrets. Butler-Sloss LJ (at 435) stated that trade secrets included "highly confidential information of a non-technical nature or a non-scientific nature". For a Scottish definition see *Malden Timber Ltd* v *McLeish*, 1992 SLT 727, 734–5. It must be stated that it is still not easy to state whether something is a trade secret or highly confidential information. A ruling from the House of Lords is urgently required.

A Selection of English Trade Secrets Rulings

This section notes some examples of information which on the facts of the case have been held to constitute trade secrets, together with case law. Not all of the cases concern employees but the authorities are applied to all alleged confidence-breakers:

- drawings of machine tools: *Saltman*, above, *Brian D Collins (Engineers) Ltd* v *Charles Roberts Ltd* [1965] RPC 420, and *Weir Pumps Ltd* v *CML Pumps Ltd* [1984] FSR 33;
- dimensions of engines: *Merryweather* v *Moore* [1892] 2 Ch 518;
- copies of forms used in process serving: *Louis* v *Smellie* (1895) 73 LT 602;
- templates and patterns: *Peter Pan Manufacturing Corp* v *Corsets Silhouette Ltd* [1963] 3 All ER 402;
- circuit diagrams, magnetic tapes and specifications: *STC plc* v *Plessey Semi-conductors Ltd*, 11 November 1982, LEXIS;
- the test apparatus for heating air (no matter if unreliable): *Industrial Furnaces Ltd* v *Reaves* [1970] RPC 605;
- the correct type of plastic clamping strips for swimming pool walls: *Cranleigh Precision Engineering Co Ltd* v *Bryant* [1965] 1 WLR 1293;
- secret processes: *Amber Size & Chemical Co Ltd* v *Menzel* [1913] 2 Ch 239, which was approved in *Faccenda*, above (at 136), and several other cases including *British Industrial Plastics Ltd* v *Ferguson* [1940] 1 All ER 479 (HL), *Yates Circuit Foil Co* v *Electrofoils Ltd* [1982] FSR 345, *Standex International Ltd* v *Blades* [1976] FSR 114, and *Balston Ltd* v *Headline Filters Ltd* [1986] FSR 330;
- secret formulae, for example *Williams* v *Williams* (1817) 3 Mer 157, 36 ER 1 (remedy for eye diseases), *Morison* v *Moat* (1851) 9 Hare 241, 68 ER 492 and *Johnson & Bloy (Holdings) Ltd* v *Wolstenholme Rink plc* [1987] IRLR 499;
- an invention and the problem necessitating it: *Reid* v *Moss* (1932) 49 RPC 461, approved in *Faccenda* above (at 136);
- a "mechanical conception" (a pig rearer): *Nichrotherm Electrical Co Ltd* v *Percy* [1957] RPC 207;
- "customer distribution": *High Speed Printing Ltd* v *Mendoza*, 26 September 1986, LEXIS;
- sources of supply and the size and frequency of orders: *Ackroyds (London) Ltd* v *Islington Plastics Ltd* [1962] RPC 97 (swizzle sticks): *cf. Faccenda*;
- balance sheet: *Jarman* v *I Barget Ltd* [1977] FSR 260;
- budgetary information: *Fisher-Karpark Industries Ltd* v *Nichols* [1982] FSR 351;
- identity of employees: *G D Searle & Co Ltd* v *Celltech Ltd* [1982] FSR 92;

- "reader service cards": *International Scientific Communications Inc* v *Pattison* [1979] FSR 429;
- customer lists: cases are legion and include *Robb* v *Green* [1895] 2 Ch 315, *Faccenda* itself, and *Roger Bullivant Ltd* v *Ellis* [1987] ICR 464;
- names of contacts: *Smith* v *Du Pont (UK) Ltd* [1976] IRLR 107. In *Office International (London) Ltd* v *Palm Contract Furniture Ltd*, 2 December 1985, LEXIS, Falconer J said that a list of persons approached by sales staff but who had not given their business to the employers was "confidential information": a negative list was as valuable as a list of existing clients.

As W R McComas, M R Davison and D M Gonski in *The Protection of Trade Secrets* (Butterworths Australia, 1981) 7, wrote: "Over the years the courts have recognised the increasing complexity of modern industrial society and have been prepared to hold that any technical, trade, commercial or other information or device occurring or utilised in the day-to-day activities of the home or a business may be the subject of an action for breach of confidence".

The Extent of Protection

The form of the subject-matter of the information is irrelevant. Hirst J in *Fraser* v *Thames Television Ltd* [1984] QB 44, 66, said: "neither the originality nor the quality of an idea is in any way affected by the form in which it is expressed". The form in which the trade secret is expressed is irrelevant. It might be a blueprint, a model, a machine. See below for memorisation. There is a debate whether purely abstract ideas can be trade secrets. It was said in Anon, "Nature of Trade Secrets and their Protection" (1928) 42 Harv LR 354 4 that abstract ideas could not be trade secrets but some English cases come close to holding differently, for example *Nichrotherm*, above. Such cases may constitute the prelude to a development whereby purely abstract ideas receive protection (*cf.* copyright law and its protection for the expression of ideas). For a comment see J Stuckey-Clarke "Remedies for the Misappropriation" [1989] EIPR 333.

Development of Trade Secrets

As Megarry J said in *Coco*, above (at 47), confidential information can comprise an item which has been developed from information which is in the public domain. "Whether it is described as originality or novelty or ingenuity or otherwise, ... there must be some product of the human brain which suffices to confer a confidential nature upon the information ... ".

A Simple Matter can be Confidential

Under Water Welders and Repairers Ltd v *Street* [1968] RPC 498 (Ch D) exemplifies the proposition that a simple matter can have the quality of confidence. The solution to a problem may be self-evident but it remains confidential.

"Trivial Tittle-Tattle, However Confidential"

This phrase appears in the judgment of Megarry J in *Coco*, above. The principal exponent is Lord Goff but an example occurs at first instance in *Attorney-General* v *Guardian Newspapers Ltd (No 2)* [1990] 1 AC 109 where Scott J refused *obiter* to protect "useless information" such as "the contents of the daily menu in MI5's London office". What is trivial, useless or absurd may be dependent on the standpoint of the observer.

The Memory Rule

An employee may leave her job with printed details of trade secrets or with a list of customers. An employee can during employment be restrained from copying a list for use afterwards. What about the situation where the defendant consciously memorises the information? The preponderance of authority is that the employee can be restrained. In *Printers & Finishers Ltd* v *Holloway*, above, Cross J said: "the mere fact that the confidential information is not embodied in a document but is carried away by the employee in his head is not, of course, in itself a reason against the granting of an injunction to prevent its use or disclosure by him" (at 255). He considered that the true distinction lay between information which a person "of ordinary honesty and intelligence would recognise as belonging to the employer and that which he would not". Such a person would recognise a memorised list as belonging to the employer. This test was applied in *Poly Lina* v *Finch*, above at 762.

There are, however, cases to the contrary. In *Baker* v *Gibbons* [1972] 1 WLR 693 Pennycuick V-C refused to grant the third defendants an injunction pending trial against the plaintiff, one of their former directors, to prevent his soliciting their employees to leave them and join him. He held that an injunction was always directed at a written list (at 701–2). The judgment was upheld on appeal but without reference to this point. There is some support for *Baker* v *Gibbons* in other cases such as *Merryweather* v *Moore*, above (at 524) where Kekewich J said: "if he can carry them [that is details of a table of dimensions] in his head, no one can prevent his doing that and making use of them". It should be noted that *Printers & Finishers* was not cited in *Baker* v *Gibbons*, and there are other contrary statements such as that of Astbury J *arguendo* (at 242) in *Amber Size & Chemical Co Ltd* v *Menzel*, above, who stated: "how can it possibly matter whether the servant learns the process by heart or writing it down? It is an equal breach of confidence to use or disclose it in either case". Cases after *Baker* v *Gibbons* continue to hold that it is immaterial that the defendant has memorised the list or other trade secret: see, for example, *Johnson & Bloy (Holdings) Ltd* v *Wolstenholme Rink plc*, above (at 502) (interlocutory appeal).

A summary of present law was provided by Speight J in *Westminster Chemical New Zealand Ltd* v *McKinley* [1973] 1 NZLR 659, 666 (Sup Ct), who attempted to reconcile *Baker* v *Gibbons* and *Printers & Finishers*. He stated: "I do not go so far as to say that I would restrict the matter only to written material if it could be shown that information used even from memory was of such a specialised nature that the former employee could not have known of it but for his employment". This distinction between memorising the list for present employment and doing so for future competition was emphasised by Megarry J in *British Northrop Ltd* v *Texteam Blackburn Ltd* [1974] RPC 57, 76. The employers must prove that the employee *consciously* memorised the names, etc, for this purpose: *Coral Index Ltd* v *Regent Index Ltd* [1970] RPC 147, 149 (Stamp J). If, however, the list if not so memorised but the employee recalls the customers' names, no injunction will lie – the information has become part of the employee's skill and knowledge, as occurred in *Faccenda* itself. The former employees were free to use the sales information gained during employment without memorising it for the benefit of a competing business. An interesting Commonwealth case, which demonstrates that the employee did not learn a list, is *A C Gibbons Pty Ltd* v *Cooper* (1980) 23 SASR 269 (Sup Ct, South Australia) where the ex-employee stated that he had gone through the Adelaide phone book to recall customers' names. In *Louis* v *Smellie* (1895) 73 LT 226, 228, Lindley LJ said: "if the defendant happens to remember that there is an agent whose address he can find out from the ordinary directories he is at liberty to do it". Another issue which was seen in *Baker* v *Gibbons* is that where there is a list, not every name on it may be confidential. The employers must prove that it is so.

The rationale behind the law that an injunction is not to be granted in relation to memorised lists is that it would be impractical to issue an injunction because the plaintiffs would have to prove that each name of the customers that the defendant had memorised was on the list: see *Baker* v *Gibbons*, above (at 702). The wording of the injunction may also be important in this context even if the former employee has memorised the list, no injunction ought to be granted for those parts of the list which are common knowledge; so, the injunction cannot in these circumstances affect all the names on the list. Another rationale is that the memory rule allows the employee access to clients he or she has personally acquired but not ones he or she did not.

It is thought that this memory rule does not adequately represent the law. What if the employers have only a short list of customers, say, because their work is specialised? Why should they not receive protection when a firm with a lengthy list does because the employee cannot memorise such a list? What if in the same firm one employee has a good memory and another has not and so has to write down a list? The District Court for New Jersey in *Midland-Ross Corp* v *Yokana*, 185 F Supp 594 (1960) thought it an "absurdity" to grant an injunction against matters which the former employee could recall. Certainly if as in *Best Dairy Farms Inc* v *Houchen*, 448 P 2d 158 (1968) (Mont) the information in the employee's memory is readily available to others, it is not sensible to issue an injunction. Compare the view of the Supreme Court of New York in *Palmer* v *Dewitt* (1871) 23 LT 823, 827 (a case on common law copyright): "The objection is not to the committing of a play to memory, for over that no court can exercise any control, but in using the memory afterwards as the means of depriving the owner of his property". The memory rule may also lead to perjury. In *Sperry Rand Corp* v *Rothlein*, 241 F Supp 549 (1964) (D Conn) the court disbelieved the employee's statement that he could recall without memorisation tolerances of 1,000ths of an inch. It may also be that an employee memorises the names of the biggest customers and makes a list of the rest; presumably the employers will want protection for the memorised list more than for the written one. It is arguable that the reasoning behind the memory rule is deficient in that if one has memorised some names on a written list, surely it ought to be open to the inference that other names were also confidential. After all, the employers' economic interests may be the same in both instances. The length of an employee's memory seems irrelevant to "what is or is not fair post-employment activity" (H M Blake, "Employee Agreements not to Compete" (1960) 73 Harv LR 625, 656). Estey CJHC inquired in *Alberts* v *Mountjoy* (1978) 79 DLR (3d) 108, 115 (Ont) why the law should provide "a remedy against the departing employee with a poor memory, but none against one with a good memory". Why should it matter that one employer has a long customer list, which cannot be recalled, and another has a short list? And why should it matter how the information was obtained?

In the context of written and memorised lists there is much sense in what Field J said over 60 years ago in *Di Angeles* v *Scauzillo*, 191 NE 426 (1934) (SJC Mass):

> The significance of the possession by an employee of a written list of his former employer's customers, as distinguished from the retention of their names in memory, in any particular case where the information is not confidential, lies in the fact that the employee is the owner of the written paper ... in the fact that the list of customers was copied or written out in violation of a duty to the employer, or, perhaps, in the fact that the employee, in carrying off the written list, is carrying off something more than experience gained by him in the business

Leaving aside property rights in the papers neither the second nor the third ground distinguishes between written and memorised lists. Provided that the names are confidential there is no distinction. The distinction lies between confidential information and skill and experience. The problem arises – and it is not one which has been tackled by the English courts – when some names are confidential but some, for instance, are household ones. Why should a former employee be enjoined from contacting famous-name customers? More towards the borderline are names which persons in the industry alone would know, but again these seem to be part of the ex-employee's skills and experience. To stop him or her using these names would be to deprive the employee of working at the trade in which the skill or experience was gained. Similarly, with regard to a route which a salesperson followed. A rival could "follow the van" and so trace customers with little expenditure or time wasted. Why cannot the salesperson recall the route? The answer must lie in whether each of these aspects of competition is regarded as legitimate or not. From the viewpoint of the employee and employer, the answer is easy. As for the public, in a Western economy, such competition seems not improper, though some may have their doubts.

Is Detriment Necessary?

There is some debate whether detriment is required: see, for example Lord Denning MR in *Seager* v *Copydex Ltd* [1967] 1 WLR 923, 931, where he stated that "prejudice" was required. The *obiter* reference in *Coco* v *A N Clark (Engineers) Ltd* [1969] RPC 41 that equity will not protect tittle-tattle, however confidential, may be explained as a requirement of detriment, but it may be a reference to equitable remedies. In *Ashmore* v *Douglas-Home* (1982) [1987] FSR 533 the court required detriment but it did not involve a trade secret, though *Coco* did. Trivial "tittle-tattle" seems to relate to the protectability of the information. The old Victorian case of *Prebble* v *Reeves* [1910] VLR 88 and the more recent *Pacifica Shipping Co Ltd* v *Andersen* [1986] 2 NZLR 328, 342, both required detriment as do a substantial number of other Commonwealth cases including *Breeze Corp* v *Hamilton Clamp & Stampings Inc* (1962) 30 DLR (3d) 685, 697, *Conveyor Co* v *Cameron Bros Engineering Co Ltd* [1973] NZLR 38, 41, *Castrol Australia Pty Ltd* v *Emtech Associates Pty Ltd* (1980) 33 ALR 31, 48, *Talbot* v *General Television Corp Pty Ltd* [1981] RPC 1, 8, and *LAC Minerals Ltd* v *International Corona Resources Ltd* (1989) 61 DLR (4d) 14. Scots law would seem to require "prejudice" at least in governmental secrets cases: *Lord Advocate* v *Scotsman Publications Ltd* [1990] 1 AC 812. As Lord Coulsfield said, "useless or trivial" information will not be protected. Some US cases require detriment, for example *Crouch* v *Sewing Machinery Co Inc*, 468 SW 2d 604 (1971) (Tex) and *Hickory Specialities Inc* v *B & L Laboratories Inc*, 592 SW 583, 586 (1977). The duty of fidelity has been said to require detriment, for example *Reid* v *Moss* (1932) 49 RPC 461, 480, *obiter*.

Despite the plethora of authority, other cases have either not mentioned detriment or have rejected it. In the case which relaunched breach of confidence, *Saltman Engineering Co Ltd* v *Campbell Engineering Co Ltd*, above, Lord Greene MR did not refer to detriment, while in *X* v *Y* [1988] 2 All ER 648, 657, Rose J specifically rejected detriment as an element; *obiter* he said that in any case there was detriment.

The lengthiest English assessment is found in the speech of Lord Keith in *Attorney-General* v *Guardian Newspapers Ltd* [1990] 1 AC 109, the "Spycatcher" case. He stated that detriment was "presumably" needed for damages, but that perhaps nominal damages would be available where there was no detriment. He said (at 256): "I would think it a sufficient detriment to the confider that information given in confidence is to be disclosed to persons whom he would prefer not to know it, even though the disclosure would not be harmful to him in any positive way". This definition would largely obviate any need for detriment in trade secrets law. Lord Griffiths (at 270) required "detriment or potential detriment", while Lord Goff (at 281) wished to reserve the question. Lord Keith thought it possible that no detriment was required in personal information cases.

Lord Keith placed on one side the governmental secrets cases, where it is accepted that detriment is necessary. This rule is based on *Commonwealth of*

Australia v *John Fairfax & Sons Ltd* (1981) 147 CLR 39, which has been approved in *Attorney-General for England & Wales* v *Brandon Book Publishers Ltd* [1986] IR 597 and by all the judges in *Attorney-General (UK)* v *Heinemann Publishers Australia Pty Ltd* (1987) 75 ALR 353 (NSW Sup Ct).

The difficulty would not exist if the action were easily classifiable. If it were a tort, presumably detriment would be required. If it were a proprietary action, any interference would be a detriment. If the action is one involving equity's exclusive jurisdiction, there is no need for any damage to a proprietary interest. Equity acts against the wrong, not against the damage. If the action is *sui generis*, the breach would be sufficient damage alone. Gurry, the principal English commentator, stated that detriment is not required and deals with detriment as part of the process of granting an injunction: *Breach of Confidence*, (Clarendon, 1984) 407–8. Such is this writer's view too. Therefore, the view of J Hull in "Speed Seal v Paddington" [1986] 8 EIPR 249 that detriment is required is incorrect.

In sum, except in governmental secrets cases there is no separate condition of detriment. Even if detriment were required, there would normally be little difficulty in employers proving that the employee's use or disclosure has prejudicially affected them. For example, if the employee leaves and joins a rival, the revelation of confidential information to her new employers would almost automatically be a detriment to her former employers because they will have been deprived of their competitive edge. If detriment is necessary, the lack of such a requirement in restraint of trade cases is one advantage which covenants have over implied contractual clauses.

Communication of Information in Circumstances Imparting a Duty of Confidentiality

In relation to employees these circumstances are fulfilled by disclosure of trade secrets by the employers to the employee in the context of a contract of employment.

Unauthorised Use or Disclosure: The *Breach* of Confidence

The employee must breach the duty of confidentiality. In relation to restraint of trade covenants (depending on the wording) it need not usually be demonstrated that the former employee used or disclosed the data. An express term is thus more advantageous than an implied one to employers, for employers need prove less with the former than with the latter.

The "*actus reus*"

If the plaintiffs have established that the information is confidential, before they can succeed they must show that the defendant has acted in breach of her duty to preserve confidentiality. The concept of "breach" is a simple one: has the defendant disclosed or used the information for a purpose other than that which it was given? Alternatively, did the plaintiffs consent to the use or disclosure? Use or disclosure may be inferred from the circumstances. It does not matter that the defendant did not realise that the information was confidential (*National Broach & Machine Co v Churchill Gear Machines Ltd* [1965] 1 WLR 1199 (CA); the defendant accepted that decision: [1967] 1 WLR 384 (HL)) or that the defendant acted unknowingly (see The "mens rea" below). Similarly, the motive of the defendant is immaterial. There is no breach if the defendant did not obtain the information by breach of confidence but by, for example, independent discovery. As will be seen an injunction may be obtained to prevent a threatened use or breach.

One matter which requires discussion at this juncture is the nature of the duty not to use the confidential information. As Megarry J pointed in *Coco v A N Clark (Engineers) Ltd* [1969] RPC 41 the obligation not to use or disclose secret commercial information resembles more closely a duty not to use the information without paying for it rather than a duty not to use the information at all. In this respect the action is like a forced sale or licensing. Megarry J distinguished personal information, where the duty was one not to reveal the secret at all. His postulation of the nature of the duty may be criticised thus: he defines the duty in terms of remedy; however, the commercial value of the information is relevant to the remedy, not to the duty itself. Similar is J Stuckey "The Equitable Action for Breach of Confidence" (1981) 9 Syd LR 402, 408. His approach is also out of line with the definition of the action of Lord Greene MR in *Saltman Engineering Co Ltd v Campbell Engineering Co Ltd* (1948) [1963] 2 All ER 413, which is quoted above. Megarry J's difficulty stemmed from the springboard doctrine. If one cannot use information without consent, an injunction will lie to prevent the use. If, however, the duty is phrased as one not to use without payment, there arises the issue of whether the injunction will lie. If the defendant pays, why have an injunction? If she does not, an injunction ought to last for only as long as the headstart remains. In this way Megarry J reconciled the springboard principle with the duty and the breach aspects of the action.

It is for consideration whether the notion of a "forced licence" might be preferable to that of a forced sale. A forced licence would recognise that the employers retain an interest in the trade secret while allowing the employee to exploit it.

Evidence of a breach may not be hard to find. It would seem not to matter that, for example, the ex-employee does not copy every point from the secret. In a US case, *Northern Petrochemical Co v Tomlinson*, 484 F 2d 1057 (1973), the Court of Appeals for the Seventh Circuit said *obiter* that "the test for illegality is whether a supposedly different process ... was derived from a wrongfully obtained secret process". In that case the former employee was held to have given to his new employers the process which they modified before using. That the process was substantially different was immaterial because the misappropriated process was the "cornerstone" of the new. Often the facts speak for themselves. In *Kubik Inc v Hull*, 224 NW 2d 80 (1974) the Michigan Court of Appeals related trial testimony to demonstrate that the defendant gave his new employers the plaintiffs' technical information, and provided information permitting his new employers to give a lower quote than his old. In *Aries Information Systems Inc v Pacific Management Systems Corp*, 366 NW 2d 366 (1985) (CA Minn), the court was asked to determine whether the appellants had misappropriated confidential information contrary to the Minnesota Trade Secrets Act 1984. It held that they had used software without the respondents' consent. There were no material differences between the software of the parties and the appellants did not show how they had developed or acquired the process. Therefore, there was an appropriation. A comparison case is *de Filippis v Chrysler Corp*, 159 F 2d 478 (1947), where the Court of Appeals for the Second Circuit held that there were material differences between the plaintiff's and defendants' overdrive mechanisms. There was no breach despite the defendants retaining the plaintiff's drawings for nine months.

A case where the evidence showed that the defendant had copied formulae from his former employers and not from public sources is *Heatbath Corp v Ifkovits*, 254 NE 2d 139 (1969), a decision of the Illinois Appellate Court. Seidenfeld J noted that the plaintiff's formulae were held in confidence and no one had competed with them, until the employee left. "He showed no expense for research and development, but rather was able to make a significant profit almost immediately by selling products to plaintiff's old customers at half the plaintiff's price. [D]efendant copied, rather than developed, the formulas of the plaintiff by independent legal methods ... ". The employee is liable even though there was no "slavish" copying: *Richardson v Suzuki Motor Co Ltd*, 868 F 2d 1226, 1244 (1989) (Fed Cir). A contrasting case comes from the Supreme Court of Oregon. In *North Pacific Lumber Co v Moore*, 551 P 2d 431 (1976) the plaintiffs did not contend that the employee had copied or removed a large number of customer cards with detailed data about lumber transactions, and the employee could not have memorised such technical information. Accordingly the employers could not prove that the information had been appropriated.

Evidence may show that, though there are differences in the two systems, those were put there to disguise copying, as occurred in the District Court of Massachusetts case of *Dickerman Associates Inc v Tiverton Bottled Gas Co*, 222 USPA (BNA) 529 (1984). Zobel DJ also accepted evidence that the defendants could not have produced the system in the time they did without copying from the plaintiffs.

The question whether the defendant used the plaintiffs' confidential information is one of fact: *Terrapin Ltd v Builders' Supply Co (Hayes) Ltd* (1960) 77 RPC 128, 135.

The *"mens rea"*

Is a defendant liable only when he or she knowingly broke the duty of confidentiality or does liability also arise where that person has acted unwittingly? English cases support the view that the latter version is correct. In *Terrapin Ltd* v *Builders' Supply Co (Hayes) Ltd*, above, Roxburgh J said *obiter* that subconscious use of information about a type of portable buildings was caught by the action, and as stated above the Court of Appeal came to the same conclusion in *Seager* v *Copydex Ltd* [1967] 1 WLR 923. Unintentional use also gave rise to liability in *National Broach & Machine Co* v *Churchill Gear Machines Ltd* [1965] RPC 61, 78, 83. The CA and HL decisions, above, did not refer to this issue. One case is to the contrary. *Paul (K S) Ltd* v *Southern Instruments Ltd* [1964] RPC 118 held that the defendants were not liable if they were entirely innocent, but, as Gurry, *Breach of Confidence* (Clarendon, 1984), 265, pointed out, the report is so truncated that it is difficult to see how the court reached its conclusions and so the case is not of the same authority as *Seager* v *Copydex Ltd*, which like *Paul* is a Court of Appeal decision.

The liability of an employee even where he or she has acted subconsciously may be defended on the grounds that without such liability the defendant might unfairly take advantage of the information.

The Boundaries of the Duty of Confidentiality

However secret and confidential the information there can be no binding obligation of confidence if that information is blurted out in public or is communicated in other circumstances which negative any duty of holding it confidential (*per* Megarry J in *Coco*, above, at 47–8).

Furthermore, if the trade secret is derived independently by another company the employers cannot restrain that company, for example *James* v *James* (1872) LR 13 Eq 421. The information must have been "directly or indirectly obtained from a plaintiff": *per* Lord Greene MR in *Saltman*, above (at 415).

"Common Knowledge" or "Public Property"

If a trade secret is revealed, the owners lose the competitive edge that secrets gave them over rivals. For this reason one has to decide whether information is confidential or public. The law is stated thus: "Something which is public property and public knowledge cannot *per se* provide any foundation for proceedings for breach of confidence. However confidential the circumstances of the communication, there can be no breach of confidence to reveal to others something which is already common knowledge". So said Lord Greene MR in *Saltman*, above (at 415). (Donaldson MR in *Attorney-General* v *Guardian Newspapers*

Ltd [1987] 1 WLR 1248, 1275 (CA), sought to draw a line between "public property" and "public knowledge" but no other judge did at any level in the case or before or since: it is suggested that Lord Greene MR was simply finding synonyms for common knowledge.) Accordingly the information must remain secret. If there is no secret, there is no protection. For example, the half-size tennis courts in *Half Court Tennis Pty Ltd* v *Seymour* (1980) 53 FLR 240 (Qd Sup Ct) were public knowledge as to their construction and the prices were not *per se* confidential because they were in the public domain. Accordingly putting products onto the market destroys confidentiality (unless the secret is not revealed). In its more modern guise of information "in the public domain" (for example *Potters-Ballotini Ltd* v *Weston-Baker* [1977] RPC 202, 206) this limitation on the duty of confidentiality received its imprimatur in the judgment of Megarry V-C in *Guinle*, above. To take a matter out of the public domain (a term which Simon Brown J in *Attorney-General* v *Turnaround Distribution Ltd (1986)* [1989] FSR 169, 172, called a "fashionable idiom" though it has since been used without opprobrium) the employers must have used their brains (*Saltman*) or exercised the human brain to produce something with "originality, novelty or ingenuity" (*Coco*, above). "Novelty" simply means that the item is not common knowledge in the trade. An invention in patent terms is not necessary. By taking over this information without expenditure of time and money, the defendant may gain a competitive advantage by spending less on research and development and by seeing whether the process would be commercially profitable. Accordingly, if work must be done on publicly available material to transmute it into the information sought to be protected, that information will be confidential and not in the public domain. Therefore, the fact that the defendant could have lawfully acquired the material is irrelevant if she did acquire it unlawfully. (It should be said that early cases did not investigate the accessibility of the information: they merely inquired whether the information was in the public domain.)

A good illustration of the application of the principle, though not of a case involving an employee, is *Coco* v *A N Clark (Engineers) Ltd*, above. The parties agreed to collaborate on the design for a moped. Negotiations collapsed, and the defendants brought out their version which was similar to the original agreed design. Megarry J refused to grant the plaintiff an injunction because the plaintiff had not satisfied him that the defendant company had used his ideas as opposed to information which they could have obtained independently both through their own expertise and from publicly available material. So although the plaintiff had given the defendant some information in confidential circumstances, that situation was insufficient. He also had to show that the information was not in the public domain. Megarry J said (at 47): "something which has been constructed solely from materials in the public domain may possess the necessary quality of confidentiality: for something new and confidential may have been brought into being by the application of the skill and ingenuity of the human brain. Novelty depends on the thing itself, and not upon the quality of its constituent parts". (Certainly novelty in the patent sense is not required, for an independent discoverer can have a trade secret which someone else first created, and technical know-how and customer lists can be protected even though there is no originality.) Had Mr Coco been an employee of the defendants, the same principle would have applied. If the employee had not used confidential information obtained from the employers, he or she would not be liable, subject of course to his or her not breaching the duty of fidelity through spare-time work. Clause 2(2) of the Law Commission's draft bill, Report no 110, *Breach of Confidence* (Cmnd 8388, 1981), would put in statutory form the quote, above, from *Coco*. For criticism, see Scots Law Commission, Report no 90, *Breach of Confidence* (Cmnd 9385, 1984) 48.

Another illustration of the principle is *Robb* v *Green* [1895] 2 Ch 315. The employer had compiled a list of customers for his live pheasants and eggs. The defendant, his former manager, took the list. The Court of Appeal held that he was in breach of his duty to his ex-employer, even though the information was publicly available. His misappropriation of the list had saved him the trouble of discovering the information from public sources such as directories. As Gurry wrote in his book, *Breach of Confidence* (Clarendon, 1984) 71, "the defendant was not permitted to short-circuit this process by taking advantage of the list which had been communicated to him in confidence".

The fact that there has been some communication does not necessarily destroy the plaintiff's right to confidentiality, at least if that publication is only a limited and impermanent disclosure, for example in a co-development. Amedee Turner wrote that not everything in a Chinese library is in the public domain: "The Law Commission's Proposals on Confidential Information" [1976] Jo of CIPA 293, 300. Donaldson LJ in *Sun Printers Ltd* v *Westminster Press Ltd* [1982] IRLR 292, 294 said: "there is nothing . . . to prevent the fullest communication between management and the workforce under a seal of confidentiality". The information does not have to be known to everyone to lack the attribute of confidentiality. This principle was taken further in *Schering Chemicals Ltd* v *Falkman Ltd* [1982] QB 1, where Shaw LJ controversially held that the need to remind the public of facts forgotten meant that the information was not public. He further said that, "it is not the law that where confidentiality exists it is terminated or eroded by adventitious publicity" (at 28). This view would seem to be incorrect. By it the person who by those means acquired the information could not use it even though it has become public knowledge with the result that everyone except him or her could use it. If one discloses information for the purposes of licensing, one does not thereby given the licensee carte blanche to reveal that information. In *Falkman*, however, it might be said that the position was essentially different – there was public knowledge but one person in the world was restrained, and contract law permits one party agreeing to maintain silence about what one has found out. The other members of the court did not, it seems, necessarily agree with Shaw LJ: indeed, Lord Denning MR dissented. Browne-Wilkinson V-C explained the case as an application of the springboard doctrine (see below) in *Attorney-General* v *Guardian Newspapers Ltd* [1987] 1 WLR 1248, 1263. It was not followed by the New South Wales Supreme Court in *Attorney-General (UK)* v *Heinemann Publishers Australia Pty Ltd* (1987) 75 ALR 353.

It should be noted that the mere fact that the information was simple does not mean that it was public property. In *Cranleigh Precision Engineering Co Ltd* v *Bryant* [1965] 1 WLR 1293 the designs of the clamp and the overlapping strips were simple but nevertheless confidential. As Megarry J said in *Coco*, above (at 47) "the simpler an idea, the more likely it is to need protection". However, the fact that a process or design is simple may go towards showing that allegedly confidential matter is part of public knowledge and does not have a quality of confidentiality. Certainly a trade secret need not be technical. An idea for a television series is protectable. And the fact that something is complex does not *per se* make it confidential information.

Whether a matter is secret may depend on whether the information is generally or substantially known throughout the industry concerned, for example in the woodworking trade as in *Berry* v *Glidden Co*, 92 F Supp 909, 914 (1950) (SDNY), or whether knowledge is restricted to certain parties. It is suggested that the phrase "matters of general knowledge within the industry" better epitomises the law than "common knowledge" or "information in the public domain". The phrase occurs in *Whitmyer Bros* v *Doyle*, 274 A 2d 577, 581 (1971) (NJ). Turner, *The Law of Trade Secrets* (Sweet & Maxwell, 1962) 16, wrote: "Secrecy among potentially interested persons is the material criterion". The courts do not inquire whether every person knows the details of designs and processes. In this sense the secrecy need not be absolute: see Turner, *The Law of Trade Secrets* (1962) 16–7, 81–6, and 1967 Supplement. For instance, if information is available in technical papers, it remains confidential if a person would have to work to make the information of use to the public (*Ackroyds*, above), though trade secrets can be discovered fortuitously. "Secrecy is a relative term. What is known to several persons may no longer be secret in the strictest sense. But we are concerned with its meaning in the legal and equitable sense", *per* Cororan J in *Rabinowetz* v *Dasher*, 78 USPW 163 (1948) (SCNY), quoted by D E Fisher "From Secrecy to Plagiarism" [1968] U Qu LJ 60. In more general terms, "the confidential nature of the document is not dependent on whether the information which it contains is available elsewhere, but on the question of whether it contains useful information which has been compiled by the plaintiffs for a particular purpose", *per* Plowman J in *Suhner*, above. The test laid down by the Court of Appeals for the Ninth Circuit in *Clark* v *Bunker*, 453 F 2d 1006, 1010 (1972) represents English law: "there must be a substantial element of secrecy so that a third person would have difficulty acquiring the necessary information . . . without resorting to the use of improper means of acquiring the secret". A considerable number of persons may know of the secret process or formula but nevertheless it may still be confidential information. It is "a question of degree" *per* Donaldson MR in *Attorney-General* v *Guardian Newspapers Ltd* [1990] 1 AC 109, 177 (CA) *cf. Sun Printers Ltd* v *Westminster Press Ltd*, above. However, what is generally available is not protected by the implied term of confidentiality, for example *Weir Pumps Ltd* v *CML Pumps Ltd* [1984] FSR 33, 39.

If the information is part public and part secret, an employee must use only that knowledge which is not confidential, according to *Seager* v *Copydex Ltd* [1967] RPC

349, 360. If common knowledge did amount to a trade secret, competition would be stifled. It should be noted that the application of the springboard doctrine is difficult where the information is part public, part secret.

Some of the law in this section is aptly summarised by Unverzagt J in the Appellate Court, Illinois, in *Hayden's Sport Center Inc v Johnson*, 441 NE 2d 927, 932 (1982): "[i]nformation will not be considered a trade secret if its contents are generally known within an industry, fully and completely disclosed by the company through its catalogues or literature disseminated throughout the industry, or disclosed by the products themselves" (spelling anglicised). Donaldson MR summed up English law in *Attorney–General v Guardian Newspapers Ltd* [1990] 1 AC 109, 177 (CA): the implied term no longer applies when the information is "made generally available to the relevant public".

The Secret has Ceased to Exist

The noblest of human productions – knowledge, truths ascertained, conceptions and ideas – become, after voluntary communication to others, free as the air to common use" *per* Brandeis J (dissenting) *International News Service v Associated Press*, 248 US 215, 250 (1918).

How far does the law reflect these sentiments? (This area of law is sometimes seen as independent from the previous topic, sometimes as part of it. It is treated separately here for ease of exposition.)

At times there may be no confidential information because the employers have disclosed the material (see also later for consent to disclosure). For example, they may have distributed a confidential report too widely for confidentiality to continue to exist (*Sun Printers*, above). Scottish law is the same: *Lord Advocate v Scotsman Publications Ltd*, 1988 SLT 490 (2nd Div). In that eventuality the duty formerly owed to the employers is terminated and the employee has the same rights as the rest of the world, who are strangers to the obligation. The subject of an expired patent cannot be a trade secret: *Newberry v James* (1817) 2 Mer 446. In *Mustad & Son v Dosen* (1929) [1964] 1 WLR 109, the House of Lords held that if information previously confidential is disclosed to the public by the acquisition of a patent, the employers can no longer restrain an employee from using or disclosing the secret process or design. The position, said Lord Buckmaster, would have been different if the ex-employee had acquired knowledge of secrets ancillary to a patent. An application for a patent would not end confidentiality. He stated: "after the disclosure had been made by the appellants to the world it was impossible to them to get an injunction restraining the respondents from disclosing what was common knowledge. The secret, as a secret, had ceased to exist". The plaintiffs had made the secret public knowledge. *Mustad*'s case was applied by Cross J in *Franchi v Franchi* [1967] RPC 149 to foreign patents. He followed the well-known New York case of *Vulcan Detinning Co v Assam*, 185 App Div 399 (1918) to hold that the plaintiffs could not recover damages because "by applying for the Belgian patent they set in train a process which would, in the ordinary course of events, lead to the process becoming known to their competitors at or shortly after the publication date in Belgium" (at 153). The judge said *obiter* that if relative secrecy remained, the plaintiffs would have succeeded as is consonant with the previous section. Accordingly a matter may be confidential in one area of England and Wales but not in another area, as may be seen from the news cases such as *Exchange Telegraph Co Ltd* v *Gregory & Co Ltd* [1896] 1 QB 147. The necessary quality of confidentiality was preserved despite the widespread dissemination of news items. In *Franchi* Cross J said that secrecy ended once the foreign specification became open to inspection in England. See too section 2(4) of the Patents Act 1977.

The principle here mentioned has been said to be in conflict or at least apparent conflict with another, the so-called "springboard" or "head start" doctrine, which derives from the judgment of Roxburgh J in *Terrapin* (1959) [1960] RPC 128, 130.

> A person who has obtained information in confidence is not allowed to use it as a springboard for activities detrimental to the person who made the confidential communication, and springboard it remains even when all the features have been published or can be ascertained by actual inspection by any member of the public . . . The dismantling of a unit might enable a person to proceed without plans or specifications, or other technical information, but not, I think, without some know-how, and certainly not without taking the trouble to dismantle . . . Therefore, the possessor of the confidential information still has a long start over any member of the public . . . It is, in my view, inherent in the principle upon which the *Saltman* case [above] rests that the possessor of such information must be placed under a special disability in the field of competition in order to ensure that he does not get an unfair start . . .

(*Terrapin* was not an employment case but has been applied to employees from as early as *Cranleigh*, 1965.)

One problem with this statement is that Roxburgh J did not limit expressly his remarks to limiting the injunction to the period necessary for competitors to catch up on the head start but rather the disclosee is bound, and he or she alone, beyond that time. The principle was approved by Lord Denning MR in *Seager* v *Copydex Ltd* [1967] RPC 349 (CA) and has been applied several times, for example *Harrison* v *Project & Design Co (Redcar) Ltd* [1978] FSR 81 (Graham J).

The springboard doctrine limits the time during which the employee may be restrained, whereas the grant of a patent ends the secrecy and everyone has access to the confidential information but cannot use it for a certain period. One problem with the doctrine is its width. It applies where the advantage is simply knowing how to apply information which is accessible to the public, as in *Cranleigh*, above, and where the information is not of major importance, as in *Seager*, above. These effects are severe on a defendant who may not be dishonest. The law is designed to protect those employers who were ahead of their competitors and would have remained ahead, had the employee not revealed the secret. The injunction on this view should last as long as that benefit would have lasted, had there been no disclosure. For this reason the injunction ought to be limited in time. Whether it is so limited or not, it may be dissolved when the head start has come to an end. There is, therefore, no need for there to be a secret remaining at the time when the injunction is granted. Compare *Allen-Qualley Co* v *Shellmar Products Co*, 31 F 2d 293 (1929): a court of equity cannot approve a breach of confidence even where the plaintiff later reveals it to the world, since the defendant cannot complain that he or she had been deprived of the opportunity open to everyone else.

In *Mustad* publication destroyed the confidentiality; in *Terrapin* it did not. In *Peter Pan*, above, Pennycuick J, who did not have the transcript of *Terrapin* before him, saw the conflict but refused to choose between the principles (assuming that he had a choice, because *Mustad* is a House of Lords decision) because to do so was unnecessary on the facts as he had them before him. It should be remembered that putting a product on the market does not *per se* destroy its confidentiality. It is only if no "work would have to be done upon [the information] to make it available" (*per* Havers J in *Ackroyds*, above) to the public that the product loses its confidentiality. This approach explains *Terrapin*. If the two cases as stated do conflict, Roskill J, as he then was, suggested a reconciliation in *Cranleigh*, above, namely that in *Mustad* it was the plaintiffs themselves who published the information while in *Cranleigh* the disclosure was by a third party. He held that *Terrapin* applied to only the latter eventuality. If *Terrapin* applies, therefore, an injunction may be awarded which restrains the defendants for an unlimited time, a state of law which has been criticised as penalising the employee when it should be protecting the employers: W J Braithwaite "Trade Secrets: The Spring-Board Unsprung" (1979) 42 MLR 94, 96. Accordingly the fact that publication is made by a third party does not by itself release the employee from the duty not to disclose. Whether a plaintiff in that situation needs protection depends on the market: *Speed Seal Products Ltd* v *Paddington* [1986] 1 All ER 91. Fox LJ (at 95) approved the reconciliation attempted in *Cranleigh*.

The court in *Speed Seal* listed three situations:

(1)   published by the plaintiffs, as in *Mustad*: no protection;
(2)   publication by a stranger: protection;
(3)   publication by a person under a duty of confidentiality (for example an ex-employee): protection (*cf.* the Spycatcher litigation).

In the second and third situations it was not the voluntary act of the employers which placed the information in the public domain. Hull "Speed Seal v Paddington" [1986] 8 EIPR 249 noted the "curious" result of those cases. The defendant alone was under a disability: he or she was restrained from using publicly available information. Fox LJ in *Speed Seal* noted that the purpose of the injunction was to protect the plaintiffs. If the defendant is the sole other party with the information, the injunction will protect the plaintiffs. See further Lord Goff in *Attorney-General* v *Guardian Newspapers Ltd (No 2)* [1990] 1 AC 109, 285, discussed in Chapter 13.

The Law Commission, *Breach of Confidence*, Report no 110 (Cmnd 8388, 1981) paragraphs 4.31, 6.70, proposed that restraint should last only so long as the head start would have remained, for the purpose of the doctrine was to protect plaintiffs, not punish defendants. They considered that this approach was in line with the full text of *Terrapin*. Therefore, the disclosure would not be bound for all time though he or she would be liable for damages for the breach of confidence. Some English cases have adopted this line. The fullest argumentation appears in *Roger Bullivant Ltd* v *Ellis* [1987] ICR 464, 476. Nourse LJ made the following points:

(1)   the springboard, that is the advantage which the defendant has gained, cannot last forever;
(2)   the law does not restrain lawful competition;
(3)   in forbidding unlawful competition, the law seeks to protect the injured, not punish the guilty.

Therefore, the injunction should not extend "beyond the period for which the advantage may reasonably be expected to continue". The court fixed that time as 12 months, which was the duration of a covenant in restraint of trade which may have been part of the defendant's contract of employment. (However, this approach was limited by May LJ to confidential information as distinguished from "true trade secrets".) An example from the Commonwealth of the Law Commission's proposal occurs in *Fractionated Cane Technology Ltd* v *Ruiz-Avila* [1988] 1 Qd 51, 69: the springboard would have been useful for one month; that time had already elapsed; therefore no injunction was granted.

The Law Commission recommended the retention of the rule that if the disclosure is not by the secret holder or by the divulgee but by a third party, the secret has entered the public domain (for example publication, patents).

The springboard doctrine is in employment cases of narrow width. "However, the sphere in which it can be applied as between master and servant is considerably limited by the servant's freedom, after lawful termination of his employment, to compete with his former employer and to solicit the latter's customers, unless, of course, he has been restrained by express contract from doing so" (*per* Goulding J at first instance in *Faccenda* [1984] IRLR 61, 66).

The head start doctrine may also be criticised on the grounds that (1) damages may not recompense the owner of the secret; (2) it presumably acts as a brake on research and development; and (3) it would seem to be in conflict with the reasons for patents.

In summary unlike most covenants in restraint of trade the implied duty of confidentiality after employment is not restricted in terms of time or area. However, it is in the nature of things that matters which once constituted trade secrets or highly confidential information lose their quality of confidentiality over time. For example, other firms may work out the details of a secret process which until that moment a company had kept as a closely guarded secret. Then the implied duty between the former employers and the ex-employee evaporates (provided that the information has entered the public domain), unless the springboard doctrine comes into play.

The Employee's Stock of Knowledge

The same approach to the employee's personal skill, knowledge and experience is taken in actions for breach of confidence as in the area of covenants in restraint of trade. The duty of confidentiality extends to matters that constitute a "separate part of the employee's stock of knowledge which a man of ordinary honesty and intelligence would recognise to be the property of his old employer" (*per* Cross J in *Printers & Finishers*, above). It does not however include matters which can reasonably be regarded as part of the employee's expertise. The knowledge is no longer confidential, if it ever was. (The effect of a covenant is considered elsewhere.) Presumably the nearer the information comes to pure science or basic research, the less likely it is to be a trade secret. Circumstantial evidence may point to where trade secrecy ends and skill and expertise begin. The line "is notoriously difficult to draw" (*per* Marais J in *Northern Office Micro Computers (Pty) Ltd* v *Rosenstein* [1981] (4) SA 123 (Sup Ct CPD)), and the cases are not easily reconcilable. "To acquire the knowledge of the reasonable mode of general organisation and management of a business ... and to make use of such knowledge cannot be regarded as a breach of confidence in revealing anything acquired by reason of a person having been in any particular service, although the person may have learnt it in the course of being taught his trade ... " *per* Wilson J in *Reliable Toy Co Ltd* v *Collins* [1950] 4 DLR 499, approving Lord Atkinson in *Herbert Morris Ltd* v *Saxelby* [1916] 1 AC 688, 705, a restraint case.

A small number of cases will be outlined to illustrate the present principle. In *United Sterling Corporation Ltd* v *Felton & Mannion* [1974] RPC 162 the second defendant was in charge of production of a process for making polystyrene. He had not been involved in the development of the new design but had attended meetings on its introduction. He visited the first defendant, the former general works manager, who had gone to the United States to work for a competitor. The plaintiffs sought an interim injunction to restrain the second defendant, whom they had dismissed, from divulging their confidential information. The judge, Brightman J, refused the injunction. He said (at 179):

> there is no evidence that Mr Mannion was given any special information which he ought to have regarded as a separate part of his stock of knowledge of polystyrene plants, information which an honest and intelligent man would have recognised as the property of the employer and not of the employee ... There is no evidence that he has done more during the years of his employment than add to his general stock of knowledge and experience of polystyrene plants in the ordinary way that any intelligent employee would naturally do.

Brightman J followed *Printers & Finishers*, above. The plaintiffs sought an injunction to restrain their former employee from revealing to a competitor information which he had acquired during his employment. They were successful in relation to some documents but other information had become part of his stock of knowledge and was no longer the property of the former employers. Cross J was quick to point out that such a result need not harm employers. They may resort to a covenant in lawful restraint of trade.

A case to contrast with *Printers & Finishers* is *B O Morris Ltd* v *F Gilmore (BST) Ltd* (1943) 60 RPC 20 where Asquith J held that machinery which two employees had copied constituted trade secrets. In that case, however, the employees were engaged to copy German machines before the outbreak of the Second World War, whereas in *Printers & Finishers* the defendant acquired knowledge of the machine simply as part of his job as general manager. Both *Printers & Finishers* and *United Sterling* should be contrasted with *Cranleigh*, above. In that case Roskill J held that the defendant's knowledge of the design for swimming pools could reasonably be regarded as part of the employers' property and so was not part of the employee's stock in trade. The defendant was the managing director of the plaintiffs and he had realised the importance of the clamps and interfaces he had designed. On the other hand the defendants in *Printers and Finishers* and *United Sterling* were not such senior employees and were not part of the research and development structure of their companies. Accordingly it is suggested that the courts will investigate the role the employee played in the firm to determine whether the information formed part of that employee's knowledge or whether it was confidential. The point remains that it is not always easy to categorise information as protectable or not post-employment, and slight variations in facts can alter cases.

Cranleigh, Printers & Finishers and *United Sterling* all involve employees who for one reason or another have left the company. What if the defendant remains an employee of the company? In *United Sterling* above, Buckley J said (at 166–7): "There can be little doubt that it would have been breach of Mr Mannion's contract of service for him to have lent assistance with the installation of the . . . process at a time when Mr Mannion was still an employee of the company".

To sum up one may cite the words of Peterson J in *Alperton Rubber Co* v *Manning* (1917) 86 LJ Ch 377, 379: "a man can use in one employment the ordinary experience which he gains in another". From the viewpoint of the principal remedy, an injunction, this dictum makes practical sense. The court would be unable to enforce an injunction against the use of knowledge which had become the employee's own. The court cannot stand over the employee and stop him or her using his or her knowledge though it would be easy to draft some injunctions, for example to stop an employee selling certain information. Similar practical problems have already been seen with regard to the memory rule, which applies here. On this ground among others it is hard not to criticise a dictum of the Court of Appeal in *Faccenda*, above (at 138–9) that there may be a distinction between using skill and selling information to a third party. The effect may be the same.

The Law Commission, above, Recommendation 33, propose to retain the distinction between trade secrets and the "enhancement of the personal knowledge, skill or experience".

One issue that is hard to fit elsewhere is when the employee knows the information before being engaged by the employers or before the problem attracted their attention. Here the information belongs to the employee. For example, in *Reliable Toy Co Ltd* v *Collins*, above (at 512) Wilson J in the Ontario High Court ruled that one part of the employers' claim failed because the employee "obtained the information about the lacquer long before the problem became one for the laboratory".

Consent to Disclosure by Employers and Statutory Disclosure

Those things which only one man can truly and properly call his must remain his, till he agrees to part with them by compact or donation (*per* Aston J in *Millar* v *Taylor* (1769) 4 Burr 2303, 2338)

The employers may authorise the employee to disclose the confidential information either expressly or impliedly. A contract is not needed. In *Schering Chemicals Ltd* v *Falkman Ltd*, above (at 227), Shaw LJ said: "the communication in a commercial context of information which at the time is regarded by the giver and recognised by the recipient as confidential, and the nature of which has a material connection with the commercial interest of the party confiding that information, imposes on the recipient a fiduciary obligation, to maintain that confidence thereafter unless the giver consents to relax it".

It is a question of fact whether there has been implied consent to disclosure of use, and it may be that only an act will suffice; an omission will not, but this proposition has not been tested.

By putting a product on the market, employers are taken to have consented to reverse engineering by which the trade secret loses its confidential quality. Of course if disclosure is for a limited purpose only the process will remain secret as stated above, for example disclosure for the purposes of advertising *per se* does not make the product public.

Disclosure may also be a legal requirement, for example where it is required by statute (for instance, section 168(2)(b) of the Road Traffic Act 1972) or by court order as in discovery (see, for example, *Alfred Crompton Amusement Machines Ltd* v *Customs and Excise Commissioners* [1974] AC 405 (HL)). There may also be a defence of privilege. Disclosure on the grounds of public interest (see next section) is permitted, but disclosure under statute and at law is a duty.

Just Cause or Excuse

At times the disclosure of confidential information is mandated by law. The *fons et origo* of this doctrine is a dictum of Page-Wood V-C in *Gartside* v *Outram* (1856) 26 LJ Ch 113: "there can be no confidence as to the disclosure of iniquity ... ". The defendant, formerly employed by the plaintiffs, Liverpool woolbrokers, revealed confidential business and accounting documents which showed that the plaintiffs had conducted their trade fraudulently. The judge refused an injunction to restrain the defendant from revealing more information.

For the next century disclosure was permitted only where the employers' proposed crimes or torts were revealed. The law has, however, developed in the last 30 years and is no longer so restricted. In a case which was a staging post towards present law, *Initial Services Ltd* v *Putterill* [1968] 1 QB 396, 405, Lord Denning MR said that the law *should* provide a defence to those who revealed "crimes, frauds and misdeeds, both those actually committed as well as those in contemplation, provided always – and this is essential – that the disclosure is justified in the public interest". The first defendant, formerly employed as the plaintiffs' sales manager, left, taking with him documents revealing a cartel among laundries to support prices. He revealed the documents to a national newspaper. The plaintiffs sought an injunction, damages and delivery up, contending that the former employee was in breach of his implied contractual duty of confidentiality. On a motion to strike out the first defendant's allegations that the cartel was contrary to statute and that the plaintiffs had sought to mislead the public by blaming the increase on selective employment tax, the Court of Appeal held that there should be no striking out. Lord Denning MR permitted disclosure where the revelation showed misconduct. The other members of the court adopted a different stance. Salmon and Winn LJJ (at 410, 411) inquired whether an express term preventing disclosure would be void for illegality. Judgments were unreserved and on an interlocutory matter.

Lord Denning MR's judgment is open to criticism. He did not define misdeeds. In the context of his speech they are not crimes or frauds. Are they torts other than deceit or are they wrongdoings which do not amount to torts? The misdeed revealed in *Initial Services* was not a crime or a tort, except perhaps a breach of statutory duty in that the members of the price-fixing cartel had not registered the arrangement under the Restrictive Trade Practices Act 1956. Critics of judicial discretion could certainly attack the liberty accorded to the judges by the "just cause or excuse" exception: should unelected persons be the guardians of the public interest, which is an unruly horse? It should also be noted that it is difficult, if not impossible, to weigh misconduct against the public interest, for the two are not commensurable. Lord Denning MR had not at this time diverged far from "iniquity" within *Gartside* v *Outram*. This exception is sometimes known as the "iniquity rule", but as Kerr LJ in *Petranol plc* v *Mountford*, 22 May 1985, LEXIS, had it, the phrase should be in inverted commas because it is not restricted to iniquity in any narrow sense. In the *Spycatcher* case, *Attorney-General* v *Guardian Newspapers Ltd (No 2)* [1990] 1 AC 108, 259, Lord Keith spoke of the "so-called iniquity defence". Another term which has been used is "higher duty": see *Weld-Blundell* v *Stephens* [1920] AC 956, 985 (HL), a phrase which has been taken up in other cases, notably *Tournier* v *National Provincial and Union Bank of England* [1924] 1 KB 461, 473 (CA).

Lord Denning MR took his views further in *Fraser* v *Evans* [1969] 1 QB 349, 362. Iniquity was "merely an instance of just cause or excuse for breaking confidence.

There are some things which may be required to be disclosed in the public interest". There was no restriction to crime, fraud or wrongdoing. Griffiths LJ said in *Lion Laboratories Ltd* v *Evans* [1985] QB 526, 550, that: "it may be vital in the public interest to publish a part of [the] confidential information" even though "there has been no wrongdoing on the part of the plaintiff". On the facts of this case there was a public interest in remedying unlawful convictions which overrode the confidential nature of the information. See also *Hellewell* v *Chief Constable of Derbyshire* [1995] 4 All ER 473, 479 (QBD). Now that there is no restriction to iniquity judges have adopted the name given by Lord Denning MR in *Fraser* v *Evans* for this defence: "just cause or excuse". This appellation is nowadays usually used, as by Stephenson LJ in *Lion* (at 536). As might be expected, Lord Denning MR favoured a balancing approach.

Most cases on just cause or excuse do not involve employees (for example the "Scientology" cases, *Hubbard* v *Vosper* [1972] 2 QB 84 (CA) and *Church of Scientology of California* v *Kaufman* [1973] RPC 635 (Goff J) and *Lion*), but the principle does apply to them as *Initial Services Ltd* v *Putterill* demonstrates.

The law remains at the developmental stage, and it is not always possible to state in advance of litigation whether or not an employee will be permitted to reveal information. There have been proposals that the law should be put on a statutory footing but it is suggested that the judges would prefer to retain their discretion when balancing the public interest in disclosure against the public or private interest in confidentiality rather than see this exception put on a statutory footing. Peter North, "Breach of Confidence: Is there a new Tort?" (1972) 15 JSPTL (NS) 149, 169, inquired: "If an invention is bought up by a large firm in order to prevent its manufacture and resultant competition, is disclosure of the information in apparent breach of confidence justified by grounds of 'public interest'?" A quarter of a century later we still find difficulty answering this question. The gynaecologist who invented forceps kept them secret for some years until his son revealed why his father was having great success with live births. Balancing disclosure on these facts against confidentiality may seem evident, but the outcome is not always certain.

Judges other than Lord Denning MR have essayed definitions. The lengthiest was that of Ungoed-Thomas J in *Beloff* v *Pressdram Ltd* [1973] 1 All ER 241, 260: "matters carried out or contemplated in breach of the country's security or in breach of law, including statutory duty, fraud or otherwise destructive of the country or its people, including matters medically dangerous to the public and doubtless other misdeeds of similar gravity ... Such public interest does not extend beyond misdeeds of a serious nature and importance to the country". This definition is narrower than the one in *Fraser* v *Evans* in that it is restricted to misconduct. It would not permit an employee to reveal confidential information on the basis that there was a public interest in its dissemination. W R Cornish in "Protection of Confidential Information in English Law" (1975) 1 IIC 43, 48–9 (repeated in *Intellectual Property*, 2nd ed (Sweet & Maxwell, 1989) paragraph 8–015) suggested that there were two streams of authority: one restricted to misdeeds (*Beloff*), one not (*Fraser*). Recent cases have not resolved the issue of which line of cases is to prevail. P D Finn, "Confidentiality and the 'Public Interest'" (1984) 58 ALJ 497 suggested three strands: iniquity, higher duty, and balancing interests, all of which may be found in Lord Denning MR's speeches. There have been other attempts at definition but that in *Fraser* v *Evans* now constitutes the accepted criterion. However, as Sheppard J said in *Allied Mills Industries Pty Ltd* v *Trade Practices Ltd* (1981) 34 ALR 105, 126: "I do not believe that the authorities are necessarily consistent with one another. I think that this is because the courts have to grapple with the problem in a variety of situations and have done their best to do justice between parties taking into account the public interests that are in play in the different sets of circumstances that have arisen for consideration". As Roger Rideout put it in his review of the first edition of Cripps' *The Legal Implications of Disclosure in the Public Interest* [1988] LMCLQ 105, 106, policy considerations change with the context.

The defence does have boundaries but it is hard to state them. One problem is the nature of the exercise the judge has to go through before determining whether the disclosure of confidential information should be allowed. There is debate as to the nature of the task. The House of Lords in the Spycatcher case, *Attorney-General* v *Guardian Newspapers Ltd* (*No 2*), above, considered that the judge had to balance interests. Lord Griffiths (at 269) spoke of "balancing the public interest in upholding the right to confidence, which is based on the moral principles of loyalty and fair dealing, against some other public interest, which will be served by publication of the confidential material". While Spycatcher did not involve an ordinary employee and although the balancing equation has been criticised as leaving too much discretion in the hands of the judiciary, modern authority supports the requirement of balancing interests. Therefore, one limit is that the public interest in disclosure must outweigh the private (or as Lord Griffiths would put it public) interest in confidentiality. The more serious the wrongdoing, the greater the public interest: *Attorney-General* v *The Observer and Guardian Newspapers Ltd, The Times,* 16 July 1986.

A second limitation concerns the content of the public interest in revealing confidences. This constraint was aptly summed up by Lord Wilberforce in *British Steel Corp* v *Granada Television Ltd* [1981] AC 1096, 1168: "there is a wide difference between what is interesting to the public and what is in the public interest to be made known". No doubt gossip about the royal family is interesting to the public but it is not of public interest in the appropriate sense. An application of this principle is *Stephens* v *Avery* [1988] Ch 449. Browne–Wilkinson V-C held that details of lesbian behaviour among adults was not legitimately to be revealed. Perhaps *Woodward* v *Hutchins* [1977] 1 WLR 760 (CA) would now fall within this category, for it is not a matter of public interest to reveal the details of what pop stars did on jumbo jets. In the *British Steel* case the Lords held that disclosure of mismanagement, however serious, was not justified in the public interest. Carelessness, therefore, cannot be revealed unless it constitutes the tort of negligence. It was suggested by Megarry V-C in *Malone* v *MPC* (*No 2*) [1979] Ch 344, 377, that disclosure of an impending disaster was the sort of situation where the exception applies, but the law may be narrower. A third limitation is that confidential information may not be revealed in the public interest if the danger to which it relates has passed: *Schering Chemicals Ltd* v *Falkman Ltd* [1982] QB 1 (CA). Accordingly, information about a drug could not be revealed as a matter of just cause or excuse when it had already been withdrawn.

Another limitation is that there is no defence where the employee acts "upon a mere roving suggestion", as Page-Wood V-C put in *Gartside* v *Outram*, above. In Spycatcher, Lord Goff (at 283) said: "a mere allegation . . . is not of itself sufficient to justify disclosure in the public interest. Such an allegation will only do so if, following such investigations as are reasonably open to the recipient, and having regard to all the circumstances of the case, the allegation in question can reasonably be regarded as being a credible allegation from an apparently reliable source". Lord Keith (at 262) spoke of a *prima facie* case. There may be a difference in the amount of evidence sufficient to disclose lawfully when the disclosure is to a body charged with the duty of investigating matters, provided that the information falls within its jurisdiction. In *Re a Company's Application* [1989] 2 All ER 248, Scott J said that the law in Spycatcher was restricted to instances where the disclosure threatened was to the whole world. Peter Wright's book threatened to reveal secrets of the United Kingdom security services to the world. However, in the instant case the disclosure was correctly to the relevant regulatory body, FIMBRA.

The modern understanding is that the motive of the discloser is irrelevant. For example, Stephenson LJ said so in *Lion Laboratories*, above (at 536). It is, however, possible that when a person acts *mala fide*, the public interest in disclosure may be outweighed by the interest in preserving confidentiality where there is no strong case for the disclosure: *Schering Chemicals*, above (at 23). As stated and criticised elsewhere in this work, Lord Denning waged a campaign seeking to make motive material. He wanted the law to refuse a defence to an employee who had revealed information relating to his employers for money. In *Initial Services*, above, he stated: "I say nothing as to what the position would be if [the employee] disclosed [the confidential information] out of malice or spite or sold it to a newspaper for money or for reward". When the *British Steel* case, above, was in the Court of Appeal he called the conduct of the "steel mole" irresponsible, deplorable, and disgraceful (at 1131–2), though he later recanted: *What Next in the Law* (Butterworths, 1982) 251. Later cases such as *Hubbard* and *Church of Scientology* did not apply this exception to the exception, and in *British Steel* (at 1202) Lord Fraser said: "the informer's motives are . . . irrelevant". Surely it should not matter that the employee has revealed information about lack of safety at her employers' works for payment. If it is in the public interest to reveal misdeeds, it should not matter that the employee's motives were "impure". After all, she may be dismissed or otherwise suffer financially for her public spirit.

Burden of Proof of the Public Interest

Lord Widgery C J in *Attorney-General* v *Jonathan Cape Ltd* [1976] QB 752, 770, suggested that the burden of proving that the public interest required the restraining of publication and that "there are no other facets [the Report says 'facts'] of the public interest contradictory of and more compelling than that relied on" rested on the plaintiff. If Lord Widgery CJ was correct, the law of breach of confidence may be less of a restraint on the exploitation of industrial ideas than it might otherwise have been, for the employee–defendant does not have to show affirmatively that the revelation was in the public interest. Lord Widgery's proposition was approved by Bingham LJ in *Attorney-General* v *Guardian Newspapers Ltd (No 2)*, above, (at 218) and by the House of Lords (at 257, 270 and 283); by the Scottish courts in *Lord Advocate* v *Scotsman Publications Ltd* [1990] 1 AC 812, 828; and by Australian courts in *Commonwealth of Australia* v *John Fairfax & Sons Ltd* (1980) 147 CLR 39, *Attorney-General in and for the UK* v *Heinemann Publishers Australia Pty Ltd* (1988) 78 ALR 449 (NSW Sup Ct) and *A* v *Hayden (No 2)* (1985) 59 ALJR 6 (HCA). Jones, however, criticised the approach of Lord Widgery, which the Law Commission had approved, on the grounds that: "freedom of information does not entirely explain why the burden of proof should lie upon the plaintiff to demonstrate that his confidence should still be protected. After all it is the defendant who is the 'statutory wrongdoer' and it is he who had undertaken, expressly or by his conduct, the obligation of confidence which he now rejects": "The Law Commission's Report on Breach of Confidence" [1982] CLJ 40, 46). Donaldson MR stated that the burden was on the party asserting the public interest exception in *Attorney-General* v *Guardian Newspapers Ltd* [1987] 1 WLR 1249, 1275 ("Spycatcher (No 1)"), and he said that simply alleging the public interest exception was insufficient. But his remarks were made in the context of what he called "the need for confidentiality [which was] so overwhelmingly and so strongly necessary in the national interest". Russell LJ thought the same (at 1281).

If one views the public interest exception as a narrow defence used only in exceptional cases, perhaps the burden of proof should lie on the defendant for it is that party who is seeking to disrupt the obligation of confidentiality. The law in the employment law context (*Jonathan Cape* being a case on governmental secrets where different principles may apply: see Lord Ackner in Spycatcher (No 1), at 1303). And even in the area of government secrecy the Court of Appeal in *Fraser* v *Evans*, above, (at 362) said that the defendants had not made out the public interest exception.

In the context of commercial secrets one might expect the courts to put the onus on the plaintiffs to uphold a public interest in non-disclosure where the disclosure would reveal, for example the ill-effects of drugs. Instead the courts have directed their minds at considering whether a public interest in disclosure overrode private rights: *Distillers Co (Biochemicals) Ltd* v *Times Newspapers Ltd* [1975] QB 613, 623 (Talbot J). There is, however, a strong dictum of Lord Griffiths in *Attorney-General* v *Guardian Newspapers Ltd (No 2)*, above (at 269) that in a case not involving governmental secrets the burden of proof is on the defendant; that is the employee must show why the public interest overrides the right to confidentiality. The position as to who bears the burden of proof in trade secret cases is at present unclear but could be resolved by the enactment of clause 1(2) of the draft bill proposed by the Law Commission, Report no 110, *Breach of Confidence* (Cmnd 8388, 1981): " . . . a defendant raises the issue of public interest in relation to a disclosure or use of information if he satisfies the court that, in view of the content of the information, there was (or in the case of an apprehended disclosure or use), will be, at the time of the disclosure or use a public interest in the information being so disclosed or used". Once the issue was raised, the plaintiffs would have to establish that the restraint was required in the public interest and that that interest was not outweighed by the public interest in disclosure or use. This formulation would apply to both commercial and government secrets and would enact *Jonathan Cape*.

Reasonable belief in the employers' wrongdoing would seem to be the standard required, though no case directly treats of the issue. In *Gartside* v *Outram*, above, Wood V-C said (at 114) *obiter* that "a mere roving suggestion" was not sufficient evidence to justify the disclosure of confidential information. Taking the words of Goff J in *Butler* v *Board of Trade* [1971] Ch 680 slightly out of context, Gibbs CJ in *Attorney-General* v *Hayden (No 2)*, above, said that at least what has to be shown *prima facie* is a "*bona fide* and reasonably tenable charge" of wrongdoing.

To Whom Should the Information be Revealed?

The "just cause or excuse" exception is potentially of wide scope. It is, however, subject to limits, as seen above. The present rule is a serious restriction and a trap for employees. Even if the public interest exception applies, the information must be disclosed to the correct person or authority. The leading judgment is that of Lord Denning MR in *Initial Services Ltd* v *Putterill*, above (at 405), which, though criticised by P M North, "Further Disclosures of Confidential Information" [1968] JBL 32, 38–9, has been adopted in English cases such as *Malone* v *MPC (No 2))*, above (Megarry J) and *Francome* v *Mirror Group Newspaper Ltd* [1984] 1 WLR 892 (CA): "the disclosure must . . . be to one who has a proper interest to receive the information. Thus it would be proper to disclose a crime to the police; or a breach of the Restrictive Trade Practices Act to the registrar. There may be cases where the misdeed is of such a character that the public interest may demand, or at least excuse, publication on a broader field, even to the press". Salmon LJ (at 409) thought that on interlocutory appeal he ought not to strike out the defence that the press was a proper authority to which to give details of a fraudulent circular blaming tax, not a cartel, for increasing prices. Winn LJ (at 411–2) was unimpressed by a law that information had to be disclosed to the correct body. This restriction of the defence is particularly important for the media: see, for example *Attorney-General* v *The Observer and Guardian Newspapers Ltd*, above, which deals with MI5 and national security. The Court of Appeal decided that the public interest exception did not apply in the circumstances where newspapers had printed the details of allegations made by Mr Peter Wright about the British Security Services: instead, the newspaper should have given the information to the Prime Minister, the Privy Council, the police, or the DPP. This doctrine was approved in *Attorney-General* v *Guardian Newspapers Ltd (No 2)*, above, in all the courts.

Who is a proper person would seem to vary according to the just cause or excuse. The DPP and the police would seem to be proper parties to whom one might divulge a crime; it would seem that a tort should be disclosed to the aggrieved party: in *Gartside* v *Outram*, above, Wood V-C said that frauds on customers should be revealed to them; if the misconduct affects society, there are statements that disclosure may be to the public, for example via the press: *Church of Scientology* v *Kaufman*, above (at 649); *Woodward* v *Hutchins*, above (at 754); but the police may not always be the correct party, for example in *Lion Laboratories*, above, the police were an interested party. In that case and in *Cork* v *McVicar, The Times*, 31 October 1984, LEXIS, the courts emphasised the role of the media in publishing information which the public had an interest in receiving. In *Re a Company's Application*, above, disclosure of confidential information about clients' personal affairs by the employee of a financial services company to the regulatory authority, FIMBRA, and the Inland Revenue was permitted by Scott J, though without reference to *Putterill*.

The Law Commission, in clause 11 of the draft bill attached to their Report, supported the *Initial Services* approach. One of the matters to be considered by the courts in determining whether the public interest exception applies is "the extent and nature of the particular disclosure or use in question". That is, a breach of confidentiality may be justified in the public interest if the information is revealed to the proper person or body (for example the police) when it would not be justified if revealed to the public.

Conclusion

It is sometimes suggested, for example by S Ricketson "Public Interest and Breach of Confidence" (1978) 12 MULR 223, 229, that public interest does not form a defence to the duty of confidentiality but is taken into account when considering the remedy. There is some judicial support for such an approach in Australia: see *G* v *Day* [1982] 1 NSWLR 24, 36 (CLD) and *A* v *G Hayden (No 2)*, above (at 9), for example. In *Woodward* v *Hutchins*, above, an English case, Bridge LJ seemed to posit that the public interest was a defence where equitable remedies were sought, but not a defence to common law damages. It is not always clear what the judges are thinking. For instance, in *Schering Chemicals Ltd* v *Falkman Ltd*, above, it cannot be conclusively stated whether the majority relied on public interest as an exception or as an element in deciding whether to award an injunction. Cases such as *Fraser* v *Evans*, above (at 362) are unambiguous: the defence is not discretionary. It is suggested that English law is to that effect. The issue whether the public interest operates as a (confession and avoidance) defence or as preventing the obligation from occurring in the first place is well-discussed by Cripps in *The Legal Implications of Disclosure in the Public Interest*, 2nd ed (Sweet & Maxwell 1994). The cases are not easy. In *Gartside* v *Outram*, above, Page

Wood V-C said that there was no property in iniquity, implying that employers had no cause of action, whereas in *Woodward* v *Hutchins* injunctions were refused but damages given, implying that the obligation exists but the remedy for breach is restricted.

The Law Commission's Proposals

The smooth running of businesses may be undermined if employees can easily use the public interest exception (and there is a public interest in the smooth running of businesses). This is why reform proposals in this area bear scrutiny. In their 1981 Report, above, paragraphs 6.77 and 6.131, the Law Commission recommended a new start in the law, jettisoning the "iniquity" rule as broadened in recent years (see clause 11(3) of the draft bill) and proposed that: "the courts should have a broad power to decide . . . whether in the particular case the public interest in protecting the confidentiality of the information outweighs the public interest in its disclosure or use". The Commission (at paragraph 6.133) considered that its recommendation was analogous to public interest in covenants in restraint of trade. This reform would apply to both the contractual and general confidence actions. The aim would be to open up the free circulation of information. The proposal was criticised by the Law Society's Law Reform Committee because the setting aside of confidentiality provisions in commercial contracts would put trade secrets at risk: Memorandum of Comments (1982) 79 LSG 1576. The change would be major. There would be an excuse for disclosure: the plaintiff would not succeed in the new tortious action. They propose that the restriction of the public interest defence to misconduct ought to be abolished, and that the courts should take into consideration how the material was acquired, the extent of the disclosure and the time since the information became public, as part of the process of deciding whether it should be disclosed. The burden of proof would be on the defendant to show that the public interest demanded disclosure. Then the plaintiff bears the burden of showing that that interest is outweighed by the public interest in the confidentiality of the information. Depending on how the judges were to use such a power, more employees than at present would presumably be allowed to reveal mismanagement and carelessness by their employers, but whether the result reached in cases under the present law would be altered is open to doubt: W L Grant "In the Public Interest?" [1985] JML&P 178, 185. The employee's interests may in any case be thwarted by judicial interpretation (*The Guardian*, leader, 30 October 1981), and there are sanctions other than legal ones for the disclosure of confidential information even when the public interest demands it, for example dismissal, no promotion. J Michael "Breach of Confidence" (1981) 131 NLJ 1201, 1202, did not accept *The Guardian*'s view which was put by a leader writer who considered that the tightening up of the law may be beneficial to employers: "a potentially deadly Armalite" may be better than "an unsatisfactory blunderbuss".

The provision that the courts should take into account the manner in which the information was acquired may be criticised on the ground that there may be a public interest in disclosure even though the information was obtained in breach of confidence. The Scots Law Commission, Report no 90, *Breach of Confidence* (Cmnd 9385, 1984) 43, criticised the approach of the Law Commission:

> we have had some difficulty in accepting the distinction which the Law Commission drew between the public interest in the use or disclosure of information and the public interest in protecting confidentiality. The essence of our difficulty is that we regard the latter less as a matter of public interest than as a private interest ... We think, too, that it ... is somewhat artificial to require a person to establish that the public interest involved in protecting confidentiality outweighs that involved in disclosure ... The court will, in our view, be able to take account of all ... the evidence without being directed to consider any special onus of proof.

G Jones "The Law Commission's Report on Breach of Confidence" [1982] CLJ 40, 47, criticised the balancing approach because judges do not possess the required economic skills. The Scots Law Commission generally agreed with the Law Commission about the breadth of the defence, and they accepted the view of the latter body that the defence should not be restricted to the proposed statutory tort of breach of confidence but should apply also to contractual obligations of confidentiality: "[w]e ... think it desirable to preclude arguments about the correct classification of the obligation. It is preferable ... that the appropriateness of a defence be justified against a background of the whole circumstances of the case and not, at least in part, on whether a pursuer [that is plaintiff] can establish that there was an express or implied contractual form of confidentiality" (at 45). The Commission arrived at this conclusion "with considerable hesitation" in the light of freedom of contract. They considered that the courts should not be restricted by a statutory formulation of how they should balance the individual interest in confidentiality and the public interest in free access to and dissemination of information. They preferred to adopt the reasonable man test, a test which would take account of different relationships (at 19–20).

The Law Commission briefly adverted to the rationale behind their proposed change in the law. "Breach of confidence ... is a not insubstantial check on freedom of speech and on the exploration of ideas in the commercial and industrial spheres" (paragraph 4.4). This is one of the few references to policy in the Report. Gurry in his book, *Breach of Confidence* (Clarendon, 1984) trenchantly criticised this reasoning (at 477–8, footnote omitted). His argument deserves stating at length.

> Certainly, it is a check for the very good reason that a check provides an incentive to the production of new information in a system dependent on technical progress for productivity increases. The law also provides an indispensable framework for the operation of such enterprises. By removing protection for trade secrets to the extent

that there is some (however measured) benefit to the public interest, two consequences would follow. In the first place, paradoxically, greater secrecy and greater inefficiency would ensue ... [for example through segregating departments, keeping matters in house]. Secondly, the United Kingdom would suffer under such a proposal. Why would any multinational firm base a research and development department in the UK if aberrant employees can justify the disclosure of information? ... Additionally ... [h]ow are courts in an adversary system to decide whether it is in the public interest to disclose information if there is no demonstrable detriment but a benefit?

A M Tettenborn "Law Commission reports on Breach of Confidence – at last" (1982) 3 Co Law 81, 82, provided a more down-to-earth criticism of the Law Commission's proposals – businessmen would not like a law which obliged them to reveal secrets when it was reasonable so to do. The present law merely allows disclosure of confidential information which is detrimental to the public: it is not a charter for roguish employees.

The Law Commission (paragraph 6.130) recommended that its proposals on the public interest should apply both to contractual and non-contractual confidences. This proposal is out of line with its other recommendations which draw a line between contractual and non-contractual sources of obligations of confidentiality, but in the opinion of the writer it is not the public interest exception which is out of joint but rather the distinguishing of contractual and non-contractual obligations. On the facts of a particular case it may be difficult to distinguish them, and the arguments which limit non-contractual confidences apply equally to contractual ones.

The Canadian *Report on Trade Secrets*, no 46 (1986) 178, said that the "only alternative to a public interest type defence would appear to be reliance upon the general discretion of the court with respect to various specific remedies. For instances, if a newspaper 'steals' and publishes a secret formula to prevent the common cold, a court might conceivably, in its discretion, refuse to grant an injunction restraining publication". However, the working party was of the view that a public interest defence should apply, but that it ought to be restricted to situations where "the trade secret is tainted by crime, fraud or other unlawful conduct, or involves some matter going to public health or safety", a narrow definition which would exclude the defendant in *Lion*, above. It would not apply to the tort of improper acquisition. A Coleman wrote "Reform of Canadian Trade Secrets Law" [1987] EIPR 228, 231, "This could lead to much heart-searching if, for example, a person steals the formula for a cure for cancer of [*scil* or] AIDS from the safe of another who intends not to exploit his discovery, and the thief then discloses it, without reward to a manufacturer who distributes it free to sufferers". On the Canadian proposals the thief is liable for the improper acquisition but not for the improper disclosure. Another view would be to say that the assumed facts and similar ones must be very rare. In the civil law, however, such a view would not stop litigation. A Bradley, "Constitutional Law" [1988] All

ER Ann Rev 55, 62, wrote that because of the sensitive nature of the duty of confidentiality in the context of MI5 agents, "it is unlikely that the government will wish to introduce legislation directly on the civil law of breach of confidence".

Part 3

PRACTICE AND REMEDIES

Contents of Chapter Twelve

PRACTICE IN RESTRAINT OF TRADE AND BREACH OF CONFIDENCE

Chapter Twelve

PRACTICE IN RESTRAINT OF TRADE AND BREACH OF CONFIDENCE

Introduction

This section investigates procedural safeguards for employers seeking to protect (highly) confidential information before, during, and after trial, and considers the mode of trial.

Particulars and "Controlled Discovery"

The employee as defendant is entitled to particulars of the trade secret alleged to have been misappropriated. In *Sorbo Rubber Sponge Products Ltd* v *Defries* (1930) 47 RPC 454 the order for particulars was made with the provisos that disclosure would be to lawyers and three named experts who were not competitors of the parties, that the order was formulated so that persons to whom the secret was communicated were prevented from disclosing it, and that copies of particulars were to be returned to the plaintiffs on close of proceedings. *Cf. Centri-Spring Corp* v *Cera International Ltd* [1979] FSR 175, where the employee was permitted to inspect. See also *Format Communications Ltd* v *ITT (UK) Ltd* [1982] FSR 473. As always disclosure will not be granted in order that the employers may uncover sufficient evidence to found a claim: *A-Z Couriers Ltd* v *Comspec Computer Software Ltd*, 9 November 1988, LEXIS.

At the interlocutory stage the position seems to be that there must be alleged enough detail to permit the court to discover "precisely what information is said to be confidential": *Suhner & Co AG* v *Transradio Ltd* [1967] RPC 329, 333. (But a speedy trial was ordered.) Accordingly in *Diamond Stylus Co Ltd* v *Bauden Precision Diamonds Ltd* [1973] RPC 675 Graham J refused an interlocutory injunction on the grounds that the plaintiffs had not disclosed sufficient information to enable the court to judge whether the plaintiffs had a serious case (the case was pre-

American Cyanamid [1975] AC 396, so the judge was looking for a *prima facie* case but the principle appears to be the same after that case). There are other similar cases. Recent ones include *Schering Chemicals Ltd* v *Falkman Ltd* [1982] QB 1 (CA), *Saratoga Automation Ltd* v *Clark*, 25 November 1982, LEXIS, *Lock International plc* v *Beswick* [1989] 1 WLR 1268, 1274, *Ixora Trading Inc* v *Jones* [1990] FSR 251, and *Mainmet Holdings plc* v *Austin* [1991] FSR 538. It has been said that the law is not as insistent on precisely framed injunctions as it was 20 years ago but the judge excluded trade secrets from this analysis. *John Zink Co Ltd* v *Lloyds Bank Ltd* [1975] RPC 385 goes further: pleadings were struck out as being an abuse of process where the statement of claim was not particularised, and the further and better particulars did not remedy the situation. Discovery will not be awarded if it would be oppressive: *Ashworth* v *Roberts* (1890) 45 Ch D 625, 627. See also the section on injunctions, where it is stated that the court must be able to frame the remedy so that the ex-employee knows precisely what he or she must not do. If that does not happen, the employers will lose, though *Amber Size & Chemical Co Ltd* v *Menzel* [1913] 2 Ch 239 is to the contrary; but even there Astbury J said (at 247–8) that: "in the event . . . of any breach of the order . . . there will be no difficulty in the plaintiffs supplying the Court, under proper safeguards . . . with the details of their process in the event of their alleging disobedience to my order". See also *Aubanel and Alabaster Ltd* v *Aubanel* (1949) 66 RPC 343, 347, for a very widely drafted order ("any trade secret or confidential information").

In the *Diamond Stylus* case, above, Graham J distinguished *Under Water Welders and Repairers Ltd* v *Street* [1968] RPC 498, 507. In that case Buckley J granted an interlocutory injunction even though the plaintiffs did not condescend to specifying the confidential information. The information was considered to be confidential by both sides. He said that such condescendence as to commercial secrets was not to be expected at that stage. Any difficulty could be sorted out. However, Graham J thought that Buckley J may have been correct on the facts of that case, but "there are other cases where . . . depending on the surrounding circumstances and the state of knowledge generally in the art, [the plaintiff] may have to go further and disclose at any rate the essential features of his process . . . " (at 677). He emphasised that each case should be judged on its own facts. In *Lawrence David Ltd* v *Ashton* [1991] 1 All ER 385 the court thought that Megarry V-C was wrong in *Thomas Marshall (Exports) Ltd* v *Guinle* [1979] Ch 227 to award an injunction without defining the prohibited material.

Gurry in his book *Breach of Confidence* (Clarendon, 1984) 457, postulated that a plaintiff is more likely to succeed despite revealing few details "where the confidential information consists in a large, generalised body of information, such as complex schemes for tax avoidance" rather than where it consists of a specific piece of data, but his sample of cases is too small for this proposition to be accepted. He also suggested in a footnote to his statement (note 28) that the courts will be especially vigilant where the defendant is an employee because of the courts' desire to protect skill and experience, but there is no supporting argument.

Returning to the problem of expert inspection, the law was laid down in *Printers & Finishers Ltd* v *Holloway* [1961] RPC 77. The Court of Appeal held that the plaintiffs had clearly to specify the alleged piece of confidential information to the expert. The case can be adjourned to allow this identification to take place after discovery. Any specially important information was to be revealed only to an agreed independent expert reporting only to lawyers. At trial Cross J considered that the appointment of the expert was to be seen as a substitute for better particulars and so the plaintiffs had to inform the expert precisely what they claimed to be secret. If they did not do so, the defect could not be remedied at trial by adducing evidence. On the facts, since the plaintiffs could not identify what was confidential and what was not, no injunction was granted over the material allegedly confidential.

The law was summarised in the now classic patents case of *Warner-Lambert Co* v *Glaxo Laboratories Ltd* [1975] RPC 354, where, after reviewing previous authorities, the Court of Appeal permitted disclosure to quite a large number of the plaintiffs' "side": solicitor, counsel, patent agent, company chairman, and so on. Asked what would happen if an employee came to the chair with an idea involving a technique similar to that used in the secret process, the court said: "[t]his is a difficulty which he must resolve as an honourable man: he must be poker-faced, just as he must if quizzed by members of his Board". The court had to determine which form or order was best on the facts of each case. There was no order for universal use (at 361). The case was applied in *Format*, above, where the employee was permitted to inspect, subject to five conditions. In *Hydro-Dynamic Products Ltd* v *A H Products Ltd*, 21 August 1986, LEXIS, the court held that there was a risk of misuse. Accordingly, the information was not revealed to the defendants. Evershed MR in *Printers & Finishers*, above (at 79) said that the court should at the discovery stage consider justice to the defendants, protection for the plaintiffs, and any delay to the court. *Warner-Lambert* extends these considerations to inspection.

At the pleading and disclosure stage, Edmund Davies LJ relying on *Helps* v *Mayor etc of Oldham* (1923) 40 RPC 68 and *Printers & Finishers*, said that there was no basic difference between trade secrets cases and others: *John Zink & Co* v *Wilkinson* [1973] RPC 717, 725. As Russell LJ put it in that case (at 723) the difference was in the safeguards, but that does not affect the general law. More detail of alleged secrets is needed to stop fishing expeditions: *per* Edmund Davies LJ (at 727). See also *Napp Research Centre Ltd* v *Ethical Genetics Ltd*, 27 July 1987, LEXIS. Purely speculative actions are to be discouraged, as he said. Whitford J said the same thing with reference to *Wilkinson* in a case where the plaintiffs merely alleged that the defendants were making use of the information without putting forward evidence of a reasonable belief: *Reinforced Plastic Applications (Swansea) Ltd* v *Swansea Plastics & Engineering Co Ltd* [1979] FSR 182.

The policy in the area of disclosure of documents and inspection besides that mentioned above is to prevent the defendants obtaining the secret. The implied obligation not to make use of the information except for the purposes of litigation may be insufficient to prevent the defendants from gaining a competitive edge over the plaintiffs (see below).

In Camera Hearings

Exclusion of Public

The motion for an injunction may be heard in camera: *Mellor* v *Thompson* (1885) 31 Ch D 55. The trial can take place also in camera, for example *Badische Anilin und Soda Fabrik* v *Levinstein* (1883) 24 Ch D 156, a patents case. There is no need for the consent of the defendant: *Mellor* (at 56). In that case the whole matter was heard privately. However, the court may order that only the part dealing with the information is to be heard privately, for example *Industrial Furnaces Ltd* v *Reaves* [1970] RPC 605. The court cannot order the hearing to be behind closed doors merely because both parties so desire. If the order was wrongly granted, the trial is void. The fact that trial was in private does not prevent judgment from being delivered in open court. Certainly the order is to be given in public.

The power to exclude is part of the inherent jurisdiction of the court: *Attorney-General* v *Leveller Magazine* [1979] AC 440, 450.

The exclusion of the public has been extended by statute substantially since the early years of this century, but the privacy of trade secrecy hearings has been unaffected by subsequent developments. The principle has not been challenged judicially or academically, and has been applied to requests for Anton Piller orders in relation to trade secrets, for example *Vapormatic Co Ltd* v *Sparex Ltd* [1976] 1 WLR 939.

Statute

By section 12(1) of the Administration of Justice Act 1960: "publication of information relating to proceedings before any court sitting in private shall ... be contempt ... (d) where the information relates to a secret process, discovery or invention which is at issue ... ". "Sitting in private" covers both hearings in camera and in chambers. There is also section 11 of the Contempt of Court Act 1981. This prohibits the revelation of names of witnesses, but it is expressed to cover "other matter". This terminology could cover trade secrets, though no court has so far held thus.

The Justification of Secret Trial

Without secrecy the confidential information would be disclosed to the world. Therefore, no breach of confidence actions would be commenced. The basic rule of English law was laid down in *Scott* v *Scott* [1913] AC 417, a House of Lords case concerning nullity of marriage. As Lord Halsbury C put it (at 443): "[i]t would be the height of absurdity as well as of injustice to allow a trial at law to protect [trade secrecy] to be made the instrument of destroying the very thing it was intended to protect". These statements were echoed by Viscount Haldane (at 437–8). The presumption therefore is in favour of public trial but a trade secrets trial may as an exception be in private. Similarly the fact that there is a trade secret does not *per se* mean that it will not be disclosed on discovery: *Reddaway & Co Ltd* v *Flynn* (1913) 30 RPC 16.

Viscount Haldane in *Scott* based the exception on the interests of justice and this rationale was used in the *Leveller Magazine* case, above.

Collateral Purposes

There is a well-known rule of law that information disclosed in the course of proceedings must not be used for other purposes: *Riddick* v *Thames Board Mills Ltd* [1977] 3 All ER 677. This duty arises impliedly. The courts may also require defendants to give an express undertaking on the same terms, as occurred in, for example *Sorbo*, above, and *John Zink Co Ltd* v *Wilkinson*, above (at 724). This requirement may take place on an order for further particulars or on inspection during discovery (see *Church of Scientology* v *DHSS* [1979] 1 WLR 723, which was followed in the patents case of *Roussel Uclaf* v *Imperial Chemical Industries plc* [1990] RPC 451).

Other Measures to Safeguard Trade Secrets

The courts have various other powers, for example to order the particulars not to be filed as part of the proceedings, as in *Sorbo*, above, and *Wilkinson*, above. Note also the following:

(1)   The record of evidence of the trade secret may be sealed: *Badische Anilin*, above, where the shorthand writer's notes were impounded.
(2)   The details of the secret may be printed separately from the record: *A G für Anilin* v *Levinstein Ltd*, above.
(3)   The details of the secret may be left unrevealed in the judgment: *Yates Circuit Foil Co* v *Electrofoils Ltd* [1976] FSR 345, 348–9. This whole case was heard *in camera* at the request of both parties.
(4)   The secret may be designated by a letter, as in *Reaves*, above.
(5)   In a libel case, *Malan* v *Young* (1889) 6 TLR 38, 39, Denman J ordered a barrister to leave the court when he had nothing to do with the case. No doubt the same can occur in a breach of confidence action.
(6)   Under the inherent jurisdiction the court could prohibit a report of the proceedings which was a cover for the disclosure of trade secrets: *per* Lord Shaw in *Scott*, above (at 483).

Commonwealth Jurisdictions

Commonwealth courts adopt procedures similar to those in England. The British Columbia Supreme Court in *Terrapin Ltd* v *Tecton Structures Ltd* (1967) 59 WWR 374, 376, (affirmed 68 DLR (2d) 326, 328) made orders for full inspection at the suit of both parties. Inspection was to be by an agreed expert, or by one independent expert appointed by each side and reporting only to that party. Experts and not employees were appointed both to preserve secrecy and "to provide the court with skilled and, if possible, unbiased witnesses capable of testifying as to the dissimiliarities in, as well as resemblances of, the products or processes". The BC Supreme Court ordered the discovery of documents allegedly containing trade secrets in *Forestral Automation Ltd* v *RMS Industrial Controls Inc* (1978) 80 DLR (3d) 41, 52–3. Inspection was by named persons with undertakings not to disclose the information except for the purposes of the proceedings. *Reddaway & Co Ltd* v *Flynn*, above, was cited approvingly and *Warner-Lambert Co* v *Glaxo Laboratories Ltd*, above, was applied, with Bouck J noting that there was no universally applicable form of the order. On the facts discovery was made to the president, expert, and legal adviser, and copies could be made. Discovery was to be ordered so that legitimate claims were not frustrated (at 51).

Cases in Canada can be heard in secret as in *Terrapin*, above, though whether the case should be heard *in camera* or not was for the trial judge.

And as in England an express undertaking could be given, indeed "in most cases ... should be given ... " to protect the secret, as the Supreme Court put it in *Forestral*, above.

The Supreme Court of New South Wales Equity Division in *General Motors-Holden's Ltd* v *David Syme & Co Ltd* [1985] FSR 413 relied on *Scott* v *Scott*, above, holding that justice could be done only by holding the trial in camera as well as holding that the evidence disclosed should not be used for any purpose other than the proceedings. In line with English authority Australian cases also demand that plaintiffs clearly specify the material alleged to be confidential, for example *Independent Management Resources Pty Ltd* v *Brown* [1987] VR 605, 610 (Sup Ct).

Mode of Trial and the Appropriate Courts

The Supreme Court Act 1981, section 69(3), states that actions in the Queen's Bench Division, except for the various exceptional categories laid down in section 6(1) of the Administration of Justice (Miscellaneous Provisions) Act 1933, are to be heard by judge alone unless the court otherwise orders. This subsection largely codifies the well-known House of Lords authority of *Williams* v *Beesley* [1975] 1 WLR 1295, 1298. RSC Order 33 confers a similar discretion, but actions concerning trade secrets are heard by judge alone in practice.

The appropriate courts are the civil courts. The High Court, Chancery Division, is the usual one but the action could be brought in the Queen's Bench Division. If the amount of damages claimed for the breach of the contractual duty of confidentiality is under the relevant limit the county court has jurisdiction.

It should be noted that the county courts are not empowered to order the equitable remedies by themselves; they must be ancillary to a money order. For the county courts' power to award damages in lieu of an injunction and to grant an account, see the Law Commission's Report, no 110, *Breach of Confidence* (Cmnd 8388, 1981) 84 n 170.

Raising the Issue

Lack of enforceability should be pleaded. It cannot be raised by the court: *ex proprio motu*: *Petrofina (Great Britain) Ltd* v *Martin* [1966] Ch 146, 180, followed by Parker J in *Panayiotou* v *Sony Music Entertainment (UK) Ltd* [1994] EMLR 229, 341. Therefore, despite the gravity of the public policy underlying the doctrine "our judicial procedure is based on the principle that in fairness a litigant should have due notice of the issues that are to be raised in order that he may prepare himself with the evidence necessary to present his case fittingly to the court, and it would indeed be strange to hold that this wholesome rule should be relaxed when he is charged with something so grave as acting against the common weal" (*North Western Salt Co* v *Electrolytic Alkali Co Ltd* [1914] AC 461, 476 (HL), *per* Lord Moulton).

Compromise

A compromise on a restraint issue cannot be challenged on the ground that it too is in restraint of trade; otherwise such an issue could never be compromised: *Panayiotou*, above at 346. For criticism of the application of the law to the facts, see Coulthard, "*George Michael* v *Sony Music*" (1995) 58 MLR 731, 737.

Contents of Chapter Thirteen

INTERLOCUTORY RELIEF

Chapter Thirteen

INTERLOCUTORY RELIEF

Specific Performance and Negative Injunctions

Section 236 of the Trade Union and Labour Relations (Consolidation) Act 1992 reads in part:

> ... no court shall whether by way of
>
> (a) an order for specific performance ... of a contract of employment or
> (b) an injunction ... restraining a breach or threatened breach of such a contract, compel an employee to do any work or attend at any place for the doing of any work.

This section is the statutory embodiment of the judge-made rule that an employment contract, being a contract of personal service, cannot be enforced specifically.

The rule in section 236 is bolstered by the common law rule most authoritatively laid down in *Ridge* v *Baldwin* [1964] AC 40 that with regard to a "pure" or "ordinary" contract of employment neither party can oblige the other specifically to perform her side of the bargain. Lord Reid (at 65) said: "The law regarding master and servant is not in doubt. There cannot be specific performance of a contract of service ... ". This principle is not in doubt with respect to employers; however, sometimes an employee may be able to obtain a remedy equivalent to specific performance. It has been held that the position is different where there exist statutory underpinnings to public employment, the job is an office, where mutual trust and confidence remains, and where the relationship remains a workable one. Injunctive relief is available to employees (but not employers). This area, which is beyond the scope of this book, is considered in the labour law encyclopedias.

The legal rationale for the courts' incapacity to grant specific performance stems from the now rather old-fashioned view that an employment contract is one of personal service. The employee is under a duty to serve her employers personally. Her engagement with the present employers cannot be transferred to others without her consent (*cf.* the Transfer of Undertakings (Protection of Employment) Regulations 1981 as amended by the Trade Union Reform and Employment Rights Act 1993). Judges will not oblige employers specifically to perform their contractual obligations because there is no mutuality of obligations. Since they cannot specifically enforce the contract against an employee, the mutuality argument means that the contract cannot be enforced against the employers. A more modern rationale is that the courts are unable to supervise the enforcement of contracts of employment, and courts do not grant specific performance of any type of contract which requires the supervision of the court to ensure that the obligations are correctly fulfilled. Another, more practical, point is that if the employee refuses to obey the court's order, the court may commit her for contempt. If she is in prison, she can hardly serve her employers! They would obtain the opposite of what they wanted.

To the rule that an employment contract will not be specifically enforced, there is an exception relative to terms expressed in a negative fashion ("do not … "). The granting of an injunction may be virtually equivalent to specific performance. This jurisdiction originates from *Lumley* v *Wagner* (1852) 5 De G & Sm 485, 64 ER 1209 (Ch). The defendant, an opera singer, undertook "not to use her talents at any other theatre, nor in any concert or reunion … ". She was persuaded to sing at Covent Garden. Knight Bruce V-C held that if the defendant promised one thing and agreed not to do another, an injunction could be given to prohibit her from acting in breach of her promise. The court granted an injunction to prevent the defendant from working for others. In other words, an injunction may be granted when the worker can earn money by doing something other than performing the contract. In accordance with normal principles the court refused to order specific performance of the employee's obligation to sing. A similar outcome was reached in *Warner Bros Pictures Inc* v *Nelson* [1937] 1 KB 209. The film actress Bette Davis was restrained by Branson J from performing for any film production company except the plaintiffs on the grounds that she could work in any film production company except the plaintiffs in any other capacity and thereby not starve. The decision has been trenchantly criticised for making the injunction virtually into an order of specific injunction (for what else could she do in practice?).

A negatively expressed term will not be enforced if it obliges the employee to choose between working for her employers or starving. In *Rely-a-Bell Burglar & Fire Alarm Co* v *Eisler* [1926] Ch 609, Russell J held that a clause during the currency of the contract to prohibit the defendant from entering into another's service was not invalid but the remedy was damages, not an injunction. See also *Whitwood Chemical Co* v *Hardman* [1891] 2 Ch 416 (CA), where an injunction was refused to enforce a "whole time" clause. In summary, an injunction to work for the employers will be refused, but one to prevent the employee working for others may be granted.

The courts will not, it has been said, enforce a term which, though expressed in negative form, is positive in nature. An example is a clause that an employee must not work for any other person except her employers: the clause can be rephrased as ordering her to work for her employers only: see the clauses in the previous paragraph. However, the courts have not really always enforced this principle for sometimes clauses to devote one's whole time and attention to the employers' business are upheld.

Similarly, an interlocutory injunction will not be granted when to do so is the equivalent to the award of an order for specific performance. An example is *Page One Records Ltd* v *Britton* [1968] 1 WLR 157 (Ch D). The plaintiffs' managers of the Troggs, sought to restrain members of the group from engaging another as their manager. Stamp J (at 165) said that the case "is clearly distinguished, in principle, from such cases as *Lumley* v *Wagner* [above], for there the only obligation on the part of the plaintiffs seeking to enforce the negative stipulation was an obligation to pay remuneration and an obligation which could clearly be enforced by the defendants. But here the obligations of the first plaintiff, involving personal services, were obligations of trust and confidence which, plainly, could not be enforced at the suit of the Troggs". The negative stipulations were ones intended to bind the parties into a relationship of mutual trust. Unlike in *Warner Bros*, above, the issue of an injunction would either amount to an order for specific performance of the positive covenants or result in the defendants remaining idle or performing the positive covenants. The members of the band would be obliged to continue to use the plaintiffs as their managers if relief were granted.

Interlocutory Injunctions

The primary remedy in a restraint of trade case is the equitable one of an interlocutory injunction. Final remedies are often otiose because damages are irrecoverable against a man of straw, as an employee is likely to be, and an injunction is not granted when the period stated in the contract has elapsed. If, for example, the covenant is to last for 12 months after termination but trial does not take place until two years after the alleged breach, there is no period remaining during which the injunction prevents the former employee from acting in breach of the covenant, for the period runs from the termination of the contract, not from the date of trial. Accordingly, a provisional remedy, the interlocutory injunction, is needed. Moreover, the immediate award of this remedy may give the employers exactly what they desire. An interlocutory injunction preventing a former employee from soliciting customers for the period stated in the contract will prevent her using the influence she had acquired over customers she came to know while working for her ex-employers. Accordingly, the grant or refusal of an interlocutory injunction is of the greatest importance. If the former employee loses at the interlocutory stage, she may feel that defending the action at full trial is not worth powder and shot. Similarly, should the employers lose, they may well not proceed to trial but cut their losses. It is possible for the parties to agree that the interlocutory proceedings be treated as trial of the action.

Interlocutory injunctions protect the plaintiff against irreparable damage (that is the loss cannot adequately be repaired by damages at trial) pending trial. The relief is temporary and is necessitated by the inability of the parties and the courts to proceed to full trial immediately on the employee's actual or threatened breach of contract. One aspect of the lack of readiness is that material on which to base final judgment is not available. In theory, therefore, no "mini-trial" can take place. In practice, however, the parties may not proceed beyond the interlocutory stage.

Procedure

Jurisdiction for the High Court to grant an injunction whether interlocutory or final now derives from section 37(1) of the Supreme Court Act 1981. An interlocutory injunction may be granted swiftly and may be awarded *ex parte*: see RSC Order 29 and CCR Order 13. The application is heard in chambers in the Queen's Bench Division but in open court in the Chancery Division unless the judge orders otherwise. In the county court the hearing is in open court unless the judge orders differently. Evidence is normally given by affidavit, on which see RSC Order 41 and CCR Order 20. Affidavits must include material covered by the duty of full and frank disclosure. In relation to trade secrets *Warner-Lambert Co* v *Glaxo Laboratories Ltd* [1975] RPC 354 (CA) permitted the confidential information to be included in a separate affidavit disclosed only to the defendants' solicitors and expert witnesses, and there may be undertakings by the solicitors not to photocopy the details and to deliver up the documents at the end of the trial. There is also the rule that a party may use documents obtained by disclosure only for conducting her own case and not for any collateral purpose. The principal authority is *Home Office* v *Harman* [1983] 1 AC 280 (HL) (not a restraint of trade case). There is no cross-examination to test the evidence.

If the plaintiffs obtain an interlocutory injunction, they must give a cross-undertaking as to damages. They undertake that if at full trial the court decides that the interlocutory injunction was improperly awarded, they will recompense the defendant for any loss suffered by her as a result of the award of the remedy. In a case where the former employee will be put out of business if the remedy is granted, liability under the cross-undertaking can be substantial, and the plaintiffs have to demonstrate that they are good for the damages. A bank guarantee may be required. The enforcement of the damages under the undertaking is at the discretion of the court: *F Hoffman-La Roche & Co AG* v *Secretary of State for Trade and Industry* [1975] AC 295, 361, *per* Lord Diplock. Consent to the grant of an interlocutory injunction does not prejudice the defendant's claim under the undertaking: *Universal Thermosensors Ltd* v *Hibben* [1992] 1 WLR 840, 857 (Nicholls V-C).

American Cyanamid

The discretionary grant of interlocutory injunctions including ones in restraint of trade and breach of confidence cases is governed by the speech of Lord Diplock in the House of Lords in *American Cyanamid Co* v *Ethicon Ltd* [1975] AC 396, hereinafter *American Cyanamid*, a patents case. The plaintiffs, owners of the patent on a type of sterile absorbable surgical suture sought an interlocutory injunction against the defendants, who were about to launch a similar product on the UK market. The plaintiffs contended that the defendants had infringed their patent. For the purposes of this book the law is that ex-employers must show that they have a good arguable case. This hurdle is sometimes phrased as they must demonstrate that there is a serious issue to be tried. This test is less stringent than the previous one, a *prima facie* case (*cf. J T Stratford & Son Ltd* v *Lindley* [1965] AC 269 (HL)) to which reference was not even made. Indeed, Lord Diplock said (at 407) that the good arguable case test could only not be met by claims which were frivolous and vexatious. Very few restraint of trade cases are frivolous and vexatious even when the covenant is found to be unenforceable. A major difficulty from the employee's point of view is that the courts should not investigate the merits of the case at this stage. Therefore, logically, even though it is evident that the covenant is too wide to be valid, the court should not take legal merits into account. Not all judges have been ready to do so.

If the employers demonstrate that their claim constitutes a good arguable case the next stage of the *American Cyanamid* jurisprudence comes into play no matter how strong the plaintiffs' case. As laid down by Lord Diplock there are several sub-tests. If damages are an adequate remedy, no interlocutory injunction will be granted. Since the employee is likely to be a person of straw, damages will rarely be an adequate remedy. If damages will be difficult to quantify at trial, the remedy is likely to be granted. If an interlocutory injunction were granted but the employers would be unlikely to be able to pay damages awarded under the cross-undertaking (above), it is unlikely that the remedy will be awarded.

In a non-restraint of trade case the Court of Appeal held that courts may take into account whether more harm than good will be done by the award or refusal of the interlocutory injunction: *Cayne* v *Global National Resources plc* [1984] 1 All ER 225. Eveleigh LJ (at 232) said that where the grant or refusal of an inter-locutory remedy would dispose of the case, the "broad principle" was "what can the court do ... to avoid injustice?".

There may be special factors (at 409). In a trade secrets case the position of innocent third parties may be relevant: *STL plc* v *Plessey Semiconductors Ltd*, 11 November 1982, LEXIS. It should be noted that these special factors are ones in the balance of convenience under the *American Cyanamid* test, as Stamp LJ said in *Hubbard* v *Pitt* [1976] 1 QB 142, 185 (CA), and not as the route to an exception to

American Cyanamid, as Lord Denning MR postulated in *Fellowes & Son* v *Fisher* [1976] QB 122, 133, and *Hubbard* v *Pitt*, at 178. Orr LJ (at 188) concurred with Stamp LJ and applied *American Cyanamid*.

As a last resort the court may consider the merits. Lord Diplock said (at 409):

> if the extent of the uncompensatable disadvantage to each party would not differ widely, it may not be improper to take into account in tipping the balance the relative strength of each party's case as revealed by the affidavit evidence adduced on the hearing of the application. This, however, should be done only where it is apparent upon the facts disclosed by evidence that there is no credible dispute that the strength of one party's case is disproportionate to that of the other party.

The *American Cyanamid* approach is more structured than the previous test of a *prima facie* case, which often led the judges to agglomerate all the factors. However, the sequence in *American Cyanamid* has not always been adopted. *American Cyanamid* is directed at preserving the *status quo ante* the alleged breach, not the time of the application: *Perceptual Development* v *Versi* (1987) 11 IPR 758.

American Cyanamid and Restraint of Trade

The applicability of *American Cyanamid* to interlocutory injunctions against former employees in restraint of trade cases was finally settled by the Court of Appeal in *Lawrence David Ltd* v *Ashton* [1991] 1 All ER 385. The remainder of this section deals with prohibitory interlocutory injunctions; that is, those which pending trial seek to prevent the former employee from doing something such as dealing with customers. The law may be different with regards to interlocutory injunctions which seek to oblige the defendant to do something (mandatory orders). In cases such as *Films Rover International Ltd* v *Cannon Film Sales Ltd* [1987] 1 WLR 670 (Ch D) it has been said that the court should investigate whether if relief were granted but the plaintiff failed at trial, injustice to the plaintiff would be greater if no relief were granted but she succeeded at trial.

In *Fellowes & Son* v *Fisher* [1976] 1 QB 122 (CA) Lord Denning MR decided that there were special factors within *American Cyanamid* to allow him to apply the previous test of a *prima facie* case. The majority followed *American Cyanamid*, though Sir John Pennycuick wished to see it revised so as not to apply to cases where resolution of the interlocutory motion would end proceedings. In *Office Overload Ltd* v *Gunn* [1977] FSR 39 (CA) the defendant was licensed to carry on the plaintiffs' business in their name in Croydon. He covenanted that he would not for one year after the termination of the agreement be connected with "any business competitive with" them within a radius of six miles of Croydon. Lord Denning MR said that if a covenant was *prima facie* valid and if the defendant had *prima facie* breached it, the courts would grant an interlocutory injunction to prevent a continuing breach (the defendant had set up in competition in

Croydon and had solicited his former customers). Therefore, covenants in restraint of trade fell outside the *American Cyanamid* principles, said Lord Denning.

Balcombe LJ stated in *Lawrence David* (at 392) that the professional opinion that *American Cyanamid* did not apply to covenants was incorrect and lawyers should disabuse themselves of so thinking. The plaintiffs manufactured and sold bodies for lorries. The defendant, a sales director, covenanted *inter alia* thus:

> For a period of two years after the termination of this agreement for whatever reason whatsoever, Mr Ashton shall not without the consent of the board either alone or in partnership undertake to carry on or be employed in any capacity or be interested directly or indirectly in the design and development, manufacture or supply of any sliding door vehicle body, tension or sliding curtain vehicle body or any other vehicle body for which a patent has been applied for or granted in the name of the company or any part of the aforementioned bodies in the UK.

There were three main companies in this line of work. The employee left and joined one of them. The plaintiffs sought interlocutory injunctions to enforce the covenants including the one quoted. Balcombe LJ (at 392) stated that "*American Cyanamid* did change radically the approach previously taken on the grant or refusal of an interlocutory injunction ... ". He noted that the majority in *Fellowes & Son* v *Fisher* had followed *American Cyanamid*. Furthermore, in *Office Overload Ltd* v *Gunn* Bridge LJ had said that *American Cyanamid* applied where "either there is an unresolved dispute on the affidavit evidence before the court, or a question of law to be decided". On the facts of *Office Overload* the affidavit of the defendant showed that he was infringing the covenant. Accordingly Balcombe LJ was able to say (at 393) that there was nothing in that case which created an exception to *American Cyanamid*. He concluded " ... 13 years have gone by since *Fellowes & Son* v *Fisher*, and 12 since *Office Overload Ltd* v *Gunn*, and ... it should now be firmly stated that the principles of *American Cyanamid* apply as well in cases of interlocutory injunctions in restraint of trade as in other cases". He added that he had said the same in *Dairy Crest Ltd* v *Pigott* [1989] ICR 92, 97 (CA). If the grant or refusal of an interlocutory injunction would not effectively dispose of the action with the result that nothing remained to be dealt with at trial, then *American Cyanamid* governed. Fox LJ (at 396) briefly concurred. He regarded the court bound by the majority in *Fellowes*.

Dairy Crest itself exemplifies the application of *American Cyanamid*. Balcombe LJ (at 95–6) quoted from the speech of Lord Diplock (at 407):

> It is no part of the court's function at this stage of the litigation to try to resolve conflicts of evidence on affidavit as to facts on which the claims of either party may ultimately depend nor to decide difficult questions of law which call for detailed argument and mature considerations ... So unless the material available to the court at the hearing of the application for an interlocutory injunction fails to disclose that the plaintiff has any real prospect of succeeding in his claim for a permanent

injunction at the trial, the court should go on to consider whether the balance of
convenience lies in favour of granting or refusing the ... relief ...

On the facts there was an issue of law to be decided, namely whether a period of
two years from termination was unreasonable. That question could be determined only at trial when the judge would investigate by considering the evidence
"whether or not, in the circumstances of these particular employees, these
particular employers, and the area in which they operate, this was a reasonable
period for restraint" (at 96). Since there was a serious issue to be tried, Balcombe
LJ considered the adequacy of damages. If the employers' contention that the
covenant was valid was correct, but no remedy was given at the present stage, they
would lose their trade connection by the time full trial took place. The former
employees were in no position to pay damages. If the employers failed at trial,
they were financially able to pay the damages under the cross-undertaking.
Damages would adequately compensate the employees if they were found at trial
to have been wrongfully restrained. The stage of the balance of convenience was
therefore not reached. The two-man court dismissed the employees' appeal.

Since the significance attached to the factors varies from case to case it is not
proposed to deal with all cases in which the principles of *American Cyanamid* have
been adopted in breach of confidence cases. Instead I choose *Potters-Ballotini Ltd
v Weston-Baker* [1977] RPC 202 simply on the grounds that it is illustrative of the
general run of these cases and that it involves a factory which I used to pass every
weekday. The plaintiffs sought to prevent the defendants from producing ballotini – glass beads used in making white lines on roads and cleaning jet engines.
The plaintiffs contended that three former employees had used confidential
information to set up a rival plant. Lord Denning MR (at 207), noting that "there
has been much discussion about the decision of the House of Lords in *American
Cyanamid*", said that there were difficult points of fact and law involved and that
an interlocutory injunction which had the effect of closing down the defendants'
factory would be disastrous, so the balance of convenience was against the grant
of the injunction. Instead a speedy trial was ordered. Scarman LJ (at 208) said that
there were serious questions of fact and law to be tried and that the defendants
would be put out of business. (His remark about the closure of the factory was
disapproved by May LJ in *Roger Bullivant Ltd* v *Ellis* [1987] ICR 464, 482. He
considered that such a fact related only to duration of the interlocutory injunction, not to the decision to grant it.) He also (at 209) noted that according to Lord
Diplock one can look at the chances of success at trial only as a last resort.
Nevertheless it was unlikely that the trial court would award an injunction on the
facts; damages were the more likely remedy (at 210). Sir John Pennycuick
concurred (at 210–11). All judges mentioned *American Cyanamid* and all loyally
followed it. Lord Denning MR (at 207) said that the case "straight and plainly"
fell within *American Cyanamid*; Scarman LJ (at 208) said that he had to adopt "the
approach that the House of Lords has said this court must adopt"; and Pennycuick said (at 210) that "the *American Cyanamid* case must be applied to and is

wholly appropriate to the circumstances of the present case". The judges thought that at trial damages would be a more appropriate remedy than an injunction, and Pennycuick thought that this factor could be thrown into the equation because it was a matter of remedy, not of merit – a perhaps doubtful distinction.

A second illustration in restraint cases of the application of the effect of *American Cyanamid* is *Business Seating (Renovations) Ltd* v *Broad* [1989] ICR 729. The law was stated to be well-settled that *American Cyanamid* governed "at least where there is some reasonable period of restriction which still lies ahead" (at 732). In the present case, there were 10½ months left of a 12-month covenant. Even with a speedy trial more than half of the covenanted period would have elapsed. Damages would not be adequate to the plaintiffs if they succeeded at trial but were not granted an interlocutory injunction: business would be lost and the ex-employee could not pay damages if an injunction were granted but the plaintiffs lost at trial; the cross-undertaking in damages would not adequately compensate the employee. He would not have suffered loss except the ability to carry out his duties effectively – it would be his new employers who would have suffered the loss through his not being able to work for them fully. The judge, Millett J, called what he was doing the balance of convenience but in reality he was running the stages of damages and the balance of convenience together. On the facts he thought that he had to look at the merits, especially as the prospects of success at trial did not depend on any further investigation of the facts (at 733). On those facts the covenant was enforceable and accordingly the interlocutory injunction was granted.

American Cyanamid has also been used in unreported first instance cases. It is in such cases that the importance of *American Cyanamid* is seen for the judges are going through the various parts of Lord Diplock's judgment and are taking care to apply all the stages which are appropriate on the facts. An example is *Flexiveyor Products Ltd* v *Herbert Owens*, 4 May 1982, LEXIS. The defendant had risen to become managing director of the plaintiffs who manufactured flexible conveyors which moved cartons to a delivery point. He was made redundant and he started a competing business. The plaintiffs alleged *inter alia* that the defendant had solicited distributors in breach of his duty of confidentiality. He contended that he had no case to answer. On the motion for an interlocutory injunction Falconer J applied *American Cyanamid*. The first step was to discover whether the action was frivolous or vexatious which he equiparated with whether there was a serious question to be tried. He stated that Lord Diplock said:

> in [1979] AC; page 408 'So unless the material available to the court at the hearing of the application for interlocutory injunction fails to disclose that the plaintiff has any real prospect of succeeding in his claim for a permanent injunction at the trial the court should go on to consider ... the balance of convenience ... '. When his Lordship talks about a serious question to be tried the touchstone is whether the plaintiff has any real prospect of succeeding in his claim for an injunction.

Since the defendant argued that the plaintiffs had no prospect of success the judge considered the evidence in some detail. He held that the evidence did not establish anything like a case that the defendant had solicited even one of the plaintiffs' distributors. In the eventuality that he might be wrong, Falconer J went through the other steps of Lord Diplock's approach to interlocutory injunctions. The plaintiffs had large overdrafts and the defendant was not financially sound. The judge said:

> If there is no injunction and the plaintiff wins the action the defendant is not going to be likely to meet the extra damages which would be accruing in the interim if no injunction is granted now. Against that, his operation is a small one. The plaintiff company is well established. I cannot see that there could be any real irreparable damage done to the plaintiff company . . . If an injunction, however, is granted and the defendant wins at trial his small but established business will undoubtedly be stopped . . . [T]here would [word missing: presumably "be"] unquantifiable damage to him.

The judge also considered that the defendant's competition until trial would not harm the plaintiffs too much and such competition would stop at the trial if judgment went in their favour. Accordingly, *obiter*, the judge thought that the balance of convenience was in favour of the defendant. The *ratio*, however, was as previously stated that the defendant had not used any of the plaintiffs' confidential information, and the motion for interlocutory injunctions was dismissed.

Falconer J also looked at the delay of the plaintiffs in bringing the action. It was not until 10 months after they became aware of the defendant's competition that the writ was issued. The judge considered that such delay *per se* debarred them from success on a motion for interlocutory injunctions. If the action had been commenced immediately, the status quo to be preserved under *American Cyanamid* would have been different. The defendant would not have gone so far in this competition. Therefore, because of the delay the status quo had changed and was at the date of the motion in favour of the defendant.

In *STL plc* v *Plessey Semiconductors Ltd*, above, the same judge held that there was a serious question to be tried but he dismissed the motion on the balance of convenience: the defendants could not be adequately protected by the cross-undertaking.

There have been exceptional cases where the application of *American Cyanamid* has worked in favour of employees. In *Lock International plc* v *Beswick* [1989] 3 All ER 373, a breach of confidence case, an interlocutory injunction was refused. While it was true that damages would not adequately compensate the employers because the loss of the allegedly confidential information could not easily be quantified, damages would also not be adequate for the employees because they would not be able to show how many products they would have sold, had the remedy been granted; on the balance of convenience the employers' business was established and so would survive if no relief were given, whereas the employees' was not firmly established and would collapse if the remedy were awarded.

If the trial judge does not apply *American Cyanamid* in a case where it should have been applied, the Court of Appeal is entitled "to review the judge's exercise of what is undoubtedly a discretionary jurisdiction, and to substitute its own discretion" (*per* Balcombe LJ in *Lawrence David* (at 393)).

Lawrence David, therefore, emphatically held that *American Cyanamid* applied to covenants, a matter which had previously been unclear: for example, the Court of Appeal as late as *Rockall Ltd* v *Murray*, 1 March 1988, LEXIS, was uncertain which test applied. Other similar Court of Appeal cases are *Milthorp International Ltd* v *Mann*, 19 May 1982, LEXIS, *Certified Laboratories Ltd* v *Mugleston*, 28 September 1982, LEXIS (by concession), and *Pritchard Services Ltd* v *Sieben*, 26 May 1988, LEXIS. In *Rex Stewart Jeffries Parker Ginsberg Ltd* v *Parker* [1988] IRLR 483 the same court discussed both the merits and severance at the interlocutory stage. In some Court of Appeal cases it did not matter which test was adopted: *Superprints Ltd* v *Woods*, 23 April 1986, LEXIS, and *Horsell Graphic Industries Ltd* v *Slattery*, 4 February 1988, LEXIS. However, even before *Lawrence David* there was strong support in restraint of trade and breach of confidence actions that *American Cyanamid* applied in those areas. See, for example, *Dunford & Elliott Ltd* v *Johnson & Firth Brown Ltd* [1977] 1 Ll LR 505, *Potters Ballotini Ltd* v *Weston-Baker*, above, *Transatlantic Records Ltd* v *Bulltown*, 28 February 1980, LEXIS, *Baron Meats Ltd* v *Siequien*, 11 May 1983, LEXIS, *Cord Designs Ltd* v *Greenless*, 24 October 1985, LEXIS (restraint of trade), *Schering Chemicals Ltd* v *Falkman Ltd* [1982] QB 1, *per* Shaw and Templeman LJJ, *Balston Ltd* v *Headline Filters Ltd* [1987] FSR 330, and *Evening Standard Ltd* v *Henderson* [1988] ICR 588. Quite often the relevant test was not discussed, and sometimes they were run together, as occurred in *Office International (London) Ltd* v *Palm Court Contracts Furniture Ltd*, 2 December 1985, LEXIS (Falconer J). *Lawrence David* cut through this difficult law, replacing it with simplicity.

In *Lansing Linde Ltd* v *Kerr* [1991] 1 All ER 418 (CA) the court held that trial could not take place until the period stated in the covenant had elapsed, and therefore judgment at the interlocutory stage would in effect dispose of the issue. Accordingly, *American Cyanamid* did not apply. Instead the court should assess whether it was more likely than not that had trial taken place, the employers would have obtained an injunction (disregarding the fact that the contractual period would have expired). The defendant was a former employee of the plaintiffs, fork-lift truck manufacturers. He left. Four days later he was appointed managing director of a rival firm. He was subject to covenants, one of which prohibited him for 12 months after termination of the contract from being engaged or concerned in any business competing with the plaintiffs. He had left on 26 June 1990. The covenant would therefore end on 25 June 1991. Trial would not be possible until March or April 1991. The judge, Knox J, did not apply the *American Cyanamid* test of whether there was a serious question to be tried but inquired whether the covenant would be upheld at trial. He held that at trial a worldwide covenant against competition would probably not be upheld and accordingly on the balance of convenience the plaintiffs failed: the covenant, being too wide in area, was unreasonable. Staughton LJ (at 423–4) said:

> If it will not be possible to hold a trial before the period for which the plaintiff claims to be entitled to an injunction has expired, or substantially expired, ... justice requires some consideration whether the plaintiff would be more likely to succeed at a trial. In those circumstances it is not enough to decide merely that there is a serious issue to be tried. The assertion of such an issue should not operate as a *lettre de cachet*, by which the defendant is prevented from doing that which, as it later turns out, he has a perfect right to do ... On a wider view of the balance of convenience it may still be right to impose such a restraint, but not unless there has been some assessment of the plaintiff's prospects of success ... I do not doubt that Lord Diplock, in enunciating the *American Cyanamid* doctrine, had in mind what its effect would be [with regard to discouraging "prolonged interlocutory battles on affidavit evidence"].

Lord Diplock himself in *NWL Ltd* v *Woods* [1979] 1 WLR 1294, 1306, had said that a judge should "give full weight to all the practical realities of the situation to which the injunction will apply". On the facts of *NWL* "the grant or refusal of an injunction ... would, in effect, dispose of the action finally in favour of whatever party was successful in the application, because there would be nothing left on which it was in the unsuccessful party's interest to proceed to trial". *Cayne* v *Global Natural Resources plc*, above, was a similar case. One of the practical realities in *Lansing Linde* was "delay caused by congestion in the court's lists". Staughton LJ said that the prospect of success at trial was only a factor in the equation, not conclusive. On the facts Staughton LJ considered it unlikely that full trial would occur before April 1991. While the defendant could give an undertaking as to damages, he may well not have been able to finance a five-day trial in which he would be seeking damages and freedom from the restraint (at 424).

> So if an injunction had been granted by the judge, or is now granted, the likely effect would be to decide the dispute against Mr Kerr for good and all. In those circumstances justice requires ... some assessment of the merits and more than merely a serious issue to be tried. But the situation would have been different if, in early September, there had been a prospect of a trial in November. Lansing Linde would have been obliged to proceed to trial if they wished to maintain their injunction for more than a small proportion of the 12-month period ...

Accordingly, the strength of the plaintiffs' claim could be considered. It should be remembered that the strength of the claim is only one factor in the equation: however, that factor may outweigh others. The worldwide covenant was unlikely to be upheld at trial. Fox and Butler-Sloss LJJ concurred. The court remained of the opinion that on interlocutory motion judges should not consider too closely the details of the case. The effect of *American Cyanamid* is to streamline applications, an effect which would be rendered nugatory if judges expended their time on detailed study of the evidence. This rationale does not, however, justify the grant of interlocutory injunctions in restraint cases. The doctrine of restraint of trade works in favour of the employee, whereas *American Cyanamid* works in favour of employers.

This approach was taken substantially further by Lord Jauncey in the House of Lords in *R v Secretary of State for Transport ex p Factortame Ltd (No 2)* [1991] 1 AC 603, 677, which is not a case on covenants. In reference to *American Cyanamid* Lord Jauncey said:

> it is not the function of the Court to try to resolve conflicts of evidence at an interlocutory stage but I would demur to any suggestion that in no circumstances would it be appropriate to decide questions of law. If the only question at issue between the parties is one of law it may be possible in many cases to decide this at the stage of a contested application for an interim injunction. For example, where an employer seeks to enforce a restrictive covenant in a former employee's contract of employment and the only defence is that the covenant by reason of its wide terms is unenforceable it would be wholly illogical to grant to the employers an interim injunction on the basis that there was a serious question to be tried when the question could at the same time be resolved as [a] matter of law in favour of the employee.

When reading this passage one should bear in mind the caveats "in many cases"; no "conflict of evidence"; only questions of law. Indeed Lord Diplock in *American Cyanamid*, above (at 407), spoke of "conflict of evidence on affidavit as to facts". Moreover, since reasonableness is a question of law, some questions of validity could be settled at the interlocutory stage using Lord Jauncey's suggestion. The effect would be that more employees would win than at present because of the low threshold question in *American Cyanamid*. Unfortunately, however, there may well be substantial disputes as to reasonableness which ought not to be determined "on the hoof".

There are a number of areas where it has come to be accepted that *American Cyanamid* does not apply. The first context is where there is no disputed question of fact. Hirst J accepted counsels' agreement that this exception applies in *Haarhaus & Co GmbH* v *Law Debenture Trust Corp plc* [1988] BCLC 640, 646. Accordingly he went straight on to discuss the merits of the case as to whether there was confidential information.

Lord Denning MR in *Woodward* v *Hutchins* [1977] 1 WLR 760, 764 (CA), a breach of confidence case involving personal, not trade, secrets, said that no injunction should be granted where there was a public interest in favour of disclosing confidential information. The issue of defences was not raised in *American Cyanamid*. It is suggested that investigation into the merits of a defence is inconsistent with the refusal to consider the merits of the claim. Lord Denning MR in *Schering Chemicals Ltd* v *Falkman Ltd*, above (at 21) (CA), a breach of confidence authority, suggested that *American Cyanamid* did not apply when relief was sought against the media. The majority did not support him. However, in the patents case of *Roussel-Uclaf Ltd* v *G D Searle & Co Ltd* [1977] FSR 125 Graham J stated *obiter* that no remedy should be awarded when the effect was to deprive the public of a life-saving drug. The public interest was not referred to by Lord Diplock in *American Cyanamid*. Only the interests of the parties were considered. It is unfortunate that no reference was made to the former employee's use of the skill and experience she acquired in her previous employment: such knowledge is stymied by the grant of interlocutory relief. The public interest in the free flow of information was also not mentioned. Perhaps, if the facts had raised them, Lord Diplock might have addressed these issues. It should be added that the structured approach in *American Cyanamid* sits oddly with the discretionary nature of the remedy.

It may be that the case is a simple one where affidavit evidence is sufficient to determine whether or not the covenant is enforceable. In those circumstances the case can be heard and determined at what would otherwise be the interlocutory stage. In *Business Seating (Renovations) Ltd* v *Broad*, the facts of which are given above, Millett J (at 733) said that he could not "avoid taking into account the likely prospects of success at the trial, particularly since they do not depend on any further investigation of the facts". The covenant prevented the defendant from canvassing or soliciting the plaintiffs' customers or the customers of any company associated with them. The judge held that the extension to associated companies was unjustified. "That aspect of the case does not depend on facts which require further investigation at the trial. It is as easy or as difficult a matter to decide on motion as at the trial of the action. Accordingly, I see no real prospects of the plaintiff succeeding in upholding the covenant in its full width at the trial and I would for that reason alone refuse interlocutory relief ... " (at 734). In *Lawrence David* Balcombe LJ (at 393) himself saw this point: "if there is no serious issue to be tried because the case is an open and shut one, then it is a case where an interlocutory injunction should be granted". A mini-trial has proved useful to the parties, and will not easily be foregone. It is useful whether or not a speedy trial can be arranged, and is a great cost-saver.

The issue whether *American Cyanamid* applies to covenants has not been considered by the Lords. It would be a good idea for the House to clarify the width of the exceptions to *American Cyanamid*. For example, in *Fellowes & Son* v *Fisher*, above at 141, Sir John Pennycuick thought that some cases could be competently settled at the interlocutory stage such as the construction of documents, which may occur in a restraint case, and some cases call for decisive early action such as a continuing trespass. Scotland retains the *prima facie* test: see for example *WAC Ltd* v *Whillock* [1990] IRLR 23, 26 and *Scotcoast Ltd* v *Halliday*, 10 January 1995, LEXIS and *Aramark plc* v *Sommerville*, 1995 SLT 749: see also below.

Speedy Trial

Where the covenant is of a suitable length, it may be possible for a speedy trial to be ordered under RSC Order 29 rule 5 (which applies too in the county court: County Courts Act 1984, section 76). If there is a speedy trial, the *American*

Cyanamid principles apply. In *Lawrence David Ltd* v *Ashton*, above, Balcombe LJ stated that the ex-employee should consider offering an undertaking until trial, provided that the former employers are likely to be able to pay compensation on their cross-undertaking. He said (at 395):

> cases of this type are singularly appropriate for a speedy trial . . . This case has already occupied four days of court time . . . which is four-fifths of the time counsel have estimated the trial of the action will take. I do not accept that the courts are unable to adapt their procedures so that, if time is not taken up by argument at the interlocutory stage, where the application of *American Cyanamid* indicates the desirability of an interlocutory injunction, provided that a speedy trial is possible, time cannot then be made available for a speedy trial.

Practitioners should pay heed to this heartfelt plea. He had earlier stated in *Dairy Crest*, above, that if there had been an application for a speedy trial the case might have been resolved before the interlocutory appeal in which he was delivering judgment (at 98).

A Summary of the effects of *American Cyanamid*

(1) The burden of proving that there is a good arguable case is a low one. Employers should be able to shoulder it in most cases.
(2) At the balance of convenience stage employers again will normally succeed because employees will usually be unable to pay damages at trial. The loss may be substantial if relief is not granted.
(3) Even if there is a speedy trial, because of (1) and (2) employers will be able to prevent employees competing until trial, which is precisely what they want. Employees will be restrained for the period immediately after employment. Moreover, since the court cannot deal with difficult questions of law at the interlocutory stage, matters such as repudiation by the employers which constitutes the destruction of the covenant are not investigated.

Employers will also be advantaged by the possibility of speedy trial: employees' rights will be subjugated to their rights for a short period, and so in the court's view it does not matter that employees lose out for a short period. Indeed in *Dairy Crest Ltd* v *Pigott*, mentioned above, the Court of Appeal seemed to hint that one factor in the grant of the injunction was that a speedy trial would have occurred had the employee not appealed!

Consistency of the Remedy with General Law and the Terms of Interlocutory Injunctive Relief

In a breach of confidence claim, if an interlocutory injunction is to be granted, it must of course be consistent with the law on trade secrets (for example no remedy will be granted to restrain information in the public domain), and it must identify the material to be restrained: *Amway Corp* v *Eurway International Ltd* [1973] FSR 213. Otherwise the judge would not be able to see whether the defendant had acted in contempt of court. As Lord Penrose put it in *Malden Timber Ltd* v *Leitch*, 1992 SLT 757: "One cannot stipulate for the protection of 'confidential' information and leave it to the court to find content for that expression ...". *Amway* has been followed in the Commonwealth: *O'Brien* v *Komesaroff* (1982) 150 CLR 310, a decision of the High Court of Australia. See also *Pioneer Concrete Services LGA* v *Galli* [1985] VR 675. Similarly, no interlocutory injunction will be granted where the information is not at least *prima facie* confidential: *Petranol plc* v *Mountford*, 22 May 1985, LEXIS. Accordingly, as Hoffmann J put it in *Lock International plc* v *Beswick*, above (at 378): "[t]he terms of any injunction must be capable of being framed in sufficient detail to enable the defendant to know exactly what information he is not free to use on behalf of his new employer". The order "must be capable of being framed with sufficient precision so as to enable a person injuncted to know what it is he is to be prevented from doing", as Balcombe LJ put it in *Lawrence David Ltd* v *Ashton*, above (at 393). Precision is a prerequisite because otherwise the employee will be uncertain whether what he or she is doing will breach the order and so be in contempt of court. The same principle applies to final injunctions: see below. For a Scottish case see *NCH (UK) Ltd* v *Mair*, 20 September 1994, LEXIS. Contempt is rare. For a reported case see *C R Smith (Dunfermline) Ltd* v *Anderson*, 1993 SLT (Notes) 592.

If the employers cannot so identify the trade secret, there is a way round the problem. Employers should incorporate a covenant that the employee will not work for a rival in trade as occurred in *Lawrence David*. Therefore, even if the employers cannot rely on the general law of confidentiality or on a covenant framed to protect trade secrets, they can still rely on an order preventing the employee from working for herself or for a competitor in breach of the express covenant. The terms of that injunction can ensure that the employers suffer no loss until trial.

There can be an appeal concerning the terms of the interlocutory injunction. For example, the judge in *K S Paul (Printing Machinery) Ltd* v *Southern Instruments (Communications) Ltd* (1961) [1964] RPC 118, on appeal 122, granted one that the defendants would not use confidential information "relating to machines manufactured by the plaintiff company under the trade name of 'Recordacall' ''. The Court of Appeal narrowed the injunction to information obtained from "machines of the type hired by the plaintiffs to the second defendant ... and obtained by the defendants ... from any unlawful inspection of any such machines".

The Terms of the Interlocutory Relief when an Injunction is Refused

A topic rarely discussed is that of the phrasing of the interlocutory relief. One case which does deal with the matter is the inventor case of *Coco* v *A N Clark (Engineers)*

Ltd [1969] RPC 41, 54, a case from the era before *American Cyanamid* but one which is not affected in this regard by that authority. The plaintiff had submitted an idea for a moped engine to the defendants. He alleged that they had used the idea which he had supplied to them: they denied both the supply and the use. Megarry J refused an interlocutory injunction partly on the ground that an idea was less worthy of protection than a product already on the market, and partly that the grant of such a remedy would halt the defendant's production line thereby making idle 35 to 40 workers and stopping the production of the sole British moped engine. Nevertheless, in case he was wrong and judgment at trial would be for the plaintiff, he accepted the proposals of counsel, who later became president of the Bar, that the defendants should pay a royalty on each engine into a special joint bank account held on trusts that would protect the plaintiff in the event of the defendants' insolvency and that the plaintiff's solicitors would be provided with information about the number of engines produced each month on their undertaking not to divulge the figure to the plaintiff or any other person without the consent of the defendants or leave of the court. These sensible arrangements could easily be adopted in the employers – employee situation.

It is instructive to compare *Coco* with another judgment of Megarry J, that in *British Northrop Ltd* v *Texteam Blackburn Ltd* [1974] RPC 57, where he rejected the evidence of the defendants that damages would adequately compensate the plaintiffs and that the defendants would be put out of business by the grant of an interlocutory injunction for, he said, the defendants could buy the parts they needed to continue production from the defendants. The distinction seems to lie in the plaintiff's information being only an idea in *Coco* while in *British Northrop* it was a list already in use by the plaintiffs.

If an interlocutory injunction was properly granted under *American Cyanamid* but the plaintiff fails at trial either because the complicated issues which could not be resolved at the interlocutory stage are settled in the defendant's favour or because the question of fact are resolved in the employee's favour, there will be an inquiry as to damages, and the questions will relate to causation and quantum: see *Zygal Dynamics plc* v *McNulty*, 20 June 1989, LEXIS (CA).

Undertakings to the Court

The former employee may agree pending trial to an undertaking given to the court that she will obey the whole or part of what the former employers would obtain if an interlocutory injunction were granted. An undertaking to the court is equivalent to an injunction. Breach of either is a contempt of court.

Courts may accept an undertaking in lieu of an interlocutory injunction but the undertaking must be in terms which protect the plaintiffs. So in *Brian D Collins (Engineers) Ltd* v *Charles Roberts & Co Ltd* (1965) 82 RPC 429 the plaintiffs designed a tank truck for carrying bulk liquids and the defendants manufactured them. When the plaintiffs cancelled their contract, the defendants continued to manufacture the trucks in competition with the plaintiffs, who sought an interlocutory injunction. The defendants offered an undertaking not to manufacture the trucks but reserved the right to sell the trucks they had made. Had this undertaking been accepted, the market for the trucks would have been satisfied. The court held that the undertaking was insufficient and granted the interlocutory injunction.

Commonwealth Authority

Canadian cases have tended to rely on and follow English cases. An example from the era after *American Cyanamid* is *Tenatronics Ltd* v *Hauf* (1979) 27 DLR (3d) 60, a decision of the Ontario High Court. The plaintiffs sought an interim injunction to restrain their former general manager from acting in breach of an express term that he would not disclose confidential information. He had joined a company which had then copied the plaintiffs' products. Hughes J noted that damages would not adequately compensate the plaintiffs because they would lose their market position if the defendants continued in production. He approved the English case of *Terrapin Ltd* v *Builders' Supply Co (Hayes) Ltd* [1967] RPC 128 that at the interlocutory stage a judge should not prejudge the outcome but that on the present facts the defendant had used the confidential information to enable the company to gain a market share. The remedy was granted accordingly. Similar is *Polyresins Ltd* v *Stein-Hall Ltd* (1972) 25 DLR (3d) 152, a decision of the same court. Galligan J adopted the pre-*American Cyanamid* law that a good arguable case or a strong *prima facie* case was necessary. He did however go on to mention the next stage, that of irreparable harm, and he held that two former employees of the plaintiffs would cause a loss which it would be impossible to quantify in damages through the loss of their competitive advantage. He too granted an interim injunction. For academic comment see R G Hammond "Interlocutory Injunctions" [1980] UTLJ 240 (noting at 251 the need in England to combat the litigation explosion); G M Rogers and G W Hateley "Getting the Pre-Trial Injunction" (1982) 60 CBR 1, especially 16–7; P Carlson "Granting an Interlocutory Injunction" (1982) 12 Man L J 109; and P M Perell "The Interlocutory Injunction and Irreparable Harm" (1989) 68 CBR 538 (remedy should be granted only if full trial would come too late to do justice).

Scottish law adheres to the *prima facie* reasonableness test with regard to covenants, and the courts have looked in depth at the reasonableness of the clause and a higher court will overrule a lower one if it believes it has ruled wrongly, for example *Bluebell Apparel Ltd* v *Dickinson*, 1978 SC 16.

Such an approach is consonant with a basic point about trade secrets. Once they are disclosed, no court order can retrieve that secrecy. However, if one is granted and subsequently it is found that it was wrongly granted the ex-employers may suffer only delay (though also they could be put out of business). It is here that the balance of convenience test demands that the facts ought to be closely scrutinised.

The Springboard Injunction

Employers who seek an injunction against an employee who has used or disclosed or who threatens to use or disclose trade secrets or other highly confidential information may rely on what is called the springboard doctrine. The law was first stated by Roxburgh J in *Terrapin Ltd* v *Builders' Supply Co (Hayes) Ltd* quoted in [1960] RPC 128, 130:

> ... a person who has obtained information in confidence is not allowed to use it as a springboard for activities detrimental to the person who made the confidential communication, and springboard it remains even when all the features have been published or can be ascertained by actual inspection by any member of the public ... [He] ... still has a long start over any member of the public ... [T]he possessor of such information must be placed under a special disability in the field of competition to ensure that he does not get an unfair start.

The employee cannot make use of the unfair start, and she is enjoined even though all others including trade rivals are free to use the information for their purposes including competition with the employers who have obtained the injunction. It is this special disability which is controversial, and it remains controversial even though it was the employee who put the information into the public domain. What the ex-employee has gained (and any new employers gain) is the saving of the trouble, time, and expense of replicating the former employers' confidential information. They cannot use the data even though the product which contains it has come onto the market in the meantime and can now be reverse-engineered.

Since the aim of the springboard injunction is to remove a head start, relief is limited to the head start period. A permanent injunction is inappropriate. In *Fisher-Karpark Industries Ltd* v *Nichols* [1982] FSR 351 Whitford J ordered that an interlocutory injunction should last only as long as the defendant retained an unfair advantage from the information he had improperly obtained. One year from termination was appropriate. In *Roger Bullivant Ltd* v *Ellis* [1987] ICR 464 the Court of Appeal held that the duration of the interlocutory injunction should be limited to the time the advantage to the former employee would last. On the facts a covenant limited the period of non-dealing to 12 months. That time was taken to be the reasonable period. Since that time had expired, the injunction was discharged. Nourse LJ (at 477) said: "the injunction should not normally extend beyond the period for which the unfair advantage may reasonably be expected to continue. That is ... the period for which an injunction would normally be granted in springboard cases". Similar is *Potters-Ballotini Ltd* v *Weston-Baker* [1977] RPC 202 (CA).

The springboard doctrine does not apply where the employers themselves have put the confidential information into the public domain. In *O Mustad & Son* v *Dosen* (1928) [1964] 1 WLR 109 the House of Lords held that the grant of a patent to the plaintiffs destroyed confidentiality for the information thereby lost its quality of confidence. "The secret, as a secret, had ceased to exist" (*per* Lord Buckmaster at 111).

Speed Seal Products Ltd v *Paddington* [1985] 1 WLR 1327 (CA) exemplifies the situation where the former employee, the first defendant, disclosed the information to his new employers, the second defendants. The defendants had published the information before the former employers sought an injunction. On the defendants' application to strike out the claim Fox LJ stated (at 1331–2) that publication by a stranger to the obligation of confidentiality does not release the ex-employee from that obligation. The court approved *Cranleigh Precision Engineering Ltd* v *Bryant* [1965] 1 WLR 1293, a case where, again, a stranger to the duty published the information. The employee was bound despite the knowledge being available to everyone else in the world. Roskill J granted the plaintiffs an injunction.

As a result of *Mustad* and *Cranleigh* Fox LJ summarised the law thus:

> (1) The publication is made by or with the consent of A (the person to whom the obligation is owed) ... B, who previously owed A a duty not to disclose the information, is released from that duty: see *Mustad & Son* v *Dosen* ... He has the same rights as every other member of the public. (2) The publication is made by or with the consent of X (a stranger) ... The court will prevent B from abusing his position of confidence. (3) The third case is where the publication is by or with the consent of B ... He ... cannot be in a better position than he would be if the publication had been made by a stranger.

Accordingly, as *Cranleigh* showed, "the mere fact that the publication has been made by a third party does not necessarily release from his obligations a person who previously owed a duty not to disclose". Whether an injunction was to be granted depended on whether the plaintiffs needed protection. On the facts that issue could not be resolved by an application to strike out (at 1332).

Lord Goff in *Attorney-General* v *Guardian Newspapers Ltd (No 2)* [1990] 1 AC 109, 285, criticised *Speed Seal.* He said that *Speed Seal* had decided that:

> if the confidant is not released when the publication is by a third party, then he cannot be released when it is he himself who has published the information ... [H]owever, ... the true basis of the decision [in *Cranleigh*] was that, in reliance on the well known judgment of Roxburgh J in the springboard case, *Terrapin Ltd* v *Builders' Supply Co (Hayes) Ltd* [1967] RPC 373, the defendant was in breach of confidence in taking advantage of his own confidential relationship with the plaintiff company to discover what a third party had published and in making use, as soon as he left the employment of the plaintiffs company, of information regarding the third party's patent which he had acquired in confidence ... The reasoning of Roskill J ... should be regarded as no more than an extension of the springboard doctrine, and I do not consider that it can support any general principle that, if it is a third party who puts the confidential information into the public domain, as opposed to the confider, the confidant will not be released from his duty of

confidence. It follows that ... the reasoning in the *Speed Seal* case ... cannot ... be supported.

The secret, therefore, does not exist when a third party publishes it.

It should be remembered that a springboard injunction may be granted even when the information is contained in a product which has come onto the market, as in *Terrapin* itself. In *Ackroyds (London) Ltd v Islington Plastics Ltd* [1962] RPC 97 (QBD) Havers J (at 104) said that the product, swizzle sticks, had not come onto the market generally because information is not available to the public when work has to be done on it to make it available. Therefore, "the mere publication of an article by manufacturing it and placing it upon the market ... is not necessarily sufficient to make such information available to the public".

It may be that the doctrine is limited to continuing breaches of confidence. Scott J was so minded in *Balston Ltd v Headline Filters Ltd* [1987] FSR 330. If the breach of confidence occurred in the past and is not continuing Scott J thought that no springboard injunction could be granted. In his opinion such a remedy could not be granted to deprive the employee of the benefits which accrued through his breach of contract. Scott J's dicta may be criticised. It is precisely past breaches to which the springboard injunction relates. If the breach is continuing, there is no need for such an injunction. The employers may obtain an ordinary interlocutory and final injunction. What, it is suggested, Scott J meant was that an employee will lose any competitive advantage she has acquired through breach of confidence in the past and continues to take advantage without breaching the duty not to use or disclose highly confidential information acquired during employment.

There is also debate over another statement of Scott J in *Balston*. He said that springboard injunctions could be used only for breaches of confidentiality and not to restrain other aspects of the duty of faithful service. The employee has broken that obligation by establishing during his garden leave a business which could compete with his employers after he had left and by soliciting customers for his new business. Scott J refused to grant a springboard injunction against these breaches of the duty of fidelity.

The Memory Rule and the Springboard Doctrine

In *Roger Bullivant Ltd v Ellis*, above, the Court of Appeal granted an injunction restraining the defendant, the former managing director of the plaintiffs, from dealing with clients whose names were on a card index he had taken from them including names which he could remember. Nourse LJ (at 495) explained: "Having made deliberate and unlawful use of the plaintiffs' property, he cannot complain if he finds that the eye of the law is unable to distinguish between those whom he could ... have contacted lawfully and those whom he could not". It was lawful for him to contact former clients whose names he could recall (and whose names he did not memorise). The interlocutory injunction was thus framed to cover unlawful and lawful use of names, the reason being that an injunction covering only the former would be difficult to enforce, for it would be hard to check whether the former employee had acquired the name legitimately or not. Approval for *Roger Bullivant* has come from the Court of Appeal. In *Johnson & Bloy (Holdings) Ltd* v *Wolstenholme Rink plc* [1987] IRLR 499 Fox LJ said that, although some of the information might have been carried away in the former employed director's head when he left the plaintiffs, the law was as stated in *Bullivant* as quoted above. In *Universal Thermosensors Ltd* v *Hibben* [1992] 1 WLR 840 Nicholls V-C (at 857) emphasised that the former employee's statement that he did not refer to a list but used his memory was likely to be greeted with circumspection, even scepticism.

There is authority for the proposition that an injunction cannot be granted to forbid an ex-employee from using the names of customers which he can remember. In *Louis* v *Smellie* (1895) 73 LT 226 Lindley LJ (at 228) stated that: "[i]f the defendant *happens* to remember that there is an agent whose address he can find out from the ordinary directories, he is at liberty to do so" (my emphasis). Pennycuick V-C applied *Louis* v *Smellie* in *Baker* v *Gibbons* [1972] 1 WLR 693. He held (at 702) that what Lindley LJ had said was part of the *ratio* of the case, that the ruling was correct in principle, and that the ruling was consistent with the springboard doctrine. He said that: "even where there is a list, one cannot regard every name and address on it as being *ipso facto* confidential. *A fortiori* where there is no written list ... ". There is therefore an unfortunate conflict of authority as to the confidential nature of the contents of a list where those contents are readily available to the former employee.

Springboard Injunctions and Fulfilling Contracts

The order in a springboard case may have the effect of preventing the defendant from fulfilling orders for customers. In *PSM International plc* v *Whitehouse* [1992] IRLR 279 Lloyd LJ (at 283) said that an interlocutory injunction is an equitable remedy, that it may be granted where the defendant has already contracted with customers and that it is not limited to situations where the employee has not yet reached the stage of negotiating contracts. "The arm of equity is not so short." As Lloyd LJ pointed out the position had already been dealt with in restraint cases. "Take the ordinary case of an employee who enters into a fresh contract of employment for, say, five years in breach of a valid covenant in restraint of trade. The new employer may be entirely innocent. Yet an injunction to restrain the ex-employee from continuing with his new contract of employment would undoubtedly affect the new employer's rights. He would be deprived of the services of the ex-employee which he had obtained by contract."

In a case heard after *PSM* but before it was reported, *Universal Thermosensors*, above, Nicholls V-C (at 853–4) said that fulfilling orders, whether present ones or future ones, was not to be restrained because doing so was not a breach of confidence. The breach occurred when the employee had taken and used the employers' lists of customers. However, it is suggested that the fulfilment of orders is legitimately restrained, for it demonstrates that the breach of confidence is a continuing one; that is, the defendant is still taking advantage of a prior breach. The relief in effect deprives the employee of her wrongful gains which are continuing, and is not directed at breaches which no longer have effect.

Garden Leaves and Interlocutory Injunctions

Actions to enforce covenants in restraint of trade normally take place after the contract of employment has terminated. An injunction to enforce a garden leave clause, however, is based on the theory that the contract is in existence. See Chapter 4. By their suit the employers are seeking to oblige the employee to abide by her agreement at a time when she wishes to join a rival or set up her own business in competition. Employment of the term leads to: (1) the employee receiving her contractual benefits such as salary; (2) her not rendering performance of part of the contract, the duty to work for the employers; and (3) her not leaving the employers and entering into competition.

A garden leave clause is not enforced when the employee has a contractual right to work. The situations where she has such a right are expanding, and it is not always clear whether the employee falls within one of the categories recognised in law. For greater detail see Chapter 3. This issue is picked up in the cases next discussed.

The law is to a large degree laid down in *Evening Standard Co Ltd* v *Henderson* [1987] ICR 588 (CA) and *Provident Financial Group plc* v *Hayward* [1989] ICR 160 (CA). In the former case the court allowed an appeal from the refusal of an interlocutory injunction to enforce a contractual clause that the defendant would give one year's notice. Lawton LJ noted that the plaintiffs could not gain an injunction to enforce a negative stipulation in a contract of employment where the award would leave the former employee in the position that he had to work for his former employers or starve (or be idle). On the facts the plaintiffs promised to pay the defendant during the notice period. Therefore, he would not starve. The plaintiffs would suffer damage if he left within the notice period and joined a rival firm. Accordingly, applying *American Cyanamid* the balance of convenience was tilted in favour of granting relief. Lawton LJ (at 594) was exercised by the employee's disloyalty. Without a garden leave clause or the existence of trade secrets included within the implied term of confidentiality, employees "can snap their fingers at their old employers because they can say: 'You cannot obtain an injunction against me which will have the effect of forcing me either to come back and work out my notice or starve ... ' This seems to me to be a most unsatisfactory situation". Balcombe LJ (at 595) concurred and added *obiter* that the evidence did not disclose that there was no alternative employment. Therefore, the defendant was not forced to choose between working for the plaintiffs or starving. He would have applied the Bette Davis case, *Warner Bros Pictures Inc* v *Nelson*, above.

Evening Standard and *Provident Financial* emphasise that enforcement is not granted when the employee's skills will atrophy during the garden leave. "The employee has a concern to work and a concern to exercise his skills. That has been recognised in some circumstances concerned with artists and singers who depend on publicity, but it applies equally ... to skilled workmen and even to chartered accountants", said Dillon LJ in *Provident Financial* (at 168). Taylor LJ said that "the defendant's skills as an accountant or financial director are unlikely to atrophy in a period of three months. Nor is he likely to suffer severe withdrawal symptoms for loss of job satisfaction over that period" (at 170).

The courts are loath to enforce garden leave when the period is a lengthy one: see Dillon LJ in *Provident Financial* (at 168). He stressed that the effect of the duration was a matter to be taken into account by the first instance judge. It was not decisive *per se*.

There are statements in the authorities that the clause is more likely to be enforced when the employee has acquired the employers' confidential information than otherwise. Dillon LJ in *Provident Financial* (at 169) stated that "the amount of confidential information that he [the employee] must have in his head, which would be highly prejudicial to the employers if he is working for a rival, is such that, on the mere principle of policing [the employers'] confidential information, it is right that the covenant should be enforced to prevent him working for a rival until the expiration of a reasonable period of notice". Dillon LJ emphasised that this matter too was one for the discretion of the judge.

Courts do not enforce garden leave clauses when the employee joining the employers' rival would not harm them. Fears that she will reveal confidential information must be real. On the facts of *Provident Financial* the confidential information was not relevant to the competitors, who operated an estate agency chain out of supermarkets, not from high street branches.

Anton Piller Orders

This section looks at Anton Piller orders in relation to the protection of confidential information. For more general treatment see Ough, *The Mareva Injunction and Anton Piller Order* (Butterworths, 1987).

The order is named after the case in which it was first granted, *Anton Piller KG* v *Manufacturing Processes Ltd* [1976] Ch 55 (CA). An *Anton Piller* order, which is discretionary, is granted by the High Court, normally in the employee's absence on affidavit evidence. The essence is surprise. The county court has no jurisdiction. It permits the employers, through a fixed number of persons and with a fixed number of their solicitors, to search the employee's premises, both business and private, and seize documents. Usually entry to business premises is made during office hours and must be made through normal doors (and not, for example, through the roof). In the context of restraint of trade the facts may be that the employee is alleged to have misappropriated confidential information from her employers or is using such material for purposes other than her job. The order places her under a duty to permit the search or reveal the documents immediately. However, the employers must not search through the employee's papers in an effort to stop her competing against them. Their solicitors may take the documents and copy them, but they must not allow their clients to read them until the judge grants leave for the employers to inspect them: *Lock International plc* v *Beswick* [1989] 1 WLR 1268. The search and seizure must be executed without force, but the sanction is contempt of court. If, however, the refusal of the former employee is upheld at trial, the contempt remains unpunished, and costs may be awarded against the plaintiffs. The order normally provides that the employers will pay for the disruption they cause. Therefore while the order is not a search warrant (because force cannot be used), in substance there is little difference. The appropriation of items not covered by the order is a contempt of court: *Columbia Pictures Industries Inc* v *Robinson* [1987] Ch 38 (Scott J). A list of material taken should be given to the employee: *Universal Thermosensors Ltd* v *Hibben* [1992] 1 WLR 840. Documents seized should be photocopied and the originals returned, unless they belong to the employers. If the parties dispute ownership, a neutral third party takes control of them: *Columbia Pictures* (at 77).

The requirements for the order were laid down by Ormrod LJ in *Anton Piller* (at 60). The employers must have a good reason to believe that the employee has the material. There must be a real possibility that the employee will destroy the material before any hearing. The fact that evidence has not been destroyed before the application is evidence that the order should not be granted for the order may not be needed. There must be "an extremely strong *prima facie* case" and "the damage, potential or actual, must be very serious for the applicant". However, because the remedy is one granted in the court's discretion, the judge is not bound to apply these conditions religiously. For example, an *extremely* strong case is not always required; see especially *Roamer Watch Co SM* v *African Textile Distributors* [1980] RPC 657, 675 (Cilliers J). The standard of proof is reduced where proceedings are *inter partes*. Even if she has acted dishonestly, her dishonesty does not demonstrate that she will destroy the confidential information: *Lock International* (at 1283). If the defendant is reputable it is unlikely that the order will be granted: *Booker McConnell plc* v *Plascow* [1985] RPC 425, 438–9 (CA), a breach of confidence case. Hoffmann J said in *Lock International* (at 1281) that "there must be proportionality between the perceived threat to the plaintiff's rights and the remedy granted". They cannot use an Anton Piller order to mount a fishing expedition against the defendant to gain evidence of any breach: *Hytrac Conveyors Ltd* v *Conveyors International Ltd* [1989] 1 WLR 723 (CA). The documents sought must be particularised as far as possible.

The Anton Piller order is in reality a series of orders. One is to sanction search and seizure, but this order is normally coupled with an injunction to restrain the employee from acting in breach of contract or in breach of confidence or both (for example, to prohibit her from disregarding a covenant in restraint of trade and by means of a springboard injunction to restrain her from utilising the competitive edge she has acquired through breaking her duty of confidentiality) and an injunction to restrain her from warning others of the award of the Anton Piller order: for example, the employee will be restrained from informing colleagues that their premises are about to be raided, though practice seems to be that all relevant premises are raided at the same time. There may be an order that the former employee divulges the names and addresses of suppliers and clients: *EMI Ltd* v *Sarwar* [1977] FSR 146. The duration of this order is limited. In *Universal Thermosensors*, above, Nicholls V-C (at 860) thought that a week was too long. There will also normally be an order that the employee disclose the names and addresses of those involved in the breach or breaches such as the company which induced her to break her contract by revealing her employers' trade secrets to it. This order is known as a Norwich Pharmacal order after *Norwich Pharmacal Co* v *Customs and Excise Commissioners* [1974] AC 133 (HL). An example is *Gates* v *Swift* [1982] RPC 339. Graham J (at 342) ordered the defendant to disclose the names and addresses of customers. The case involved copyright in respect of computer software but is applicable generally. If the employers exceed the powers in the order, they may be liable for torts such as trespass.

In the order there is a cross-undertaking as to damages. The employers promise to make good the employee's loss if the court subsequently holds that the order ought not to have been granted. The employers have to show that they can pay any damages awarded: *Vapormatic Co Ltd* v *Sparex Ltd* [1976] 1 WLR 939 (Graham J). They also undertake to serve a writ as soon as practicable, if they have not already done so.

The judiciary has developed safeguards against abuse of the order. The most important one is that the employers must make full and frank disclosure when applying for the order. Even material which seems irrelevant is subject to this obligation. In *Columbia Pictures*, above, Scott J (at 79) held that the plaintiffs had not made full and frank disclosure when they stated that the defendant's trade was being undertaken in a clandestine manner when it was not. In *Manor Electronics Ltd* v *Dickson* [1988] RPC 618, a breach of confidence case, Scott J said that the plaintiffs had failed to reveal their financial situation, which was that they were not good for paying damages on the cross-undertaking. A similar case is *Lock International*, above. If the applicants do not make full and frank disclosure, the order is discharged, and it is discharged, even though the failure was innocent. However, if the failure was innocent they may reapply for the order, for example *Brink's Mat Ltd* v *Elcombe* [1988] 1 WLR 1350 (CA). The time for making an order to discharge is at the interlocutory stage, provided that there has definitely been a failure to make full and frank disclosure or that there are grave consequences to the non-disclosure: *Tate Access Floors Inc* v *Boswell* [1991] Ch 512, 533 (Browne-Wilkinson V-C).

One issue requiring consideration is that the employers may have to reveal the trade secret which, they allege, the employee has misappropriated when applying for the order. Donaldson MR in *WEA Records Ltd* v *Visions Channel 4 Ltd* [1983] 1 WLR 721 (CA) thought that a judge was wrong to rely on evidence which was not incorporated into the plaintiffs' affidavits. It is suggested that one way of avoiding this difficulty is to put details of the confidential information into an affidavit separate from that used to support the application for the order.

A solicitor serves the Anton Piller order on the defendant. She is under a duty to explain the order to her in ordinary language and must advise her to seek legal advice: *Booker McConnell*, above. The employee can seek that advice before she complies with the order but she must do so immediately. She cannot do anything else (such as warn her friends). In relation to the solicitor Nicholls V-C in *Universal Thermosensors*, above (at 861), said: "judges should give serious consideration to the desirability of providing, by suitable undertakings and otherwise, (a) that the order should be served, and its execution supervised, by a solicitor other than a member of the firm of solicitors acting for the plaintiff ... ; (b) that he or she should be an experienced solicitor having some familiarity with the workings of Anton Piller orders, and with judicial observations on this subject (*e.g.* as summarised in the notes in the *Supreme Court Practice* ... to Ord 29 r 3". Nicholls V-C warned against the order being executed in a private dwelling in the early morning when sole persons in the house were a woman and her children. He suggested that in such a situation the solicitor, if a man, should be accompanied by a woman (at 860).

If the employee refuses to comply with the order, she commits contempt of court, unless she persuades the judge that the order should be discharged. If the employee meanwhile destroys the evidence, she will suffer "consequences ... of the utmost gravity": *WEA Records*, above (at 726). An application to discharge may be made *ex parte*, though usually evidence by affidavit will have to be provided: *Hallmark Cards Inc* v *Image Arts Ltd* [1977] RPC 150. An Anton Piller order may be discharged retrospectively: *Booker McConnell*, above (at 434–5). The defendant may be cross-examined as to whether she has complied with the order, though such procedure rarely happens. Normally the employers apply for committal for contempt or apply for an order to disclose.

Current judicial attitudes to Anton Piller orders in restraint of trade and breach of confidence cases is much less "gung ho" than earlier ones. Judges have said that the orders have been granted too readily in the past (for example Scott J in *Columbia Pictures*, above at 76). The defendant is not heard before the order is made and her privacy is invaded. Furthermore, as Browne-Wilkinson J stated in *Thermax Ltd* v *Schott Industrial Glass Ltd* [1981] FSR 289, 291, " ... it is capable of being abused. A plaintiff engaged in trade who obtains an order enabling him to enter the business premises of a competitor and reach that competitor's documents may obtain a quite unfair and wrongful commercial advantage". Courts nowadays are more ready than previously to adhere to the stringent conditions for the grant of the order. The effect is that orders are granted more rarely now than before: *Universal Thermosensors*, above (at 860).

Hoffmann J stated in a highly significant judgment, *Lock International*, above (at 1280–1), that:

> Anton Piller orders are frequently sought in actions against former employees who have joined competitors or started competing businesses of their own ... There is a strong incentive for employers to launch a pre-emptive strike to crush the unhatched competition in the egg ...
>
> Some employers regard competition from former employees as presumptive evidence of dishonesty. Many have great difficulty in understanding the distinction between genuine trade secrets and skill and knowledge.

Hoffmann J called for a proportionate response. If the employee would destroy the evidence, an order for delivery up suffices, and an Anton Piller order will not be granted. He continued (at 1281):

> [t]he more intrusive orders allowing searches of premises or vehicles require a careful balancing of, on the one hand, the plaintiff's right to recover his property to preserve important evidence against, on the other hand, violation of the privacy of a defendant who has had no opportunity to put his side of the case . . . The making of an intrusive order *ex parte* even against a guilty defendant is contrary to normal principles of justice and can only be done when there is a paramount need to prevent a denial of justice to the plaintiff. The absolute extremity of the court's powers is to permit a search of the defendant's dwelling house, with the humiliation and family distress that frequently involves.

An addition to Hoffmann J's graded response is an order for inspection under RSC, Order 29. Since the Anton Piller order is "a nuclear weapon of the law" (*Bank Mellat* v *Nikpour* [1985] FSR 87, 92), its use must be strictly controlled.

Contents of Chapter Fourteen
FINAL REMEDIES

Chapter Fourteen

FINAL REMEDIES

The principal remedy desired by former employers at the final stage of proceedings is an injunction. However, many enforceable covenants have run their course before the date for trial arrives. For this reason an interlocutory injunction is of far greater importance than a final one. Where time has not elapsed, the injunction lasts for no longer than the contractually stipulated period. Where the claim is for an injunction restraining a breach of confidence, it seems that the normal approach is to grant a permanent injunction with liberty to apply or to grant an order restraining the former employee for a time limited to the estimated length of the head start. Other remedies are also available. Commonly damages are awarded for past loss coupled with an injunction to forestall future lose.

Injunction

A final injunction is used to prevent continuing or future breaches of contract. It is not the appropriate remedy when the employee has gained the whole benefit from the breach at one time. An injunction may be granted against a minor: *Bromley* v *Smith* [1904] 2 KB 235.

This relief, being equitable in origin, is discretionary. Surprisingly Donaldson P said in *Attorney-General* v *Guardian Newspapers Ltd (No 2)* [1990] 1 AC 109, 196, that "[e]quity in this context equates with fairness and common sense", rather than with the doctrines of equity. This dictum, if correct at all, must be seen in its context, that of government secrets. The judge may refuse an injunction and award damages in lieu if she considers that the plaintiffs would thus obtain justice and no undue hardship would be caused to the defendants, that a maxim of equity has been infringed (such as "he who comes to equity must come with clean hands"), that the wrongdoing will not be repeated (see the previous paragraph), or that the confidential information has been widely disseminated (see, for example, *Sun Printers Ltd* v *Westminster Press Ltd* [1982] IRLR 292 (CA) and *Attorney-General* v *Guardian Newspapers Ltd (No 2)*, in which Bingham LJ (at 226) said that it would be "futile" to grant this remedy) or that it is about to become public knowledge. A judge may refuse the remedy if the defendant has acted inadvertently or innocently.

The exception for damages in lieu is now found in the Supreme Court Act 1981, section 50. This type of damages may be awarded both to remedy past wrongs and (unlike common law damages) wrongs to be committed: *Leeds Industrial Co-operative Society Ltd* v *Slack* [1924] AC 851 (HL), approved in *Johnson* v *Agnew* [1980] AC 367 (HL). Grounds for exercising the jurisdiction to award damages in lieu were succinctly put by A L Smith LJ in *Shelfer* v *City of London Electric Lighting Co* [1895] 1 Ch 287, 322–3: " . . . (1) if the injury to the plaintiff's legal rights is small, (2) and is one which is capable of being estimated in money, (3) and is one which can be adequately compensated by money payment, (4) and the case is one in which it would be oppressive to the defendant to grant an injunction – then damages in substitution for an injunction may be given". A L Smith LJ referred to "money payment" but in *Seager* v *Copydex (No 2)* [1969] 1 WLR 809, a breach of confidence case, damages on a capitalised royalty basis were awarded by the Court of Appeal. Damages may also be awarded in addition to an injunction under the Supreme Court Act. Damages may thus be awarded in respect of past breaches of contract and an injunction against future breaches.

"Unclean hands" is a ground for refusing an injunction. The defence is an equitable one, focusing on whether the plaintiffs have acted improperly. Generalised misconduct is insufficient: there must be a connection between the wrongdoing and the action (*Church of Scientology* v *Kaufman* [1973] RPC 627 (Goff J)). The impropriety must be worse than "an error of judgment": *Stevenson Jordan & Harrison Ltd* v *McDonald & Evans* (1951) 68 RPC 190, 196 (first instance). Plaintiffs will succeed even if they have behaved badly if the defendant's misconduct is worse than theirs: *Argyll* v *Argyll* [1967] Ch 302, 331. The judge further held that unclean hands in the present did not mean that past confidential information could be revealed. Attempts at self-preservation are not *per se* unclean hands: *Castrol Associates Pty Ltd* v *Emtech Associates Pty Ltd* (1980) 33 ALR 31, 58.

In principle the distinction between unclean hands and the public interest exception ("just cause or excuse") is clear. Unclean hands deals with the plaintiffs' personal misconduct, whereas the public interest as its name suggests provides the defendant with a good reason not relating to the misconduct of the plaintiffs for revealing information. Sam Ricketson, "Public Interest and Breach of Confidence" (1979) 12 MULR 176, 184, gave this illustration. If a scientist discovers matters which may be dangerous if misused, the research should be made known in the public interest, but the good faith of the scientist is unquestioned. Unclean hands does not cover matters which ought to be revealed for the sake of third parties such as defective processes. Nevertheless, the same facts may give rise to both defences: see *Hubbard* v *Vosper* [1972] 1 QB 84 and *Church of Scientology of California* v *Kaufman*, above.

In *Hubbard* v *Vosper* Megaw LJ (at 101) held that a confidence was not protectable when the plaintiff had used "deplorable means". Goff J in *Kaufman* (at 634) approved this statement. The Court of Appeal seems to have treated unclean hands and deplorable means as the same in *Hubbard* v *Vosper*, but Goff J seems to have treated them as separate defences. Methods used to suppress information were deplorable, but they did not constitute unclean hands. If this analysis is correct, Goff J instituted a novel defence. The deplorable means in both cases were the cult of Scientology's penal and disciplinary codes, which permitted members to attack, both metaphorically and literally, "suppressive persons", that is those opposed to Scientology.

Goff J in *Kaufman* did not determine whether either unclean hands or deplorable means or both deprived plaintiffs of their common law damages. However, in *Weld-Blundell* v *Stephens* [1919] 1 KB 520 (CA) Warrington LJ treated *Gartside* v *Outram* (1856) 26 LJ Ch 113 as a case on unclean hands and, since the maxim applied only to equity, he held that the plaintiff retained his legal remedy. Lack of acquiescence and lack of delay (laches) are also conditions for the grant of an injunction. In *Church of Scientology of California* v *Miller, The Independent*, 23 October 1987, LEXIS, Vinelott J held that the plaintiffs had delayed too long in seeking an interlocutory injunction. They had delayed until close to the date of a publication of a book about the founder of Scientology, a delay which would cause the second defendants the greatest possible financial loss, inconvenience, and damage to their reputation. The Court of Appeal approved the judgment and refused to allow the plaintiffs to adduce evidence as to the reason for their failure to commence proceedings promptly on the grounds that they were under a duty to make full disclosure of all relevant material when making the application. A contrasting case is *Schering Chemicals Ltd* v *Falkman Ltd* [1982] QB 1 (CA). Templeman LJ said that the plaintiffs had not delayed too long in seeking to prevent a television company from making a programme about a certain drug because they had signified throughout that they would see if the film made use of confidential information.

An injunction will not be granted to protect "utterly absurd" information: *Kaufman*. No injunction is awarded where the court cannot enforce it (see specific performance and negative injunctions, above at pp 285–7).

An injunction may be granted against a third party who has derived information from an employee who acquired it in breach of confidence, if that person is aware of the injunction: *Electronic Applications (Commercial) Ltd* v *Toubkin* (1962) 79 RPC 225, 226 (Wilberforce J). It may be granted in favour of a third party injured by a covenant: *Nagle* v *Feilden* [1966] 2 QB 633 (CA).

The Terms of the Injunction

The injunction must be formulated in such a manner that the defendant knows what she must not do; see for example *Bjorlow (Great Britain) Ltd* v *Minter* (1954) 71 RPC 321, 323; *Suhner & Co AG* v *Transradio Ltd* [1967] RPC 329, 334; and *Searle &*

Co Ltd v *Celltech Ltd* [1982] FSR 92, 104. For a Scottish case see *Aramark plc* v *Sommerville*, 1995 SLT 749. The injunction must state what the confidential information is. If the plaintiffs cannot do so, they will not be awarded a final injunction, even if they have received an interlocutory one: *P A Thomas & Co* v *Mould* [1968] 2 QB 913.

In breach of confidence cases the injunction can be phrased to fit the facts and necessities of each case. In the old case of *Yovatt* v *Winyard* (1820) 1 Jac & W 394, 37 ER 425, Lord Eldon C granted an injunction to restrain the defendant, the plaintiff's former assistant or journeyman, from selling veterinary medicines, the recipes for which he had surreptitiously appropriated while in the plaintiff's employment, but he decided not to forbid the administration of the medicine to any animal which was on a course of it. The injunction must not infringe the general law such as that concerned with the employee's skill and knowledge.

The form of the injunction will vary with the facts of the case. For instance, in *Electronic Applications (Commercial) Ltd* v *Toubkin* (1962) 79 RPC 225 the injunction restrained the party in breach of confidence from "manufacturing or attempting to manufacture or selling or canvassing, concerning any of the plaintiffs' products or products similar thereto based on the plaintiffs' processes or designs". This wide form was however cut down by Wilberforce J who refused an injunction which would have prohibited the defendant from making use of the information. He demanded "a clear case" (at 227) before granting an injunction in those terms, and the plaintiffs failed in that endeavour. A similar injunction was granted in *Peter Pan Manufacturing Corp* v *Corsets Silhouette Ltd* [1963] 3 All ER 402 where Pennycuick J accepted the argument of plaintiffs' counsel that the words "merely colourably differing therefrom" were appropriate. The form of words prevented the defendants from slightly altering the articles to evade the injunction. He did not wish to reject a "time-honoured expression".

There is New Zealand authority on the duty of fidelity for the proposition that an injunction ought not to remain in effect for a long time because if the employers cannot recover lost custom within a short time, little will be gained by an injunction for a lengthy period: *A M Satterthwaite & Co Ltd* v *Gay* (1987) 1 NZEL c78–060.

In restraint of trade cases, the injunction must be "expressed in the very words of the clause – for that is what the parties agreed": *per* Lord Denning MR in *Littlewoods Organisation Ltd* v *Harris* [1977] 1 WLR 1472, 1483. Provided that the covenant is suitably drawn, the remedy can prevent an employee working for a competitor. Such a remedy is wider in scope than an injunction which prohibits an employee from using or disclosing the information at issue. Since employers may wish to stop a former employee from working for a rival, it is advantageous to them to have a restraint clause and not rely on breach of confidence. Banning employment would stop the leakage of confidential information, such leakage being almost inevitable in a new job.

There was no argument as to the scope of the injunction in *Littlewoods* because the injunction had to be phrased as per the clause. The result was ably criticised by M W Bryan, "Restraint of Trade: Back to a Basic Approach" [1980] JBL 326, 334.

> By forbidding an employee from working for its principal rival the plaintiffs were making it difficult for him to work in that field at all and were threatening to sterilise completely for a time the use of his general skills. An injunction restraining disclosure of confidential information would have enabled him to ply his chosen trade with another firm but would also have provided some protection for the employers for their secrets.

Bryan noted, however, that on the facts the court was probably correct to frame the injunction in terms of the covenant because it was probably inevitable that the ex-employee would disclose the information to the new firm because of the nature of his job. Furthermore, the sterilisation was for a year only, and he may well not have suffered too much financially because of his large salary. Nevertheless it must be said that in other fact situations a different outcome may be desired, and that outcome may be impossible since the courts have to follow the terms of the covenant. Moreover, if the covenant is unenforceable, no injunction is possible. There is therefore no middle way. If the covenant could be granted on narrower terms than the clause, employers could get what they want without oppression to employees.

If the injunction is couched in such terms that the process is protected as long as it remains secret, the process will cease to be protected once there has been an independent discovery of it.

In England the injunction runs to the end of the contractual period. There have, however, been American cases where the injunction lasts for the contractual period not beginning at the date when the employee leaves employment but from the date of judgment. For example, by a four to three majority the Supreme Court of Florida ruled in *Capelouto v Orkin Exterminating Co of Florida*, 183 So 2d 532 (1966) that the Chancellor was correct in dating the decree to run for two years from a date over a month after judgment rather than from the date of termination of employment or judgment. The period from judgment to the commencement of the injunction was to be used by the employee to settle his affairs. O'Connell J said:

> the appellee–employer was entitled to have a period of two years during which the appellant–employee would not be in competition with it ... In as much as the appellant had been in competition with the appellee continuing since his resignation, the Chancellor must have determined that this was the only way to give the appellee its two competition-free years. We can find no fault with this theory ... We think that the procedure followed by the Chancellor is the only way by which the provisions of the contract and the statute could be effectuated. ("The statute" is a reference to Florida Statutes section 542.12, Florida Statutes Annotated, which permitted reasonable covenants.)

The dissentients said (spelling anglicised): "it is not our function to trim and pad our conclusions to fit the curves and dimples of fairness nor to otherwise temper the rigours of express agreements. *Stare decisis* is preferable to the Napoleonic idea of meting fairness in accordance with the passing whim of each judge in each case". There would seem to be something to be said for both approaches.

A contrasting case is *A-Copy Inc* v *Michaelson*, 599 F 2d 450, 452 (1978), where the Court of Appeals for the First Circuit applying Massachusetts law followed *All Stainless Steel Inc* v *Colby*, 308 NE 2d 481, 485, 487 (1974), a decision of the Supreme Judicial Court which held that "when the period of restraint has expired, even when the delay was substantially caused by the time consumed in legal appeals, specific relief is inappropriate and the injured party is left to his damages remedy". However, the court thought that a time period which might otherwise be unreasonable was reasonable if the time left to enforce was reasonable: *Marine Contractors Inc* v *Hurley*, 310 NE 2d 915, 921 (1976). This is an interesting idea and one which could deter unmeritorious appeals. However, it does perhaps leave too much power in the hands of employers.

Construction

The question of the construction of an injunction was raised in *Clark* v *Electronic Applications (Commercial) Ltd* [1963] RPC 234. In a memorandum of agreement Clark, a director, agreed that his inventions should belong to the company. On resigning he consented to an injunction preventing him from disclosing anything to anyone in connection with the work he had performed while employed by the company. He later claimed that the restraint was unlawful because the terms of the injunction prevented him from practising as an electrical engineer. The court held that the injunction was to be construed in the light of surrounding circumstances. Therefore the ex-employee was restrained only from revealing the novel feature of the products he had worked on.

Reform

The Law Commission Report, *Breach of Confidence* (Cmnd 8388, 1981), 109, recommended that the final injunction should last "so long as the requirements of the action for breach of confidence continue to be fulfilled". In conformity with the springboard doctrine and with the Uniform Trade Secrets Act of the United States and the proposed Canadian Trade Secrets Act the defendant who put the information into the public domain is to be restrained until her commercial advantage has ceased to exist.

Unliquidated Damages for Breach of Covenant in Restraint of Trade during and after Employment and for Breach of the Contractual Duty of Faithful Service

Where a contract of employment is broken, whether in respect of implied terms or express ones, the remedy of damages is always available. Damages may also be granted as a substitute for or in addition to an injunction: Supreme Court Act 1981, section 50. The quantum of damages for a breach of covenant or breach of the duty of confidentiality is assessed in the usual contractual manner within *Hadley* v *Baxendale* (1854) 9 Exch 341, 156 ER 145. Since the relationship is governed by contract, there is no need to discuss other possible bases of jurisdiction such as equity: *Vokes Ltd* v *Heather* (1945) 62 RPC 135 (CA) and *Faccenda Chicken Ltd* v *Fowler* [1987] Ch 117 (CA). In the latter case Neill LJ said (at 135), referring to *Vokes Ltd* v *Heather*, that: "Where the parties are, or have been, linked by a contract of employment, the obligations of the employee are to be determined by the contract between him and his employer".

In a breach of covenant action damages for loss flowing naturally from the breach include compensation for the loss of clientele by which the employers' profits are diminished. "Special circumstances" damages include loss caused to them by using or disclosing their confidential information. What are the circumstances reasonably in the contemplation of the parties is determined by reference to the time when the parties made the relevant agreement. Damages are assessed at the date of breach.

It may be that there is no loss which is definite. For example, the employer may have lost the chance of acquiring contracts. In that situation *Chaplin* v *Hicks* [1911] 2 KB 786 (CA) applies. In *Sanders* v *Parry* [1967] 1 WLR 753 the defendant breached his duty of faithful service by acquiring a client of his employer for himself. Havers J awarded £502 damages, being the amount for loss the breaches of the duty of fidelity caused the plaintiff. Even where the employers would not have obtained the contract because the firm which had dealt with the employee would not deal with them, they have a remedy in damages. In *Industrial Development Consultants Ltd* v *Cooley* [1972] 1 WLR 443 (Assizes) Roskill J said *obiter* (at 456) that the plaintiffs had only a 10% chance of acquiring the relevant contract because the third party had strongly expressed the view that they would not deal with the plaintiffs. (The case largely deals with breach of fiduciary duty and the obligation to account by a director but in case he was wrong the judge considered damages.) *Chaplin* v *Hicks* was mentioned in argument but not by the judge.

A recent illustration of damages for breach of confidence is *Universal Thermosensors Ltd* v *Hibben* [1992] 1 WLR 840. Nicholls V-C (at 851) stated that the basis of the claim was "for loss of profits which [the plaintiff] would have earned but for the defendants' misuse of confidential information by soliciting orders from the customers . . . In addition, the plaintiff claims to have suffered general loss of profits by diminution of its trade". The judge said (at 852) that if the employers cannot show that specific contracts were lost through the breach of confidence, they can recover damages for the general diminution of their trade, but they had to demonstrate that the loss was occasioned by the defendants' misconduct and it was not misconduct when employees left to set up their own competing business and targeted former customers (in the absence of a covenant).

It has been suggested that if the former employers did not intend to retain the information for their own use, but to sell or license it, the proper basis of damages is a capitalised royalty: *Seager* v *Copydex Ltd (No 2)* [1969] 1 WLR 809 (CA). This issue is discussed below in the context of the non-contractual claim for damages. This notion has not been used in restraint cases.

As in other claims for damages for breach of contract the plaintiffs are under a duty to mitigate loss. Mitigation may be problematic. If the employee has left to join a competitor and takes a confidential list of customers, surely the employers are not under a duty to entice her back, especially as such persuasion may constitute the tort of inducing breach of contract.

One rule of general contract law limits the employers' duty to mitigate. There is no duty until they accept the breach: *White and Carter (Councils) Ltd* v *McGregor* [1962] AC 413 (HL). The effect of this rule may be that by the time the employers accept the breach, it is too late to mitigate.

There may be situations in which the relationship between the parties is not governed by contract. Perhaps the agreement is void for illegality. It might be argued that since there is no contract, there can be no breach of contract and therefore damages cannot be awarded. Alternatively, one might contend that illegality does not affect confidentiality. Illegality is built on public policy (see *Hewcastle Catering Ltd* v *Ahmed* [1992] ICR 626) and public policy does not demand that employers lose their right to confidentiality.

Another situation where there is no contract occurs during pre-contract negotiations between the employers-to-be and the employee-to-be such as at an interview. There can be no covenant for that is a contractual matter but there is another juridical base for the remedy. In *Nichrotherm Electrical Co Ltd* v *Percy* (1957) 74 RPC 207 the Court of Appeal (at 212, 215) found that there was a contract but in relation to the situation where there was no contract, as the first instance judge had found ((1956) 73 RPC 272), Lord Evershed MR (at 214) inquired:

> Is the remedy . . . to be found at common law or in equity or, possibly, both? If the confidence . . . is imposed by or arises out of contract, express or implied, then the remedy would . . . be by way of damages at law . . . If . . . the confidence infringed is one imposed by the rules of equity, then the remedy would be, *prima facie*, by way of injunction or damages in lieu of an injunction under Lord Cairns' Act.

Lord Cairns' Act, the Chancery Amendment Act 1858, is now in substance section 50 of the Supreme Court Act 1981. In a second case involving an inventor, *Seager* v *Copydex Ltd*, above, the Court of Appeal granted an inquiry as to damages but did not state whether damages were common law ones or in lieu of an injunction. In

English v *Dedham Vale Properties Ltd* [1978] 1 WLR 93, 111, Slade J read *Seager* as being an instance of damages in lieu. In *Harrison* v *Project & Design Co (Redcar) Ltd* [1978] FSR 81 Graham J granted damages but he left open for argument "the basis on which damages should be assessed ... " (at 90). Moreover, in *Malone* v *Metropolitan Police Commissioner* [1979] Ch 344 Megarry V-C stated (at 360): "Where there is no breach of contract or other orthodox foundation for damages at common law, it seems doubtful whether there is any right to damages as distinct from an account of profits".

The courts seem to be edging their way towards saying they can award damages for breach of non-contractual duty of confidence. Sometimes reference is made to Lord Cairns' Act, the Chancery Amendment Act 1858, sometimes not. See further D Capper "Damages for Breach of the Equitable Duty of Confidence" (1994) 14 LS 313.

Cases on Crown Service are ones where there may be no contract. In *Attorney-General* v *Guardian Newspapers Ltd* [1987] 1 WLR 1248 (HL), an interlocutory appeal, there is support for damages. Lord Goff (at 307) said that account of profits was not an adequate remedy, not that there was no remedy in damages, while Lord Bridge (at 1285) considered that an account was appropriate: since an account is available only as an alternative to damages, there is support for damages as a remedy. When the case was determined finally, it was Lord Goff who best saw the issue. In *Attorney-General* v *Guardian Newspapers Ltd (No 2)* [1990] AC 107 (at 186) he stated that damages were available when the jurisdiction lay in equity because there was no contract as a result of "a beneficial interpretation" of the 1858 Act.

If damages may be awarded for breach of a non-contractual duty of confidence the question arises as to how they are to be assessed. The sole judge to have tackled this issue in any depth was Lord Denning MR in *Seager* v *Copydex Ltd (No 2)*, above (at 813):

> The value of the confidential information depends on the nature of it. If there was nothing very special about it, that is, if it involved no particular inventive step but was the sort of information which can be obtained by employing any competent consultant then the value of it was the fee which the consultant would charge for it; because in that case the defendant company, by taking the information, would only have saved themselves the time and trouble of employing a consultant. But, on the other hand, if the information was something special, as, for instance, if it involved an inventive step or something so unusual that it could not be obtained by just going to a consultant, then the value of it is much higher. It is not merely a consultant's fee, but the price which a willing buyer ... would pay for it.

Salmon L J agreed (at 814): "the damages ... are equal to the market value of the confidential information wrongly taken by the defendant company – the market value, that is to say, as between a willing buyer and a willing seller", while Winn L J said (at 815) "since the basis on which damages are to be recovered in this case is a tortious basis, where there is insoluble doubt between any two possible versions or assessments ... *omnia praesumuntur contra spoliatorem*''. The court, as it were, wished damages to be assessed as if there was a notional sale by the inventor of the carpet grip to the defendants who had used the idea and it rejected the argument of the defendants that damages on the facts of the case should be calculated in accordance with a sum which would be reasonable remuneration for a consultant.

The Court of Appeal thought that the most appropriate remedy would be a royalty, which it could not award. It could however give an equivalent sum based on the capitalisation of a royalty. It did not attempt to quantify the damages because patent proceedings were pending, and the court said that the patent judge should calculate the damages in accordance with its judgments. A market value calculation may yield more to employers than common law damages, which are assessed at the date of breach.

This idea of a notional sale deserves consideration. Lord Denning MR drew (at 813) an analogy between the damages awarded in *Seager* and the way in which damages are calculated in conversion. In conversion when damages are paid, the goods become the property of the tortfeasors; so Lord Denning MR argued, when damages have been paid for breach of confidence, ''the property, so far as there is property in it [that is the confidential information], would vest in them. They would have the right to use that information for the manufacture of the carpet grips ... ''. Criticism may be directed at this statement.

(1) The forced sale is not the remedy which the plaintiff wanted or required. Having failed to obtain an injunction, at an earlier stage in the proceedings, he could not stop the company making the grips, yet the company had misused the information the plaintiff had provided. It may be that the Court of Appeal was wrong not to award the injunction.

(2) At that time the tort of detinue still existed. In detinue plaintiffs could obtain specific restitution of the chattel. If one likes, the plaintiff in *Seager* wanted specific restitution of his lead, but the court did not consider this analogy. Perhaps they did not wish to stop the commercial production of the carpet grips, or perhaps they were not willing to ''restore'' an idea when the defendants had not consciously used it.

(3) Lord Denning MR's reference to property was ill-considered. One ought not to make too much of an unreserved judgment, but if the law of confidential information is to be seen as part of intellectual property, it is substantially different from other parts of intellectual property. If a patent or copyright is infringed, an injunction is virtually automatic, yet one was not given in *Seager* v *Copydex Ltd*. There is no forced sale as happened in that case. And defendants who satisfy the judgment do not obtain ownership of the property. Lord Denning MR indeed went further in saying that if the information was patentable, the defendants ''would be entitled to the benefit of the patent as if they had bought it'' (at 813). This concept of damages for breach of confidence would mean that the plaintiff would lose

her right to a patent and the defendants could use the patent monopoly against her to prevent her manufacturing the products. This idea does not seem to have been well thought-out. Since it has not been considered recently, perhaps it should be left to die a decent death. It has, however, not been overruled.

(4) If the capitalised royalty mode is used, for how long is the royalty to be capitalised? No answer was given.

(5) In *Levin* v *Caledonia Produce (Holdings Ltd)*, 1975 SLT 69, 71, Lord Robertson wondered whether *Seager* was limited to cases where the market value was readily ascertainable. There is no English case but the idea is sensible.

Seager (No 2) was discussed and distinguished in *Dowson & Mason Ltd* v *Potter* [1986] 1 WLR 1419, like *Seager* a decision of the Court of Appeal. The facts of the case were very simple and are an epitome of the fact situation which arises in breach of confidence actions. The plaintiffs had developed a new type of "landing leg" for use on articulated lorries, that is the prop which is used when the two halves of the lorry are separated. The idea was a simple but sound one; the leg was constructed in several parts, each of which could be separately replaced if damaged. The first defendant, an employee of the plaintiffs, gave to the second defendants a list of suppliers and prices. The second defendants used these items of information to gain a competitive advantage. The district registrar made an order which stated *inter alia*: "the proper basis for the assessment of damages . . . is the loss suffered by the plaintiffs which fails to be assessed according to their loss of profits resulting from the wrongful disclosure and use of the confidential information".

The second defendant appealed to the Chancery Division and then to the Court of Appeal on the grounds that damages ought to be assessed in accordance with the willing buyer/willing seller formula in *Seager (No 2)*. The court held that the purpose of damages was to place plaintiffs in the position they would have been in had the defendants not used the confidential information. Their loss, therefore, was the loss of manufacturing profits. The court was strongly of opinion that *Seager (No 2)* did not lay down any general rule of law but was concerned with the approach to be used when faced with the particular facts of that case. The present facts were not, in the court's view, in the contemplation of the judges in *Seager (No 2)*. In the instant case, where the plaintiffs and defendants competed, the defendants deprived the plaintiffs of their manufacturing profits, whereas in *Seager (No 2)* no such profits were assessable because the plaintiff did not manufacture the article himself but would license it; his loss was the loss of royalties. The distinction between the present case and *Seager (No 2)* was simply one of fact, dependent on the fact situation as to what loss the plaintiffs suffered. The judgments in *Dowson & Mason Ltd* v *Potter* were unreserved. It should be noted that if the object of a breach of confidence case is to put the plaintiffs in the position they would have been in had the wrongdoing not occurred, damages constitute the appropriate redress and a restitutionary remedy is inappropriate.

If damages are awardable for non-contractual breach of confidence, presumably exemplary damages are also available under the law as laid down in *Rookes* v *Barnard* [1964] AC 1129 (HL).

Two Subsidiary Points

Can damages in lieu be awarded only when the plaintiffs can show that the court would exercise its discretion in their favour or where they have a cause of action but the court might refuse an injunction? The statute on which jurisdiction is now taken, the Supreme Court Act 1981, section 50, says merely that damages may be awarded where the court "has jurisdiction to entertain an application for an injunction", and so is not helpful. If the first view is adopted, damages will only rarely be awarded, for then damages would be granted only where an injunction would be granted! That result would be silly, and so it is suggested that the second approach is preferable.

Both Lord Cairns' Act and the Supreme Court Act mention damages in addition to an injunction. Presumably the aim in 1858 was to stop the Chancery having to send the plaintiffs to the common law courts for damages. The Act however has been interpreted as allowing the court to award damages in addition for breach of an equitable duty of confidence. This now would explain the first instance decision of *Nichrotherm Electrical Co Ltd* v *Percy* mentioned above as well as several others.

Commonwealth Authority

Gummow J in the Australian case of *Concept Television Productions Pty Ltd* v *ABC* (1989) 12 IPR 129 said that damages were available under the inherent jurisdiction of equity, as Lord Haldane had said in *Norton* v *Ashburton* [1914] AC 932, 958. Therefore, there was no need to look at Lord Cairns' Act for that dealt with equity's auxiliary, not exclusive, jurisdiction. The cases of *Talbot* and *Interfirm*, dealt with below, were inapposite. On this approach, one can have cumulative damages for breaches of confidence and copyright, not as was held in *Interfirm* that there was only one head of damage.

Victoria has permitted the remedy of damages for breach of a non-contractual confidence. The case is *Talbot* v *General Television Corporation Pty Ltd* [1980] VR 224, a decision of Harris J in the Supreme Court. The plaintiff, a film producer, thought up an idea for a television series concerning how millionaires made their money. He negotiated with the defendants for the sale of his concept and a pilot script was written. Some time later the defendants began to advertise a series based on the same concept. The plaintiff sought an injunction and damages. The defendants contended that the court could not award damages in lieu of or in addition to the injunction because the Victoria version of Lord Cairns' Act, the Supreme Court Act 1958, section 62(3), permitted damages only if there was a "wrongful act". "Wrongful act" meant a tort; and breach of confidence was not a tort. (This phrase does not appear in the Supreme Court Act 1981.) Harris J had little difficulty in rejecting this contention, and he ordered an inquiry as to damages. The judge based himself on the history of the provision, and he noted that in *Seager* v *Copydex Ltd*, above, damages were awarded.

Harris J died, and the inquiry as to damages was undertaken by Marks J. The defendants appealed from his judgment to the Full Court [1981] RPC 20. Lush J (at 30) said that there was not one single way of assessing damages for breach of confidence but he considered that in the instant case it was appropriate to award damages on a depreciation basis. Young CJ pointed out (at 29) that a depreciation basis was not appropriate if one considers the right in a breach of confidence action as a right to have one's confidence respected, for if the confidence is broken, the right is "hardly capable of being depreciated in value". He considered that the plaintiff ought to have a proportion of the profit which he would have made (80,000 Australian dollars) plus damages for the loss of his chance of breaking into television production (applying *Chaplin* v *Hicks*, above). The figure arrived at was 15,000 dollars. Leach J agreed with both judgments.

The fullest appreciation of how damages were to be assessed was in fact given by Marks J. He too thought that there was no simple basis and he dealt with several possible modes.

(1)   *Damages should be assessed on the market value of the information as between a willing seller and a willing buyer.* This was the method adopted in *Seager* v *Copydex Ltd (No 2)* above, though as the Court of Appeal noted the market value might be the capitalised value of the royalty payable on sale of an invention if the information involved an inventive step or a reasonable fee for a consultant if the information involved was only a small step forward (see above). Marks J held that the Court of Appeal did not intend to lay down an assessment basis for all possible cases; rather the assessment they adopted was appropriate to the facts of that case. Obviously if there is no market, a market assessment is at best artificial, at worst impracticable.

(2)   *Damages should be assessed on the basis of giving a fair remuneration for the defendant to have paid the plaintiff for a licence to use the information.* This was the basis adopted by the Supreme Court of New South Wales, Equity Division, acting in exercise of Federal jurisdiction in *Interfirm Comparison (Australia) Pty Ltd* v *Law Society of New South Wales* [1977] RPC 137. Bowen CJ in Eq held (at 152) that there was no need for an injunction and ordered (at 157) damages to be assessed on the basis of fair remuneration as had happened in the English copyright case of *Stovin-Bradford* v *Volpoint Ltd* [1971] Ch 1007. His reasoning was that the plaintiffs could not have damages for both breach of copyright and breach of confidence when the damages for both actions related to the same breach. Therefore, the same measure of damages was appropriate to both claims. *Interfirm* was followed by Jeffries J in *Wilson* v *Broadcasting Corp of NZ* (1989) 12 IPR 173 on this point.

(3)   *Damages should be assessed on the basis of the loss of value to the plaintiff caused by the breach.* This was the method adopted in *Talbot.*

As a result of *Talbot* it may therefore be said that there are a number of possible bases for the award of damages in Victoria and presumably throughout Australia. England lags behind on this point. A New Zealand court has also ruled that damages can be awarded for misuse of confidential information. The Court of Appeal in *Van Camp Chocolates Ltd* v *Aulsebrook Ltd* [1984] 1 NZLR 354, 361, expressly approved *Seager (No 2).* Cooke, Richardson and McMullin JJ accepted that the principle may be wrong historically but there was nothing to stop a court from awarding damages for past loss. Damages could also be awarded for future injury in lieu of an injunction. The case itself was a follow up to *A B Consolidated Ltd* v *Europe Strength Food Co Pty Ltd* [1978] 2 NZLR 515 where these remedies had been given. The Court of Appeal cut through the jurisdictional problem by holding that it did not matter whether the award was described as damages for tort or equitable compensation for breach of duty. The New Zealand Court of Appeal followed *Van Camp* and *A B Consolidated in Agriculture Corp* v *N Z Green Mussel Co Ltd* [1990] 3 NZLR 299 to hold that damages can be awarded for breach of confidence arising from equity because of the merger of law and equity, and that exemplary damages may be granted.

Liquidated Damages

General contractual principles apply to liquidated damages clauses consequent on a breach of a contract. Such a term is not upheld if it is in truth a penalty: *Dunlop Pneumatic Tyre Co Ltd* v *New Garage and Motor Co Ltd* [1915] AC 79 (HL). A clause which is a genuine pre-estimate of loss is upheld, but one which is a penalty clause is not. Lord Dunedin said (at 86–7): "[t]he essence of a penalty is a payment of money stipulated as *in terrorem* of the offending party; the essence of liquidated damages is a genuine covenanted pre-estimate of damage ... The question whether a sum stipulated is a penalty or liquidated damages is a question of construction to be decided upon the terms and inherent circumstances of each particular contract, judged at the time of the making of the contract, not as at the time of the breach ... ". He continued by stating various principles of interpretation.

Liquidated Damages and Injunctions

The law appears to be that employers cannot have both an injunction and liquidated damages (as expressed in the contract). They must elect. Wright J in *General Accident Assurance Corp* v *Noel* [1901] 1 KB 377 reviewed previous cases from the nineteenth century and so decided. However, if there is an express clause in the contract permitting the award of an injunction, that remedy can be awarded: *Sharp* v *Cain* [1924] SASR 203, 219.

Account of Profits

General Matters

Unlike damages for breach of a contractual duty of confidence, the remedy of account of profits, being equitable, is discretionary. This remedy obliges the defendant to disgorge any profit she has made from the plaintiff's confidential information (*cf.* damages, which are compensation for loss). The employers need not have lost anything. Because the plaintiffs do not need to prove that the defendant has caused them any loss, it is immaterial that they would not have received the contract in any case: *Industrial Development Consultants Ltd* v *Cooley*, above. Moreover, they are not under a duty to mitigate because the remedy is not to compensate them for loss. The remedy is also useful when the employee's profits exceed the employers' loss.

If both damages and an account are available, the plaintiff cannot have both remedies to avoid double compensation for the same loss. The plaintiff must elect: *Neilson* v *Betts* (1871) LR 5 HL 1 and *De Vitre* v *Betts* (1873) LR 6 HL 319, both patent cases. The choice will depend on how much the plaintiff can get from each remedy.

An illustration of the process is *Peter Pan Manufacturing Corp* v *Corsets Silhouette Ltd* [1963] 3 All ER 402. Pennycuick J held that the defendants were not entitled to use confidential information in relation to the manufacture of two styles of bras. The plaintiffs claimed damages for their past losses or alternatively an account of profits. The judge said "What a plaintiff who elects in favour of an account of profits is entitled to is simply an account ... that is, what has the plaintiff expended on manufacturing these goods? What is the price which he has received on their sale? And the difference is profit".

He rejected the defendants' counsel's arguments that a different meaning should be attributed to profit, namely, the amount by which the defendants profited from the use of the confidential information exceeded the profit they would have made, had they not used the information. Pennycuick J said that this approach was not in accord with previous authorities and was "perfectly impossible" to use because it was hypothetical: the defendants had used the information. He thought that there would be no serious difficulty in determining the profit. However, he did not reject the alternative mode in all cases: it might be used where the defendant had used the idea not to start production but to produce more cheaply.

It is uncertain whether modern courts would adopt the simplistic definition of profit in *Peter Pan*. As Reid wrote in Confidentiality and the Law (Waterlow, 1986) 188: "accounting techniques have become more sophisticated since" (spelling corrected).

If profits were derived from both the plaintiffs' confidential information and, say, the defendant's expertise, the courts calculate the amount by which the information increased the profits. There is no requirement that an exact sum is appropriated to the use of the particular information and the courts are ready to draw inferences in favour of the plaintiffs. In *Normalec Ltd* v *Britton* [1983] FSR 318 Walton J used this presumption in favour of the plaintiffs as the innocent parties to hold that the defendant's business belonged to them when he had used their confidential information. What is surprising is that he so determined even though the defendant's business was wider than that of the plaintiffs.

It is the aspect of the difficulty in uncovering the profit which has caused problems in some cases. As Lindley LJ said in *Siddell* v *Vickers* (1892) 9 RPC 152, 163, a patent case: "the difficulty of finding out how much profit is attributable to any one source is extremely great ... The litigation is enormous, the expense is great, and the time consumed is out of all proportion to the advantage ultimately attained ... ". Nevertheless, there are cases such as *Peter Pan* where an account is a straightforward matter, and it may be that this remedy could deter those who might make more in profit out of the breach of confidence than they would lose in damages. A plaintiff would be well-advised to seek an account where the defendant made more use of the knowledge than she would have done.

There would seem to be two restrictions on the award of an account of profits. First, the remedy will not be granted where the defendant acted innocently. In *Seager* v *Copydex Ltd* [1967] 1 WLR 809 an account was refused because the defendant did not act *mala fide*. *Peter Pan* is distinguishable on this basis. See also *Attorney-General* v *Guardian Newspapers Ltd (No 2)* [1990] 1 AC 109, where the defendants kept the Crown in the dark about publication. Secondly, an account will not be granted where no profits have been made, or no profits have been made which are attributable to the defendant's breach of confidence. The law cannot be said to have crystallised as yet.

An account of profits may also be defeated by delay or acquiescence because the remedy is an equitable one and is accordingly subject to equitable principles. Damages, being a common law remedy, are not subject to the maxims of equity.

Is the Remedy Available for a Breach of the Contractual Duty of Confidence?

The common law remedy for a breach of contract, including thereby a breach of contract referable to an express or implied contractual term, is damages. Is the equitable remedy of an account of profits also available? The answer is unclear, and certainly there is a dictum against the answer being in the affirmative in the Victoria case of *Deta Nominees Pty Ltd* v *Viscount Plastics Products Pty Ltd* [1969] VR 167, 180. Nevertheless, it is arguable that the remedy could be available as ancillary to an injunction where a legal right has been infringed. If so, plaintiffs would receive more than the sum they would receive if in a contractual claim they suffered no damage from the breach. Plaintiffs would be able to recover the infringer's "ill-gotten gains": *Colbeam Palmer Ltd* v *Stock Affiliates Pty Ltd* (1968) 122 CLR 25 (HCA).

Peter Pan, above, shows that an account of profits is available in breach of industrial confidence cases. The two bases for the remedy in that context were stated by Scott J in *Attorney-General* v *Guardian Newspapers Ltd (No 2), obiter*, to be these, above (at 161):

> ... the account of profits serves to compensate the owner of the information for the unauthorised use that has been made of it. The profit, in equity, belongs to the owner of the information. There is, however, also a deterrent effect provided by the remedy. The wrongdoer, who has misused the information, is not permitted to retain a a profit made by means of his own wrongdoing.

Similar remarks were made by Lord Keith in the House of Lords. In commercial cases damages were the main form of compensation for loss; account of profits, being founded on the maxim that no person should profit from her wrong, was to deter people from misusing information for profit.

The Law Commission in its Report, no 110, *Breach of Confidence* (Cmnd 8388, 198) paragraph 6.107, proposed that employers should continue to be put to their election between damages and account. The Canadian Report, no 46, of a Federal/Provincial Working Party on Trade Secrets Law, Institute of Law Research and Reform, Alberta (1986) paragraph 10.37–8, recommended that both should be available but there should be no double recovery.

Practical Considerations

A major drawback of an account is that the plaintiffs are put to their election between this remedy and damages when the trial is over. At that time they may not know which relief is the more profitable. Plaintiffs will therefore have to be alert to the fact configurations in each case to see whether for example the defendant was able to exploit the market successfully, in which case an account of profits may be the better remedy, or whether the defendant was inexperienced.

Undoubtedly in the normal run of cases it will be easier for the plaintiffs to calculate their loss rather than seek to determine the profit made by the defendant, but if the courts are seeking to deter the improper acquisition of confidential information, this remedy would seem to have a part to play where the profit to the defendant is greater than the loss to the plaintiffs.

As already stated, the remedy is a discretionary one and is granted on equitable grounds. Delay will therefore be a reason for the refusal of an account, as occurred in the trade mark case of *Electrolux Ltd* v *Electrix Ltd* (1953) 70 RPC 158 and accordingly plaintiffs in this situation have to be content with damages. The practical point, then, is that plaintiffs must seek the remedy as soon as they know of the breach. Delay in breach of confidence cases is seen as acquiescence in the wrongful use of the confidential information: *International Scientific Communications Inc* v *Pattison* [1979] FSR 429. Delay may be relevant in another context as accounting takes a long time.

The main drawback of the remedy was noted by Lord Goff in *Attorney-General* v *Guardian Newspapers Ltd (No 2)*, above at 286. It was technical, indeed technical to excess. Therefore, unless an account promises a large sum, employers may be well-advised not to go for it. Moreover, it does not seem acceptable to base a remedy on a former employee's bookkeeping skill, and it may be difficult to extract profit figures from a recalcitrant defendant. Alternatively, the former employee may have made a loss, and so this remedy is useless, or the profit may be insufficient to indemnify the plaintiffs.

Order for Delivery up or Destruction

Such orders, which are granted under RSC Order 29, rule 2A, are ancillary to one of the previous remedies, usually an injunction. Being equitable, they are discretionary. Delivery up, which is to the plaintiffs, not the court, is used where the employee is not trustworthy: *Industrial Furnaces Ltd* v *Reaves* [1970] RPC 605, 627. Graham J said that in the normal run of cases "property" in the confidential information remained in the plaintiffs, who could resume ownership by that order. The position was different where the court by awarding damages in lieu granted the defendant the right to use the information as in *Seager* v *Copydex (No 2)* [1969] 1 WLR 804. Delivery up will not be refused simply because information belonging to the defendant is incorporated into the design or product: *Industrial Furnaces*. If the ex-employee has made copies, they must be surrendered too, for example *Prince Albert* v *Strange* (1849) 1 Mac & G 25, 41 ER 1171. In their discretion the courts may refuse the order when delivery up may sterilise enterprise. The famous case of *Saltman Engineering Co Ltd* v *Campbell Engineering Co Ltd* (1948) 65 RPC 203 illustrates this proposition. The Court of Appeal decided that the defendants had misused drawings which the plaintiffs had entrusted to them. From the drawings they had prepared tools to manufacture leather punches. The court ordered them to deliver up the drawings but not the tools, and damages under Lord Cairns' Act were awarded for damage suffered in the past or which might be suffered in the future out of both the drawings and the tools. *Cf. Peter Pan*, above, where presumably the bras were burnt. It should be noted that the order may be made even though the items contain the former employees' own confidential information.

A Commonwealth illustration of delivery up is *Ansell Rubber Co Pty Ltd* v *Allied Rubber Industries Pty Ltd* [1977] VR 37. Gowans J ordered the defendants to dismantle machines for making gloves and hand them to the plaintiffs for destruction. The machines could not be retained or used by the defendants because they had "no property in them". Severance was adopted: only the offending parts were handed over. This doctrine may apply in England. For another Commonwealth illustration see *Franklin* v *Giddins* [1978] Qd R 72. Like English cases early Commonwealth ones do not discuss the juridical basis of the remedy, but *cf. Lindsey* v *Le Sueur* (1912) [1911–16] MacG Cop Cas 118 (Ont): the plaintiff was entitled to delivery up because he was the absolute owner of the archives which the defendant was using.

Declaration

Normally plaintiffs in breach of confidence actions will be seeking an injunction and damages or an account of profits, but at times they may wish for the discretionary remedy of a declaration. Jurisdiction is found in RSC Order 15, rule 1. This relief may be useful in test cases: a declaration against a former employee in one case may be valuable against others in subsequent cases. Similarly, a declaration may be of worth to the plaintiffs in one case to show that their trade secret still exists when they wish to sue in relation to that confidential information subsequently.

The employers obtained a declaration in *Marion White Ltd* v *Francis* [1972] 1 WLR 1423 (CA), although the covenanted period had expired. An injunction would have been of no use to the plaintiff but a declaration was useful because it demonstrated that the covenant was valid against the defendant's former colleagues. Stephenson LJ (at 1430) had doubts about the jurisdiction. Davies LJ (at 1431) had had doubts but in the end he agreed that the court had the power. A declaration is an available remedy in pension and commission cases: *Bull* v *Pitney–Bowes Ltd* [1967] 1 WLR 273.

The remedy is available to both employers and employees. In *Greer* v *Sketchley Ltd* [1979] IRLR 445 (CA) the plaintiff, the managing director of the defendants, sought a declaration that a covenant enduring for 12 months after employment not to "engage in any part of the UK in any business which is similar to any business involving ... trade secrets and/or secret processes carried on by the Company ... " was invalid. The court dismissed the employers' appeal from Fox J who granted a declaration. It may also be granted to a third party: *Eastham* v *Newcastle United Football Club Ltd* [1964] Ch 413 and *Greig* v *Insole* [1978] 1 WLR 302.

There are some statements in the case that the remedy is an equitable one with the effect that the maxims of equity such as "he who comes to equity must do equity" apply. In general, however, judges treat the remedy as discretionary, but not equitable, with the result that the maxims do not apply.

This remedy may be refused at the court's discretion. In *Seager* v *Copydex (No 2)*, above, the Court of Appeal refused a declaration on the ground that when the defendants satisfied the judgment for damages, they acquired property in the confidential information, and so none was needful. There is no power to determine hypothetical questions. The breach must be actual or threatened.

Constructive Trust

English law has not developed the constructive trust in pre-contractual and contractual relationships: see, for example *Nichrotherm Electrical Co Ltd* v *Percy* (1956) 73 RPC 272. In an interesting development the Supreme Court of Canada has, no doubt under the influence of its neighbour's jurisdiction, used the device in the context of the disclosure of confidential information in pre-contractual negotiations which did not ripen into a contractual relationship: *LAC Minerals Ltd* v *International Corona Resources Ltd* (1989) 61 DLR (4th) 14. Corona had identified land which it thought might be gold-bearing. It interested a larger company, LAC, in the land with a view to a joint venture and disclosed confidential data during negotiations. LAC acquired the land for itself and developed it as a goldmine. Corona sought delivery up of the land and offered to pay some of the defendants' developmental costs. The court held 3:2 that the equitable remedy of a constructive trust was available.

The principal judgment delivered by La Forest J noted that in the industry there was a practice not to use confidential information obtained in serious negotiations and that information could be confidential, though partly derived from the public domain. The judge considered that there was a range of remedies, for example damages, account of profits. One of those remedies, a proprietary one, was the imposition of a trust. No English authority was cited. That remedy was warranted for breach of fiduciary duties. Since the law of fiduciaries and breach of confidence was based on good conscience, a constructive trust was available. The choice of remedy lay with the court. A remedy *in rem* would be inappropriate in "the vast majority of cases". On the facts, however, it was the sole appropriate remedy. The plaintiffs wanted that parcel of land: compensation based on the unknown value of the mine would be difficult to assess; a remedy *in rem* would deter defendants who acted as LAC did, and the wrongdoers were deprived of ill-gotten gains, something which damages could not do. The restitutionary remedy was therefore appropriate. It will not be appropriate for the same reasons in all fact configurations. LAC involves bad faith bargaining. The defendants were penalised to prevent them from profiting from their own wrong. The remedy of an account was not urged in LAC. Compare *Boardman* v *Phipps* [1967] AC 46, where the plaintiffs obtained the defendant's gain at their expense despite the fact that the estate could not lawfully have done what the defendant did, and the defendant's gain was partly the estate's gain. A company would not be deterred from using confidential information by the institution of a joint venture, for that would have arisen had the confidence not been broken.

Two judges, Sopinka and McIntyre JJ, also decided that the plaintiffs won, but dissented as to remedy. In their view the jurisdictional foundation of the plaintiff's right was not contract, equity, or property. It was similar to tort, where the focus is on loss to plaintiffs. Therefore, a right *in rem* was inapplicable. A constructive trust was "ordinarily" appropriate only where jurisdiction was based on property or a fiduciary relationship. It was not available for breach of confidence, damages being the conventional remedy. The focus is on the plaintiffs' loss. They should be put into the position they would have been in, had no wrong occurred. On the facts a joint venture could have been created. Corona would have had a 50% interest or less. (The majority contended that, but for the breach, Corona would have held the whole interest.) In accordance with English and Commonwealth authorities in the view of the minority, a monetary award (including an account of profits which would deprive the defendants of the whole value of the mine but not ownership of it) alone could be granted. The minority therefore looked at the plaintiffs' loss, while the majority looked to compensate them and deter later defendants. Sopinka J thought that a restitutionary remedy would overcompensate because it was impossible to determine how much confidential data was mixed with public information. Grant Hammond wrote in "Equity and Abortive Commercial Transactions" (1990) 106 LQR 207, 212, (emphasis in original): "[E]ven with respect to a breach of confidence (supposedly historically, a *personal* obligation ...) the court can impose a constructive trust as a remedy. But, given that courts are now awarding damages for breach of confidence, perhaps that extension was always going to come, given the right sort of case." J D Davies added "Duties of Confidence and Loyalty" [1990] LMCLQ 4,5: "if a ground of liability is established, then the remedy that follows should be the one that is most appropriate on the facts of the case rather than one derived from history or over-categorization". For other comments see W L Hayhurst "The Supreme Court of Canada on Confidential Information" [1990] EIPR 30, P C Wardle (1990) "Post Employment Competition" 69 CBR 223, D W M Walters "LAC Minerals Ltd" (1990) 69 CBR 458, and P Birks "The Remedies for Abuse of Confidential Information" [1990] LMCLQ 460.

There are, however, disadvantages. It may be difficult to see when the pre-contract stage matures into a contract. Once there is a contract, one is looking for a remedy for breach of contract, should the defendant divulge confidential information. A constructive trust, a remedy *in rem*, is not available for a breach of contract. Yet that may be the remedy which, more than a contractual one is, is the best remedy for the breach of confidentiality. The outcome of *LAC Minerals* is also hard to square with that applying where there is a contractual relationship. La Forest J said that at the pre-contractual stage the court chose the remedy. However, as we have seen it is at the contractual stage for plaintiffs to elect between damages and an account of profits. There is also the difficulty as with any selection from a broad range of remedies that it is difficult to advise clients and negotiate a settlement when lawyers do not know the bottom line. Moreover, as Birks put it, above at 461, the use of a proprietary remedy leads to "surprising and undeserved priorities in the event of insolvency". The availability of a constructive trust would also differentiate breach of confidence from other forms of intellectual property.

Remedies Against Third Parties

Inducing a Breach of Contract

This is an action in tort against the trade rival who persuades an employee to reveal confidential information. The principal English authority is *British Industrial Plastics Ltd* v *Ferguson* [1938] 4 All ER 504 at the Court of Appeal level. One defendant, who had been an employee of the plaintiffs for 16 years, left, and two years later applied to the first defendant, who was the managing director of the corporate defendants. He offered to bring over the knowledge which he had acquired while works manager of the plaintiffs. The first defendant suspected that some of the information was secret, and told the employee to see the corporate defendant's patent agents. He thought that if the information was patentable, it was therefore not secret! As the trial judge, Joyce J, put it (quoted at 507), he was "muddle headed". There was no doubt that the employee had breached the implied term of fidelity by revealing the plaintiff's secrets, but had the other defendants induced that breach? The appeal court held not, on the grounds that they had acted *bona fide* and so had not wilfully and knowingly procured the breach. They did not act with actual knowledge that the employee would breach his contract; neither did they act with wilful blindness. All three members of the court agreed with this analysis. Slesser LJ (at 510–11) went further and said that if he was wrong, the defendants had the defence of justification following the well-known authority of *Brimelow* v *Casson* [1924] 1 Ch 302. As Slesser LJ put it:

> [i]t would be impossible as a matter of business . . . for any person to whom a process was offered, who wished *bona fide* to be sure before receiving it that it was not secret, to send the vendor to an expert in order that the proposed purchaser might be advised on such a matter, if, the advice being unfavourable and technically amounting possibly to a breach of contract of secrecy [*sic*] on the part of the vendor as a confidential servant of others, the purchaser were to be subjected to a risk of action in a case where his whole proceedings were entirely *bona fide* and founded on a desire to act lawfully.

Two judges, Slesser and MacKinnon LJJ, also held that special damage was not necessary, provided that damage was likely to be caused. The third judge, Finlay LJ, did not mention the point.

On appeal the House of Lords ([1940] 1 All ER 479) agreed that the defendants did not know, either actually or constructively, that the process belonged to the partners, and that they had acted honestly, though stupidly. Accordingly the employers' appeal was dismissed.

No doubt this remedy is apt to be used against "head-hunters".

Several US authorities deal with inducing breach of contract. In one of them, *Coleman* v *Morris*, 279 AD 656 (1951), the Appellate Division of New York in a memorandum opinion said that "mere inducement to an employee at will to discontinue such employment is not actionable, at least unless the purpose of the action was solely to produce damage, or unless the means employed were dishonest or unfair".

The *Restatement of Torts*, section 766 (1939), states:

> ... one who, without a privilege to do so, induces or otherwise causes a third person not to
>
> (a) perform a contract with another, or ...
>
> is liable to the other for the harm caused thereby.

The comment notes that the tort of inducing a breach of contract is, as now in England, seen as an instance of unjustified interference in business relations. In *Walt Peabody Advertising Service Inc* v *Pecora*, 393 F Supp 328 (1978) the District Court for the Western District of Kentucky followed "the celebrated case of *Lumley* v *Gye*" (1853) 2 El & Bl 216, 118 ER 1083, the *Restatement*, and recent Kentucky authority instead of old cases to rule that the action was not restricted to breaches occasioned by fraud or coercion.

Injunction

Employers may obtain injunctions against third parties who induce breaches of contract: such occurred in one of the most famous cases on the duty of fidelity, *Hivac Ltd* v *Park Royal Scientific Instruments Ltd* [1946] 1 Ch 169. The Court of Appeal granted an injunction to restrain the defendants from continuing to employ the plaintiffs' employees. Similarly but in relation to confidential information an injunction was granted in *Bents Brewery Co Ltd* v *Hogan* [1945] 2 All ER 570 to restrain a union official from obtaining details of weekly sales and wages bills from pub managers employed by the plaintiffs.

For the position of third parties in a breach of confidence action see Gurry, *Breach of Confidence* (Clarendon, 1984) 269–83 and the House of Lords in *Attorney-General* v *Guardian Newspapers Ltd (No 2)*, above. The *bona fide* purchaser for value without notice apparently is not bound.

If the defendant is aware of an injunction binding on a third party, he may be restrained from aiding or abetting that party in breaches of the injunction: *Electronic Applications (Commercial) Ltd* v *Toubkin* (1962) 79 RPC 225.

Negligent Misstatement

Moore & Co Ltd v *Ferrier* [1988] 1 All ER 400, an unreserved decision of the Court of Appeal, raises the spectre of employers suing those who draft restraint clauses, *in casu* solicitors. The plaintiffs instructed the defendant solicitors to prepare a covenant to restrain an employee, who was also one of their directors. The defendants drew up a clause which bound the employee for three years after termination within 15 miles of a town where their business was situated. The employee resigned as employee and director. The covenant, however, applied only when he ceased "to be a member of the company". Since he remained a shareholder, he remained a member of the company and the clause did not take effect. The plaintiffs sued the solicitors for negligence.

In fact the defendants were not liable because of the Limitation Act 1980: the plaintiffs had suffered damage through the negligence at the date of the drafting, which was more than six years from the commencement of action, and so the action was time-barred. The Latent Damage Act 1986 did not apply because the cause of action accrued before the coming into force of that statute. Accordingly in the absence of fraud, concealment or mistake, the plaintiffs' claim failed despite their not knowing of the damage. Bingham LJ said (at 411) that the case was one which reached a "wholly unreasonable result", as Lord Reid put it in *Cartledge* v *Jobling & Sons Ltd* [1963] AC 758.

If the Limitation Act had not applied, the employers would have had a right of action. To avoid negligence drafters might:

(1)   discuss the difficulties with the employers;
(2)   advise them of the problems;
(3)   not use a precedent from the books or data bank;
(4)   draft the clause with regard to the rules relating to covenants.

In many cases *Moore* will not help employers because the employees will have left employment more than six years after the clause was written.

General View of the Problems

As can be seen from this exposition of the law the courts are not restricted by a limited range of remedies. They have a wide enough choice to enable them to select the one which is appropriate to the circumstances. However, because of the difficulty of assigning a jurisdictional basis to the non-contractual duty of confidence, there are problems in determining whether a certain remedy was given correctly. In law damages are the relief given for breach of a common law right, whereas an account of profits is available for the breach of an equitable duty of confidentiality. The theory is clear-cut, but as we have seen the present position is unclear as to whether damages are available as of right for a non-contractual obligation of confidence. As Gurry wrote, *Breach of Confidence* (Clarendon, 1984), 395: "[t]he authorities cannot be simply explained away as repeated misconceptions, and it is becoming increasingly tempting to conclude that a fusion of law and equity is taking place under the notion of confidence in the breach of confidence action". If so all the energy which has been expended in seeking the jurisdictional foundation of the claim has been wasted. The law has refused to be bound by theory.

The Canadian Trade Secrets Protection Act proposed in a Report of the Federal-Provincial Working Party on Trade Secrets in 1986 would authorise the court to grant one or more of the following remedies – injunction, damages, an account of profits (which it cannot do at present), an adjustment order, and delivery up or destruction. On this approach both damages and an account could be awarded, as could damages and an injunction. The adjustment order, partly defined in clause 10, would permit the court to grant a royalty and expenses. Exemplary damages might also be awarded (clause 9). The idea of an adjustment order, also taken up by the Law Commission (and, indeed, both bodies favour the creation of a statutory tort) is similar to the notion of Lord Denning MR in *Seager* v *Copydex Ltd (No 2)* mentioned above, but this Canadian proposal is a continuing, not a capitalised royalty.

Appendix

PRECEDENTS

The use of precedents for covenants in restraint of trade is fraught with difficulties. Among the problems are:

(1) a covenant successful in one case may not be successful in another with slightly different facts;
(2) a covenant which would have been successfully enforced at the commencement of employment may have minimal relevance to the employee's job at termination: a tea boy may have become the managing director, or a covenant expressed to operate within a radius of seven miles from Tamworth Town Hall is useless if the employee was moved to Brighton;
(3) English courts are unlikely to enforce covenants which seek to apply to all employees of whatever job and status in the firm's hierarchy.

For these reasons precedents are not as reliable in this area of law as they are in, say, commercial property. Drafters must study the whole of the law, for a precedent from a database may be of little help.

A simple example illustrates this aspect of the law. In *Littlewoods Organisation Ltd v Harris* [1977] 1 WLR 1472 (CA) the relevant clause read in part: " ... the Divisional Director shall not at any time within twelve months after ... determination:– i Enter into a Contract of Service ... with Great Universal Stores Limited or any company subsidiary thereto or be directly or indirectly engaged concerned or interested in the trading or business of the said Great Universal Stores Ltd or any such company aforesaid ... ". By a majority the court upheld this covenant. It is, however, improbable that a similarly worded clause would be upheld today even after substituting the employers' main competitor and deleting the reference to subsidiary companies, since the covenant will most likely be interpreted as one applying throughout the world (see Chapter 6), and most companies do not operate worldwide.

The principal drafting advice (after an admonition to use good English) is for the employers not to attempt to overreach themselves. Area and duration should be the minimum reasonably necessary for the protection of their interests. The sphere of activity should be narrowly stated. One possible method of predisposing the court to enforce the covenant is to use provisos which state that certain activities which would otherwise fall within the prohibition are allowed, such as ownership of shares (to a certain percentage, say 5%) in publicly quoted companies and work may be performed for various bodies, which are listed. Other drafting techniques have been noted throughout the book in relation, for example, to the various types of covenants, reasonableness in the interests of the parties, construction and severance. The reader is referred to those chapters.

Restrictive Covenants for Contracts of Employment

1. Duty of Confidence during Employment

You shall at times during the term of your employment with the Company keep secret (except to the extent that disclosure is authorised by the Company), and use only for the purposes of the Company all information which is of a confidential nature and of value to the Company, including without limitation:

(1) business methods and information of the Company (including prices charged, discounts given to customers or obtained from suppliers, transport rates, marketing and advertising programmes, costings, budgets, turnover, sales targets or other financial information);

(2) lists and particulars of the Company's suppliers and customers and the individual contracts at such suppliers and customers;

(3) secret manufacturing or production processes and know-how employed by the Company or its suppliers;

(4) confidential details as to the design of the Company's or the Company's suppliers' products and inventions or developments relating to future products;

[And other specific confidential information should be added to the list as necessary.]

whether or not in the case of documents or other carriers of information they are or were marked as confidential.

Upon termination of your employment howsoever arising you shall forthwith return all documents or other carriers of information in your possession, custody or control which contain records of such information and all property in your possession, custody or control of the Company or its customers or suppliers.

2. Duty of Confidence after Termination of Employment

You shall at all times after the termination of your employment keep secret and not use any information obtained by you during the term of your employment which is of a confidential nature and of value to the Company including without limitation:

(1) business methods and information of the Company (including prices charged, discounts given to customers or obtained from suppliers, transport rates, marketing and advertising programmes, costings, budgets, turnover, sales targets or other financial information);

(2) lists of particulars of the Company's suppliers and customers and the individual contacts at such suppliers and customers;

(3) secret manufacturing or production processes and know-how employed by the Company or its suppliers;

(4) confidential details as to the design of the Company's or the Company's suppliers' products and inventions or developments relating to future products;

[Again, any other specific confidential information should be added to the list as necessary.]

whether or not in the case of documents or other carriers of information they are or were marked as confidential. This restriction shall apply without limit in point of time but shall cease to apply to information or knowledge which shall come (otherwise than by breach of this clause) into the public domain.

3. Representing a Continuing Connection

You shall not, at any time after the termination of your employment, represent yourself as being in any way connected with or interested in the business of the Company.

4. Poaching of Staff

You shall not for a period of [12] months after the termination of your employment directly or indirectly, on your own behalf or on behalf of any person, firm or company employ or offer to employ or entice away any employee of the Company who was to your knowledge employed by the Company in a sales, technical or management capacity at the time of the termination of your employment with the Company.

5. Garden Leave During Notice Period

Upon notice to terminate your employment being given by the Company or you then if requested by the Company you shall:

(1)   forthwith return all documentation, articles or property in your possession, custody or control of the Company;

(2)   forthwith return all documentation or articles which contain records of confidential information concerning the business of the Company;

(3)   not during the notice period enter onto the premises of the Company without their prior consent;

(4)   not during the notice period contact or deal with the Company's customers suppliers or employees;

(5)   not during the notice period set up, carry on, be employed in, provide services to, be associated with, or be engaged or interested in whether as director, employee, principal, agent or otherwise howsoever (save as a shareholder of not more than 3% of any public company whose shares are quoted on any recognised Stock Exchange) any other business and in particular but not by way of limitation any other business which is or is about to be similar to or competitive with any type of business carried on by the Company and with which you were concerned at any time during the [12] months immediately preceding the date of the notice to terminate your employment.

Provided that during the notice period your salary and other contractual financial benefits are continued to be paid by or on behalf of the Company.

For the avoidance of doubt it is agreed that:

(1)   your other duties and obligations whether contractual or otherwise and which are not inconsistent with the terms of this clause shall continue in full force and effect during the notice period; and

(2)   the Company has no duty to provide you with work during the period of your employment and in particular but not by way of limitation during the notice period.

6. Customer Non-Solicitation/Dealing (Requiring Personal Contact, for example Sales Representative)

You shall not for a period of [12] months after the termination of your employment in relation to any goods or services similar to or competitive with those sold or provided by the Company at the time of such termination, directly or indirectly, on your own behalf, or on behalf of any person, firm or company:

(1)   solicit or canvass the custom of or entice away

or as a separate obligation

(2)   deal with

any person, firm or company who at any time during the [12] months prior to the termination of your employment was a customer or potential customer of the Company and (in the case of a customer) from whom you had obtained business or to whom you had provided services on behalf of the Company at any time during that [12] month period, or (in the case of a potential customer) with whom you had dealt with with a view to obtaining business at anytime during that [12] month period.

7. Alternative Customer Non-Solicitation/Dealing (Requiring Knowledge, for example Sales Manager)

You shall not for a period of [12] months after the termination of your employment, in relation to any goods or services similar to or competitive with those sold or provided by the Company at the time of such termination, directly or indirectly, on your own behalf or on behalf of any person, firm or company:

(1)   solicit or canvass the custom of or entice away

or as a separate obligation

(2)   deal with

any person, firm or company who at any time during the [12] months prior to the termination of your employment was a customer or potential customer of the Company, and (in the case of a customer) who had to your knowledge done business with the Company or (in the case of a potential customer) with whom to your knowledge the Company had had dealings with a view to obtaining business.

8. Geographic Non-Competition

You shall not for a period of [12] months after the termination of your employment and within [define area] set up, carry on, be employed in, provide services to, be associated with, or be engaged or interested in, whether as director, employee, principal, agent or otherwise howsoever (save as a shareholder of not more than 3% of any public company whose shares are quoted on any recognised Stock Exchange) any business which is or is about to be similar to or competitive with any type of business carried on by the Company at the date of termination of your employment and with which you were concerned at any time during the [12] months immediately preceding such termination.

9. Working for Specified Competitors

You shall not for a period of [12] months after the termination of your employment, on your own behalf, or on behalf of any person, firm or company seek employment from or accept employment by or offer or provide services to the following persons, firms, or companies

[Here list out the names of any specific competitors you do not wish the employee to work for.]

This list of competitors may be amended or added to during the period of your employment by notice to you in writing.

Provided that this restriction shall not apply if your duties and responsibilities do not involve or concern you in the manufacture sale or provision of any goods or services which are similar to or competitive with those sold or provided by the Company at the time of the termination of your employment and with which you were concerned at any time during the [12] months immediately preceding such termination.

NB   (a)   Clauses 6 and 7 can be readily adapted to cover solicitation/
              enticing away/dealing with suppliers where this is appropriate.
      (b)   All clauses can be adapted to take account of any relevant asso-
              ciated or subsidiary companies.

Bibliography

The following is a list of selected books and articles.

Books: UK and Commonwealth

P S Atiyah, *The Rise and Fall of Freedom of Contract*, 1979

J Bell, *Policy Arguments in Judicial Decisions*, 1983

K Brearley and S Bloch, *Employment Covenants and Confidential Information*, 1993

College of Laws Lecturers, *Commercial Contracts: Restraint of Trade*, 1987

Y Cripps, *The Legal Implications of Disclosure in the Public Interest*, 2nd ed, 1994

R Dean, *The Law of Trade Secrets*, 1990

M G Fox, *The Law of Master and Servant in relation to Industrial and Intellectual Property*, 1950

F A Gare, *The Law relating to Covenants in Restraint of Trade*, 1935

F Gurry, *Breach of Confidence*, 1984

J D Heydon, *The Restraint of Trade Doctrine*, 1971

W R McComas, M R Davison and D M Gonski, *The Protection of Trade Secrets*, 1981

S Mehigan and D Griffiths, *Restraint of Trade and Business Secrets*, 2nd ed, 1991

C Osman (ed), *Butterworths Employment Law Handbook*, 1990

Sir David H Parry, *The Sanctity of Contracts in English Law*, 1959

B C Reid, *Confidentiality and the Law*, 1986

S Ricketson, *The Law of Intellectual Property*, 1984

W Sanderson, *Restraint of Trade in English Law*, 1926

M J Trebilcock, *The Common Law of Restraint of Trade: A Legal and Economic Analysis*, 1986

A Turner, *The Law of Trade Secrets*, 1962, and 1967 Supplement

Books: American

D Dessemontet, *The Legal Protection of Know-how in the USA*, 2nd ed, 1976
E G Fiorito, *Sorting out the Ownership Rights in Intellectual Property*, 1986
M F Jager, *Trade Secrets Handbook*, 1983 (as updated)
R Milgrim, *Trade Secrets*, 1967 (with updates)
H A Pooley, *Business Information and Trade Secrets*, 1987
A C Valiulis, *Covenants not to Compete*, 1985
A N Wise, *Trade Secrets and Know-how throughout the World*, 1974

Reports: England and Scotland

Law Commission, *Breach of Confidence*, WP no 58, 1974
Law Commission, *Breach of Confidence*, Report no 110, 1981, Cmnd 8388
Scots Law Commission, *Breach of Confidence*, Memo no 40, 1977
Scots Law Commission, *Breach of Confidence*, Report no 90, 1984, Cmnd 9385

Reports: Canada

Institute of Law Research and Reform, Report for Discussion no 1, *Protection of Trade Secrets*, 1984
Institute of Law Research and Reform and a Federal Provincial Working Party, Report no 46, *Trade Secrets*, 1986
Law Reform Commission of British Columbia, *Report on Covenants in Restraint of Trade*, LRC 74, 1984

Reports: New Zealand

Torts and General Law Reform Commission of New Zealand, *Protection of Trade Secrets*, 1973

Articles Specifically on Covenants

England

Anon, Competition: The Law of Restrictive Covenants (1983) IRLIB 230
Anon, Employee Competition and Restraint of Trade (1993) IRLB 486
Anon [A L Goodhart], [Untitled] (1933) 49 LQR 465
J Bowers, Covenants in Restraint of Trade [1983] LSG 1268

J R Bradgate, Restraining the Ex-employee [1986] LSG 1615

M W Bryan, Restraint of Trade: Back to a Basic Approach [1980] JBL 326

J Carby-Hall, Contracts in Restraint of Trade (1983) 25 Man L 5

A Coulthard, *George Michael* v *Sony Music* – A Challenge to Artistic Freedom? (1995) 58 MLR 731

P L Davies, Post Employment Restraints: Some Recent Developments [1992] JBL 490

F Dawson, Contracts in Restraint of Trade: Meaning and Effect (1974) 90 LQR 455

M Edwards, Restrictive Covenants and Employment: Recent Developments [1991] Bus LR 3

Restrictive Covenants in Employment Contracts: Current Trends [1994] (October) L Ex J 14

A Evans, Freedom of Trade under the Common Law and European Community Law: the Case of the Football Bans (1986) 102 LQR 510

S Gild, Restraint of Trade Agreements in Medical Partnerships [1986] LSG 2081

R N Gooderson, Restraint of Trade in the Field Code (1963) 79 LQR 410

A G Guest, The House of Lords and the Law of Contract (1968) 2 JALT 3

J D Heydon, The Frontiers of the Restraint of Trade Doctrine (1969) 85 LQR 229

J Hull, Employees' Know-how and Secrecy Covenants [1988] EIPR 387

M Jefferson, Evading the Doctrine of Restraint of Trade (1990) 134 SJ 532

Interlocutory Injunctions and Covenants (1989) 133 SJ 232

Restraint of Trade Update (1991) 135 SJ 47

K L Koh, Restraints against undertaking Work during Currency of Service (1970) 4 JALT 67

A Korn, Losing Staff and Trade Secrets (1991) 135 SJ 484

Restrictive Covenants and Employee Shareholders (1990) 134 SJ 851

M McLean, Contracts of Employment – Negative Covenants and No Work, No Pay [1990] CLJ 28

N S Marsh, The Severance of Illegality in Contract (1948) 64 LQR 242 and 367

P Molyneaux, Recent Problems on Restrictive Agreements in Service Agreements [1980] LN 23

A E Randall, Covenants in Restraint of Trade in relation to Personal Services (1915) 31 LQR 187

J Richards, Recovering the Costs of Staff Training (1991) 135 SJ 678

P Sales, Covenants restricting Recruitment of Employees and the Doctrine of Restraint of Trade (1988) 104 LQR 600

E Slade, Restrictive Covenants in Employment Contracts [1982] Bus LR 261

S A Smith, Reconstructing Restraint of Trade (1995) 15 OJLS 565

A Spowart-Taylor and B Hough, The Client and Restraint of Trade (1984) 47 MLR 745

M Walsh, Thou shalt not covet the Boss's Clients or Employees [1995] NLJ 1400

Articles: Scotland

S Woolman, Restrictive Covenants 1985 SLT 253

Articles: Australia

J G Collinge, The Modern Doctrine of Restraint of Trade (1968) 41 ALJ 410

A Humphreys, Sport, Restraint of Trade and the Australian Courts (1993) 15 Syd LR 92

Articles: Canada

J D Heydon, Recent Developments in Restraint of Trade (1975) 21 McGLJ 327

Articles: Ireland

J Phillips, The Construction of Contracts in Restraint of Trade (1978) 13 IJ 254

Articles: Switzerland

R Cuvillier, Non-competition and Non-disclosure Obligations: Bond or Bondage for the Employee? (1977) 115 ILR 193

Articles: USA

M L Agee, Covenants not to Compete in Tennessee Employment Contracts (1988) 55 Tenn LR 341

I Alterman, Trade Regulation in Michigan: Covenants not to Compete (1977) 23 Wayne LR 275

Anon, Employment Contracts – Covenants not to Compete (1970) 45 Wash LR 210

Anon, Enforceability of Covenants not to Compete (1928) 28 Col LR 81

Anon, On Contracts in Restraint of Trade (1890) 4 Harv LR 128

Anon, Specific Performance of Employee's Covenant not to Compete (1928) 41 Harv LR 782

D R Aplington, Validity of Covenants not to Compete [1978] U Ill LF 249

M R Barrick, An Employer's Competitive Restraints on Former Employees (1967) 17 Drake LJ 69

H M Blake, Employee Agreements not to Compete (1960) 73 Harv LR 625

T A Briody, Employment Agreements not to Compete (1972) 47 Cal SBJ 319

G L Bryenton, Validity and Enforceability of Restrictive Covenants not to Compete (1964) 16 W Res LR 161

M B Callahan, Post-Employment Restraint Agreements (1985) 52 U Chi LR 703

C E Carpenter, Validity of Covenants not to Compete (1928) 76 U Pa LR 244

A M Cerino, A Talent is a Terrible Thing to Waste (1986) 24 Duq LR 777

W F Clark and D H Reynolds, The Underbrush grows deeper (1984) 21 GSBJ 28

P J Closius and H M Schaffer, Involuntary Nonservitude (1984) 57 S Cal LR 531

S E Corisis, Postemployment Restrictive Covenants (1990) 65 Wash LR 209

C F Cowan, Covenants not to Compete after Termination of Employment (1941) 5 Peabody LR 79

C T Drechsler, Enforceability of Restrictive Covenants, Ancillary to Employment Contracts, as affected by Territorial Extent of Restriction (1953) 43 ALR (2d) 94

A M Eaton, On Contracts in Restraint of Trade (1890) 4 Harv LR 128

K B Fisher, Post Employment Restraints (1981) 17 Tulsa LJ 155

A W Gans, Statutes prohibiting Restraints on Profession, Trade or Business as applicable to Restrictions in Employment or Agency Contracts (1948) 3 ALR (2d) 522

P Garry, The Relationship between Employment Agreements and Trade Secret Litigation in Minnesota (1985) 11 W Mitchell LR 501

J G Grody, Partial Enforcement of Post-Employment Restrictive Covenants (1979) 5 Col JLSP 181

M Gunter, Restraints on Trade – Covenants in Employment Contracts not to compete within the entire United States (1971) 49 NCLR 393

M Handler and DE Lazaroff, Restraint of Trade and The Restatement (Second) of Contracts (1982) 57 NYULR 669

F B Harty, Competition between Employer and Employee (1985–6) 35 Drake LJ 261

M J Hutter, Drafting Enforceable Employee Non-competition Agreements to protect Confidential Business Information (1981) 45 Alb LR 311

A M Kales, Contracts to Refrain from doing Business or from entering or carrying on an Occupation (1917) 31 Harv LR 193

S E Kalish, Covenants not to Compete and the Legal Profession (1985) 29 St Louis LJ 423
Restrictive Covenants among Solicitors in England (1985) 10 JLP 27

G P Kreider, Trends in the Enforcement of Restrictive Employment Contracts (1966) 35 U Cinn LR 16

R and C S Krendl, Non-competition Covenants in Colorado (1975) 51 Denver LJ 499

R D Lewis, Contracts in Restraint of Trade (1967) 21 Ark LR 214

C E McTiernan, Employees and Trade Secrets (1950) 41 JPOS 820

J D Mullender, Contracts – Legality – Contracts in Restraint of Trade (1953) 26 SCLR 208

S L Pachman, Accountants and Restrictive Covenants (1983) 13 Seton Hall LR 312

J R Parker, Injunctive Russian Roulette and Employment Noncompetition Cases (1984) 63 NCLR 222

D M Rapp, Contracts – Partial Enforcement of Restrictive Covenants (1970) 50 NCLR 689

P J Richey and M J Bosik, Trade Secrets and Restrictive Covenants (1988) 4 Lab Law 21

D T Roach, Contracts – Agreements not to Compete – Powers of Equity to scale down unreasonable Terms (1951) 1 Buffalo LR 181

T Robison, The Confidence Game (1983) 25 Ariz LR 347

P H Rubin and P Shedd, Human Capital and Covenants not to Compete (1981) 10 JLS 93

A G S, Covenant – Not to Engage in Business (1918) 4 ALR 1073
    Validity and Enforceability of Restrictive Covenants in Contracts of Employment (1920) 9 ALR 1456

S D Shadowen and K Voytek, Economic and Critical Analyses of the Law of Covenants not to Compete (1984) 72 Georgetown LJ 1425

R A Spanner, Improvements on the Noncompetition Agreement [1984] March/April Harv Bus Rev 8

F S Tinio, Enforceability, insofar as Restrictions would be Reasonable, of Contracts containing unreasonable Restrictions on Competition (1978) 61 ALR (3d) 397 and Supplement

P Walter, Employee Restrictive Covenants (1986) 91 Comm LJ 321

C R Wetzel, Employment Contracts and Noncompetition Agreements [1969] U Ill LF 61

INDEX

Index compiled by Kim Harris